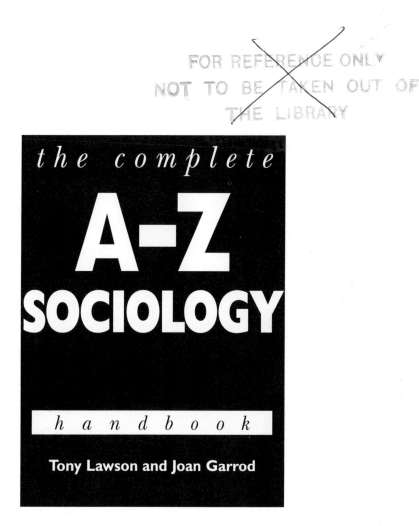

the complete

A-Z
SOCIOLOGY

handbook

Tony Lawson and Joan Garrod

Hodder & Stoughton

A M̶ ̶ ̶ ̶ ̶ ̶ ̶ ̶ ̶ ̶ OUP

British Library Cataloguing in Publication Data

Lawson, Tony
    Complete A–Z Sociology Handbook
    I. Title   II. Garrod, Joan
    301.03

ISBN 0–340–65832–0

First published 1996
Impression number   10 9 8 7 6 5 4 3 2 1
Year 1999 1998 1997 1996

Typeset by GreenGate Publishing Services, Tonbridge, Kent.
Printed and bound in Great Britain for Hodder and Stoughton Educational,
a division of Hodder Headline plc, 338 Euston Road, London NW1 3BH,
by Redwood Books, Trowbridge, Wiltshire.

HOW TO USE THIS BOOK

The *A–Z Sociology Handbook* is an alphabetical textbook designed for ease of use. The major concepts which you will come across in your study of sociology have been included. The Handbook therefore constitutes an important reference work for sociology students, helping them to grasp the basic concepts of the sociological approach.

Each entry begins with a one-sentence definition. This should help you to gain a good understanding of the concept in a precise way. The length of an entry usually depends on the relative importance of the concept and often on the degree of controversy it arouses. Entries therefore try to provide illustrative examples of the concept or introduce you to the major points in support or criticism of it. Illustrations and tables have been provided where they help you to understand the concept.

Your understanding of sociology can be increased by making use of the cross-referenced entries. These are to be found in italics either in the main body of an entry or in brackets at the end of the entry. These cross-references direct you to related concepts. The authors have restricted the use of cross-references so that important link-ways are highlighted. By looking up cross-referenced concepts you will gain a more complete understanding of the issues you are exploring.

While the *A–Z* is therefore a glossary which will aid your study of sociology, it is important to recognise that it is not a textbook. This means that you will require further reading to complete your grasp of the subject. However, the more substantial entries will give you a sound introduction to the debates and issues in which sociologists engage and will provide a handy reference when you come across concepts of which you are unsure. It also makes sense to check the entries of concepts which you think you know, to ensure that you have a good understanding of the basic tools of the sociological approach.

To help you in your revision, the authors have provided lists of the most important concepts in each of the topic areas of sociology. We have used the most popular A level syllabus – the AEB – as a guide for the structure of these revision lists, but have woven the themes of the Interboard and NEAB syllabuses into them. You should find these lists valuable when you come to do your revision.

Most importantly, we hope that you enjoy using the *A–Z* on a daily basis and find that it is an invaluable resource in your studies. We have certainly enjoyed compiling it.

Tony Lawson and Joan Garrod

ACKNOWLEDGEMENTS

Though we have worked closely as a team, we could not have carried out the work for the *A–Z* without many invisible supporters, too numerous to mention. However, we would like to record our gratitude to Ray Garrod and to Tim Gregson-Williams for their encouragement and faith over the last year. The most important thanks should go to the hundreds of students we have taught over the years who, through their questions, have honed our sociological understanding. Nevertheless, we recognise that sociology is not an exact science and that not everyone will agree with the way we have defined every concept. We have taken every care to be as factual as the subject allows and any mistakes are our responsibility.

Tony Lawson and Joan Garrod

A

abortion: the termination of a pregnancy by artificial methods, it has been the subject of often violent disagreement about the morality of allowing legal termination. This has been an important debate for sociologists to study. The debate arouses such passion that *new social movements* have been founded on the back of the debate.

absenteeism: the extent to which workers take time off work without any real reason. The degree of absenteeism in a firm is difficult to determine, because it is problematic whether a worker absent from work with 'a bad back' is genuinely sick or taking time off without good cause. The degree of absenteeism is sometimes used as a measure of *work satisfaction*. For example, a great increase in absentee rates on the shop-floor following a change in work practices may indicate unhappiness with the new arrangements. (See *industrial action*.)

absolute poverty: the lack of the basic necessities (food, shelter and access to clean water and medical care) with which to sustain a healthy existence. Absolute poverty tends to be associated with certain developing countries, but it can be argued that this type of poverty also exists in many developed *industrial societies* among the destitute and the *homeless*. (See *relative poverty; poverty of lifestyle*.)

absolute rate of mobility: this is the total number of movements up and down the *class structure* within a given period. It is distinct from the *relative rate of mobility*. The absolute rate since the Second World War has been large, with a great deal of upward social mobility occurring. (See *forced mobility*.)

abstainers: those who are registered to vote in elections, but do not do so. Abstentions range from around 50% in local elections to between 20% and 30% of the electorate in *General Elections*. (See *avoidable abstainers; unavoidable abstainers; negative abstention; positive abstention*.)

abstracted empiricism: used by C W Mills to describe the collecting of empirical evidence for its own sake without the context of a *theory* to make sense of it. (See *theory*.)

academic machismo: the domination of education by men, and agendas set by men. (See *androcentricity*.)

academic subculture: a pupil subculture identified by Hargreaves characterised by the pupils' identification with the *ethos* of the school and their acceptance of its principal values of hard work and competitiveness. The subculture was almost exclusively found among pupils in the top A/B streams, and was sustained by *peer group* pressure. Hargreaves identified another pupil subculture, the *delinquescent*, and argued that the device of *streaming* by supposed academic ability was primarily responsible for the creation of the subcultures.

accommodation: the process whereby different social groups come to live together peacefully without resolving their differences or losing their distinct identity. It is often used in describing the mutual tolerance of different ethnic groups living in the same society. (See *assimilation*.)

accounting process: the way in which individuals have *commonsense* understandings which 'account for' or make sense of the activities they undertake. In the sociology of organisations, the accounting process has been used by Garfinkel, amongst others, to show how individuals in a *bureaucracy* have a commonsense understanding of how bureaucracies work, which they employ to make sense of what they actually do in their everyday lives. That is, individuals call upon the concept of bureaucracy when they try to explain what they are doing in their work lives.

accreditation of prior learning (APL): the opportunity to have qualifications and skills gained at an earlier time recognised and therefore to be given full or partial exemption from current learning and training. APL is increasingly used in vocational courses such as *NVQs, GNVQs* and *BTEC.*

acculturation: see *enculturation*

achieved status: a position in society which individuals gain through their own efforts, rather than being born into it. In modern industrial societies, education is the main way in which individuals can achieve a particular *status* through acquiring qualifications. The greater the importance of achieved status in a society, the more open that society is likely to be. (See *ascribed status.*)

achievement: an ideological formation of industrialised societies, which states that individuals ought to be rewarded for their efforts and attainment, rather than for being born into a particular background. The idea is important ideologically because it provides the *legitimation* for industrial societies. The education systems of industrial societies are based on the idea of achievement; that is, by providing children with the opportunities to fulfil their abilities, they will rise in the social structure to their appropriate position, according to their *talent.* (See *ascription.*)

achievement principle: developed by Offe, the achievement principle is argued to be a central ideological construct of contemporary society, which states that rewards given to individuals in capitalist societies are a result of effort or qualifications, rather than *particularism.* However, Offe argued that the achievement principle cannot work in practice, because of the multi-skilled nature of contemporary societies, in which there are so many different skills that the notion of a *hierarchy* of skill becomes meaningless.

act: the basic unit of social life, this is a unit of behaviour which usually involves some purpose or meaning attached to it by the person carrying it out (the actor). (See *behaviour.*)

action: one of the basic concepts of sociology, this describes the capacity of the individual actor to do something. The concept implies a contrast with instinct, where *behaviour* is unthought. Action therefore implies intention or meaning, with the actor being purposeful in what he or she does. Giddens argues that action should also be seen as implying two other things:

- that everyone is a highly skilled, knowledgeable agent
- that everyone is a capable human agent. That is, action implies the capacity to do otherwise, to choose not to do the action, but something else instead

action research: where sociologists introduce planned changes into people's behaviour, so that the effects can be studied. It is often to be found in classroom research, where changes are introduced in the attempt to improve educational attainment.

action theory: a perspective that begins from individuals and the way that they interact with each other to create society through their everyday actions. It is in contrast to structural theories which begin at the level of society. There are many forms of action theory, and although they have a long history, they rose to prominence in the 1970s, in reaction to the dominance of *functionalism*. Action theories are *voluntaristic*, in that they emphasise the free will of the individual and the view that the activities of individuals make a difference in society. (See *dramaturgy; phenomenology; ethnomethodology.*)

active citizen: a concept used to describe a member of a society's duties and responsibilities towards others. The concept is associated with *New Right* sociologists, who argue that rather than being concerned with their rights, citizens should focus on how they can contribute to the well-being of society in an activist way. It is therefore a contrast to the idea of a *dependency culture* and constitutes a moral commitment by citizens to their compatriots.

active society: see *post-industrial society*

activism: see *political participation*

actor: see *act*

adaptation: one of Parsons' *functional prerequisites*, it relates to how societies adapt to the external environment and shape that environment to their own ends. In practical terms, Parsons was referring to economic institutions such as factories. (See *latency; goal-attainment; integration.*)

adequate at the level of meaning: the idea that, in order to be a proper scientific study of society, sociology must take account of the intentions and motivations of the individual. This view was strongly put forward by Weber, who followed Dilthey in arguing that, unlike the *natural sciences*, the social sciences need to examine both the subjective and the objective worlds.

adolescence: an imprecisely-defined period between *childhood* and adulthood. Many important physical changes occur in this period, but most attention has been focused on the emotional and behavioural problems allegedly associated with the teenage years in modern western societies. In many simple societies the period is marked by *rituals*, with ceremonial *rites de passage* marking the transition between childhood and adulthood.

adult baptism: a practice particularly associated with those religious *sects* in which converts are regarded as having been 'born again', and undergo a ceremony of baptism, often by total immersion, to symbolise the washing away of sins and the process of rebirth.

advanced capitalism: see *late capitalism*

advanced supplementary (AS) level: an academic qualification which covers half the content of an Advanced (A) level course. When AS qualifications were first introduced in the 1980s, there was a relatively modest take-up, but the growing availability of modular A level courses seems likely to increase the popularity of AS levels. The advantages of AS levels are that students may enjoy a broader Advanced level curriculum than that provided by the traditional three-subject A level course. (See *gold standard*.)

advertising industry: used by sociologists to denote the powerful position of advertisers and marketing personnel in the *post-modern* world. Post-modernists argue that, in contemporary society, surface images are just as powerful and important as any underlying forces which structural sociologists might identify. In a post-modern world advertising is therefore more than just the promotion of products, it is an important part of reality in its own right. By promoting certain images and *discourses*, advertisers help to shape the reality in which individuals live and mould their *identities*. Advertising companies are also, however, concerned with making profits and therefore they form their own industry, with their own *culture* and *structure*, providing employment and income for a large number of people in *capitalist* societies.

aestheticisation: the process whereby everyday features of social life become open to artistic and aesthetic influences, such as the principles of design and art appreciation. This has had the effect of countering the notion that art is somehow the prerogative of an *elite*, but rather that artistic considerations are both social and political, with the ability to create environments which are either brutal or appealing.

aetiology: the doctrine of specific aetiology states that specific germs cause specific diseases. It thus tends to ignore other factors, such as psychological and environmental, which may have an influence on the causes and nature of disease. (See *germ theory of disease*.)

affective action: one element of Weber's typology of action, it is behaviour carried out at the whim of the individual, without thought. It is also known as emotional action, and was seen by Weber as characteristic of pre-modern societies, where *rationality* was less common as a source of behaviour.

affective-neutrality: where emotional life is controlled and under constraint. It was said by Parsons to be one of the important features of modern societies that emotions became privatised, with fewer public displays of emotions such as grief. (See *affectivity*.)

affectivity: where emotional life is carried out publicly, with little restraint. It was identified by Parsons as one of the pattern variables associated with traditional societies. (See *affective-neutrality*.)

affirmative action: a series of programmes in the United States designed to increase the prospects of minority groups by preferential treatment. Measures range from granting government contracts to minority or female-owned firms to providing target quotas to firms for the employment of minority workers. Affirmative action is under attack from members of the *New Right* as part of the *'whitelash'*. They argue that affirmative action programmes discriminate against white males in the labour market. (See *positive discrimination*.)

affluence: literally meaning prosperity, it is used in sociology to describe the relative prosperity of groups who previously may have been poor, in particular the working class and the young. Affluence has often been associated by conservative commentators with 'having it too easy' and has been cited as one of the reasons for increases in *juvenile delinquency* and the loss of respect for established authority.

affluent society: that period during the 1950s and 1960s when people in Britain were claimed to have 'never had it so good' in terms of material prosperity. In the post-war boom, labour shortages ensured that high wages were paid to many manual workers, so that prosperity reached further down the class structure than ever before. This was in sharp contrast to the pre-War situation, where mass unemployment had seen large numbers of the *working class* in dire poverty. The notion of an affluent society was discredited with the re-discovery of poverty in the 1970s and the re-emergence of mass unemployment in the 1980s.

affluent worker: a type of worker who developed in the post-war era and was paid relatively high wages, compared to the traditional manual worker. Affluent workers were the subject of keen sociological interest in the 1960s and 1970s, to see whether they would develop middle-class characteristics. Sociologists such as Zweig argued that such workers were becoming middle class and that the future of industrial societies would be to have a large middle class and a small working class. Goldthorpe and Lockwood argued that affluent workers were becoming a new type of working class rather than middle class. Other sociologists suggested that the attitudes exhibited by the affluent workers had always been held by the group of skilled workers known as the *aristocracy of labour* and therefore were not new at all.

Afro-Caribbean: a term used in Britain to describe black people, whose origins were originally in Africa, but who arrived in Britain via the Caribbean colonies such as Jamaica or Barbados. Some sociologists are critical of the term because it hides real differences between groups who originated from different areas of Africa and from different islands of the Caribbean.

age: the biological basis for *age-groups*, age describes the journey between birth and death in years. While there is an objective factor to age, in that any person has been alive for a fixed number of years (though this may be lied about), there are important subjective factors involved also. For example, how old a person feels may not correspond to their biological age. There are also important *social construction* aspects to the concept of age. (See *generation*.)

age at marriage: the median (average) age of spinsters and bachelors at the time of marriage. This is influenced by a number of social and economic factors. In Britain, as in many other Western societies, men are on average some two years older than women when they marry for the first time. In 1946, the median age at marriage in the UK was 23 for spinsters and 26 for bachelors. In the late 1960s this had fallen to 21 for women and 23 for men, but by 1992 had risen significantly to 26 and 28 respectively. This rise is partly attributable to the growing trend among young people to cohabit before marriage and also reflects the greater likelihood that many women will wish to establish a career before embarking on marriage. (See *cohabitation*.)

age group: a socially constructed collection of people, who are seen by society as occupying a similar position according to their age. Such groups are differentiated from others primarily on account of their age. For example, adolescents would constitute an age group in Britain, but would not necessarily do so in other societies. Different societies therefore construct age groups in different ways and treat members of age groups differently, according to custom, tradition, religion, opportunities etc.

age profile of the population: a breakdown of the population into different age groups. The age profile of a population has a significant effect on many other aspects of a society, including economic development and the way in which resources need to be allocated. Problems can occur if there is too great an imbalance between the different age groups, such as a disproportionate number of young people, as is the case in many developing countries, or elderly people, as in many western industrialised societies. (See *ageing population*.)

age sets: groups of people of a similar age who have shared status and roles. Age-sets are usually found in simple or non-industrial societies, where the transition from one age-set to another is often accompanied by *rites de passage*.

ageing population: a population in which the proportion of people aged 65 and over is increasing. This is a common feature of most industrial societies, and is a result of relatively low birth rates and increased life expectancy. By 2031, almost a quarter of the population of Britain will be aged 65 and over.

	Aged under 16	Aged 16–64	Aged 65+
1961	24.9	63.4	11.7
1991	20.3	64.0	15.7
2031 (projection)	18.4	59.1	22.5

(Source: Social Trends 24, 1994)

Age structure of the United Kingdom (percentages)

There are considerable implications for society arising from this pattern. There will be a significant shift in the *dependency ratio*, and consideration will need to be given to the cost of retirement pensions and the health and housing needs of the ageing. However, it is a mistake to see this pattern in only negative terms. Many retired people have a reasonably large disposable income, and form an important consumer group, particularly of leisure goods and services.

ageism: negative feelings towards, and/or discriminatory behaviour against a person or group because of their age. The term is almost always used to refer to such feelings or behaviour towards older people. In Britain, finding employment is sometimes difficult even for people still in their forties, and the older age groups are increasingly stereotyped as having physical and mental disabilities despite the fact that many of them are healthy and lead active and fulfilling lives. In some societies, such as ancient China, the elderly were viewed as a valued and respected group whose accumulated wisdom could be used to benefit society. It is notable that, despite ageism, some groups of people, such as politicians and judges, continue to wield power and command respect to a much greater age than the majority of citizens. (See *ageing population*.)

agency: a term used by Giddens to indicate human action which has the possibility of transforming social arangements, through the intended or unintended consequences of that action. Agency also has the effect of reproducing structures as well as containing the possibility of changing them.

agenda setting: where the news media bring issues to the forefront of public debate by choosing to give those issues prominence in their reporting. The power of agenda-setting is important, because it allows the media to determine what we should think about, even if we reject the particular line taken by the media with which we have contact. The process occurs because the news is socially constructed through a whole series of choices in the news-gathering process. Decisions are taken all along the line from the actual event to its eventual appearance in the media, any one of which may lead to the item being 'spiked'. Editorial control is the final and crucial stage in deciding how prominent a story should be, if it is to appear. (See *gatekeepers*.)

aggregate: used in sociology to depict a collection of individuals which usually does not have some formal or informal structure. It is used to distinguish collectivities such as groups, which always have an internal structure, from chance collections of individuals, thrown together in fortuitous circumstances.

aggression: see *frustration-aggression theory*

AGIL: the four systems needs of society identified by Parsons and referred to in this way by their initial letters: *Adaptation, Goal-attainment, Integration* and *Latency*. (See *functional prerequisites*.)

agrarian societies: where the major form of *employment* in a society is agriculture. Agrarian societies are characterised by subsistence farming and traditional, settled social relationships, with low rates of geographical and *social mobility*.

agribusiness: the development of farming away from small family-owned businesses with a notion of stewardship of the land, towards a system where large farms are owned by absentee companies and farmed only for profit. Agribusiness is associated with the extension of capitalist relations of production from the factories of the towns to the farms of the countryside. Agribusiness has been opposed by many traditional farmers because it leads to non-traditional practices which are claimed to ruin the land. However, the efficiency of agribusiness in producing cheap food has led to its inexorable rise.

agricultural revolution: that period around the eighteenth century, when traditional land patterns and production methods were subject to fundamental and far-reaching changes. In terms of the pattern of land ownership, the enclosure movement destroyed the strip-farming methods of the feudal system, in exchange for the development of larger, privately-owned agricultural units. Production method changes included the introduction of increasingly efficient and sophisticated machinery and rotation methods, which allowed the production of larger amounts of food to feed the growing population of the towns.

ahistoricity: having no sense of history. In sociology, this has been a critique of functionalist thinking, which tends to take an existing society as the best one possible, with little feeling for the past and how societies have developed into their present state.

aid: a blanket term for various kinds of assistance given to *third world* countries by the *first world*. Aid covers the direct transfer of financial resources, such as charitable donations, the transfer of material goods, such as industrial plant, and the provision of loans and credit. Aid can be given by individual countries or by international organisations such as the World Bank. Sociologists are interested in the way that aid affects the *development* of the third world. There is disagreement amongst sociologists as to the most effective use of aid.

- Some *modernisation theorists* see aid as the main vehicle of development in the third world, with the emphasis on large infra-structure projects.
- Some 'green' sociologists argue for intermediate development aid, with resources going to smaller, locally sustainable projects.
- Some *dependency theorists* suggest that aid is used mainly as an instrument of policy by the first world, with projects being financed which assist the first world to exploit the resources of the third world.

AIDS (Acquired Immune Deficiency Syndrome): an illness which has raised a number of important issues for sociologists. Initially identified as exclusively associated with homosexual men, AIDS increased the *stigmatisation* of this group. Some even saw what they referred to as 'the gay plague' as a form of divine retribution. The 'at risk' category was then widened to include intravenous drug users, another group held in generally low social *esteem*. Recent statistics of the actual and projected incidence of AIDS, however, show a fall among homosexual men, a continued rise among intravenous drug users, and a growing increase among the heterosexual population. Sociologists have focused on AIDS as an example of a *moral panic*, on the further stigmatisation of certain groups in society, on how people who have AIDS or who are HIV positive cope with this, and how it has altered the doctor-patient relationship. The inability (as yet) of the medical profession to find a cure, and the fact that many AIDS patients are articulate, well-educated and successful people, has meant that the usual power relationship between doctor and patient, in which the doctor is the more powerful partner, has undergone changes. (See *epidemiology*.)

alienation: according to Marx, the result of capitalist organisation of industry which increases the separation of workers from the fruits of their labour. Central elements in the condition of alienation are the separation of workers from their tools and from the final product. Alienating conditions stem from the ownership of the *means of production* by the capitalist class, who therefore control the conditions of work, as well as expropriating the *surplus value* of the worker. The conditions of work which are alienating are increasing mechanisation and specialisation. These transform the active satisfaction of the worker in work into passive resentment at the monotony of work. Alienation is therefore the totality of the objective conditions of capitalist production, which translate into subjective features of deprivation, loss of dignity, sense of a lack of wholeness and most of all, a feeling that one's life is controlled by impersonal forces. (See *anomie*.)

alienative involvement: the way in which individuals are committed to a society in which *coercion* is the mechanism of control. Because individuals share a common threat, they are likely to be committed in a way which does not engage their feelings. Such an involvement is likely to be limited and lead to weak feelings of loyalty to society from individual members.

allocation process: the ways in which individuals are sifted and sorted by the education system to produce different types of workers for the economy. The crucial part of the allocation process is the certification of individual students, which codifies the skills they can bring to work. However, there are also non-tangible factors in the allocation process such as co-operative ability, work discipline and attitudes and other personality traits. Schools are concerned with the development of these non-tangibles as much as they are about the actual knowledge that they give students.

allocation role: the capacity of the education system to select individuals and place them into appropriate occupational positions.

allocative control: the power to determine the resources given to particular activities in an organisation. Sociologists have identified allocative control as the more powerful form of control in companies. By being able to decide the distribution of priorities, those who hold allocative control can influence the direction of the organisation in a strategic sense. Owners of companies do not therefore need to control the day-to-day activities of the company in order to retain control over what goes on. Allocative control ensures that the interests of those who hold such control are met. (See *operational control; managerial revolution.*)

allopathic medicine: the type of medicine primarily associated with western industrial societies. It is based on the principle of finding a treatment (usually a drug) with an opposite effect to the symptoms of the disease or illness to counteract these symptoms. Recently, more western doctors have shown an interest in, and sometimes a willingness to prescribe, *homeopathic medicines.* (See *aetiology; germ theory of disease.*)

alternative medicine: a general term to describe those forms of treatment which are not recognised by the official medical profession. These include acupuncture and aromatherapy amongst others. The boundary between mainstream and alternative medicine is constantly shifting. (See *allopathic medicine.*)

altruism: feelings that place the welfare of others above a person's own interests. Comte saw the development of altruistic feelings as a measure of the civilised nature of a society, influenced by positivistic values.

altruistic suicide: self-inflicted death where the integrating forces of society are so powerful that they overcome the individual's instinct for self-preservation. This form of *suicide* is usually bound up with the concept of *honour* and involves an over-identification with the group. So, soldiers performing hopeless rearguard actions are committing altruistic suicide. (See *hara-kiri; suttee.*)

American dream: a central ideological construct of the United States, the dream offers all Americans the chance to pursue their own happiness. Its main promise is that any individual can rise to the top of American society if they work hard enough and have the talent. It is the openness which the American dream promises that ensures the allegiance of the many diverse groups which make up the United States.

amplification of deviance: the idea that the media, through their reporting activities, contribute to the escalation of activities of which the majority population disapproves. The process begins with an actual event or phenomenon, which the media report and headline. The reporting arouses concern in the majority of the population, who demand that something should be done about it. The police respond by placing more resources in the area of concern, consequently catching more individuals committing the illegal activity. In reporting this development, the media give the impression that the number of occurrences of the initial activity is on the increase. Individuals who are pre-disposed to the initial illegal activity may also gravitate to the places where reporting is taking place, thus actually increasing the incidence of the phenomenon. The amplification of deviance can be represented as a spiral. (See *moral panics; folk devils.*)

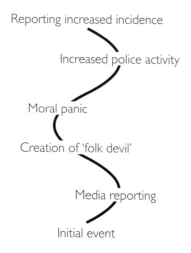

Reporting increased incidence

Increased police activity

Moral panic

Creation of 'folk devil'

Media reporting

Initial event

Amplification of deviance spiral

analogy: the use of a comparison to illustrate a social phenomenon. The classic analogies in sociology are the comparison of society to a biological organism or a machine.

anarchism: a political philosophy which advocates social life without the *State*. It argues that rules of social life should be negotiated between the participants of inter-actions rather than being imposed by an alienative State. While it is usually accused of being disruptive of social arrangements and leading to disorder, anarchism claims to be about setting up an alternative social order, based on individual freedom with each person taking responsibility for their own actions.

anarchy: the condition of being without *social order*, state justice or the force of law. Anarchy is similar to the *state of nature*, though it is the result of a break-down in or overthrow of the apparatus of the *State*, rather than a hypothetical position.

ancient society: used by Marx to delineate the period of history associated with slave-based production and usually identified with the Greek and Roman civilisations.

androcentricity: viewing things from a male perspective or being biased towards male points of view. In the sociology of education, traditional text-books are said to be androcentric in that they encode a particular masculinity and femininity, in which females are seen as subservient and passive. (See *malestream sociology.*)

animism: a belief that plants and animals are endowed with a spirit, or life-force, usually accompanied by the idea that people must learn to live in harmony with the animal world. In some societies, certain plants or animals are regarded as particularly sacred, and are the object of *rituals*. (See *totemism.*)

anomic suicide: self-destruction which results from the lack of social regulation in society. It is related to the appearance of *normlessness* in society, for example in times of crisis or in times of rising prosperity. In both cases, there is a loss of social identity and control, which results in increased *suicide rates*, as individuals are frustrated through the non-realisation of their expectations.

anomie: a concept used by Durkheim to describe a society in which individuals do not have any firm guidelines about the way to behave with each other. This *normlessness* is characteristic of those societies in which *individualism* predominates, with no counter-values of *social solidarity* to tone down the emphasis on individual satisfaction, at the expense of others.

antagonism: where a *respondent* shows hostility to the interviewer or to the topic under question. Antagonism can taint the results of sociological enquiry as it creates resistance by the respondent.

antagonistic co-operation: a feature of *pluralist theory of industrial relations*, in which the opposing sides of management and workers in a firm work together only in so far as it is necessary to achieve whatever their aims are. They therefore engage in conflict in a restricted way.

anthropocentric: looking at phenomena from the viewpoint of the human race, in contrast to other species. The term is used to denote a selfish perspective which does not take into account the interests of the other species that share the planet. It is thus mainly associated with the *new social movements* which surround the issue of *environmentalism.*

anthropologically strange: treating a familiar situation as if we had never encountered it before and it therefore needs explaining as a completely alien phenomenon.

anthropomorphism: the attribution of human characteristics to animals or other non-human forms, especially supernatural beings.

anti-clericalism: a political attitude which is opposed to the Church's interference in politics. It is particularly strong in France and Spain, where a strong Roman Catholic Church has attempted to influence *social policy* over such issues as education, abortion and morality.

anti-racism: a particular approach to *race relations*, which argues that the important issue is the prejudiced attitudes in every one of us and therefore racist groups and opinions should be confronted and challenged at every opportunity. Though it has led to a particular form of education, anti-racism has many manifestations, from challenging racist groups for control of the streets, to agitating against discriminatory legislation. (See *anti-racist education.*)

anti-racist education: education which actively tries to combat racism and prejudice and promote positive images of people from different ethnic groups.

anti-school culture: a pupil *sub-culture* identified by Stephen Ball in his 1970s study of a comprehensive school. Ball found that the system of *banding* in the school contributed to the formation of two distinct pupil sub-cultures, which he termed pro-school and anti-school. Those pupils in the latter sub-culture were either passive, i.e. had drifted into largely apathetic attitudes and behaviour, or active, i.e. were actively and deliberately rejecting the values of the school. (See *delinquescent sub-culture.*)

anti-sexism: policies and behaviour consciously geared towards the prevention of sexist images, language and practices. It is likely to be a combination of legislation (e.g. the Equal Pay Act) and initiatives such as *anti-sexist education* programmes.

anti-sexist education: education which actively tries to combat *sexism* and sexist practices in schools, e.g. by ensuring that all pupils have equal access to the curriculum, by using text books and other teaching materials which do not contain sexist language or images, and by raising the awareness of pupils to sexism as an issue.

anticipatory socialisation: the process whereby individuals alter the patterns of their behaviour to conform to those of a superior social group in the hope of joining it at a later time.

anticipatory widowhood: a concept developed by Jacobsohn to explain why many middle-class women are reluctant to retire from work early, when their husbands do. Their reluctance is based on the apprehension of isolation should their husband die, which statistically they are likely to do before the women themselves. Women in work therefore remain more attached to their work relationships to keep contact with the non-domestic world, should they be left as widows.

apartheid: the system of racial segregation which operated in South Africa until the 1990s. Apartheid was maintained through the use of force and legal sanctions, which included imprisoning its opponents such as Nelson Mandela. It was the release of Mandela which heralded the end of apartheid and the emergence of democracy there.

apolitical: the condition of being uninterested in politics. It is usually applied to women and the young, but many sociologists have been critical of this view, arguing that it is better applied to the vast majority of the population, who exhibit little interest in politics beyond voting.

apprenticeship: the provision of on-the-job training for young people leading to a craft or skill. Apprenticeship took a relatively long time and was seen in the 1980s as a traditional route into work, which led to restrictive practices and less effective production. The provision of alternative training schemes funded by central government persuaded many employers to abandon their own apprenticeship schemes in favour of the cheaper alternative. (See *training.*)

appropriate technology: see *intermediate technology*

appropriation: the taking of the *surplus value* of the labour of the non-owners of the *means of production* by the owners, to be disposed of as they see fit. The exploitation of the subordinate class is a central feature of capitalist society according to the Marxists. It is achieved by capitalists forcing the labourer to work beyond what is necessary for survival and then taking away the value of the excess for their own. (See *labour theory of value.*)

arbitration: the appointment of an independent person or group to try to bring two parties in a dispute to an agreed compromise. It is a feature of *industrial relations* and is often carried out by an agency called ACAS – the Advisory, Conciliation and Arbitration Service.

archaeology of knowledge: the methodology associated with Foucault, which consists of peeling back the additions which time collects on social and cultural ideas to reveal the origins of those ideas in their socio-economic context. Foucault was particularly interested in using the archaeological method to examine the development of conceptions of punishment and of sexuality in society.

areligiosity: the state of being without religious belief and thus without religious practices. It is claimed by some sociologists that the extent of areligiosity is growing as *secularisation* becomes more widespread. However, this claim is disputed.

aristocracy: a traditional noble stratum, whose power over society stemmed from their control of agricultural production. The power of the aristocracy reached its climax in the feudal system, but it was slowly supplanted by new social groups emerging from the industrial revolution. However, many aristocratic families were also in the forefront of industrial developments and remained individually powerful. The aristocracy still retain enormous *wealth* in the form of land and are held in high regard by many subordinate groups in society.

aristocracy of labour: that section of the skilled working class who see themselves as separate from the rest of the working class on account of their high level of skill. They tend to be status-conscious and instrumental in their attitudes. Their trade union organisations tend to defend the pay differentials of the aristocracy of labour from other less skilled workers. (See *deferential workers*.)

arranged marriage: a marriage in which the partners have been chosen by the respective parents and in which the bride and groom will often not have met until shortly before the wedding ceremony. Although now mainly associated with Eastern cultures, arranged marriages used to be quite common among the aristocratic and royal families of Europe, where marriages were seen as alliances between families and groups, and a way of creating or perpetuating dynasties rather than a romantic attachment between two people. Defenders of arranged marriages today argue that they are much more likely to last than relationships based on physical attraction and notions of romantic love, while critics say that many such marriages are unhappy, and can be particularly hard for the women involved who may be completely subject to their husband and mother-in-law.

artefact: an object produced by a *culture*, which can have an existence beyond the life of that culture. Although usually associated with physical objects, sociologists also recognise non-tangible artefacts such as ideas, which can also survive the culture which produced them.

artefact explanation of health inequalities: see *Black Report*

asceticism: the practice of self-denial of worldly comforts and pleasures arising from a belief that this is a means to religious salvation. Traditionally, in Christianity, the monks and nuns were those who practised asceticism, often by a complete withdrawal from the world. However, after the Reformation a form of Protestant asceticism developed in which self-denial was practised without withdrawal from the world. Indeed, with the notion of the 'calling', this self-denial was applied to work, with the result that a group of people emerged who worked hard, but re-invested the profits of their labour rather than spending them. (See *Protestant ethic thesis*.)

ascribed status: a position in society which is the result of a fixed characteristic given at birth, such as gender or class of origin. (See *achieved status*.)

ascription: where an individual's status is fixed by the social characteristics with which they are born. These characteristics may be a person's gender or ethnicity. They may also be the social standing of the parents. (See *achievement.*)

ascriptive socio-political deference: the acceptance of a high-born social elite as being particularly fitted for high political office. The central idea is that this elite is 'born to rule'. (See *socio-cultural deference; political deference.*)

Asiatic stage: one of Marx's eras of history, which was distinguished by the hold of the State over schemes of irrigation and the ownership of the land by self-sufficient village communities. Though there is little empirical evidence to support the existence of the Asiatic mode of production in any widespread way, the term was used by Marx to indicate the relative stability of societies in Asia, in contrast to the dynamic societies of Western Europe. It has been criticised as a *Eurocentric* view of development.

aspiring professions: see *semi-professions; personal service professions*

assembly-line systems: a form of production in which the product is sent down a continuously moving line, with workers arranged down the line performing a limited number of routinised tasks. The classic assembly-line is associated with car production during the 1960s. Sociologists are interested in the effects of assembly-line production on workers' attitudes and it is often seen as the most alienating form of *technology*. High levels of *strikes* in the car industry tended to confirm this view. (See *continuous process production; craft industry.*)

assimilated workers: those members of the *working class* who aspire to be members of the *middle class,* economically and socially, and are accepted by the middle class as their social equals. The accepted worker is said to be assimilated into the middle class. (See *socially aspiring worker.*)

assimilation: a view of *race relations* which sees the host community as culturally homogeneous and the task of the immigrant community is to be absorbed into the host community as quickly as possible, by adopting host features. Sensitivity to cultural differences is minimal so that ethnic minority *culture* is disparaged. It can lead to the minority community being dissipated through tactics such as *bussing.* (See *cultural pluralism.*)

assisted places scheme: a scheme in which the government and local authorities provide money to allow able children from homes with modest incomes to be educated in fee-paying schools. The argument in favour of the scheme is that places at schools in the *independent sector* should be available to as many children as possible, not only those whose parents are able to afford the fees. Critics of the scheme argue that it reinforces the idea that independent schools provide a 'better' education than state schools, and the creaming-off of brighter children has a negative impact on the ability range of pupils in nearby maintained schools. It is also argued that a disproportionate number of children receiving assisted places are the children of middle-class parents such as teachers and clergymen rather than the children of manual workers. In 1995, the scheme provided places for 33,000 children at 294 independent schools, at a cost of £115 million.

association: see *Gesellschaft*

asymmetrical family: see *stages of the family*

atheism: a belief that god does not exist.

attempted suicide: an unsuccessful act of self-destruction. Sociologists are interested in attempted suicides because they give access to the motivations of would-be suicides. However, in exploring the intentions of attempted suicides, sociologists have found that it is very difficult to determine what is a serious attempt at self-destruction and what is a cry for help. (See *gambles with death.*)

attitude: a frame of mind which persists over time and which predisposes the holder to view things from a particular angle and with a particular slant. Attitudes are learned through experience and *socialisation*, but are not unchangeable.

audience: used in the sociology of the media to denote the recipients of any media content, not just cinema or theatre. Thus, sociologists would describe the readership of a newspaper as its audience, because they receive the messages which the producers of the media content wish to get across. Some sociologists are critical of the term as it implies, with its image of sitting in an auditorium listening to a concert, a passive reception of messages.

audience dependency: a view that, with the advent of the *mass media*, people increasingly rely on the mass media not only for their knowledge of the world, but also the interpretation of particular events. The mass media are therefore seen as increasingly powerful, with the ability significantly to shape people's ideas, and therefore behaviour. Others see this as a flawed view of *audiences*, arguing that people are not passive and uncritical receptors of media messages but 'filter' and even transform them in the light of their existing opinions and beliefs.

audio-visual evidence: the wealth of material now available to the sociologist which relies on the relatively new technologies of tapes and videos. It includes photographs, video-tapes and audio-tapes. For example, the cameras now located in city centres provide a rich source of ethnographic material for the sociologist.

authoritarian personality: developed by Adorno to indicate that attitude of mind which believes that society is a system of domination and submission and that some individuals are born to rule and others to obey. Authoritarian personalities can be of the dominant or the submissive kind, that is, they can expect to be obeyed or expect to obey.

authority: the possession of *power* which is seen as legitimate by those over whom it is wielded. Accepted authority can be sub-divided into two major types:

- **Sacred authority** – this can be invested in the personnel of the Church, Temple or Mosque, or in the Holy documents which a religion holds. The authority held by religious tradition is often unchallengeable and can lead to *fundamentalism*
- **Secular authority** – this is often associated with political leaders and the legitimate organs of government. Political authority can also be attached to great political leaders who, through their *charisma*, can attract legitimated support

autobiographies: written accounts of people's lives as recounted by themselves. Autobiographies can form a useful source of information, but it should be remembered that they are usually written only by those who are sufficiently well-known for their life-story to be of interest to others, and that the events recounted will be selective. (See *documents; life-histories.*)

autocracy: strong rule, it is where a society is governed arbitrarily, with little democratic accountability and where the ruler or rulers can make decisions without recourse to anyone else. Autocratic rule is often used in contrast to democratic rule.

automation: systems of production where human beings take a supervisory role and the main process of production is carried out by machines alone. There are several types of automation:

- transfer automation, which links different machines in a continuous process
- techniques of automatic control over production, with no feedback mechanisms
- computerisation, where complex work tasks are controlled by computers through feedback loops

Automation is a key area of study for sociologists of industry, as the effects of increased automation on society are likely to be long-range and fundamental. Much interest has focused on the effects on jobs, with some sociologists predicting that automation will lead to massive job losses and the creation of a society in which there are large numbers of unemployed people. Other sociologists argue that automation both destroys and creates jobs, with the newly created jobs more highly skilled than the jobs destroyed. Another area of interest has been the effects of automation on the *consciousness* of those who work with it. Some sociologists suggest that automation decreases *alienation,* as it frees up workers from the more routine aspects of work, leaving them to concentrate on more creative aspects of work. Others suggest that automation leads to even more alienation, as workers are reduced to 'appendages of the machine' with little control over their own work.

autonomy: the freedom of individuals to act in certain circumstances. Sociologists use the concept of autonomy in different contexts. Autonomy in the workplace is associated with the ability of workers to set their own pace of work and organise its activity to their own liking. In terms of *professions,* autonomy is one of the defining characteristics, in that professionals theoretically have the freedom to offer the best advice to the client, irrespective of any other pressures. Professional autonomy is defended vigorously by the professions, but is under constant threat from the bureaucratic forces with which they may work. For example, doctors have the autonomy to advise the best treatment, but whether it is actually given or not may depend on the availability of finance, either through private funds or in the *National Health Service.*

avoidable abstainers: those who register to vote and do not do so in an election, when they could very easily have cast their vote. Reasons why they did not turn out could be things like a favourite programme came on the TV when they had intended to go, they forgot etc. (See *unavoidable abstainers.*)

avoidance relationship: where an individual seeks to keep out of the way of another for usually deferential or ritualistic reasons. The classic avoidance relationship is between *caste* members and the harijan in India, where contact with the latter by the former is believed to lead to a ritual *pollution.*

B

babble of experts: a phrase which describes the state of knowledge in the post-modern world, in which a large number of apparently knowledgeable people offer contradictory opinions about the major issues facing society. For example, there are so many conflicting views about whether the 'greenhouse effect' is or is not happening that we cannot reasonably know which view is correct. (See *information overload.*)

back-fill development: building new houses between two existing rows of houses, in the space where their large gardens used to be. This form of development creates a great deal of dissatisfaction amongst those who are subject to it. Local residents often cannot withstand the pressure from developers to back-fill and they become infected with a *NIMBY* attitude.

backlash vote: the support for the racist parties of the right by mainly, but not exclusively, working-class whites, who are reacting against the presence of ethnic minorities in their localities. The strength of the racist vote varies but is most significant in local elections when the *turn-out* is low. It tends to be concentrated in white areas on the edges of high concentrations of ethnic minorities.

balkanisation: the process whereby any organisation or structure is split up into smaller separate parts, with limited connections between them. It refers to the historical development of the Balkans in Europe which changed from being dominated by a few Empires to forming many smaller States, as those Empires broke up. In sociology, balkanisation can refer to labour markets, where jobs are divided into different sectors with little interchange between the parts or it can refer to an organisation where the levels are split from each other and kept separate by the need for qualifications to advance to different parts.

banding: a system in which school pupils are grouped into broad ability bands. The system is supposed to be less rigid than *streaming*, as the bands span a wider range of abilities. However Stephen Ball's study of banding in a *comprehensive school* showed that banding can have similar effects to streaming in the creation of pupil *sub-cultures*. (See *mixed ability teaching; setting.*)

bandwagon effect: where *opinion polls* suggest that a party has a lead in voting intentions or there is a surge in support for one party at the expense of the others, then other voters may be tempted to support the winners by 'jumping on the bandwagon'.

base: see *substructure*

batch production: a manufacturing process in which goods are manufactured in small numbers. It is usually associated with craft skills or small manufacturing companies, employing skilled workers and fairly simple machinery.

batches: the way in which individuals in *total institutions* are dealt with, that is, in large groups. Given that in a total institution there is usually a small number of staff looking after a large number of inmates, social life has to be organised so that a great number of inmates can be processed quickly in any activity, for example, eating.

bearers of the mode of production: a term developed by Althusser to indicate that individuals' actions are determined by their position in the production system. It has been criticised for denying individuals choice in their actions, because it implies that an individual's position in the relations of production controls the actions he or she can take.

behaviour: as distinct from action, behaviour is the events which individuals engage in, which may or may not be intended and planned. Behaviour has thus several sources, from emotions, through instinct, to rationality. It does not have to involve purpose in the consciously planned sense.

beliefs: things which we hold to be true. The term is often used in the context of religious beliefs, which are usually concerned with beliefs in a *supernatural* power or powers, and linked to ideas concerning the origin of life, the meaning and purpose of life on earth and what happens after death.

Beruf: the calling or vocation of the professional. The Beruf defines part of the *ideology* of professionals, who claim that they carry out their job not for the good rewards they receive, but because they have a calling to practise. It is this ideology of service which informs professionals' own view of themselves. Critics of the Beruf argue that it is a smoke-screen to justify the professionals' high salaries.

Beveridge Report: a 1942 report from a Government committee chaired by Lord Beveridge, the recommendations of which formed the basis of the modern *welfare state*. The report stated that it was the duty of the modern state to eliminate what Beveridge called the 'five giant ills', namely disease, ignorance, idleness, want and squalor. The main recommendations of the Beveridge Report were implemented by the post-war Labour Government of 1945–50.

bias: a deviation from some assumed 'truth' or objective measurement. Bias in sociological research can arise at any or all of a number of stages, e.g. in the research design, the method of *sampling* and/or the choice of group to be studied, when designing *questionnaires*, in *interviews* and in the analysis and interpretation of results. Some sociologists argue that the use of quantitative methods is less likely to lead to bias than qualitative methods, but others strongly disagree. It is probably the case that truly unbiased research, whether in the natural or social sciences, is impossible to achieve, and that the methods chosen will themselves influence the nature of the results. (See *objectivity.*)

bilineal descent: where inheritance and descent are reckoned through both the male and female lines. (See *matrilineal; patrilineal.*)

bingeing: striking the upper arm of a worker to bring her or him into line with the rest of the work-group. It was one of the sanctions used by workers to establish group identity and discipline on the shop-floor.

bio-mechanical model of health: a dehumanising model of health and illness in which the doctor is viewed as a mechanic treating a defective machine. This model, associated with western industrial societies, tends to ignore links between mind and body, physical and mental well-being. Its characteristics are:

- a focus on treating the symptoms of a disease rather than finding its root cause

- belief that a particular disease is caused by a particular germ (also known as the doctrine of specific *aetiology*)
- a focus on the individual as the site of disease and the object of treatment, rather than considering the wider social, psychological and environmental milieu of the patient
- a belief in the objectivity of medical knowledge and treatment, and that the most appropriate place for treatment is in a medical environment

Critics argue that, by its focus on the effects of disease on the body, and on treating symptoms, the bio-mechanical model of health has diverted attention away from the social and environmental causes of disease and ill-health.

biological analogy: used mainly, but not exclusively by functionalists to compare society to a living organism. The idea is based on the similarities between biological organisms and social formations. In it, society is seen as a functioning entity with an existence of its own, but composed of many parts which contribute to the well-being of the whole. The analogy has been criticised because it leads to the assumption that all parts of society have a positive function to perform for society as a whole, and critics point out that some parts of the social 'body' are dysfunctional rather than functional. The analogy is drawn from biology, but other critics point out that if Darwinian selection is taken as the biological analogy, then conflict would be the main feature of the analogy rather than the inter-dependence of inter-related parts. (See *cybernetic analogy*.)

biological deviant: according to Durkheim *deviance* would occur as a natural event, even in a perfect society, because individual consciences vary enormously due to genetic inheritance and the variation in social contexts. The purpose of the biological deviant is therefore to fix the boundaries of what is acceptable in any society. The biological deviant operates on the margins of society's approval.

biological naturalness: in answering the question, 'why do people choose to interact with their kin?' some people refer to the fact that 'blood is thicker than water'. This implies that, in some basic sense, *family* is a natural phenomenon and more than just the accident of genetic inheritance.

birth rate (crude): the number of live births per thousand of the population per year. As the number of births is expressed per 1000 people, this enables a comparison to be made between countries of widely differing population sizes, such as Britain and China. The birth rate in Britain has shown an overall downward trend since the peak value of 36 in the 1870s, with a few 'bulges', such as those at the end of both World Wars and in the 1960s. The birth rate in Britain has now stabilised at between 12–14, officially categorised as 'fairly modest'. Although the availability of reliable contraception is of obvious importance to the birth rate, social factors such as religious beliefs, the level of literacy, employment opportunities for women, norms governing 'ideal' family size and views on the relative importance of males and females also have a crucial effect. Different countries show markedly different birth rates, with developed regions of the world generally having much lower birth rates than developing regions (see below). Some demographers argue that, as the total population obviously includes those who are not in the child-bearing category, (males, very young and elderly females) and as the proportion of people in these categories might differ considerably between populations, a more accurate way of measuring birth rate is the *fertility rate.*

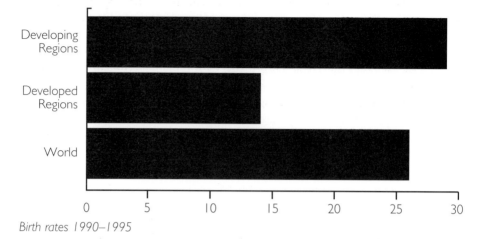

Birth rates 1990–1995

births outside marriage: the number of births to women who are not in a legal state of *marriage* at the time of the birth. This number has increased significantly since 1960, and by 1992 had risen to almost one birth in every three (31%). However, three-quarters of births outside marriage are registered by both parents (as against 45% in 1971), over half of them living at the same address, indicating that many of the parents are in a stable relationship. Much of the increase can be attributed to the growth of *co-habitation.* The younger the mother, the more likely it is that she will be unmarried. In 1992, 83.8% of all births to mothers under 20 were births outside marriage, compared with 27.4% to mothers aged 20–39.

black: a general term used to describe a number of non-white ethnic groups in Britain. In the United States black refers to those only of African descent and was developed as part of the black consciousness movement of the 1960s, in which pride in being black was developed in contrast to the feelings of inferiority associated with slavery. Because in Britain the term is more widely applied, it is more controversial, and many Indian, Pakistani and Bangladeshi groups argue that it makes invisible their particular interests and cultures.

black box view: an approach in the sociology of education which takes for granted what happens in schools and looks to the family or wider society to explain under-achievement. The black box view has been criticised for ignoring social processes within schooling and in particular what happens in the classroom.

black British: used to denote citizens of Afro-Caribbean or African descent who were born in Britain and whose loyalty and identity lie in being British.

black economy: see *informal economy*

black feminism: a branch of *feminism* which focuses on the particular concerns of black women. It is argued that, as well as experiencing the disadvantages which apply to all women in a *patriarchal* society, black women face a further form of discrimination, *racism.* They are thus doubly-disadvantaged. (See *liberal feminism; Marxist feminism; radical feminism.*)

black legend: a term used by Pollack to describe the view that children before 1900 were treated as *young adults*. She argued that this was not a true account of the way children were treated. Rather, her research showed that children were recognised as having need for play and affection and that they were treated as children not just as little adults.

Black Report: a report on inequalities in health which showed that there were marked *social class* differences in the health and health chances of the population of Britain. The report was the work of a committee set up in 1977 by the Labour Government under the chairmanship of Sir Douglas Black, President of the Royal College of Physicians and former Chief Scientist at the DHSS. The report looked at four different types of explanation to account for social class differences in health. These were:

- *The artefact explanation* – health inequalities are not 'real' but are a consequence of the use of misleading or inappropriate statistics and definitions of social class.
- N*atural/social selection* – people in the lower social groups are there as a result of their poor health, which prevents them from obtaining and maintaining higher ranking jobs, i.e. their class position is a consequence rather than a cause of poor health.
- *The structural/material explanation* – a number of factors give rise to poorer health in the lower social classes, e.g. low income and subsequent poor diet and inadequate housing, dangerous working environments, stress and depression which in turn lead to smoking and excess drinking, lack of knowledge of good hygiene and child care practices, restricted access to good quality health care.
- T*he behavioural/cultural explanation* – people in the lower social groups fail to look after themselves properly, e.g. not having medical check-ups or going regularly to the dentist, they take insufficient exercise and eat the wrong kind of food and they pass on these habits and attitudes to their children, transmitting ill-health across the generations.

The Report concluded that the first two appeared to be weak influences, and identified a need for Government action. It recommended a wide-ranging strategy to alleviate *poverty* and improve the life style and therefore the health of the working classes. The Report was published in 1980, by which time a Conservative Government was in office. Publication was delayed for four months, then 263 duplicated copies were released on the Friday of a Bank Holiday weekend with no press conference and when Parliament was not sitting. A three-paragraph foreword by a Minister suggested that the research had not been helpful, its conclusions were unclear and its recommendations 'unrealistic'. (See *inverse care law.*)

black-coated worker: a term applied by Lockwood to clerical workers. It reflects the traditional clerical 'uniform' of a long black frock coat.

blasé attitude: developed by Simmel to describe the urban sophistication which he found in large cities. It was manifested in a 'seen it all before' attitude, in which the individual affected never to be surprised by the many novel events to be found in the city.

blue-coated workers: a term used to describe the police. It is used to indicate that the police have pay issues, *status* considerations and working conditions just like other workers.

blue-collar workers: an American term for manual workers and therefore the working class.

body: in sociology this is not just the physical aspect of the human being, but is also a social construct, influenced by social processes and negotiated in interaction. The sociology of medicine has been particularly interested in concepts of the body, especially with the rise of post-modernist theories in the 1980s. For example, Foucault argues that the way people conceive of their bodies is influenced by *discourses* which define appropriate body shape and the ways in which bodies may be kept healthy and free from disease.

body language: the communication of sentiments, ideas or emotions by gestures, facial expressions and posture. Some of this communication is deliberate (e.g. waving good-bye) but much of it is unconscious. Individuals become very skilled at interpreting the body language used in their own culture, but mistakes are often made when interacting with or observing people from other cultures, where the same gesture or expression may have a quite different meaning.

Booth, Charles: a Victorian businessman and social reformer whose detailed survey of people in London at the end of the nineteenth century provided detailed statistical evidence of the extent of urban *poverty*. Booth used the concept of the *poverty line* to define and measure poverty, and his pioneering *social survey* showed that almost a third of the people in a large part of London could be defined as 'poor'. (See *Rowntree*.)

border pedagogy: developed by Giroux, it suggests that teachers should be recruited to transform the prospects of working-class children by focusing on resistance to dominant ideologies and the crossing of traditional subject divisions to show, for example that works of literature are situated in specific social and historical settings, rather than only being interpreted in a particular way.

boundary maintenance: in functionalist sociology, the tendency of a *social system* to preserve its position in relationship to its external environment. It is therefore a defence mechanism for systems to maintain their own position and ensure survival. (See *reification*.)

bounded rationality: used by March and Simon to suggest that action is never totally logical, but is limited by the partial knowledge which the individual may have about a situation. Because no one individual can know everything about a set of circumstances, there must be areas of uncertainty and chance involved in the decision-making process.

bourgeoisie: one of Marx's two main classes in society; they are the owners of the *means of production*. According to Marx the bourgeoisie are not just an owning class but by virtue of their ownership also a *ruling class* in capitalist societies. That is, economic power gives access to political power.

bricolage: in the sociology of youth culture, it is borrowing aspects of different styles of dress, music and behaviour to form new styles. Youth sub-cultural styles therefore give nods in the direction of particular cultures and modes of dress, but are creative in the pastiche of *style* which results.

bride-price: a gift from the bridegroom and his family to the father and family of the bride. The higher the *social status* of the bride, the higher the bride-price will be. The handing over of the gift is often the sign that the marriage is legally established. The notion of the bride-price is most often found in societies in which there is *patrilineal descent*, where it forms the means to attach children to lineages.

brute being: a concept used by Merleau-Ponty to describe the shadow side of the human character. In existential sociology attention should be paid to this darker side of humanity, with its passions and thoughts, about which the individual rarely tells others.

BTEC (Business and Technical Education Council): an awarding body for examinations specialising in vocational qualifications. One of the three boards, together with City and Guilds and RSA, to offer *GNVQ* examinations.

Buddhism: an Eastern religion which pre-dates Christianity based on the teachings of the Buddha, 'the enlightened one'. With its emphasis on self-denial and the finding of inner peace through meditation, Buddhism has attracted a growing number of adherents in Western societies, many of them people tired of the 'rat race' and what they see as the growing materialism of Western consumer-oriented societies.

buffer zone thesis: the argument that the amount of mobility at the manual/non-manual line is marginal and that this line forms a barrier to mobility. While this is a traditional view of the class structure as a relatively closed one, the increase in middle-class occupations has had the effect of temporarily increasing mobility rates across the manual/non-manual line. However, the long-term effect of the occupational changes has been to produce a relatively homogeneous working class, whose *self-recruitment* is high.

built environment: a term which covers sociological interest in urban planning and architecture and their inter-relationships with individuals and society. The interaction between people and the space that surrounds them is a particular interest of post-modern sociologists, but the built environment has a more general appeal to sociologists as a reflection of and background to the cultural values and activities in which people engage.

bureaucracy: a particular form of organisation which is characteristic of *modernity*. The concept is associated most of all with the *ideal type* of bureaucracy developed by Max Weber. In this ideal type, Weber defines a large number of features of bureaucracies which may then be used as a measure of how bureaucratic real *organisations* are. These features include:

- a series of official roles which are organised hierarchically
- these roles are bound by rules which define what may or may not be legitimately done by an official
- laid down procedures which theoretically cover all situations which may face the bureaucracy
- officials are subject to strict discipline
- records are meticulously kept
- there is a clear separation between what is official and what is personal

Weber claimed that bureaucracies are the most efficient form of organisation. Critics of bureaucracy have argued that they are more suited to a situation where there is predictability, for example in producing standardised goods for a mass market in which demand for the goods will be steady. Bureaucracies are said to be less efficient in the post-modern world where there are *niche markets* demanding specialised tailor-made goods. Where bureaucratic organisations survive in inappropriate situations they become *dysfunctional.*

bureaucratic personality: developed by Blau to indicate how individuals working in a *bureaucracy* tended to develop similar habits, skills and reflexes in dealing with their clients. This personality was one of the factors which made for the *dysfunctioning* of bureaucracies, as the bureaucrats became inflexible and unable to respond to new or changed conditions. (See *impersonality.*)

bureaucratisation: the process whereby society becomes increasingly subject to the control of bureaucratic organisations, with a consequent loss of *freedom* and *individualism.* The concept is particularly associated with Weber who believed that modern societies were distinguished by *rationality* and that one consequence of this was the dominance of *bureaucracy.* The result was that modern societies were subject to an '*iron cage*' of bureaucracy which stifled freedom and controlled the lives of individuals.

burgesses: identified by Watson as those individuals upwardly mobile in a particular locality. They rely on local opportunities to 'better themselves' and utilise local networks in achieving movement. (See *spiralists.*)

bussing: the transportation of schoolchildren to non-local schools to ensure an ethnic mix in schooling. Bussing was an American policy designed to avoid the ghettoisation of schools with consequent low achievement in inner-city schools.

Butler Education Act: see *Education Act 1944*

C

cabal: used by Burns to describe a network of aspiring individuals in an organisation, who use their influence with each other to further their own careers. (See *clique.*)

calculability: the possibility that social actions may be predicted by an individual as a result of their regularity. Calculability is a basic prerequisite of collective action. Working together would be difficult without some calculation by an individual as to the likely responses of those with whom he or she is working. Individuals make such calculations on the basis of a whole range of factors, from previous experience to the rules of the *organisation* in which they are working. Calculability however is not foolproof because actions can have *unintended consequences* as well as desired outcomes. (See *exchange theory.*)

calculative involvement: the way in which individuals are committed to a society where there is a self-interest operating. As individuals make a rational calculation to come together in society, they are likely to be committed in a way which engages only their self-interest. Such an involvement is likely to be conditional and lead to negotiable feelings of loyalty from individual members to society. (See *alienative involvement; moral involvement.*)

Calvinism: a form of Protestant *Christianity* with a strong commitment to self-control, self-denial and the conscientious discharge of the duties and obligations arising from work. Work was seen as another way of honouring God with the emphasis on hard work, a sober, modest life style and saving, rather than spending, money. These ideas, collectively referred to as the 'Protestant work ethic', led Weber to argue that Calvinist values had a major influence on the development of industrial capitalism. (See *Protestant ethic thesis.*)

capital: in economic terms, the money, machinery and plant needed to produce goods. In sociology it is often reified to represent a social force in its own right, with its own *class interest.* Capital is therefore supposed to operate in predictable ways which often produce *exploitation* as well as great wealth. Capital is thus the contradictory concept to 'the workers'.

capital accumulation: to Marx, this was the central dynamic in capitalist society and was the process whereby capital was expanded, so that further investment and therefore profit could be made. Capital was created by exploiting workers and expropriating the *surplus value* of their labour. This capital was collected in fewer and fewer hands, that then employed it to create further capital through increased exploitation.

capitalism: a type of society in which the private ownership of the *means of production* is the dominant form of providing the means to live. Capitalism is a 'system', that is to say it has a series of inter-locking structures which together function to produce a particular way of living and producing. What distinguishes capitalism from other types of society is the emphasis on the rights of property and the individual owner's right to employ capital as she or he thinks fit. The development of capitalism has been a focus of sociological interest, with some arguing that there is a common path of capitalist development, produced by the logic of the maximisation of profits.

Critics of capitalism have attacked its reduction of all relationships to monetary value and its apparently alienating tendency. Supporters of capitalism claim that it is through the harnessing of the profit motive that the 'good life' has been provided for so many people. (See *late capitalism.*)

carceral organisation: an institution in which individuals are held for treatment or punishment and in which they spend 24 hours a day for a set period. The usual examples given are prisons and asylums. Sociologists are interested in these because they are an extreme situation, in which the collectivity is more important than the individual inmate. They thus represent a *case study* for situations where free will is limited but never extinguished. (See *total institutions.*)

care in the community: a policy of deinstitutionalisation introduced during the 1990s which removed certain groups of people from institutional care into the care of their family and the wider community. The policy was applied to certain groups of mentally ill, the mentally handicapped and the elderly. Supporters of the policy argue that it is not good for people to live in institutions unless they really need to do so, as it robs them of their dignity and independence. While most people would agree with this, critics of the policy are concerned by what they see as the inadequate resources provided for good quality care by families and communities. Many families have found themselves unable to cope with members suffering from mental illness, particularly schizophrenia, while it is argued that the number of day centres for mentally-handicapped, severely disabled and elderly people is quite inadequate. (See *carers.*)

career: the progression which individuals go through during the course of their life. It is usually associated with an occupation, but in sociology the term is used more widely. Sociologists are interested in the way that the concept of a career has changed under the impact of post-Fordist developments in industry.

career hierarchy: a concept developed by Marsh to suggest that football hooligans graduate from one level of violence to higher stages as they grow older. (See *novices; rowdies; town boys.*)

carers: a term usually applied to informal carers, i.e. those who care for people with some kind of disability, usually relatives or neighbours, outside the system of medical or care institutions. Since the policy of *care in the community* the number of these informal carers, the majority of whom are women, has increased. The largest category of dependant is that of parent.

Dependant	In same household	In another private household	All
Parent	23	39	35
Friend/neighbour	2	25	19
Other relative	10	20	18
Parent-in-law	6	15	13
Spouse	41	0	10
Child over 16	10	10	3
Child under 16	8	0	2

(Source: Social Trends 25, 1995)

Carers: by relationship with dependant 1990 Great Britain (percentages)

cargo cult: one of a number of *millenarian movements* which existed in New Guinea in the 1930s. Cargo cults shared a belief that by engaging in particular rituals their followers would ensure that the millennium would be accompanied by the appearance of a miraculous cargo of trade goods. Cargo cults arose at a time of social and political dislocation linked to successive waves of *colonialism*.

case study: a detailed in-depth study of one group or event. The group or event is not necessarily representative of others of its kind, and case studies are sometimes used as preliminary pieces of research to generate *hypotheses* for subsequent research.

cash-nexus: a term suggesting that the only bond between employer and worker is the wage paid by the former to the latter. Where the cash-nexus is dominant employers and workers have no other obligations to each other and workers develop an instrumental attitude towards their work, in which a certain amount of effort is expended for the reward that is given.

caste: the *stratification* system of India, it is based on four traditional groups organised in a *hierarchy* and originally based on an *occupational classification*. The system is now hereditary, with caste being given at birth by parents' caste membership and cannot be changed during a life-time. The system is a complicated one with the four main castes being sub-divided into thousands of jati. The four main castes from top to bottom are:

1. Brahmin; 2. Kshatriyas; 3. Vaishyas; 4. Sudras.

Standing below the castes are the harijan, who are literally 'out-caste'. and who occupy a position in society which is unofficially much discriminated against.

casualisation of the workforce: used to describe the increasing numbers of workers who are employed on a part-time and/or temporary basis. The growth of casual labour is associated with the development of *post-Fordism* and the *dual labour market* of *core workers* and *periphery workers*.

	All part-time	Men	Women
Did not want full-time job	71.7	37.1	78.9
Could not find full-time job	2	27.9	10.8
Student	12.6	31.6	8.7
Ill or disabled	1.5	3.1	1.1

(Source: Labour Force Survey No. 14, December 1995)

Reasons for employees and self-employed people working part-time, summer 1995 (not seasonally adjusted) (percentages)

category: a logical class in which to group phenomena. In the case of sociology, categorisation is one of the main ways in which sociologists seek to understand the social world.

caucus: a meeting of members of a political party for the purpose of deciding policy or nominating members for office. The term can also be used to describe the members themselves, often in the sense of 'a group within a group'.

causal explanation: a statement which accounts for the existence of a phenomenon by identifying the events and factors which led to its occurrence. They are very difficult to establish in sociology because of the complexity of social phenomena and because human beings have enough free will to change the cause and results.

censorship: the banning or restricting of public expression regarded by those in authority as potentially dangerous to that authority or the system of which it forms a part. Most censorship is carried out by political or religious authorities.

census: a method of counting the members of a population present at a particular time. In the U.K. a full-scale national census has been taken every ten years since 1801 (except for 1941) and two sample censuses were held in 1966 and 1976. As well as counting the number of residents, census returns may also ask for other detailed information. When published, data from the census are widely used by a number of organisations, including the government, and prove an invaluable source of information, particularly for predictions of health and other social trends. However, the 1991 census in the U.K. showed a much higher than average non-response rate of over 2%, despite follow-up work and the fact that people are required by law to provide information. In all, it is estimated that over 2 million people were missing from the census returns. In many cases, the failure to complete the census form was because of objection to the community charge, or 'poll tax'. As a result, many projections about social trends in the population will be based on the 1981, rather than the 1991, returns. The census represents the largest possible survey of the population and is correspondingly expensive to administer. The 1991 census cost £135 million.

central business district: one of Burgess's urban zones, it represents the economic heart of the city in which business and commerce is conducted. While the CBD is still important in the life of cities, developments such as out-of-town shopping and business parks have undermined the centrality of the CBD to the economic success of the city. (See *urban zone theory*.)

central life interest: a concept used by sociologists of work, in particular, Dubin, to describe the main focus of concern in workers' lives. It was initially used in the debate over how important work was to factory workers. Some sociologists claimed that the informal groups which grew up on the factory floor were the most important part of workers' lives – their central life interest. Others argued that the home was the central life interest of workers, who were mainly instrumental in their approach to work.

central value system: the collection of beliefs and attitudes which make up the important core of a society's consciousness. The central value system is seen by Functionalists as a key element of social solidarity and one of the main ways that individuals are integrated, through agreeing on the most important values in society.

centralisation: the process whereby *power* becomes more and more concentrated in the hands of the few, as local sources of power and influence are neutralised and stripped of their capacity to make a difference. The process of modernisation can be seen as the increasing centralisation of power in the hands of Ministers of national governments and the emasculation of independent sources of oppositional power.

centre: in the political spectrum, the ideas and organisations which stand between the right and left and emphasise the individual and freedom. They range from social democracy to the old-style Liberal parties.

Centre for Contemporary Cultural Studies: established at the University of Birmingham, its main focus is on the contemporary cultural situation, especially with regard to popular and *youth culture*. It was influenced by a number of perspectives, most notably Marxism, but rejected the economic determinism of Marx in its insistence that cultural artefacts have an importance in their own right.

centre-periphery models: a view of social phenomena which characterises divisions between a strong, stable core and a weak, vulnerable surround to that core. It developed as a conception of world economies, where the core was seen as the industrial, mainly capitalist societies of the West and at the periphery were those countries of the *third world* dependent upon and dominated by the countries of the core. The analysis has since been applied to many other social phenomena, such as the labour force. (See *core workers; periphery workers.*)

ceremony: symbolic and ritualistic actions performed on appropriate occasions which are intended to express shared feelings and attitudes. Many important ceremonies are connected with birth, marriage and death and also the transfer of power, such as a coronation or the swearing-in of a president or chief.

certification: the granting of qualifications by appropriate examining bodies. In sociology there is also a wider meaning of certification, referring to the process whereby societies recognise the abilities of individuals through the qualifications they obtain. Certification is a crucial power of professional bodies who through the granting or withholding of certificates, determine who shall and who shall not become a practitioner.

chalk-and-talk: a method of teaching in which the students are relatively passive, the teacher controls the pace and content of the lesson and few, if any, resources are used other than the teacher and the blackboard. This method is often contrasted with so-called progressive teaching methods. (See *discovery learning; experiential learning.*)

change: see *social change*

channels of influence: the focus of lobbying work by *pressure groups*, this describes the power centres of society, which, if persuaded to a course of action, can translate influence into action. By charting the channels of influence which pressure groups act upon, sociologists claim that it is possible to map out the power centres in a society.

chaos theory: an explanation in science which argues for the difficulty in establishing invariate laws because of the operation of chance and long causal connections in the natural and social worlds. The classical conception of chaos theory is where the fluttering of a butterfly's wings in one part of the world, may, through the operation of chaos, lead to a hurricane in another part. While this may seem far-fetched, the central idea is that actions can have unintended consequences long after they occur and in seemingly unconnected phenomena, through long chains of events.

charisma: the attraction exerted by a powerful personality. In sociology, charisma was identified by Weber as one of the sources of *power* in society. It led to a particular form of social organisation, which was based on the whims of the charismatic leader, from whom all *authority* flowed. (See *rational authority.*)

chauvinism: strong ideas associated with extreme forms of nationalism and national pride. The word comes from Nicolas Chauvin, a French soldier in the Revolutionary and Napoleonic armies, and is often used to imply intolerance of those from other nationalities. It is also used in the context of male chauvinism to describe beliefs in the innate superiority of males and the corresponding belittling of females.

cheque-book voting: a model of voting which argues that one of the most important factors in deciding how people vote is their concern over which party will bring the most financial benefits to the individual and his/her family. It has been suggested that it was this concern which was a major factor in Labour's losing the 1992 election, fuelled by the Conservative election campaign which emphasised the additional tax burden people would allegedly face under a Labour government. (See *consumer voting; instrumental voting.*)

Chicago school: an important school of sociology between the two World Wars, it was prominent in the development of urban sociology, based around its study of the fast-changing nature of Chicago, and also in the theoretical development of *symbolic interactionism*, associated with Cooley and Mead.

Child Support Agency: established in 1993 by the Conservative Government to help reduce the growing cost to the taxpayer of providing financial support for lone parents and their children. The main task of the Agency was given as the tracing of absent parents (usually fathers) who were not contributing to the upkeep of their children, assessing an appropriate level of maintenance and ensuring payment. The aim was to save £500 million in 1993 alone. Almost from the start of operations in April 1993 the Agency was at the centre of a number of controversies. It was claimed that, in order to meet its targets, the CSA was focusing on middle-class men who were already paying maintenance, rather than on the more difficult task of tracing absentee fathers. Divorced and separated fathers mounted a national campaign against substantial increases in payments, arguing that these were adversely affecting the living standard of their second family. Women's groups report that many mothers are frightened to reveal details of the whereabouts of their children's father to the CSA for fear of violence. Cases have come to light in which self-employed fathers have been able successfully to conceal from the CSA details of their true income, when this is considerably higher than the one declared. Few lone parents gain any financial advantage from the operation of the CSA as payments are deducted, pound for pound from benefits. (See *lone parent families.*)

childcare: in simple terms, looking after young people, but in sociology, it has other aspects, such as whether child-care is carried out by the biological parents or others. There has been an increase in professional child-care since the Second World War as more and more mothers have gone out to work, whether in a *lone-parent* or dual parent situation. Sociologists are interested in the effects that this has on children as they grow up. They have also focused on the reasons why women are seen in society as having primary responsibility for child-care and ways that this has been challenged and changed in recent years. (See *nursery voucher scheme.*)

child-centredness: a family in which much activity and emotional energy is focused on the children, rather than adult desires. It developed with the emergence of the *nuclear family* form and stands in contrast to previous forms, where children were allegedly less important in the structure of the family.

childhood: a state which in sociological terms is both socially as well as chronologically determined. The concept is used to refer both to a period of time during which a person has not yet reached adult status and a set of beliefs regarding what it is to be a 'child'. The French sociologist Philippe Ariès argued that in medieval Europe children were both perceived and treated as young adults, and that the notion of 'childhood' as a separate status as we know it developed with the creation of a formal education system. Throughout the world there is a wide variation in notions of childhood and in some countries children remain an important part of the labour force, not always legally. The Victorians idealised childhood as a time of innocence, in which moral development should be a prime concern, and the development of psychology in the twentieth century emphasised the importance of the childhood period to the development of the adult personality. There are many current concerns regarding the physical and sexual abuse of children, and the *state* has powers to protect children, even to the extent of removing them from their family. A number of well-publicised cases in which children in care have been the victims of abuse has led to calls for an urgent review of how children's rights to protection can be safeguarded. Charities point to the growing number of children and young people homeless and living on the streets, and the large number whose lives are being blighted by *poverty*, calling into question our commitment as a nation to our expressed ideals of childhood.

Physical abuse	26%
Sexual abuse	16%
Emotional abuse	7%
Grave concern	32%
Neglect	19%

(Source: Health and Personal Social Services Statistics, 1993)

Reasons for children on child protection registers, England and Wales 1992

child-rearing patterns: a reference to social class differences in ways of bringing up children. Research by John and Elizabeth Newson in the 1960s and 1970s showed that such differences existed, with middle-class mothers more likely to follow advice from health visitors and reference books, and working-class mothers more likely to rely on advice from their mothers, sisters and friends. Middle-class parents were found to apply a more consistent approach to discipline, whereas working-class mothers showed a more arbitrary approach, veering between indulgence and strictness. Bernstein also identified social class differences in child-rearing, with middle-class mothers more likely than working-class mothers to use language to control their children's behaviour and to give reasons for their decisions. Bernstein believed that this particular use of language was one way in which middle-class children learned to use the *elaborated code.*

chiliastic movements: usually religious in origin, these are organised groups which look towards the passing of the present order and the end of the world as we know it. They tend to be enthusiastic in their services and welcome the transformation as the culmination of history.

choice: the ability to make decisions between alternatives in a free and unconstrained manner. Choice is traditionally an important concept in the sociology of *poverty*, in the sense that the poor have very little choice. However it has more recently become a central concept in *postmodernism*, where the extension of choice has been fundamental to the development of postmodern societies. The idea of choice has therefore been extended from decisions about basic foodstuffs to the choice of life styles in which the postmodern individual engages.

choice of method: the choice of a particular research method or methods may be influenced by a number of factors. These are sometimes defined in terms of constraints, either practical or ethical, but the following may also exert an influence on choice of method:

- time – some methods, such as *covert participant observation*, can be particularly time-consuming
- money – both the amount of money available to the sociologist and its source (e.g. a specific research grant, government or private funding)
- access to the group being studied – is this easy, difficult or even dangerous?
- the nature of the group being studied – factors such as their degree of literacy, their willingness to take part in research, the amount of time they have available will all need to be taken into account
- the nature of the subject matter – personal, sensitive issues may not lend themselves to a written *questionnaire* with standardised questions
- the kind of data required – do the end-users of the research need quantitative, statistical data, or more qualitative information?
- theoretical perspective – does the researcher or the person/group for whom the research is being conducted, have strong positivist or interactionist leanings?
- gender – it is increasingly acknowledged that this can exert an influence on the method(s) used; these influences include physical space (there are some places where either men or women cannot easily conduct research), and female sociologists in particular sometimes face resistance from male bosses or colleagues to their attempts to conduct the more unstructured types of research often favoured by women

Christianity: a monotheistic religion which emerged in the Near East and came to dominate the religious and civil life of Europe. Through *colonialism*, it spread to many other parts of the world in various different forms of Protestantism and Catholicism.

church: a well-established, bureaucratically-structured religious organisation with values which tend to be conservative and to support the established order in the society of which it is a part. Membership is usually by ascription, i.e. people are formally admitted into the church at birth. The term is usually used to refer to Christian churches. (See *denomination; sect.*)

church attendance statistics: figures covering attendance at church on the major Christian religious festivals, particularly Easter, and/or measures of the frequency with which members of society attend church services. Other statistical measures include the number of infant baptisms, the number of marriages solemnised in church, and Sunday school attendance figures. These statistics show, particularly for the Church of England and the major *denominations*, a steady decline, particularly since the end of the Second World War. This is often used as evidence that *secularisation* is taking place, but there is considerable disagreement regarding both the reliability of the figures and their interpretation.

Respondents were asked how often, apart from special occasions such as weddings, funerals and baptisms, did they attend services or meetings connected with their religion.

Frequency of attendance	Percentages
Once a week or more	11.7
Less often but at least once in two weeks	2.0
Less often but at least once a month	5.6
Less often but at least twice a year	10.3
Less often but at least once a year	5.2
Less often than above	3.8
Never or practically never	22.7
Varies too much to say	0.6
Not answered	0.1

(Source: Social & Community Planning Research, in Social Trends 1995)

Religious attendance in Great Britain 1993

circulation of elites: a term used to describe how *social change* may occur where there is a single unitary elite monopolising *power,* it suggests that the only possibility of change is the replacement of one *elite* by another. The concept therefore denies the possibility of democratic control in society. Where there are elections, the circulation of elites suggest that the only avenue open to electors is to choose which elite they will be governed by. Circulation may occur by the replacement of individual members of the elite by others, such as when younger members replace the older, or it may occur through a peaceful transition from one elite to a new rising one. Alternatively change may be violent, with the overthrow of one elite by another through *revolution.*

citizenship: both the legal right to count oneself a member of a particular state or commonwealth, and ideas concerning the relationship between an individual and the state. Generally, notions of citizenship involve defining the rights and the responsibilities of both the *state* and its citizens.

city: a large urban area, which is usually a focus for the surrounding hinterland of the countryside. Cities have always been of enormous interest to sociologists, because they are often exciting and vibrant places, with a great deal going on. They are also associated with social innovation, so that new ways of living are constantly being developed. Cities are also places of conflict and struggle between different social groups, so they are places of *contestation.*

City Technology College (CTC): a type of secondary school introduced in the 1980s designed to deliver high-quality teaching with a strong vocational focus, supported by the latest technology. It was intended that such schools should be built with private funding from industry, as they would deliver the kind of education which employers would wish their future employees to have. In practice relatively little private funding was forthcoming, and the government was forced to pay the major part. CTCs have been criticised for becoming privileged institutions with a predominantly middle class intake which take a disproportionate amount of government spending on education. (See *New Vocationalism.*)

civil liberties: personal and social freedoms which are guaranteed by law unless, in a particular set of circumstances, the exercise of these freedoms is deemed to be against the common good or public interest. When these freedoms are claimed and/or enforced through the legal or administrative system, they are usually classed as civil rights. Many recent events, such as the passing of the Criminal Justice Bill and demonstrations against the 'poll tax' or the export of live animals, have called into question the definition of civil rights and liberties.

civil religion: where secular symbols such as flags and national anthems function to promote social solidarity in the way that religion has traditionally done. Durkheim used the term to indicate that there were *functional equivalents* to religion in every society, even those which did not have a single or unifying religion.

civilisation: a term which describes a complex cultural and social entity which usually covers more than one society or nation-state. Thus sociologists define Western civilisation as the cultural *artefacts* associated with capitalist industrial societies of the nineteenth and twentieth centuries and which encompass such values as democracy, tolerance, liberalism and so on.

civilising process: the ways identified by Elias in which history can be seen as the progressive ability of humans to control their emotions. Elias showed how different standards of behaviour (decorum or etiquette) come into existence and create a more civilised human being.

clan: a *descent group* which claims membership from one side of the family only.

clash of cultures: an approach in the sociology of education which identifies the cause of *under-achievement* of working-class and ethnic minority children as the difference between the expectations and practices of the school and the values and attitudes of pupils from particular backgrounds. In the case of the working class it is argued that the middle-class *ethos* of the school, with its emphasis on *deferred gratification,* does not go well with the more hedonistic culture of the working class. A criticism raised against this approach is that it tends to lump all schools and all working-class children together, when there are important differences within each category. (See *cultural difference theory; cultural deprivation; cultural reproduction.*)

class: see *social class*

class boundaries debate: one of the continuous disagreements in sociology, it involves how many social classes there are in modern societies and where the distinctions between them should be drawn. It was developed as a reaction to the Marxist division of capitalist societies into two major classes and some unimportant intermediate classes. Critics have argued that this is a simplistic view of a complex social phenomenon and therefore theoretically there should be more social classes identified. Commonsense views tend to divide the *class structure* into three, the upper, middle and working classes, but sociologists are interested in how these can be justified in terms of the social situation in which members find themselves. Different sociologists have therefore developed various schema of social class, which seek to divide society into a specific and often different number of social classes according to some objective criteria. (See *contradictory class locations.*)

class cleavage: see *partisan alignment*

class conflict: see *class struggle*

class consciousness: where workers have an awareness that they have an interest in common with all other workers and bind together in collective organisations to pursue those interests. This leads to struggles on the political level, as class conscious workers seek to change their common material conditions. (See *status consciousness; trade union consciousness.*)

class culture: the shared meanings and patterns of behaviour associated with a particular *social class*. The Marxist view of this is that socio-economic factors lead to different classes having different patterns of meaning, therefore it is questioned whether an overall shared *culture* exists in society. Class culture arises out of shared interests. Others disagree, and argue that there is a dominant culture which all members of society broadly share, irrespective of differences which may arise from other characteristics such as *age*, class or *ethnic group*.

class de-alignment: represents the situation where the connection between occupation and political support for a particular party declines. The traditional alignment is between manual occupations and Labour voting, and non-manual workers and Conservative support.

class-for-itself: where members of the *working class*, as a *class-in-itself*, recognise that they share interests with all other workers and take political and *industrial action* to further their interests. Marx saw the state of being a class for itself as a crucial step on the road to a revolution in which the working class would seize power and change society in their own interests.

class formation: the Marxist view that the private ownership of the *means of production* determines the allocation of *political power* in society, and leads to the two groups, the owners and the non-owners of production, having different *class interests*, resulting in a struggle with one another. These three elements, namely the ownership of the means of production, the distribution of political power and the conflict between groups, together lead to the formation of two opposing classes.

class fragmentation: see *fragmentation theories*

class imagery: the way that individuals and groups see society as divided according to levels of subordination and superordination. The main types of class imagery are proletarian, deferential and pecuniary.

class-in-itself: a term developed by Marx and Engels to describe the situation where groups of workers have enough in common materially to share a similar objective class position. The basis for a class-in-itself was urban living, where large numbers of individuals were brought together to work in large and small factories. Thus, the material aspect of these workers' lives showed great similarity, and at the time that Marx and Engels were writing, also much poverty and misery. The concept is used in conjunction with *class-for-itself*.

class interest: a term used to denote that for each of the collectivities which exist in superordinate and subordinate positions in the economic hierarchy, there are social policies and political developments which benefit them, as opposed to others in different positions. For example, it is supposed that having a Labour government is in the working class's interest, because it would introduce reforms which would benefit them. These interests are real in that they reflect the material and economic circumstances of each class.

class structure: the distribution of groups in society according to criteria such as ownership/non-ownership of the *means of production,* control or non-control over work situations and whether the group sells or buys labour power. Traditional class structure is conceived of as a *hierarchy,* in which the largest social class is also the lowest. However, post-modern societies are alleged to have developed a different class structure, in which the largest social class is in the middle of the class structure. This can be represented as in the diagram below. (See *new middle class.*)

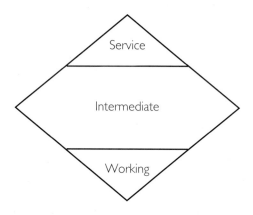

Class structure

class struggle: the conflict between economic groups which, according to the Marxists, is central to historical progress. Marx saw class struggle as the important dynamic in society, causing *social change* through the resolution of the contradictions between the interests of the *proletariat* on one hand and the *bourgeoisie* on the other. The struggle between the classes occurs on a number of levels, from the day-to-day economic conflict through the political to the sometimes violent revolutionary conflict.

class-centric: a view which is biased, in that it is taken from a particular position in the economic structure. Middle-class sociologists are often accused of being class-centric in that they view the problems of the *working class* from their particular class position.

classical criminology: the traditional approach to crime, associated with the eighteenth and nineteenth centuries and founded on the belief that all people were criminal by inclination and that therefore there must be strict controls and punishment for wrong-doing The classical criminologists assume that there is a basic *anti-social* instinct which society must control in order for there to be *social order.* There were no mitigating circumstances which might excuse the individual from crime.

classical sociologists: a term used to describe the great early sociologists, who developed and set out a distinctive way of looking at society. The canon of classical sociologists usually includes Comte, Durkheim, Marx and Weber, but may also include others such as Saint-Simon, Henderson, Vico and Tönnies.

classification: see *taxonomies*

classroom interaction: the relationships and subsequent behaviour which occur within the classroom and which can have a powerful effect on both teaching and learning. Interactionists in particular have focused on the importance of this process, and have looked at the interaction between teacher and pupils, and between groups of pupils. It is a view of education which sees it as a dynamic and constantly negotiated process, rather than the simple imparting of knowledge to pupils by a teacher. (See *labelling*.)

client mode of production: used by Marxists to indicate a productive capacity which lies outside the main capitalist *mode of production*. *Domestic labour* is one such client mode, which reproduces the labour power of the work-force.

clients: an increasingly common term used to refer to individuals and groups using particular services. These services include professional services such as health, education and social care, and a range of other services such as leisure and entertainment.

clinical sociology: a term used mainly in America to describe an approach to the subject which is aimed at intervention to solve social problems. This interventionist approach is associated with Fedcralist funding of programmes to alleviate *poverty*.

clique: a term used by Burns to describe a network of marginal individuals in organisations, who form *solidarity* friendships for mutual support. Those under threat of redundancy may therefore form cliques to give each other reassurance. (See *cabal*.)

closed questions: questions which allow the respondent only a specific range of answers, e.g. Yes/No/Don't Know.

closed shop: the situation in which being a member of a designated *trade union* is a condition of employment. The closed shop came under increasing restriction during the 1980s and only a couple remain. Sociologists are interested in how the closed shop served the interests of both trade union leaders and employers. Closed shops simplified negotiation and also gave the trade union a role to play in work discipline. However, the idea of the closed shop had been increasingly criticised as the ideology of *individualism* became dominant during the 1980s.

closed societies: societies in which there is little *social mobility* in the *class structure*. Closed societies tend to be very rigid, with individuals spending their life in the same social position into which they were born. *Status* is therefore fixed by hereditary characteristics and is given by the status of the parents. (See *ascription; open societies*.)

cluster sampling: a form of *sampling* in which the *survey population* is first divided into smaller groups, or clusters, from which *random samples* are then drawn. Cluster sampling is usually used when both the population and the desired sample size are particularly large.

co-optation: the situation in which two or more *organisations* are related through the same individuals having directorships in each of them. Though there may be no formal relationship between the organisations, some sociologists suggest that multi-directorships mean that there are informal contacts which can lead to co-ordination of some spheres of activity.

co-production: the process in late capitalist societies whereby the *State* and its citizens act together to administer society. The post-modern condition of late capitalism so fragments society that the State can no longer administer society effectively on its own. It therefore recruits the citizens into co-production, to enable the co-operation needed to ensure the smooth running of society. For example, the self-assessment of tax payments, rather than assessment by State employees, is one form of co-production.

coalition formation: a formal relationship between two *organisations*, which may range from written agreements to merger. The term is used by Thompson and McEwen to indicate one of a range of ways in which organisations might influence each other. (See *co-optation; competition.*)

coca-colonisation: the process whereby United States industry comes to dominate the economies of other countries through the penetration of their markets by American big business. The franchising of American products in other countries, while retaining overall control of the product, is a central part of the neo-imperialist process. (See *McDonaldisation.*)

code: see *language codes*

code of ethics: one of the defining characteristics of a *profession*, this regulates activity vis-a-vis the public. The code of ethics therefore sets out the moral dimension of a profession, setting standards of proper behaviour and providing guidelines for issues such as fixing charges.

coding: the way in which sociologists give numerical values to respondents' answers in order to ease the analysis of data and establish correlations of statistical significance. The development of the computer has made coding an important part of the research process and permitted the development of sophisticated mathematical models of society.

coefficient of aggravation: used by Durkheim to suggest how prone to *suicide* a particular individual might be. It was calculated by the level of involvement of individuals in integrating social contexts. Thus children leaving home increased the coefficient of aggravation of married women, who in this way lost an integrating context. (See *egoistic suicide.*)

coercion: literally force. Sociologists are interested in the way that coercion manifests itself in society. It can either be overt, as in the direct use of the police or army to control populations, or indirectly through the threat to use force. Coercion can also take a legitimated form in the law and justice system. Marxists argue that capitalist societies are coercive by nature and beneath the velvet glove of the institutions of the law lies the iron fist of the military.

cognition: the process of thinking, it is an important aspect of mental life and constitutes the conscious thought processes as against the unconscious. (See *affectivity.*)

cognitive dissonance: where there is a lack of fit between the views of an individual and the ideas in the media content to which they are exposed. Festinger argues that this is psychologically uncomfortable and that the individual will seek to reduce the dissonance, largely by selectively choosing more consonant material. (See *selective exposure.*)

cohabitation: a situation in which a couple lives together as man and wife although not legally married. This is increasingly common in Western countries, especially Britain, both among young, never-married couples and men and women separated or divorced from previous spouses. Statistics show that people are more likely to cohabit before second marriages than before first marriages. Many cohabiting couples later marry and while it might be expected that their 'trial marriage' might help to ensure a lasting relationship, figures show that couples who have cohabited have higher divorce rates than those who have not. Of couples who married for the first time in the early 1980s, those who had cohabited were 50% more likely to have divorced after five years of marriage and 60% more likely to have divorced after eight years of marriage, than those who had not. The extent to which cohabitation in Britain is increasingly the norm is reflected in the Church of England's recent decision to stop using the phrase 'living in sin' to describe cohabitation.

cohesion: literally, sticking together, it is used in sociology to describe the *integration* of a society into a unified whole. (See *solidarity*.)

cohesive mass segregation: an explanation for the high *strike-proneness* of certain groups (e.g. miners). Kerr and Siegel argued that it was the relative isolation of large numbers of workers in a single-industry town or village which led to high levels of striking. The *solidarity* which working and living together with few alternatives engendered, led to a strong propensity to act together to pursue aims.

cohort analysis: the investigation of a group who share a similar demographic characteristic, usually age. Cohort analysis is particularly used in the sociology of gender, where children born in the same year may be followed through the education system in order to chart the changes and constancies they experience. Cohort analysis is important for the *comparative method*, where two different cohorts may be contrasted and compared for differences and similarities.

Cold War: the situation which prevailed after the Second World War, when the major communist and capitalist countries (especially the Soviet Union and the United States) were in strong confrontation with each other, though not directly involved in war-like activities against each other. The Cold War was thus fought by proxies in the third world, and especially through civil wars between those sympathetic to communist ideology and those hostile to it. The Cold War ended with the collapse of *communism* in eastern Europe and the Soviet Union in the late 1980s, so that even though communist regimes survive, most notably in China, communism is widely seen as having 'lost the war'. (See *end of history*.)

collapse of communism: the momentous events of the late 1980s which saw the overthrow either peacefully or violently of the communist regimes of the Soviet Union and eastern Europe. The symbolic end of the *Cold War* came with the dismantling of the Berlin Wall. Communism continues to survive in its eastern form, in China, North Korea and Vietnam, and in the western hemisphere in Cuba.

collective bargaining: the negotiation between workers and employers which occurs through organised representatives of each side. It is in contrast to individual bargaining where single workers might seek to negotiate conditions and wages. By banding together, workers hope to receive better conditions and pay through a system of collective bargaining. For the employers, collective bargaining simplifies the process of setting conditions and pay, though it also holds the possibility of industrial action. Up until the 1980s the trend in collective bargaining was towards national agreements among groups of workers and their employers. However, in the 1990s, pressure has been growing for the dismantling of national collective bargaining arrangements and the substitution of local arrangements. This has been resisted by workers, but encouraged by Government and some employers.(See *institutionalisation of conflict.*)

collective behaviour: the actions of people when they operate together, for example in a crowd or a mob. Collective behaviour usually implies the loss of individual will in the psychology of the group, which takes on characteristics independent of the sum of the individual actions within it.

collective conscience: a term used by Durkheim to denote the existence of a social and moral order, exterior to the individual and acting upon him or her as an independent force. It is the shared sentiments, beliefs and values of individuals which make up the collective conscience and in *traditional societies* forms the basis of *social order.* As societies modernise, the collective conscience weakens and *mechanical solidarity* is replaced by *organic solidarity.*

collective consumption: developed by Castells to denote the services which need to be provided to keep a work force healthy and rested. Collective consumption therefore guarantees the reproduction of *labour power* by ensuring that the work force is housed, rested, materially content with the system and ready for a day's work. It is composed then of the agencies of the Welfare State, and provides health care, education (both vocational and ideological), housing, transport, and leisure, which are consumed by everyone in society. Critics of this concept, such as Pahl, argue that it is a very vague one, being unclear whether Castells is writing about the Welfare State or all goods consumed. This is an important distinction in Britain, where housing, for example, is provided both by the *State* and through private agencies.

collective orientation: one of Parsons' *pattern variables*, which suggests that in *traditional societies,* shared interests are more important than individual ones. (See *self-orientation.*)

collectivism: a political philosophy which covers a range of ideas which are united by their advocacy of the communal control of the *means of production* and distribution. The most common form of collectivism is associated with direct *State* control of industry, as opposed to *industrial democracy.*

collectivities: a general term to cover any grouping wider than the individual. They may range from friendship groupings to the membership of the Newcastle United Fan Club. The advantage of the term is that implies that groups are built up from individuals collected together and do not have an existence independent of the individuals.

colonialism: a world system in which European countries controlled much of Asia, Africa and Latin America. The heyday of the colonial system was in the late-nineteenth and early-twentieth centuries, when the British, French, Dutch and, until the First World War, the Germans held large Empires in the southern hemisphere. Sociological interest in colonialism has centred on the way that laws were used to establish dominant trading positions for companies in the colonial powers and the way that State power was used in a systematic way to exploit indigenous populations. The main tactic used by the colonial powers was 'divide-and-rule', setting different elements within the colonised countries against each other. The drawing up of 'national' boundaries by the colonial powers, without heed to history, *culture* or language aided this policy. The legacy of this policy is said to be the tribal and ethnic troubles which still affect much of Africa and Asia.

colonisation: a process by which a group within the middle class who are the sons and daughters of working-class parents have brought their Labour-voting traditions with them into their new class position. The emergence of the colonisers was caused by shifts in the *occupational structure* after the Second World War, which resulted in a shrinkage in manual jobs and an increase in white-collar jobs. The extra middle-class jobs were filled by the sons and daughters of the working class, benefiting from the increased education provision of the post-war era.

coming out: the process whereby lesbians and gay men reveal their sexuality to a public *audience*. It is a fairly recent phenomenon, dating in a large scale way from the de-criminalisation of certain homosexual acts and the growth of the gay movement. It is interesting to the sociologist because it involves social as well as psychological aspects. For example, the audience for the process may be confined to a few friends and not to family, or to the public at large. It may signify a personal commitment or a political statement. (See *outing*.)

command economy: a concept describing the control of the *State* over the *means of production*, so that all investment and marketing decisions are made by central State agencies in contrast to the market. (See *mixed economy*.)

commodification: the tendency for goods, services, people and relationships to become subject to the principles of the market and thus reduced to a monetary value. It is seen by Marxists as a fundamental feature of capitalist development and a sign of the increasing *alienation* associated with *late capitalism*.

commodity form of incorporation: used to describe the way in which an oppositional sub-culture is neutralised by capitalist society, through the conversion of *sub-cultural signs* into popular, mass-produced objects. The classical example is the transformation of the fashion of street punk into high fashion. (See *ideological form of incorporation*.)

common values: where people share the same set of opinions concerning the proper way to live. In any society there needs to be at least a minimum of common values if that society is to persist. Where common values are lacking or where the *consensus* over appropriate behaviour breaks down, there is likely to be conflict. Whereas in a society a degree of *conflict* is necessary to prevent it ossifying, the existence of common values ensures some continuation of society.

commonsense: what everybody knows or assumes. In sociology, commonsense is used as a contrast to sociological knowledge, which sometimes challenges commonsense and provides evidence that things are not always as people assume them to be. Commonsense explanations are therefore contrasted to sociological explanations, with the latter providing a more solid basis for knowledge.

commonsense knowledge: see *everyday knowledge*

commonsense world: the knowledge that everybody knows and takes for granted constitutes the commonsense world. It is the world where *action* is taken without deep thought but as part of the everyday activities of individuals. The knowledge of the commonsense world differs from scientific knowledge in three ways:

- Science is more formal and systematic, being precise in the way that observations are carried out. Observation in the commonsense world is haphazard and arbitrary.
- Science is more rigorous, allowing itself to be subject to critical scrutiny.
- Commonsense knowledge is practical for short-term solutions to everyday problems. Science goes beyond the pragmatic to form theoretical knowledge, which may be drawn upon for practical purposes.

(See *everyday knowledge*.)

communal economy: describes the exchange of services in a locality which does not rely on the exchange of cash. This can exist in either a semi-formal or an informal form. In the case of the former, a good example would be a baby-sitting circle in which tokens are exchanged for hours sat. For the latter, services are exchanged through friendship groupings on a basis of expertise held.

commune: a form of 'family' living in which a group of individuals, either related or not, live together and hold property in common. There are various forms of commune which vary in the amount of communal property they hold. Some for example bring up their children with all adults of the commune as the social fathers and mothers. The classic commune was the Israeli kibbutz, which emerged as an attempt to forge a new way of living in the aftermath of the holocaust.

communication: the transfer of information between individuals or groups, it is a fundamental feature of the human condition. Human beings communicate much more extensively than other animals, both verbally and symbolically, and are distinguished by their ability to use technology to reach mass audiences. (See *mass media*.)

communism: a political and social arrangement in societies characterised by State control of the *means of production* and a monopoly of *political power* by the Communist party. Derived from the work of Marx, the implementation of communism involved totalitarian control of society. The empirical manifestation of communism was in the Soviet Union and the socialist societies of eastern Europe until their collapse in 1989–90. Communism continues to dominate in the People's Republic of China, North Korea, Cuba and Vietnam.

community: a central concept in sociology, used by both the *classical sociologists* and modern sociologists, to describe a certain type of social organisation in which there is a strong sense of *identity* between individual members of the community. As with many sociological concepts, it has been defined in different ways by different sociologists:

- as locality – a given geographical area is the basis for identity
- as a local social system – a set of relationships usually, but not always, found in a given locality
- as a type of relationship – a sense of strong shared identity which may be geographically dispersed

Communities can therefore be based on day-to-day contact, religious belief, ethnic identity, national feeling etc.

community action: used where locally-based groups organise themselves to achieve objectives in a locality. It is usually associated with disadvantaged groups who seek redress for their grievances through self-help organisations. They also tend to look for funding to national or local government to help achieve their objectives.

community care: see *care in the community*

community development programmes: a U.K. Government policy in the 1970s designed to integrate a whole range of initiatives towards the inner city, in education, housing, leisure, health etc. However, many of the workers on the programmes were very critical of them, because they were inadequately funded and lacked any real power vis-a-vis the local authority. Another element of criticism was that the CDPs were designed to control the poor, rather than alleviate their poverty and were consequently funded from the Home Office rather than the social welfare agencies.

community integration: an explanation put forward by Kerr and Siegel for the low *strike-proneness* of some industries, which argued that where industrial communities were connected to the rest of society in several ways, they had less of a propensity to strike.

community languages: a generic term for those languages which do not appear in the Modern Language departments of most schools but which many students speak at home. The major community languages in the U.K. are from the Indian subcontinent, such as Urdu, Gujerati etc.

community politics: a strategy devised by the Liberal party to build up public support by concentrating on local campaigns and issues. It has been fairly successful in establishing a local power base for the Liberal Democrat Party, but has not yet produced the expected breakthrough into national power.

community power: a term used to describe the patterns of control of local areas or neighbourhoods. The concept was developed in the United States to cover those sociological studies which investigated whether there were local *elites* in control of local communities, or whether power was pluralistically dispersed among different groups.

community studies: a collective term given to a series of examinations of different localities, mainly of working-class occupational groups such as miners and fishermen. The studies, mainly carried out in the 1950s and 1960s, provide a documentary account of the experience of traditional working-class communities and in particular the male working population within them. The focus of much of the community studies was the ideologies and consciousness of members of the community. The studies have been criticised because:

- in focusing on work, they ignored the experiences of women
- they made contradictory class images into simplistic class-conscious stereotypes
- they were ahistorical, ignoring the shaping of these communities by the relationships between capital and labour

commuter zone: the outer edges of a city and its satellite towns which, according to *urban zone theory*, are the main residential areas for middle-class workers. These areas are characterised by being largely empty during the day, as workers move into the city centre to work, and have limited recreational opportunities in them for the workers who return at night.

comparative method: sometimes used as an alternative to an *experiment*, the comparative method analyses two or more different groups or institutions in terms of their similarities and differences, often with reference to statistical data. It is usually used with large groups, sometimes whole societies (e.g. Durkheim's work on *suicide*) although research in psychology has used the comparative method on a study of a relatively small number of monozygotic (identical) twins reared apart. While comparative studies can yield interesting results, there is a problem of *validity*. There are usually so many different *variables* involved that it is impossible to draw definitive conclusions.

compensation thesis: developed by sociologists of *leisure*, this argues that the main function of leisure is to make up for the frustrations which individuals experience in work. Conversely, those whose jobs are interesting do not seek compensation and therefore down-grade the importance of leisure in their lives.

compensatory education: education which has as its main aim the overcoming of perceived deficiencies in a child's education. This education is often delivered in the form of special programmes, such as the American 'Operation Headstart' and 'Project Upward Bound'. The concepts of compensatory education and the culturally-deprived child originated in the United States in the mid-1950s, and quickly became a popular way of explaining the relatively poor educational performance of certain groups of children, notably blacks and Puerto Ricans. The programmes, which received considerable financial support from the American government, developed an increasing emphasis on the pre-school years. Critics of the view that lack of educational success was a result of the 'wrong' *culture* and *values* in the homes of some children argued that it diverted attention away from the real problem, which was that of *poverty* and lack of opportunity, and also assumed that the culture of black and Hispanic Americans was inferior to that of white Americans. Some of the original 'Headstart' children were surveyed in later life, and did not show significant advantages over similar children who had not taken part in the programme, but there is disagreement regarding the interpretation of the findings. The idea of compensatory education in Britain was reflected in the implementations of the *Plowden Report*. (See *positive discrimination*.)

competences: a term increasingly used in the context of vocational education and training to refer to those skills, the effective demonstration of which renders a person able to be certified as 'competent'.

competition: a situation where industries with the same product vie with each other to attract customers to their particular brand of product. Competition is also a central ideological concept for capitalist societies as it is through competition that industry remains efficient.

competitive interest theory: an answer to the *problem of order*, this states that *society* is the unintended consequence of interaction. It proposes that in order to compete effectively and fairly for the satisfaction of desire, there must be a minimum of justice and rules, because we need order to trade.

complementary leisure: a situation where work generates neither enthusiasm nor hostility and therefore the leisure pursuits undertaken are unaffected by work. It is usually associated with routine office work and much leisure activity is carried out at home, such as watching television. (See *extension leisure; oppositional leisure*.)

compliance: see *normative power; coercive power; utilitarian power*

comprador state: a term used by to describe a *state* in the *third world* which is a client of a *first world* country. The implication of the term is that the governing *elite* of the third world country is so tied in to the interests of the first world country that the former is not truly independent. Under-development theorists argue that the advantage of a comprador relationship over direct *colonialism* is that the illusion of independence satisfies nationalist opinion in the third world society, which might otherwise be hostile to the interests of the first world state.

comprehensive schools: schools which take children of all abilities and educate them together. Primary and junior education in England and Wales has always been comprehensive (with the obvious exception of fee-paying schools), but the secondary school system created by the *Education Act, 1944* was a selective one. Although the first comprehensive secondary schools appeared at the end of the 1940s, they were relatively few in number until in 1966 the Labour Government put pressure on local education authorities to reorganise secondary schools on comprehensive lines. This process was slowed down or even halted when a Conservative government was in power, but by 1979 the majority of secondary schools were comprehensive. The debate about comprehensive schools has centred on whether they have been able to bring about greater *equality of opportunity* for secondary pupils than the selective schools of the *tri-partite system.*

comprehensivisation: the process of secondary schools being reorganised from selective schools to comprehensive ones.

computer technology: a range of machines and applications based on digital code and microprocessors, through which many millions of operations per second can be processed to achieve programmed ends. The development of computer technology has revolutionised the way that we produce goods and services in society and also affected the lives of millions of individuals, for example, in the appearance of personal computers in our homes. The development of computer technology should be one of the most important factors shaping the twenty-first century.

Comte: a French sociologist writing in the first half of the nineteenth century. Comte developed the idea of *positivism,* and believed that societies were subject to the laws of social and intellectual development, which he believed were as much 'laws' as those in *natural science.* He argued that societies passed through three stages, the last of which was the *positivist stage,* characterised by rational thinking and rational government. Many of Comte's ideas influenced the development of *functionalism* in sociological thought. (See *metaphysical stage; theological stage.*)

concentration: used by sociologists of the media to describe the way in which the media industry is increasingly dominated by a small number of large companies. Initial interest in concentration was focused on Britain, where the collapse of independent local newspapers and the shrinking of ownership in the national press meant that fewer companies were dominating media output. More recently, concentration has taken on a global dimension with increasing domination of the global media market by a few huge firms.

concentric zone theory: see *urban zone theory*

concept: a term which carries a specific meaning and stands as a half-way house between empirical facts and full-blown theories. Concepts are often used as a short-hand for more complex descriptions of social reality. Each discipline develops its own set of concepts which can sometimes be seen as the jargon of the subject. Nevertheless they are indispensable for describing and explaining the subject-matter of a discipline without having to go into long descriptions each time they are employed.

conflict: meaning disagreement, it is used in sociology to indicate the struggle between the different interests and social groups in society. The concept implies that social life is based on coercion, and generates hostility and even violence. Society is therefore fundamentally divided into sectional interests, who compete with each other by various means to protect and extend their own position. *Social systems* are therefore full of contradictions and are subject to constant change. (See *consensus*.)

conflict theory: a general term covering a number of sociological approaches, which were opposed to *functionalism* and which shared the idea that the basic feature of all societies was the struggle between different groups for access to scarce resources. They ranged from the Marxist emphasis on class conflict over economic resources, to the Weberian emphasis on the struggle between different groups over *status* and *power*, as well as *wealth*.

conformity: according to Merton, specifically where individuals are able to achieve their goals by employing legitimated ways. As their socially defined wants are met in appropriate ways, conformist individuals do not need to turn to deviant activities to satisfy their wants.

conglomeration: the bringing together of companies in different sectors to form one over-arching firm with 'fingers in many pies'. Conglomerates are of particular interest to sociologists of the media, in which a small number of firms have interests in many different sectors of the industry. (See *diversification*.)

conjecture: a logical suggestion as to why something is happening in the way that it is, which can then be subject to experimental testing. The notion of conjecture forms an important part of Popper's view regarding science and scientific method. (See *natural science; falsification; refutation*.)

conjugal: a concept referring to husband and wife. (See *conjugal roles*.)

conjugal roles: the roles played by a husband and wife within a marriage, with particular reference to the *domestic division of labour*. Elizabeth Bott suggested that there were two main types of conjugal role, *segregated* and *joint*, which her research showed to be associated with the working class and middle class respectively. Bott predicted that as the *norms* of the middle class 'filtered down' to the working class, conjugal roles would tend to become increasingly joint, though this does not seem to be borne out by the evidence. As 'conjugal roles' is a term which technically applies to married partners, and taking into account the increase in *cohabitation*, it is increasingly common to refer to the '*domestic division of labour*' rather than conjugal roles. (See *symmetrical family, New Man*.)

consanguinity: a relationship based on descent from a common ancestor. The line of descent may be lineal (i.e. a direct line of descent) or with no direct line.

consciousness: that part of the human mind which is self-aware. In sociology consciousness is used particularly, but not exclusively, by Marxists to indicate the individual's awareness of their position in the social structure of *society*. Consciousness also extends to awareness of place within the environment and with the internal workings of the individual's own mind. It is thus our knowledge about the world.

consensual view of need: a shared view of what is required to reach and maintain a minimum standard of living based not on subsistence but according to the prevailing norms of society. In the research for their 1985 book 'Poor Britain', Mack and Lansley took a *representative sample* of 1174 *respondents* and asked them to categorise a range of goods and services as either 'essential' or 'luxuries'. They found a high degree of consensus regarding items considered necessities, as shown below.

Standard-of-living items	% classing as necessity	Standard-of-living items	% classing as necessary
Heating to warm living areas of home if it is cold	97	Carpets in living rooms and bedrooms	70
Indoor toilet (not shared with another household)	96	Celebrations on special occasions such as Christmas	69
Damp-free home	96	A roast meat joint or its equivalent once a week	67
Bath (not shared with another household)	94	A washing machine	67
Beds for everyone in the household	94	New, not second-hand clothes	64
Public transport for one's needs	88	A hobby or leisure activity	64
A warm waterproof coat	87	Two hot meals a day (for adults)	64
Three meals a day for children	82	Meat or fish every other day	63
Self-contained accommodation	79	Presents for friends or family once a year	63
Two pairs of all-weather shoes	78	A holiday away from home for one week a year (not with relatives)	63
Enough bedrooms for every child over 10 of different sex to have own room	77	Leisure equipment for children, e.g. sports equipment or a bicycle	57
Refrigerator	77	A garden	55
Toys for children	71	A television	51

(Source: J Mack and S Lansley, 'Poor Britain', 1985)

The list of 'necessities' established in this way formed the basis of defining *poverty* for Mack and Lansley; people with an enforced lack of three or more items on the list (excluding public transport, a garden and a television) were deemed to be in poverty, as they were unable to reach the minimum standard of living as agreed by a majority of the sample. (See *index of deprivation*.)

consensus: literally meaning agreement, it is used in a wide sense in sociology to describe those perspectives which stress the essential cohesion and *solidarity* of society. Consensus assumes that *norms* and *values* in society are generally agreed and that social life is based on co-operation rather than *conflict*. There is usually a legitimate *authority* involved in policing the consensus, which also guarantees that societies tend to persist.

Conservative Party: a British political organisation of the right, which includes a range of tendencies from one-nation Tories to the *New Right*. It is traditionally associated with middle class support and financial support from big business. In the 1980s, the Conservative Party was dominated by Thatcherism and the *ideology* of monetarism. In the early 1990s, it was divided into pro- and anti-European Community factions.

conservatism: a political philosophy which is oriented towards traditionalism and preserving the structures and ideals of a society's past, while adapting them to the present. Modern conservative theory has become associated with the free market and the defence of capitalism.

conspicuous consumption: the use of goods and services to demonstrate actual or symbolic membership of a particular social class, especially one of high *status*. The goods and services therefore usually fall into the luxury class. Conspicuous consumption may occur in any society, but is particularly associated with consumer-oriented societies in which status is closely associated with the ownership of particular material goods. An example of conspicuous consumption is the wearing of 'designer' clothes which carry the easily-visible designer label. However, this is only effective if people can recognise which are the high-status, luxury goods, so advertising and marketing play an important role.

conspiracy theory: attached to ideas which rely on asserting that individuals in power act together secretly in order to preserve their own interests against the interests of the rest of society. The classic conspiracy theory is the belief in a global plot to dominate international and domestic politics by the *military-industrial complex*, the Zionist movement, or the capitalist class.

constituency: a geographical unit which makes up the electoral area for a single member of Parliament. A constituency contains roughly 60,000 electors, bound together in a natural unit which, as far as possible, has some sense of *identity* or logic.

constitutional typologies: an explanation of criminality which relies on the body-type of the individual as a predictor of the tendency to criminality. Of the body-types identified by Sheldon, it was the high energy of the mesomorphs (hard and round) which led into criminal activity. This did not suggest that all mesomorphs were criminal, but that they were more likely to engage in delinquency. The theory has been criticised because it does not identify the mechanism whereby the body-type is translated into particular actions. It may also lead to *stereotyping* of certain individuals on the basis of their appearance.

constructs: in sociology, any *concept* or explanation which helps individuals to understand the world around them. The term is used to indicate the artificial nature of the linguistic device which is being used. For example, the concept 'social class' is a construct, which helps sociologists classify and explain stratified societies.

consumer power: the ability we all have as buyers of goods and services to fashion the patterns of distribution in a society. While the individual purchaser may have little consumer power, the millions of consumer decisions made every day shape the economic fortunes of different firms and the country as a whole. For example, the reluctance of consumers to purchase houses in the early 1990s limited the expected recovery from recession.

consumption: used to describe the ways in which individuals use goods and services. Whereas sociologists have traditionally been interested in production, focus on consumption has increased during the 1980s and 1990s. Arising out of the increased *leisure* in society and a renewed focus on *life style* as a determinant of *social class,* consumption has become a major item of sociological research in many different areas. These range from a focus on consumption patterns by different social groups, to an interest in the sociology of food and cuisine.

content analysis: a method associated with the study of the media, in which researchers define a set of categories and then classify the material under study in terms of the frequency it appears in the different categories. For example, the *Glasgow University Media Group* used this technique in their controversial analysis of the television news coverage of *industrial relations,* and it has also been used to study newspaper coverage of different types of crime, relating the extent of coverage (in column inches) to the actual incidence of the various types of crime. One of the problems of content analysis is the difficulty both of defining the categories, and allocating the material into the appropriate category.

contest mobility: a form of *social mobility* based on the assumption that some education systems operate in a meritocratic fashion. The concept was used by R. Turner in the 1950s to describe the social mobility which he believed to operate in the USA, as a result of the fair and open competition found in American schools. Turner has been criticised for an overly-idealistic view of American education, and for ignoring the impact of *social class* on social mobility. (See *meritocracy; sponsored mobility.*)

contestation: a process described by Mandel, where workers come to challenge the rights of *capital* to determine the conditions of production. Mandel argued that, with the increase in *automation,* it would be impossible to continue to increase the real wages of workers. Therefore, the standard of living of the working class would decline and workers would begin to challenge the prerogatives of *capitalism.* (See *late capitalism.*)

contingency theory: an approach to *organisations* which examines the influence of the *environment* and *technology* (contingent factors) on organisational behaviour and structure. The importance of this perspective is that it rejects the search for the 'most efficient' form of organisation, in favour of exploring the variations which responses to the environment invoke in organisations.

continuous assessment: a form of assessment in which grades received for pieces of work done during a course of study are counted towards the final grade. The work so counted may be *coursework* or marks gained in a written or practical examination. In the early 1990s the proportion of marks allowed to be gained by continuous assessment in public examinations was significantly curtailed, as Ministers claimed that it made passing examinations easier.

continuous process production: where goods are manufactured without being touched by human hands. It is usually found in the chemical and drugs industries where the transfer of the materials from one part of the process to another could be dangerous if humans were exposed to them.

continuum: a representation of social phenomena which suggests that there are numerous variations between two opposite characteristics. It is usually drawn as a straight line, with the opposites at either end of the line. Along the line may be placed variations of the opposites and where they are placed will suggest how more of one than the other the variation is. This can be seen in the following:

Illustration of continuum

contradiction: used by Marxists to describe situations where there are disjunctions between social structures where there should be a fit. For example, Marxists argue that there is a correspondence between schools and the economy, so that schools prepare students for the world of work. However, schools are constantly changing because there are always contradictions between the type of workers an economy needs and the type of workers that schools produce. This is because capitalist economies are constantly changing under the dynamics of capitalist laws of economic development.

contradictory class locations: used by Marxist Olin Wright to describe those positions in contemporary capitalist society which are not part of the *bourgeoisie, proletariat* or *petit bourgeoisie*, but which are semi-permanent locations of the *class structure*, along the dimensions of economics, politics and ideology. The contradictory class locations are determined by a whole range of processes, such as whether a group has credentials or skills which are valuable in the labour market or some supervisory powers in the work-place, as well as whether its members are owners or non-owners of the *means of production*. These positions are only semi-permanent because they are subject to change as powerful economic, ideological and political forces act upon them. The idea has been criticised because, despite its apparent objective classification of occupations, it actually relies on the coding decisions of sociologists as to where particular occupational groups appear. (See *semi-autonomous employees*.)

control group: a group within an experiment matched as closely as possible to another group, the *experimental group*. With human groups the matching features may include age, gender, social class, ethnic group, region etc. The difference between the control group and the experimental group is that the control group is not exposed to the *independent variable*, that which is thought to be the cause of what is being investigated. Therefore if any differences emerge between the two groups it can be assumed to be because of the independent variable. The use of control and experimental groups is widely used in medicine to test the effectiveness of new drugs or a different kind of treatment. It is often much easier to control the different variables and to measure the outcome in cases such as these than in sociological research. (See *experimental method.*)

conurbation: a geographical area which covers several local government boundaries but which forms a continuous urban region.

convergence theory: an explanation of development which identifies a process whereby heterogeneous cultures develop and change in the direction of a greater likeness to each other as they industrialise. Convergence theorists argue that in important respects, industrial societies must be similar, because they adopt similar arrangements for performing important social functions in the most effective way. Convergence theory has been criticised on three main counts:

- It ignores the starting points of industrial countries, which means that they have different cultural preferences and will therefore end up in different industrial states.
- It sees the United States as the most advanced industrial society and therefore assumes that industrialising societies are converging on the American model.
- It is a crude determinist theory, ignoring the importance of political decision-making in determining social arrangements for important social functions.

Convergence theory has had a resurgence since 1989 with the collapse of the Communist regimes in the Soviet Union and eastern Europe. (See *one-way convergence; two-way convergence.*)

conversational analysis: a method associated with *ethnomethodology,* in which the commonsense rules of everyday talk are uncovered by examining the speech acts of individuals talking with each other. For example, conversational analysis might uncover the rules associated with the timing and legitimisation of turn-taking in conversation. Conversational analysis has also revealed gender differences; in mixed groups, males frequently interrupt females, who tend to stop speaking and allow the male to continue. Males are more likely to make statements of fact, while females are more likely to be tentative, e.g. 'I think that …', or 'Isn't it true that …?'. (See *sociolinguistics.*)

co-operation: where action is shared to achieve common goals. Even in high-conflict situations, some minimum of co-operation is apparent, for example in the shared principles of the Geneva Convention. (See *conflict.*)

copy-catting: the process whereby accounts of events in the media encourage people in other areas to copy the behaviour reported, leading to an increased incidence of the original behaviour. It has been used most extensively in explaining the outbreaks of urban violence which have periodically swept Britain's cities. However, critics argue that it is insufficient on its own as an explanation, as violence does not break out in all of Britain's cities following the reporting of an initial riot.

core characteristics of the professions: those features which delimit a profession from other occupational groups. (See *professions.*)

core functions of the family: are those believed to be the basic, essential functions performed by all family units. Murdock, an early functionalist writer, argued that the four basic family functions were:

- the sexual
- the reproductive
- the socialisation (Murdock referred to this as 'education')
- the economic

According to Murdock, the sexual function performed by the *family* was the social control and expression of the sex drive. All societies have rules governing sexual activity, particularly with regard to who may marry (and have legitimate sexual relations) with whom. These rules are believed to be functional in that control of sexual relations helps to avert the conflict which might arise from totally free access to sexual partners, particularly if these relations are devoid of social responsibilities. Societies also have rules about the socially acceptable expression of sexual feelings and activities which again, according to Murdock, helps to avoid conflict.

The reproduction function refers not only to the obvious fact that children are born into families, but that the rules governing *marriage* and *family structure* ensure that children are seen as the responsibility of a particular group of adults, either the parents or, as in some societies, a wider group of kin. This helps to ensure the survival of children, and thus of the society.

The *socialisation* function is seen as particularly important, as it is this process which enables children to function as members of their own society and ensures that the *culture* is passed down from one generation to the next.

The economic function refers to the work performed in family units. In simple and non-industrial societies work is largely devoted to the provision of food. This is sometimes referred to as the 'production function'. It has been argued that, in industrial societies, where few families produce their own food and household goods, the economic function is one of consumption rather than production; that is, families buy and use goods rather than produce them directly.

As in many modern industrial societies many aspects of family functions such as welfare, education and leisure are increasingly performed by more specialised agencies such as hospitals, schools and leisure organisations, it has been suggested that the family has lost many of its functions and has become correspondingly less important as an institution. However, others including Parsons, maintain that this has made the family more specialised, and that its remaining functions are more important to society than ever. A criticism of the functionalist view of families generally relates to the assumption that families are, by definition, 'good' both for society and for individual members. Sociologists such as Vogel and Bell, Leach and Laing point to the many ways in which families can be highly dysfunctional units for some people, filled with tension, misery and even violence. (See *universality of the family.*)

core skills: attempts to define what students should cover in post-16 courses, the attributes they should acquire which are useful for work. The core skills were supposed to cover both A levels and vocational qualifications, but appeared only in the latter, in the form of application of number, communication skills and *information technology* skills. Other core skill areas considered were 'life skills' and 'problem-solving skills'.

core workers: in post-Fordist production methods, these are the highly skilled workers who form the permanent members of the workforce. The cost of training and maintaining such workers is high, so that they are rewarded well in order to ensure their loyalty to the firm. (See *periphery workers; post-Fordism.*)

corporate crime: law-breaking by the executives of large work organisations, which occurs as a matter of routine in the daily discharge of their duties. Corporate crime is committed in the pursuit of *organisational goals* and the effects of it are to cause injury, sometimes fatal, and financial loss to members of the public. To theorists of corporate crime such as Box, the well-publicised effects such as the poisonings at Bhopal are merely the tip of an iceberg, because the pursuit of profit denies the rights of others who might stand in its path. His point is that corporate crime is not abnormal but a consequence of the everyday activities of organisations as they go about their normal business.

correlation: a mutual relationship between two or more *variables*, that is, one is affected by the other. For example, age and visits to the doctor are both social variables. If a study were made of a group of people and information obtained about their age and the number of visits they had made to the doctor in the past year, these variables could be examined to see whether or not there was any connection. If the *sample* were sufficiently large, it would probably be found that, the older the person, the greater the number of visits to the doctor. This would be a positive correlation, i.e. as one variable (age) increased, so did the other (visits to the doctor). Population studies have shown that, as the level of literacy in a population rises (particularly among women) the average number of children born to a family falls. In this case, as one variable (the level of literacy) rises, the other (average number of children born) falls so we say that there is a negative correlation between the two variables. We must be cautious however, in attributing a *causal relationship* to correlating variables. It would not be possible to claim that the ability to read and write in itself causes the birth rate to fall; rather, it is the effect of a more literate population on the whole economic and social structure of a society which exerts an influence on the desired number of children. (See *spurious correlation.*)

correspondence principle: developed by Bowles and Gintis to suggest that what happens in schools mirrors what happens in the work-place, so that education can be seen as a direct preparation for the child's future role in an unequal *division of labour*. For example, they argue that the system of rewards and punishments in schools echoes those of the work-place. More importantly, children of the middle class receive a different education from those of the working class. In the case of the former they have a more independent type of schooling, which prepares them for more managerial-type jobs in the future. For the latter, schools emphasise obedience and discipline to prepare them for subordinate roles in the division of labour. The idea has been criticised because:

- much more goes on in schools than just preparation for work
- if the correspondence is so good, how does change in education come about?
- it relies, at the most basic level, on some sort of conspiracy between employers and teachers

corroboration: information which lends support to or confirms existing information. For example, in *questionnaire* design, researchers sometimes include questions the answers to which check for consistency with answers given previously. Similarly, in *interviews* with people who are or have been in the same situation (such as in the same work group) one person's version of an event or situation can be checked against the answers of another member of the group. Differences do not, of course, mean that either person is lying; they may simply be reporting the situation as it seems to them.

cosmology: an aspect of a religious or philosophical belief which is concerned with the fundamental nature of the universe and with people's place within it.

cosmopolitan opinion leaders: those who stand between the media and their contacts and who are oriented towards world affairs and international news. They are often relative newcomers to a local community and tend to rely on national sources for their political information. Opinion leaders are usually asked questions about foreign affairs rather than local issues. (See *local opinion leaders*.)

cosmopolites: a concept developed by Gans to describe those inhabitants of the inner city who may be relatively poor, but who are not otherwise disadvantaged. These might include students, artists of all kinds, intellectuals etc.

cottage industry: a *mode of production* typical of pre-industrial societies, where the home was the main locus for the manufacture of goods needed in society. Such industry is small-scale and produces a limited range of goods. In modern societies, cottage industries continue to exist with some craft workers, but there is also a variation termed *out-working*.

council housing: homes built for and rented out by the local council as a low-cost alternative to buying. Public provision of housing has been one of the hallmarks of the *welfare state* and a source of major cleavage in British society. In electoral terms, council tenants have traditionally been strong supporters of the Labour Party, and owner-occupiers supporters of the Conservative Party. The policy of council house sales by the Conservatives in the 1980s was aimed at extending the idea of a property-owning democracy, by offering tenants the right to buy at discount. However, new council building was at the same time restricted, so that the public housing stock itself was reduced.

counter-culture: a general term for any sub-cultural form of ideas, beliefs and practices which is distinct from and often hostile to the dominant *culture* in society. Counter-cultures can emerge from a common interest or from *ideology* or from social experiences which differ from the normal ones in society as a whole. It is often associated with alternative cultures such as the hippie movement of the 1960s, but can also be organised around political principles such as the green movement.

countervailing power: the ability to resist dominant loci of *power* through the organisation of solidaristic groups beyond the reach of the dominant culture and the creation of alternative sources of strength to oppose official agencies. The classic example of countervailing power is the *trade unions*, who provide alternative careers for the working class outside of, but in relationship to, the dominant industrial and political forces of capitalist society.

coupe epistemologique: literally, the epistemological break, the term is used to describe the belief that there is a fundamental difference between the early work of *Marx*, represented by the Grundisse, and his later work, especially Capital. Proposed by Althusser, the epistemological break defined Marx's rejection of the romanticism of his youth, compared with the hard science of his later years. The crucial difference was his abandonment of the concept of *alienation* and all its romantic allusions to a fundamental human nature.

coursework: work done by a student during a course of study, the mark for which usually forms part of the final grade awarded for the course. Most pieces of course-work take the form of an independent investigation carried out by the student, or an artefact produced during the course. (See *continuous assessment.*)

couvade: rituals which involve husbands simulating the experience of childbirth during the pregnancy, or most usually the childbirth, of their wife. Generally associated with simple societies, the custom also existed among the Basque people of southern Europe until the middle of the 19th century, and involved the husband taking to his bed with the new baby after the birth, and being visited and complimented by neighbours, while his wife went about her normal domestic tasks. The wearing by some '*new man*' expectant fathers of water-filled harnesses to experience the sensation of the advanced stages of pregnancy may also be seen as a new western form of couvade, albeit only practised by a few.

covert participant observation: see *participant observation*

covert research: research in which those being studied are unaware of this. (See *participant observation.*)

cow sociology: a term of derision applied to the type of sociology which puts itself at the service of capitalist enterprises. The concept was developed in the sociology of work, where some sociologists were employed by industrial enterprises to develop work enrichment programmes so that workers would produce more at no extra cost. The implication of the term was that the task of the sociologist was to produce contented 'cows' who would produce more 'milk', thus denying the human qualities of workers.

CPVE (Certificate in Pre-Vocational Education): a qualification primarily aimed at one-year post-16 students. The CPVE is no longer offered, and students in the target group would now take the *GNVQ.* (See *new vocationalism.*)

craft industry: a form of production in which the work is carried out by skilled workers, fashioning the product from start to finish. Products tend to be individual or made in small *batches.* As the worker carries out a large number of varied tasks with some skill, it is said to be a less alienating form of production than others.

craft unions: trade union organisations for those workers who exercise a particular skill which is the result of long years of apprenticeship. An example might be the Boilermakers Union, which like many other unions has been losing membership and has amalgamated with others to try to preserve some industrial strength. (See *general unions; industrial unions.*)

credential inflation: a process in which higher and higher qualifications are demanded by employers, leading to a situation where many employees are significantly over-qualified in terms of the demands of their actual job. (See *credentialism.*)

credentialism: a tactic of *social closure*, in which an occupational group seeks to close off rewards from other social groups by emphasising the qualifications needed to practise. The claim to higher rewards therefore rests on the skills represented by the certificates which members of the occupation need in order to carry out the duties of the job. (See *exclusion; solidarism.*)

crime: behaviour which breaks the *law* of the land. Sociological interest in crime has tended to focus on the social context in which it occurs and the consequences of law-breaking for both criminal and victim. Recently, sociological interest has begun to focus on the process of law-making, as well as law-breaking, with sociologists such as Foucault looking at the way that the law acts as a *discourse* to criminalise or de-criminalise activities.

crime statistics: a range of official figures which encompass a number of different measurements of criminal activity. These might include reported crime broken down into constituent elements, detection rates, clear-up rates, conviction rates and so on. Crime statistics are *soft statistics* in that they are subject to *social negotiation* at every stage of their collection and compilation.

crimes of the powerful: a concept used to describe the criminal activity of those at the top of society. While their crimes are not highly visible in the way that working class crime is, Pearce argues that they account for the greatest proportion of crime in terms of material *wealth*. Thus, for example, tax evasion by the powerful is estimated to cost the country much more than welfare benefit fraud.

crimes without victims: used to describe those actions which have been criminalised by the *State*, but in which none of the consenting participants suffers any loss. The concept includes prostitution, homosexuality, drug-taking and so on. Such crimes are important sociologically because they represent the frontiers of the State's activities in policing the private actions of individuals and thus represent the struggle between the ideologies of individualism and stateism.

criminalisation: making activities unlawful in order to serve the interests of some powerful group in society, often identified as the *ruling class*. Thus criminal law categories are used to control sections of the population and sometimes to eliminate them as a social problem. Legislation in the 1990s aimed at controlling New Age travellers is a good example of this process. Criminalisation may also be aimed at individuals or groups who threaten the legitimating activities of society, such as gays, or who threaten the secrecy of the activities of the State.

critical criminology: a Marxist view of *crime* which argues that capitalism is itself the cause of crime, through its cultivation of the ethic of possessive materialism. Only by the rejection of *capitalism* and the establishment of a socialist society can the prerequisites for a crime-free society be established. However, critical criminology is criticised for being vague regarding how a crime-free society would emerge in socialism, and for side-stepping the examples of the Soviet Union and eastern Europe by arguing that they were not truly socialist societies. (See *National Deviancy Conference.*)

critical Marxism: that variant of Marxism which looks for the ways in which human history is the product of the hidden potency of people. It was humanistic in its approach and took into account the individuals who make up social classes. As such it differed from other types of Marxism in privileging the roles of individuals in the sweep of history. The critical school was represented by such Marxists as Gramsci, Sartre and the Frankfurt School. (See *Scientific Marxism.*)

critical pedagogy: developed by post-modernists, it argues that teaching should be about the possibilities in children's lives and getting children to recognise that we live in a fragmented and no longer certain world. This type of *pedagogy* does not accept that there is only one truth to be taught, rather that there is a variety of ways of looking at the world depending on the situatedness of the viewer.

cross tabulations: a simple statistical presentation which contrasts the proportions of different *variables* in a direct way. An example might be to cross-tabulate the proportion of the population of two villages engaged in mining and fishing:

	Newbiggin-by-the-Sea	Ashington
Percentage in mining	30	60
Percentage in fishing	20	2

Cross tabulation allows the direct comparison and contrasting of social variables to arrive at similarities and differences.

cross-class families: families in which the husband and wife are both in paid employment, but in different occupations, in different social classes. The implication of this formation is that when classifying *families* into social classes it is not sufficient to use only the husband's occupation as traditional *stratification* theorists have done. Feminists in particular have pointed out the importance of cross-class families when calculating the social class of individuals.

cross-class voting: where members of a particular social class vote against the party that is seen as representing their class interests. For the manual worker this would be the *working-class* Tory and for the non-manual worker this would be the *middle-class* radical.

cross-cultural comparison: the classical sociological method, rooted deep in the history of sociology, it is the examination of two or more societies to see their similarities and differences. From these comparisons sociologists hope to establish universals in human societies as well as laying bare the possible variations.

cross-sectional studies: studies of a varied *population* which divide that population into representative sub-groups with different characteristics to get a picture of the overall group. For example, a study of a multi-racial inner-city area might divide the population into different *ethnic groups,* different age groups, different types of *family structure* and so on. The aim is to make the cross-section as representative as possible of the population as a whole.

CSE (Certificate in Secondary Education): a qualification introduced in England and Wales to cater for the needs of the so-called *ROSLA* children, those who would have left school at 15 before the leaving age was raised to 16 in 1973. It was designed to place more emphasis on problem-solving and *coursework* than the traditional GCE O level examinations, which relied heavily on the regurgitation of factual material. However, as only the top grade of CSE was deemed equivalent to an O level pass, the qualification became seen as a second-best exam for less able pupils. It was replaced by the *GCSE* in 1988.

cult: either the beliefs and *rituals* associated with a particular god, as in the cult of Isis, or a type of religious group. Cults are often characterised as being relatively short-lived, having a charismatic leader and possibly having no acts of collective worship, but promising their followers access to spiritual or supernatural powers. In practice it is often difficult to distinguish clearly between cults and *sects*.

cultural accumulation: a process by which new cultural traits are added to a society, and become an accepted part of the *culture*. These additional cultural traits are often the result of borrowing from another cultural group which may live in close proximity, as with an ethnic minority within the society, or from a culture which is greatly admired, as in the case of the spread of aspects of rock culture, dress and dance forms from the USA and Europe to other parts of the world.

cultural capital: those desired *competences*, such as forms of language and expression and valued social skills, which the middle classes are able to confer on their children, together with economic capital. The concept was introduced by the Marxist writer Bourdieu, who argued that success in the education system is largely based on having and displaying these skills, which are much more difficult for working-class children to acquire, thus making it easier for middle-class children to succeed. Critics of the concept accuse Bourdieu of *cultural determinism*, i.e. the inevitability of different class cultures being transmitted from one generation to the next, and also of ignoring the significance of other factors in educational success or failure. (See *cultural reproduction*.)

cultural deprivation: the notion that the failure of certain groups of children within the education system is a result of their culturally deprived home background. The idea received widespread support in the United States in particular in the 1960s, when a number of programmes of *compensatory education* were developed to make up this supposed deficiency in the child's home background. Critics of the idea argue that it is a contradiction in terms, i.e. by definition, all social groups have a *'culture'*, and that which was actually being referred to was a white middle-class notion of desirable cultural forms such as particular kinds of literature and music. It was emphasised that children who were failing in the system, particularly black children, had a very rich culture which was ignored or misunderstood by the largely white teachers, educational psychologists and administrators. It was suggested by many that blaming educational failure on the child's home background was a way of avoiding the real issues of *poverty* and *discrimination*.

cultural determinism: a belief that the dominant *culture* or way of life of a society or group exerts a determining influence on other aspects of behaviour.

cultural difference theory: in the sociology of education, it signifies that much working-class *under-achievement* is caused by the mis-match between the culture of the working class and the middle-class *culture* of the school. In contrast to cultural deprivation theory, this therefore accepts that the responsibility for failure is at least in part to do with what happens in school. (See *black box view*.)

cultural dopes: a term in criticism of determinist theories that see individuals as unable to affect their own lives through their actions. It is often used as a critique of Marxist theories which suggest that individuals blindly follow the dictates of economics without *agency* of their own. Interactionists argue that, on the contrary, individuals do have real choices and are not determined by their social or economic position.

cultural drift: the notion that a society changes over time as a result of the large-ly unconscious, small changes to aspects of *culture*. It is believed that these changes will lead the society in a particular direction, e.g. becoming more 'westernised'.

cultural effects theory: a theory of the influence of the media, which suggests the media have long-term effects on the audience, mainly through the promotion of cultural *stereotypes*. The *audience* of these images is itself differentiated into social groups so that members receive and interpret the messages of the stereotypes accord-ing to the social position in which they find themselves. (See *drip effect*.)

cultural imperialism: the imposition by one group of its cultural forms on anoth-er group, particularly members of a different society. The term is often used in the context of the *mass media* to refer to the export of particular kinds of mass media and mass entertainment, and the products allied to them, such as certain styles of dress. With the growth of *media conglomerates* which now operate across different continents, it is alleged that cultural imperialism is increasing, and posing a real threat to indige-nous forms of *culture*.

cultural pluralism: an approach to *race relations* which acknowledges the cultural diversity of modern Britain and accepts the legitimacy of *ethnic minority* cultures. One of the implications of this is to introduce strong elements of ethnic minority culture into the *curriculum* of schools. (See *integrative race relations; assimilation*.)

cultural relativism: the view that there are no universal beliefs, but that each *cul-ture* must be understood in its own terms, because cultures cannot be translated into terms which are accessible everywhere. The implication of cultural relativism is that no one society is superior to another, they are merely different.

cultural reproduction: associated with Marxist theory, it is the process whereby social relationships of superordination and subordination in the class structure are re-created *generation* by generation. Cultural reproduction in capitalist societies is therefore associated with the establishment of *ideological hegemony* in each generation, so that working-class children end up in working-class jobs and middle-class children in middle-class jobs. The conditions of cultural reproduction are the result of perva-sive effort by the *ideological state apparatus*. It is never complete, as there are always changes in the *occupational structure* which create opportunities for *social mobility*, but the control of the *bourgeoisie* is made more secure through cultural reproduction.

cultural taboos: aspects of social life which are considered forbidden by the *norms* of society. In methodological terms, these create some difficulty in using historical or cross-cultural documents as evidence for sociological research, as the existence of cultural taboos may cause the omission of important material. For example, if talk-ing about sexual matters were a cultural taboo, it is unlikely that surviving documents would contain information about this important area of social life.

cultural transmission theory: a basic idea of the *Chicago School* that, in cities, natural areas emerge which, because of immigration patterns, are isolated from the mainstream of the rest of society. As a consequence the inhabitants develop their own knowledge, beliefs and forms of behaviour that make possible specific forms of deviant behaviour. Within each of these natural areas the cultures are transmitted to the next generation even if this is composed of a new set of immigrants. Thus it is areas of the *city*, not their populations, which demonstrate stable patterns of deviant behaviour. As populations move out into the suburbs the transmission of the deviant *sub-culture* is broken.

culture: used in sociology to denote the way of life of a society; it covers all the folk-ways of a society, such as language, customs, dress, as well as the symbols and artefacts which people develop. The concept of culture became a central organising theme of much sociology in the 1980s and 1990s, as post-modernists moved away from a focus on structure to look at cultural forms. There are different forms of culture which sociologists have identified, such as *high culture* and *popular culture.*

culture industry: a term developed by the *Frankfurt School* to denote that the pro-ducers of cultural material are embedded in economic processes and therefore to understand the media, sociologists need to look at processes of profit and loss, resourcing etc. associated with any capitalist enterprise. The importance of this insight is that it is not enough just to look at the communication processes which occur in media organisations, but the economic basis underpinning these processes must also be examined.

culture of contentment: a concept devised by Galbraith to describe the 40% of the population who are relatively well-off and will block electorally any attempt to increase taxes to pay for more welfare services for the less well-off and the poor. The term arose after the success of the Republicans in the United States and the Conservatives in Britain in the 1980s in creating the expectation of tax cuts amongst the electorate. The culture of contentment therefore represents an alternative to the post-war *consensus* that a strong *welfare state* is important for social stability.

culture of poverty: attitudes and patterns of behaviour allegedly characteristic of the poor which are transmitted from generation to generation and which serve to perpetuate the state of *poverty*. These attitudes include fatalism, dependency, apathy and despair. The concept is particularly associated with the anthropologist Oscar Lewis, who carried out research into poor families in Mexico and Puerto Rico. The concept is often used in a negative sense to imply that poverty is largely the result of these negative characteristics, i.e. is the fault of the poor themselves. However, Lewis saw these attitudes as at least partly a response to an existing situation, and argued that poverty was particularly likely to flourish in a low-wage, profit-oriented economy with minimal assistance for the poor. Some critics of the 'culture of poverty' expla-nation of poverty, argue that the real causes of poverty lie not in the attitudes and behaviour of the poor, but in the inbuilt inequalities of *wealth, income* and *power* par-ticularly associated with capitalist societies. (See *dependency culture; structural view of poverty; underclass.*)

culture of service: an ethos associated with the *New Right* sociologists, defining the appropriate way for public services to operate in relation to their *clients*. It implies that the main purpose of welfare organisations should be to serve client needs. This is in contrast to traditional ways of seeing welfare organisations as delivering State-defined services to those in need. The culture of service will be, according to the New Right, a result of the introduction of market principles into such services as the edu-cation system.

culture shock: the feeling of disruption which individuals might feel when con-fronted with a different and seemingly alien *culture,* which challenges the taken-for-granted assumptions of their own perspective. There is a tension between the unsettling effect which contact with the strange can have and the enlightenment which an alternative culture can provide.

culture structure: developed by Merton as a way of describing the relationship between means and ends in society. One half of the culture structure is the goals defined by the culture of society as the proper aims for people. The other half is the ways that individuals may legitimately pursue those goals. Where the relationship between these two is imbalanced, either because of the escalation of goals beyond the ability of many individuals to achieve them or through the blocking of legitimate means, then *deviance* is likely to result. Thus strain between ways and means leads to a state of *anomie*, to which individuals can respond in a variety of different ways. However, the idea of a culture structure has been criticised, because it takes societal goals for granted and does not ask who defines the proper aims for society or who decides which means are legitimate. The idea is therefore based on an acceptance of existing society as the best possible one. (See *institutionalised means; ritualistic deviance; retreatism; innovation; rebellion.*

curriculum: the subjects and courses offered in educational institutions which form the programme of study. These are also referred to as the 'overt curriculum'. (See *hidden curriculum; National Curriculum.*)

curriculum modernisers: those who argue that schooling should be adapted to meet the needs of a post-modern economy, mainly through the device of vocationalism.

custom: an established and traditional pattern of behaviour, which may or may not have lost its efficacy through time. Customs can provide integrative activity for a society and are often taken for granted by those who share them.

cybernation school: a theory about automation, which suggests that as it develops it will fundamentally alter society. Proponents of the Cybernation School, such as Michael, suggest that:

- automation is a radical break from previous technological developments
- that the pace of automation is accelerating
- that it will lead to chronic and continuous high levels of unemployment

Critics argue that the extent of automation has been exaggerated and that there is little evidence for an accelerating rate. Moreover, new technologies create jobs as well as destroy them, so there is little evidence for continued high levels of unemployment.

cybernetic analogy: developed from the work of Spencer, it compares society to a machine. The basic idea is that communication is essential for the system of the machine or society to hold together. Communication is provided by specialist parts of the machine which provide feedback for the system to adapt its arrangements and prevent disintegration. (See *biological analogy.*)

cycle of deprivation: see *poverty cycle*

cycle of poverty: see *poverty cycle*

D

dark figure: used to describe the large amount of criminal activity which never appears in the crime statistics. Such crimes are largely unreported either because the victim does not know that a crime has been committed (such as when price-fixing is carried out) or because the victim, for one reason or another, does not report the crime. The non-reporting of rape has been the focus of much sociological investigation, as it is the fear of being treated as the guilty party by the police and the Courts which makes the victim reluctant to come forward. The dark figure is connected to the success rate of the agencies of *social control* with regard to certain criminal acts. If the police do not catch many burglars, then the public are less likely to report burglaries where the loss is minimal.

de-capitalisation: the process whereby the natural assets of *third world* countries are exported to the *first world*, thus depriving the third world countries of the means to invest in their own development. While much de-capitalisation takes the form of the export of third world goods, especially food produce to the first world, there are also direct processes of de-capitalisation occurring. For example, the *patriation of profits* from the activities of *trans-national companies* in the third world back to countries of origin is a major form of de-capitalisation. The term is usually employed by *under-development* theorists when explaining the causes of *poverty* in the third world. New Right theorists have been critical of this process, arguing that capital flows between the first and third world are two-way, with the third world the beneficiary of capital injections from the first world through infra-structure projects etc. (See *aid.*)

de-centralisation: the dispersal of *power* away from the centre towards outlying areas. In politics, it is used when central governments give more power to regional governments or to county or town councils. In the sociology of work it is used when managements devolve responsibility for the quality of their work to the workers themselves rather than keeping power and responsibility only within management.

de-centring: used by post-modernists to indicate a moving away from traditional ways of looking at issues towards a more fragmented and oblique approach to social problems and *discourses.*

de-industrialisation: the process whereby a society loses its manufacturing capacity and concentrates on the service industries rather than a traditional manufacturing base. During the 1980s it was government policy to allow the loss of manufacturing in the belief that the service industries would compensate for this. In the 1990s there has been a shift towards seeing manufacturing as important again, especially as it is tied to the development of computer-led technologies. In terms of *gender,* the loss of manufacturing has implications for *gender codes,* as it was within heavy industries that traditional macho notions of masculinity were forged.

de-medicalisation: the process whereby sections of society turn away from traditional medicine and towards alternative medical treatment, such as acupuncture. (See *alternative medicine.*)

de-professionalisation: the process whereby professionals lose their unique status in society and become like other occupational groups. Various factors are said to be involved in this process:

- The loss of monopoly of knowledge, as other forms of service grow up. For example, *alternative medicine* offers a different route to health from that offered by the medical profession.
- A loss of public faith in the service ethic of the professionals.
- A loss of *autonomy* as professionals increasingly work in large bureaucracies.

Many sociologists dispute that de-professionalisation is happening, but argue that the form of professionalism is changing under the impact of large-scale *bureaucratisation* of the service industries.

de-schooling: a suggestion by Ivan Illich that the formal education system should be abolished, as it is damaging to pupils. Illich argues that schools indoctrinate pupils into accepting the views and interests of the *ruling class,* stifle creativity and non-conformity and train children to become mindless consumers.

de-skilling: a concept used to denote the stripping away from workers of traditional skills, through the implementation of the principles of *scientific management.* Braverman argued that increasing specialisation in modern industry results in a reduction in the skills workers can exercise. He argued that this was a deliberate policy introduced by management to increase the control they can exercise over the workers and as a result increase profits. De-skilled workers have little *power* as they are easily replaced. However, some sociologists dispute the view that the de-skilling process takes place as a matter of policy, but argue rather that technological innovation (a central part of the de-skilling process according to Braverman) both destroys old skills and creates new skills at the same time. (See *Taylorism.*)

Dearing report: a set of proposals published in 1994 following a review of the *national curriculum* carried out by Sir Ron Dearing. The review resulted in a changed, 'slimmed-down' version of the national curriculum, following complaints from teachers that the original version was proving almost unworkable. The main change was the reduction in curriculum time which had to be devoted to the national curriculum, leaving schools with time in the week to provide additional courses of their own choice.

death: the cessation of existence. Sociologists have been interested in the rituals which surround it as a *rite of passage* and more recently, in the ways that death can be defined. Whereas death might seem to be an obvious state, the development of *medical technology* has complicated the definition so that the concept of brain death has been become central to the medical profession. However, the existence of life support machines can lead to emotional complications for those who are left behind.

death of the family: a widely-expressed argument, found at all levels of society, that the *family* as an institution is 'dying'. Evidence of this is given as the high rates of *divorce* and *cohabitation* and the increase in the number of *lone-parent families.* Charles Murray argues that the root cause of what he sees as the rising *underclass* in Britain is the breakdown of the family. Critics of the 'death of the family' argument suggest that the family as an institution should be viewed as changing, rather than dying, pointing out for example that more couples remain married than get divorced, that many cohabitees later marry and that a high proportion of divorced people later re-marry. Many one-parent families are only temporarily in that state. Critics also argue that the family continues to provide a wide range of essential *welfare* and support services for its members. (See *loss of family functions*.)

death of the subject: a phrase used in connection with *structuralism*, to indicate that it tends to reduce the individual to an automaton with little ability to make free choices outside of the forces of the structures they inhabit. (See *bearers of the mode of production*.)

death rate: the crude death rate is expressed as the number of deaths per thousand of the live population per year. It takes no account of the *age structure of the population*. The standardised death rate gives rates for males and females, and people in different age groups. The death rate has been falling in Britain since about 1830. The most important cause was the decline of tuberculosis and other infectious diseases. This fall occurred before the introduction of vaccination and antibiotics, and was therefore largely a result of other social and environmental changes such as better diet and clean water. In 1992 the death rate in Britain was 11.0. However, there are still *social class* differences in the death rate, with each social class showing a higher mortality (death) rate than the class above. The major cause of death has changed from infectious diseases to degenerative illnesses, with circulatory disease, cancer and respiratory diseases now causing the greatest number of deaths for men and women of all ages. In the table below, the standardised mortality ratio means that, if there were no difference by social class, each class group would have a figure of 100. Figures below 100 therefore indicate a lower than average mortality rate, and figures above 100 indicate a higher than average rate. The degree of difference is, of course, indicated by the degree above or below 100. (See *infant mortality rate; life expectancy*.)

	Age at death				
Social Class	15–44	45–64	65–74	75 and over	15 and over
I	70	66	71	75	71
II	78	79	81	86	83
III N/Manual	91	98	92	92	93
III Manual	93	99	100	104	101
IV	113	110	108	107	108
V	152	132	117	111	117

(Source: OPCS Population Trends No. 80, Summer 1995)

Mortality of males 1976–89 by social class and age at death (Standardised Mortality Ratios)

dechristianisation: the process whereby modern Western societies, especially in urban areas, are turning away from Christianity, towards secular existence, non-standard Christian-inspired cults or non-Christian religions.(See *secularisation*.)

decoding: used by semiological analysts to indicate the process whereby the messages encoded by the producers of texts have to be interpreted by the 'reader'. The problem for analysis is that *audiences* do not always decode the messages in the way that the producer of the message intended. There is therefore always a gap between intention and effect. (See *text; encoding*.)

decomposition of capital: a term developed by Dahrendorf to describe how the capitalist class dissolves from a monolithic unity into separate and competing interests. Dahrendorf was writing particularly about the emergence of a distinct group of managers, separate from the owners of large corporations (See *managerial revolution.*)

decomposition of labour: developed by Dahrendorf to describe the breaking up of a class-conscious working-class into smaller groupings with different interests. The crucial part of the process was the development of different levels of *skill* amongst the working class, which led to differentials between them, and also the emergence of groups within the working class who saw themselves as distinct from other working-class groups. (See *aristocracy of labour.*)

deconstruction: associated with Derrida, it is the analysis of texts to demonstrate their ultimate ambiguity and *situatedness*. Derrida rejects the idea that any *text* contains some transcendental truth or meaning in favour of the idea that any meaning exists in relationships to other texts through their intertextuality. Meaning is established by social institutionalisation which privileges one interpretation of a text over others. The idea of deconstruction has been criticised as an ultimately relativist one, in which one person's interpretation becomes as valid as any other.

deference: a social value which accords reverence to social superiors, on account of their *ascribed status*. Deference was demanded and given to social superiors by those who were in established and traditional relations of inferiority with them. It is linked to the idea of *paternalism,* which is the duty superiors owed to those who gave them deference.

deferential voters: those who vote for the Conservative Party because they believe it is composed of those who are socially superior, and therefore best fitted to rule society. Although deferential voters are found in both the middle class and the working class, it was the existence of substantial numbers of deferentials amongst the working class which helped sociologists to explain the success of the Conservative Party in winning elections in the twentieth century. The deferential voters were strongest when there was a developed social *hierarchy* and they are less significant now. Deferentials therefore tend to be concentrated amongst the older population, as they grew up in a more overtly hierarchical society.

deferential workers: those in employment situations where there is a personal relationship between the employer and the workforce which is based on workers' respect for the superior employer and the employer's care for the deferential workforce. In its most extreme manifestation, deferential workers were taken care of by the employer in much wider areas of social life than just work. Deference was therefore expected from the workforce in the wider social world.

deferred gratification: the postponing of immediate satisfaction or rewards to enhance or increase those which will then follow later. An example would be a child's decision not to watch television in order to prepare for a test the following day. It is argued that teaching children to defer gratification in this way enables middle-class parents to bring about the greater success in the education system of their children compared with working-class children, as it is often viewed as a particularly middle-class characteristic. The concept is not, however, restricted to use in an educational context. Weber saw it as an important feature of the Protestant ethic. (See *Protestant ethic thesis.*)

deficit explanations: see *cultural deprivation*

definition of the situation: W I Thomas defined this as 'If men define their situations as real, they are real in their consequences.' Despite the implicit *sexism*, which was a product of the age in which Thomas was writing, the definition of the situation has been one of the most fundamental tenets of sociology. It indicates the power of the subjective in forging social relationships and influencing events.

deinstitutionalisation: see *care in the community*

delinquency: anti-social actions which range from the criminal such as vandalism to the disruptive but legal, such as messing around in the classroom. Sociological focus has been largely on rates of criminal delinquency, mostly with respect to teenagers.

delinquent drift: see *drift*

delinquescent subculture: a pupil *subculture* identified by Hargreaves in his 1968 study of a boys' secondary modern school. Boys in this subculture rejected the *values* of the school and adopted a counter-culture, with values in opposition to those of the school. Status was gained by activities such as fighting, not wearing uniform, cheeking the teachers and cheating in class. The subculture was found increasingly among boys in the lower C/D streams, and Hargreaves argued that the device of academic *streaming* led to lower-stream boys feeling increasingly inferior and alienated from the school. (See *academic subculture; labelling.*)

democracy: a system of *government* which involves some form of election of the government by the people. The emergence of modern democracies has produced a large number of different ways in which elections might be conducted, from *representative democracy* to *direct democracy*. Democracy also has an ideological aspect, in that it is seen as a valued feature of societies. Some sociologists argue that modern *capitalism* necessitates the emergence of democracy if it is to function efficiently.

democratic elitism: a *power* situation, in which there are formal electoral arrangements for the people to cast their vote, but with opposing factions of the *elite* who compete for electoral support from subordinate groups. Thus while retaining the outward form of a democratic system, the rulers of society are able to concentrate power into their hands and rule for their own benefit. The establishment of hegemonic social relationships is important in establishing the legitimacy of this arrangement. (See *hegemony.*)

democratic pluralist model: an approach to *psephology* which focuses on the statistics of voting and the correlations between particular voting habits and certain social characteristics. It is thus an empirical approach to the study of voting behaviour and uses statistical analysis to identify trends in elections.

democratic socialism: a philosophy of the collectivist left, which favours the electoral process for achieving the socialist society over the revolutionary instincts of the Communists.

demographic transition: the change in the balance of *birth rates* and *death rates* which is associated with the *industrial revolution* and which led to the different population dynamic associated with industrialised societies. The main factors in the demographic transition were firstly a fall in the death rate, which led to an increase in population. This was followed by a fall in the birth rate, which led to a stabilisation of the population at a much higher level than at the start of the process.

demography: the study of populations, with particular reference to their size and structure and how and why these change over time. This means that demographers study *birth, death* and *marriage rates,* patterns of *migration* and other important factors which affect population growth or decline such as climate, food supply and the availability of employment.

demystification: the process by which explanations based on *magic, religion* and the *supernatural* are replaced by other explanations based on logic, science and rational thought. (See *desacrilisation; disenchantment.*)

denomination: a Christian religious organisation usually thought to lie mid-way between a *church* and a *sect* in terms of its characteristics. Some denominations, such as Methodists, developed from sects. Denominations characteristically accept as members all who wish to join, and are tolerant of other religious groups, not claiming that only they know the true path to salvation. Most denominations have a professional body of ministers, but also make use of many lay (i.e. non-ordained) people as preachers. Denominations can only exist in societies with a reasonably high level of religious tolerance.

density: in urban sociology this refers to the concentration of a large number of individuals in a relatively small area, characteristically the city. This was one of the features of *urbanism* defined by Wirth and its importance lay in the fact that as the density of people increased, the possibility of meaningful relationships decreased. (See *urbanism.*)

density of membership: with reference to *trade unions,* density is the actual number of members, divided by the potential number of members multiplied by 100 to gain a percentage. This can be represented thus:

$$\text{FORMULA:} \quad \text{Density} = \frac{\text{Actual number of members}}{\text{Potential number of members}} \times 100$$

The reason for calculating the density, is that it provides a measure of how powerful a *trade union* is in relation to the employers. The higher the density the greater the trade union's power. A *closed shop* has 100% density. Density therefore represents the potential effectiveness of a trade union.

dependency culture: a view associated with the *New Right* which argues that universal welfare provision has led people to expect 'the state' to look after and provide for them, thus robbing them of self-reliance and social responsibility. The benefits of the *welfare state* are thought to be over-generous and too readily available, leading to incentives for remaining unemployed rather than seeking work. Holders of these New Right views, such as David Marsland, also believe that the culture of dependency is a cause of family breakdown, rising levels of crime and economic decline. They suggest that help should be given only to those in genuine need and that the welfare needs of the majority (e.g. education, health, pensions) should be largely met by private and voluntary organisations rather than by the state. Critics of the concept of dependency culture argue that there is no evidence to suggest that people would rather remain unemployed than be in paid work, and point out that no account is taken of the actual availability of jobs. Others point out the significance of the *poverty trap* in keeping people in *poverty*, and blame the structured inequality of a capitalist society. (See *culture of poverty*.)

dependency ratio: the ratio within a population of those under 15 and over 65 to those between those years, i.e. of working age. Those under 15 make up the 'young dependants', and those over 65 the 'elderly dependants', and together they are referred to as the 'dependent population'. The dependency ratio is a very important factor in the economy of a country, as it provides a measure of the proportion of people to be supported by the labour of others. Non-industrial and *newly-industrialising countries*, with high *birth rates* and a relatively low *life expectancy* typically have a high proportion of young dependants, while the low birth rates and low *death rates* of advanced industrial countries mean that these are all experiencing *ageing populations*. World population statistics show that in 1990, for every 100 people of working age there were 53 people under 15 and 10 over 65, while projections for 2025 suggest that there will be 38 under 15 and 15 over 65. (See *age structure of the population*.)

dependency theory: an explanation of the continued lack of *development* throughout the *third world* in the relationship between the third world and the developed capitalist societies of the West. The principal architect of dependency theory is Andre Gunder Frank. Though emerging from a Marxist perspective and concerned with the exploitation of the *third world* by the first world, Frank was not himself a Marxist, because he defined *capitalism* primarily as a market system, rather than in terms of ownership (as traditional Marxists maintained). Frank argued that the *undeveloped* state of the third world was a consequence of *first world* policy towards the third world. He argued that first world countries had 'enclaves' in the third world, usually in the capital cities, these he called '*metropolis*'. The role of the metropolis was to exploit the *hinterland* of the third world countries, concentrating capital in the metropolis. In turn, first world countries exploited the metropolis, so that capital was transferred to the capitalist countries of the West. This *de-capitalisation* was, according to Frank, the prime reason for the *under-development* of the third world.

Frank has been criticised from many different angles:

- Some Marxists, such as Brenner, argue that it is the exploitation of the *working class* in the first world which should be the focus of analysis, not the relationship between the first and third worlds.
- Other Marxists, such as Warren, argue that Frank ignores the development that is going on in the third world, because capitalism has a positive role to play in the third world in destroying traditional patterns of behaviour which might hinder development.
- *New Right* theorists, such as Bauer, argue that Frank gives too much attention to economic forces and ignores the importance of *culture* in promoting or hindering development.

Process of under-development according to Frank

dependent elderly: used to describe those old people, usually over 75, who are in need of some sort of care. The increase in the dependent elderly is argued to be one of the main reasons for the crisis in the *welfare state,* as the resources needed to target the dependent elderly have to be raised from tax-payers. (See *ageing population.*)

dependent population: see *dependency ratio*

dependent variable: that which changes as a result of changes in something else, which is known as the *independent variable.* For example, if the ability of women with children to take paid employment depended on the availability of affordable child-care, then an increase in low-cost crèches and nursery schools (the independent variable) should result in an increase in mothers taking employment (the dependent variable). This could, of course, be tested, although as there are many other variables, it would be difficult to claim that an increase in child-care facilities was the only reason for the increase in working mothers.

depth interview: see *unstructured interview*

desacrilisation: a decline in belief in the *sacred.* It is argued that this process is taking place and is part of the overall process of *secularisation.* (See *resacrilisation.*)

descent group: members of a society who can all trace their lineage back to the same ancestor.

detailed division of labour: the breaking down of a work task into its smallest and most detailed constituent parts. The term was devised as a contrast to *specialisation.* (See *social division of labour.*)

determinant level: used by Althusser to describe the economic forces in society which determine whether the political and ideological levels have *relative autonomy* or not. Economic conditions therefore determine the rest of society, including whether other spheres of social life might be dominant. (See *dominant level.*)

determinism: the belief that individuals' activities are forged by their situations and environment and that they have little free will or choice in how they behave. Different theorists have identified different forces which determine individuals. Functionalists argue that common *values* are the prime determinants of individual behaviour, while Marxists identify economics. (See *voluntarism.*)

development: usually a reference to the process whereby societies move from an agricultural base to an industrial state. The term is associated with *evolutionary theory* and is linked to the idea of progress from an undeveloped state to a superior, developed one. Sociological concern with the issue of development has been present from the very beginnings of the sociological enterprise. The *classical sociologists* were primarily concerned to explain the immense changes which Western societies were experiencing during *industrialisation* and it was on this development process that they focused in their theories. The term itself is controversial, in that sociologists often disagree about what constitutes development. Some sociologists see development as part of an inevitable convergence of all industrialising societies to an American-type society, while others see more than one way to develop a modern industrial economy. (See *convergence theory; under-development.*)

deviance: on a simplistic level, this is behaviour which goes against the dominant *norms* of the specific society or group in which it occurs. The problem with the concept from the sociological point of view is that deviance is socially constructed, that is, there are no actions which in themselves are inherently abnormal or universally condemned by all societies at all times. Deviance is thus situational and contextual. For example, killing another human being is seen as deviant in peacetime, but may be a requirement of a soldier in wartime. All social actions are rule-governed but the rules themselves are subject to change over time. Therefore, even to suggest that there are dominant norms in a society is to beg the questions: 'Who says they are dominant and how does the sociologist know that they are?' Ultimately, sociologists tend to give specific examples of deviant behaviour, which are then subject to qualification or amendment if circumstances change. There is also a further problem in that individuals who engage in what is seen as deviant behaviour are not necessarily known or labelled as deviant, because the circumstances in which they engage in the behaviour may exempt them from the label. (See *secret deviant.*)

deviance disavowal: the process whereby an individual or group comes to reject the label which is being pinned on them. While this often has an individual dimension in that individuals may engage in a self-negating prophecy, there is also a group phenomenon, where socially 'deviant' groups such as the disabled, reject the labels which 'straight' society attaches to them and seek to forge their own *identity.*

deviancy amplification: see *amplification of deviance*

deviant career: the process whereby an individual comes to accept a deviant life-style as their way of life, through the acceptance of the deviant label and the adoption of sub-cultural behaviour and values. It implies that the labelled deviant has a choice of whether to accept the label and thus embrace a deviant life-style or reject it. *(See deviant disavowal; labelling theory.)*

deviant case: in *methodology,* this is the one example which does not fit the general circumstances which have been established. It may be seen as the 'exception which 'proves' (i.e. tests) the rule'.

deviant voter: one who votes for a political party which is said not to express his or her class membership. It includes the manual worker who supports the Conservative Party and the middle-class worker who supports the Labour Party. (See *working-class Conservatives; middle-class radical.*)

dharma: a belief of *Hinduism* that everything in the universe has its proper place in an overall ranking system, with purity at one end and pollution at the other. The principles of dharma were used to rank the various *castes,* and the *rituals,* observances and avoidances which were proper to each.

dialectic: a central idea of Marxism, this argues that everything which exists is in a contradictory existence with its opposite and the tension between the two produces a new situation, which also exists in contradiction to its opposite. It is thus an explanation of how *social change* occurs in society and history is produced. It can be represented as:

$$\begin{array}{ccc} \text{thesis} & + & \text{antithesis} & = & \text{synthesis} \\ \text{[thing]} & & \text{[opposite]} & & \text{[new thing]} \end{array}$$

Dialectic

dialectical materialism: the process identified by Marxists as the fundamental principle of history, it suggests that the *contradiction* and resolution of economic forces in society is the main way that change is accomplished. The actual material forces which are in a dialectical relationship are social classes and it is the conflict between these which produces social progress.

diaries: written accounts of events as experienced and interpreted by the author, diaries are a source of *secondary data* which can be of great use to the sociologist. One of the most well-known large-scale use of diaries is the Mass Observation studies of the 1930s, in which large numbers of people were asked to keep diaries. Supplemented by *interviews* and *questionnaires*, the Mass Observation diaries provide a rich account of life in Britain in the 1930s and 1940s. Obviously, it needs to be acknowledged that diaries are subjective documents, but they provide a rich source of information if used with care, particularly for research into the past. (See *documents*.)

dichotomous models: these are representations of social formations, in which opposites are used to compare the 'before' and 'after' situations. For example, the move from an agricultural to an industrial society is often shown in dichotomous terms, with agricultural societies displaying one characteristic, (such as *ascription*) and industrial societies the opposite, (such as *achievement*). Critics of dichotomous models argue that they inevitably over-simplify what are very complex situations. An example of a dichotomous model is:

Parsons' pattern-variables

Traditional societies	Modern societies
ascription	achievement
role diffuseness	role specificity
particularism	universalism
affectivity	affective-neutrality
collective orientation	self-orientation

differential association: a theory of *deviance* developed by Sutherland, which suggests that everyone comes into contact with attitudes towards the law which are favourable or unfavourable and the deviant is one whose unfavourable contacts outweigh the favourable. The implication of this is that those areas of the city where unfavourable attitudes to the law are rife are likely to be high-crime areas. Critics argue that this theory reduces individuals to slaves of their environment, without any choice as to whether they commit deviant acts or not.

differential fertility: differences between social groups in the average number of children per family. The differences are usually examined between social class or ethnic groups. Social class differences in *fertility* were used as an explanation of *upward social mobility*, as it was argued that those in the upper and middle classes did not produce enough children, especially sons, to fill all the available white-collar, professional and managerial jobs, thereby necessitating recruitment from the working class. With the advent of more reliable and easily available birth control and a rising standard of living for many, rates of differential fertility between the social classes have declined.

differentiation: ways in which the teaching and learning process can be adapted to cater for pupils of different abilities. There are two ways in which this can happen. 'Differentiation by input' refers to ways in which the materials used in the classroom are adapted to match broad ability bands of pupils, or where more able pupils are expected to tackle more tasks. 'Differentiation by outcome' refers to a situation in which all pupils are given the same work, and then graded on the basis of their results.

diffusion: the process whereby social practices and *beliefs* are transferred from one group to another, so that similar cultural traits can be found in many different societies and levels of society. (See *stratified diffusion.*)

DINKY: an acronym for 'dual income, no kids yet' the term is used particularly in marketing to refer to a young or fairly young couple, both of whom are in well-paid employment, and who consequently have a high disposable income available to spend primarily on themselves and their home.

diploma disease: used by Dore to describe the way in which qualifications are becoming more and more important in securing employment and a decent standard of living. (See *credential inflation.*)

Diploma of Vocational Education (DVE): a post-16 vocational qualification which has now been replaced by the *GNVQ.*

direct democracy: the political situation where every citizen is involved in decision-making through the casting of a ballot. The original model of direct democracy was ancient Athens, where men who were not slaves and who held citizenship, gathered together in assemblies to decide the great issues of the day. A modern equivalent would be the Swiss system of referenda for making important decisions about the direction of the country.

direct instruction: an American system of *pedagogy* which is highly traditional and is focused on basic skills. It has been criticised because it allegedly creates dependency and a lack of initiative amongst students.

direct taxation: taxes levied directly on a person's *income* or *wealth*, e.g. income tax, inheritance tax. (See *indirect taxation; progressive taxation.*)

disability: a term used to cover a range of health problems which incapacitate the individual in some way. It has fallen into disuse, as the 'disabled' have challenged the implied contrast with being able to do things, suggesting a passivity and helplessness amongst those labelled 'disabled'. (See *handicap.*)

discourse: developed by Foucault to explain how human beings attempt to bring order out of the chaos of social life. A discourse is a collection of related statements or events which define relationships between elements of the social world. The establishment of these relationships involves the use and establishment of *power* to create knowledge. To Foucault, all knowledge establishes power over others, because discourses are used to control and channel behaviour. Those who control the discourse have the power to define the position of others.

discourse of derision: the process whereby a phenomenon is discredited through establishing ways of thinking about it which inevitably lead to negative feelings about it. It is not just constant criticism, but a way of framing problems and issues so that whatever approach is made to something, a negative result is obtained. For example, the introduction of the *National Curriculum* was made possible by the *New Right* establishing a way of thinking which denigrated the efforts of Local Education Authorities whatever they tried to achieve.

discovery learning: a pedagogical method based on the belief that children learn faster and better if they are given the opportunity to solve problems and find out information for themselves, rather than having knowledge imparted by the teacher. The method, although very successful when used by good teachers, has its critics, who argue that children need more structure and guidance in their learning. Discovery learning is often contrasted with '*chalk and talk*' as examples of progressive and traditional teaching methods respectively. The Conservative governments of the 1980s and early 1990s attributed what they saw as the decline in educational standards to the widespread use of discovery learning in schools, particularly by teachers who were trained in the 1960s and 1970s. However, research has consistently shown that most teachers use a variety of teaching methods, with a bias towards the traditional. (See *experiential learning.*)

discrimination: treating a person or group unfairly, usually because of a negative view of certain of their characteristics. Discrimination is suffered in a variety of spheres of life by certain groups, including the disabled, females, the poor, the elderly and members of ethnic minority groups. (See *positive discrimination.*)

discursive consciousness: this is where we say why we do what we do. We are being discursive when we offer reasons for our actions, and these may be bound up in formal discourse, or in humour, irony etc. (See *practical consciousness; unconscious motivation.*)

disempowerment: the process whereby marginal groups in society have the ability to influence decisions taken away from them by the powerful. This may occur through legislation or through *discourses of derision*.

disenchantment: a process described by *Weber* in which, as a result of the development of *science* and rational modes of thought, the explanations of natural phenomena provided by beliefs in *magic,* miracles and the *supernatural* are displaced. The process of disenchantment is one of the factors thought to lead to increasing *secularisation.*

disengagement: the process by which the *state* and the church become increasingly separate and distinct entities, with a corresponding loss of *power* and influence of the church over the state. Disengagement is alleged to be one of the factors in the increasing *secularisation* of society.

disorganised capitalism: the tendency in contemporary capitalist societies for structures to become increasingly fragmented and unorganised, through a variety of processes. Associated with Lash and Urry, the concept can be applied in a number of ways, but refers to three main developments in particular:

- The increasing *globalisation* of industry, which reduces the ability of any capitalist society or firm to control its own destiny. They therefore operate in conditions of permanent insecurity.
- The constant development of *new technologies* which transform production and make all investment risky.
- The continual cultural transformation and fragmentation associated with the growth of *new social movements* and the decline of traditional class-based politics.

dispensability: refers to the ease or otherwise with which an employee can be removed from work, either voluntarily or through involuntary separation. Sociologists have suggested that the young, the old, women and the disabled are more dispensable than male members of the *internal labour market*. Part of the reasons for dispensability are related to the absence of trade union organisation amongst these groups and partly to the ease with which such workers can be dismissed without recourse to industrial tribunals. For example, older workers are more likely to be persuaded to retire early than workers in middle age.

displacement effect: the argument that television has taken over from other forms of entertainment to become a central part of many peoples' lives.

displacement of goals: used by Merton to describe the situation where individuals in organisations no longer focus on the overall aims of the *organisation*, but only on the immediate task in hand. Organisational goals are displaced by immediate goals. This leads, he argues, to *formalism* by bureaucrats, in which adherence to the rules becomes more important than fulfilling the aims of the organisation. (See *ritualism*.)

disrupting normalcy: a methodological technique associated with the ethnomethodologists, it consists of deliberately upsetting the normal taken-for-granted rules that operate in everyday situations, in order to expose and explore them. The technique illuminates ordinary life in an interesting way, but it has been criticised for a lack of ethical consideration for those whose lives are being disrupted. It can be psychologically unsettling to be in a situation where the normal rules are not being applied.

diversification: the process whereby an *organisation*, originally concerned with one area of production, buys stakes in other areas of production to produce conglomerates. The process is of particular interest to sociologists of the media, where many firms have diversified their interests into several areas of the media. So companies like EMI, who were originally into the record industry, now also have financial interests in television and other media enterprises. (See *conglomeration*.)

divine right of kings: the belief that monarchs are placed on earth by God to rule and that any challenge to that rule is rebellion against God and worthy of eternal damnation. It is therefore an ideological device to legitimate monarchical rule and dissuade those ruled from revolting against the privileges of the monarch. (See *legitimation*.)

division of labour: where *specialisation* occurs, so that individuals carry out only part of the activities needed for survival and sustenance. The basic *social division of labour* is where occupations emerge, so that needs are met by a variety of people carrying out specific jobs. This creates problems for society, specifically that the division of labour creates inter-dependence between individuals, while reducing the similarity of experiences they have. This can lead to problems of *integration* in a society, as more complex divisions of labour emerge. The chains of inter-dependence grow, while the *impersonality* of participants increases. More complex formations of the division of labour lead to problems of co-ordination between individuals and increase the need for constraint over individual behaviour to achieve that co-ordination. (See *calculability; detailed division of labour*.)

divorce: the legal termination of a marriage. In the U.K. before 1857 a divorce could be obtained only by a private Act of Parliament. Over the next century a number of successive laws were passed making divorce progressively easier. Initially, it was easier for a husband to divorce his wife than vice versa, and the grounds under which divorce could be granted were not the same for both sexes until the 1920s. The cost of divorce meant that it remained largely the prerogative of the well-to-do until the passing of the Legal Aid and Advice Act in 1947, which helped poorer people with legal expenses. With each change in the law making divorce easier to obtain, the *divorce rate* has risen, leading to the suggestion that there have always been people trapped in unhappy marriages, wanting to divorce but unable to do so. A major change in divorce law was the passing of the 1970 Divorce Law Reform Act, which made the only grounds for divorce 'the irretrievable breakdown of marriage'. This went some way to removing the notion of an 'innocent' and a 'guilty' partner, and led to a significant increase in the divorce rate. There was a further increase in the number of divorces between 1984–5 following the passing of an Act which allowed couples to divorce after the first anniversary of marriage. In 1991, nearly 10% of all U.K. divorces granted occurred within the first two years of marriage. At 171,000 divorces, the 1991 figure was the highest recorded up to that date. A feature in the recent pattern of divorce is the rise in the number of women petitioners, i.e. it is increasingly likely that, in terms of the legal procedures, the woman will take the first step. (See *divorce rate; lone parent families.*)

divorce rate: a statistical measure of the number of divorces, usually expressed as the number of divorces in any one year per thousand married couples in the population.

documents: documents form an important source of *secondary data* for sociologists. However they need to be used with caution. John Scott suggest that four appraisal criteria should be used when deciding whether, and how, to use documents in sociological research. These are:

- Authenticity – is the document 'genuine', i.e. what it purports to be? Is it complete? Was it actually written by the alleged author?
- Credibility – did the author act from sincere motives when producing the document or was there some kind of pressure applied? To what extent is the material in the document accurate?
- Representativeness – is the document and its evidence typical of its kind, or if not, can the degree of its atypicality be judged? What other documents might exist of the same kind and are these available for scrutiny?
- Meaning – is this clear? Is the document written in shorthand, a foreign language or in archaic language, and if so, can it be accurately translated? What kind of interpretation needs to be placed on the document to render its meaning clear?

Scott does not suggest that negative answers to any of these questions render the document unusable, simply that the researcher has to recognise actual or potential problems and make corresponding allowance.

domestic division of labour: how household and childcare tasks are divided between the members of a *family*, particularly the adult male/female partners. Despite the prediction by Willmott and Young that families would become more 'symmetrical', with a more equitable division of domestic labour between men and women, and also the alleged appearance of the '*New Man*', research suggests that, while attitudes towards the sharing of domestic tasks have shifted, in practice women still perform a disproportionate share. (See *symmetrical family*.)

	Mainly men (%)	Mainly women (%)	Shared equally (%)
Shopping	8	45	47
Preparing evening meal	9	70	20
Doing the evening dishes	28	33	37
Cleaning	4	68	27
Washing and ironing	3	84	12
Repairing equipment	82	6	10
Taking carre of money and bills	31	40	28

Source: British Social Attitudes Survey 1991

Domestic division of labour

domestic economy: a term which describes the contributions each member of the *family* makes to the maintenance and survival of the family as a whole, through labour carried out at home. In pre-industrial societies parents and children tended to work in the home or the fields, directly producing what the family needed. The domestic economy was therefore crucial for survival. In industrial societies the domestic economy has declined, with work in outside agencies replacing work at home.

domestic gadgets: the application of *technology* to household tasks has produced a whole range of machines which are aimed at saving effort in the home. However sociological investigation suggests that gadgets have displaced rather than replaced activities while some gadgets have actually increased the burden of *housework* by raising expectations higher than previously.

domestic labour: an alternative name for *housework* and *childcare*, domestic labour is used by sociologists to indicate that it is a *social construction* and not some natural phenomenon. Sociologists have argued that domestic labour emerged with the *industrial revolution*, when surplus *wealth* allowed households to keep the female head at home engaged in running the house rather than contributing to the *household economy*, as previously.

domestic labour theory: an approach to *housework* and child-bearing which seeks to establish their importance to the maintenance and continuation of capitalist *relations of production*. Rather than dismissing housework as non-work, Marxist feminists argue that domestic labour is central to the survival of *capitalism*. Domestic labour is therefore seen as productive in itself, reproducing labour-power, both on a daily basis through the provision of food and opportunities for recuperation and generationally through the provision of the next generation of labourers.

domestic violence: usually a reference to physical abuse at the hands of a spouse or partner, although may also include the physical abuse of children by parents/step-parents. Most adult victims of domestic violence are women, and many towns and cities now have women's refuges where the victims of domestic violence and their children may stay in safety. Domestic violence is one of the most widely under-reported crimes, and even when the police are alerted they are often reluctant to become involved. Feminists argue that domestic violence against women arises out of the patriarchal system in which men are assumed to have *power* over women who are expected, and who often themselves expect, to play a subordinate role.

domestication: one of the ideological ways in which oppositional *sub-cultures* can be neutralised in capitalist society, by reducing the 'threat' seemingly posed, by making the sub-cultural style seem 'normal'. This has been described as 'otherness is reduced to sameness'. (See *trivialisation*.)

domesticity (ideology of): a set of ideas concerning women's role in society, which is seen as primarily wife, mother and home-maker. Even today when so many women are in the employed labour force the *ideology* of domesticity is widely propagated, particularly through the advertising of household products. (See *dual role of women; housework.*)

dominance: see *dominant level*

dominant level: used by Althusser to describe a situation where politics or *ideology* are allowed by the economic *determinant level* to be the most important aspect of society, with a real freedom to act independently of economic imperatives.

dominant value-system: the ideas and view-points which, taken together, form the leading set of *values* in a society. The dominant value-system is usually composed of the ideas which serve the interests of the *ruling class* and which through the effort of various agencies such as the media are also accepted as legitimate by large numbers of the subordinate groups in society. Where members of the *working class* accept the dominant value-system, it is usually because they are either deferential or aspirational. The dominant value-system therefore legitimates society and contributes to *social order*. However it is difficult to show that the dominant value-system actually exists and if it does, that it is accepted uncritically by subordinate groups. Post-modernists point to the plurality of ideas and view-points in society, rather than the existence of a single dominant set. (See *subordinate value-system; radical value-system*.)

domination: in Weber's meaning, the likelihood that an order, once given, will be obeyed. It is thus a form of *power*, which is logically distinct from the imposition of one person's will on another. There are aspects of *legitimation* involved in domination.

dormitory villages: rural residential areas where workers in towns buy up property and commute to work, leaving the villages quiet and empty during the day. The search for some idyllic countryside retreat is part the *golden age of the village community* myth which has such a hold over the consciousness of many urban dwellers.

double hermeneutic: an idea put forward by Giddens, that in order to understand meaningful *action*, we need to understand both the everyday knowledge of the individuals engaging in the action and the more technical language employed by sociologists to describe and explain it. Understanding therefore occurs on two levels.

down-sizing: see *shake-out*

downshifting: a process in which people (usually middle class) voluntarily opt for a simpler, more frugal life style. The ultimate aim is being able to opt out of the 'rat race' and take a less demanding job or voluntary work to allow more time for the things that one really wants to do. The process is gathering pace in the United States, with the American Trends Research Institute predicting that by the year 2000, 15% of people in their 30s and 40s will be choosing to live a less consumer-oriented life style, preferring to buy simple, durable products. A random sample of 800 Americans carried out in 1995 showed that 28% had 'down-shifted'.

downward social mobility: where an individual or group moves from a superordinate to a lower position in society. The causes of downward mobility are many, but ill-health is perhaps the major one. Poor investments or a tough business environment can also lead to bankruptcy and downward mobility. The amount of downward mobility in society is variable, but since the Second World War, changes in the occupational structure, (especially a shrinkage in working-class jobs) have reduced the opportunities for downward movement. (See *upward social mobility*.)

dramaturgy: the sociology of co-presence, it was developed by Goffman, using the *analogy* of social life as theatre. The focus is on what happens when people are in the presence of each other and the way that they act out roles in their social life. As an *action theory*, it starts with the individual and looks at the way that they foster and maintain specific images of the Self in different situations. The manipulation of image is a central part of the dramaturgical approach. It has been criticised for being ahistorical and episodic, focusing on the now, rather than on structures and the past.

drapetomania: literally, the running away madness, it was defined by doctors in the slave-owning southern United States as the medical reason for runaways. Despite the lack of any biological evidence of its existence, the condition functioned as an ideological device to legitimate the harsh measures taken by the owners to prevent their slaves absconding.

drift: developed by Matza as a theory of *deviance*, in which individuals do not engage in sub-cultural deviant activity, but move into deviance gradually by neutralising ordinarily accepted moral objections to deviant activity through providing some justification for the action. The focus in the theory of drift is on the type of deviance that is mundane and trivial – the everyday deviant act. Thus, there is no commitment to a *deviant career*, but rather juvenile delinquents drift back into normal society as they grow older. The idea has been criticised for trivialising much seriously deviant behaviour.

drip effect: where the effects of the media on the individual are cumulative, through continuous exposure to similar media messages. (See *sleeper effect*.)

dual career families: where both parents in a *nuclear family* situation are employed in occupations in which advancement is possible. The appearance of significant numbers of dual career families has been a significant development in the post-war period, with consequences for the way that *conjugal roles* are envisaged and child-care planned.

dual consciousness: a term developed by Mann to describe the attitudes of the *working class* towards society, in which they accept the dominant values of the *middle class* while at the same time developing their own oppositional attitudes. This holding of two sets of attitudes at the same time is a normative feature of the *proletariat* and should be seen as resolving the *contradiction* that workers generally agree that individuals are free to withdraw their labour but should not strike. (See *normative ambivalence*.)

dual economy thesis: an argument that, in *third world* countries, there are two economies operating, one a technologically advanced and urban-centred economy, the other a less sophisticated rural economy. The thesis was developed by Boeke as a counter-point to *under-development theory* which saw the relationships between these two economies as one where the urban *metropolis* exploits the rural *hinterland.* Boeke argued that these two economies, while operating in the same national and cultural space, are economically separate, inhabiting a different economic reality. The relationship between the two economies is minimal, rather than exploitative.

dual labour market: the idea that there are two separate sectors of work in the economy between which there is little movement. One part of the *labour market* is secure and provides full-time work for permanent workers while the other is composed of temporary and part-time workers. (See *internal labour market; external labour market.*)

dual role of women: the two major roles undertaken by an increasingly large proportion of women, namely those of wage-earner and housewife. Feminists such as Oakley point out that even though the majority of women of working age are now in *paid employment,* they are still expected to play the traditional role of the person primarily responsible for domestic tasks and *childcare.* Though there is evidence that the partners of women in full-time employment take a greater share of domestic tasks and childcare than the partners of women in part-time employment, most women still take the major share of the burden. One result of this is that women, on average, have less leisure time than men. (See *housework; New Man; domestic division of labour.*)

	Full-time employees				Retired	
	Males	Females	Part-time female employees	Housewives	Males	Females
Weekly hours spent on:						
Employment and travel *	47.1	42.2	20.8	0.4	0.5	0.6
Essential cooking, shopping and housework	13.0	25.5	32.5	38.1	17.0	33.0
Essential childcare, personal hygiene and other shopping	13.2	20.0	25.2	29.4	10.0	14.0
Sleep **	49.0	49.0	49.0	49.0	49.0	49.0
Free time	45.7	31.4	40.6	51.1	91.5	71.4
Free time per weekday	5.0	3.0	4.7	6.6	12.8	9.7
Free time per weekend day	10.3	8.2	8.5	9.0	13.8	11.5

Source: Social Trends 1994
* Travel to and from place of work; ** Seven hours per night

Time use in a typical week: by employment status and sex, 1992–3

duopoly: the situation where *political power* alternates between two dominant parties, so that they share the government between them and effectively squeeze out any third force. The situation in the 1950s and 1960s in Britain was an effective duopoly. Greater *volatility* since then has reduced the duopolistic tendencies in Britain, so that, for example in the 1990s, the Liberal Democrats are a significant force in local government.

dureé: the stream of experience which constitutes our everyday lives. It is the unbroken series of events which, unthinkingly, we perform and experience as our social lives. The importance of the durée is that it is broken when we stop to reflect on what is happening to us.

Durkheim: a French sociologist writing in the latter part of the nineteenth and the early part of the twentieth centuries. Durkheim devoted much of his writing to his search for an understanding of what held societies together and what caused change. Like many others writing at that time he was influenced by the enormity of the social changes wrought by the *industrial revolution*. Durkheim was influential in the development of *functionalism*, and also introduced the important concept of *anomie*. His study of *suicide* was undertaken to demonstrate his belief that even what appear to be individual acts are, in fact, governed by *society*. The suicide rate was thus an example of a *social fact*. Durkheim also published important works on the *division of labour* and *religion*.

dysfunction: where a part of the social structure does not positively contribute to the maintenance of society, but causes disharmony and *conflict* rather than coherence and *integration*. The term was used by Merton to produce a more flexible *functionalism*, by doing away with the necessity for everything which existed in society to have a positive function for the maintenance of society. The term is often employed by sociologists of organisations to explain how an organisational feature, though generally functional (helping the organisation to survive) may under certain circumstances become dysfunctional and even *pathological* for the organisation. (See *organisational rules*.)

E

eating disorders: conditions such as anorexia nervosa and bulimia, in which an individual becomes progressively unable to eat a normal, healthy diet through psychological, rather than medical reasons. Eating disorders mainly affect girls and young women and are thought to be a response to low self-esteem and the desire to achieve a 'model' figure. Recently, doctors have reported a rise in the number of boys and young men suffering from anorexia nervosa.

ecclesia: another term for *'church'*. More specifically, it is used for a universal or all-encompassing church, such as the Roman Catholic Church in medieval Europe.

echelon authority: a situation where all the members of a particular organisational position have *power* over all members of a subordinate organisational position, regardless of any other social distinctions between them. For example, warders in a prison have echelon authority over all prisoners, even those who might have had high *status* outside prison.

ecological fallacy: a methodological error, in which the characteristics of a population as a whole are attributed to groups within that population, without any real connection between them being demonstrated. For example, if we take three areas and find the following results:

Areas	Number of smokers	Number of cases of lung cancer
A	500,000	1,000
B	250,000	500
C	100,000	200

There seems to be a strong correlation between smoking and lung cancer, but we would be committing the ecological fallacy if we concluded that. What we do not know is whether the lung cancer cases are smokers. We cannot just assume that they are.

ecology: see *environmentalism*

economic power: a term which includes a number of capabilities stemming from control of material resources, such as the right to hire and fire, the ability to locate industry in particular areas and the influence that this can give over other areas of social life, such as politics. While ownership is a crucial dimension of economic power, it is not the only aspect of it. Economic power can also operate at the micro-level, for example between husband and wife, where control over domestic resources can lead to power of one over the other. (See *consumer power; institutional power; political power*.)

ecumenicalism: a process in which different Christian organisations, particularly *churches* and *denominations*, work together co-operatively, emphasising their shared characteristics. This might mean that joint church services are held, with worshippers gathering alternately at, for example, the Anglican, Roman Catholic and Methodist churches to engage in collective worship.

education: the process of acquiring knowledge and skills, both formally and informally. Although education is a life-long process which takes place in a wide variety of settings, sociologists have tended to focus on the formal education process and the specialist institutions in which this takes place.

Education Act 1944: an Act of Parliament which introduced the *tri-partite system* of secondary education. The Act created three types of secondary school, designed to cater for the needs of pupils from the age of 11 according to their age, aptitude and ability. The schools were meant to provide an appropriate education for what was seen as three different groups of children. The types of school were:

- Secondary grammar schools – designed for the top 20% children thought able to benefit from an 'academic' education.
- Secondary technical schools – designed for children with largely practical abilities thought capable of becoming technicians and skilled workers. In practice relatively few of these schools were built, largely because of the cost of equipping them.
- Secondary modern schools – a completely new type of school designed for children with practical abilities who were destined to become semi-skilled and unskilled manual workers.

Under the terms of the Act, children were meant to be selected to the most appropriate type of school according to their ability, which was usually considered to be measured by their performance in an examination taken at the age of 11-plus. In practice, the system proved to have a strong class bias, with middle-class children most likely to go to grammar schools, and secondary modern schools drawing most of their pupils from the working class. (See *comprehensive schools; parity of esteem; wastage of ability.*)

Education Reform Act 1988: hailed as the most significant and far-reaching government intervention in education since Butler's *1944 Education Act*, the Act introduced the following educational reforms:

- A *national curriculum* for children of compulsory school age in the *maintained sector*, accompanied by standardised tests (SATs).
- *Local management of schools* (LMS), under which headteachers and governors of schools were given greater control over their school's budget.
- Permission for schools to have *open enrolment.*
- A scheme under which schools would be allowed to opt out of local authority control and receive *grant-maintained status.*
- The abolition of the Inner London Education Authority.

Many of the changes introduced under the Act have been highly controversial but it is still too soon to judge clearly what the effects of the various changes have been.

Educational Priority Areas: designated areas of England and Wales identified by the *Plowden Report* of 1967 as areas in need of particular support in primary education because of their high levels of social disadvantage. The support took the form of the allocation of extra resources, including teachers, as a way of helping to overcome certain disadvantages arising from a child's *home background.* (See *compensatory education.*)

educational standards: a controversial measure of quality in educational achievement which has increasingly political overtones. There is much debate on the question of whether educational standards have or have not fallen over the years. They are usually measured by the numbers of pupils and students achieving pass grades in external examinations, and it is argued that the style and nature of examinations have undergone several changes, making it impossible to make direct comparisons. Teachers complain that when the pass rate falls they are accused of allowing standards to drop, and when the pass rate rises they are accused of making examinations too easy. (See *gold standard; National Curriculum.*)

effectiveness: applied to *organisations,* this is a measure of success of an organisation in achieving its goal. It is not the same as *efficiency,* though they are usually connected. A firm may be efficient but if the organisational goals are wider than just making profits, it may not necessarily be effective if other goals are not being met.

efficiency: an economic concept which when related to industry, is measured by the amount of resources needed to produce one unit. Efficiency is a central concept of *New Right* sociologists in the sociology of industry. The aim of industry is said to be the most efficient production possible, that is maximum production at minimum cost. In this way profits can be maximised. (See *effectiveness.*)

egalitarianism: a philosophy which focuses on social policies which introduce greater *equality* into society. It is one of the sources of inspiration for the *welfare state* and *progressive taxation* and thus is attacked by philosophers of the *New Right* as the politics of envy.

egoism: defined as the cult of the individual, it is the situation in a society where individual appetites are subject to little or no social control.

egoistic suicide: self-destruction which stems from the lack of integrating social contexts in society. Durkheim argued that individuals needed to be integrated into groups in order to be stable. Contexts which provided such integration were the *family* and *religion.* Where individuals were cut off from such contexts the possibility of suicide increased. It was therefore this type of suicide which Durkheim saw as differentiating Catholic low-suicide and Protestant high-suicide societies. (See *coefficient of aggravation.*)

elaborated code: a form of speech identified by Bernstein. It refers to a pattern of speech commonly used on formal occasions, in lectures, and between strangers. It is characterised by grammatically complex sentence structures, can describe abstract concepts (such as 'freedom') and is context-free, i.e. does not have to be tied in to a specific situation. The elaborated code is used extensively in education and while middle-class children come to school able to use both the elaborated code and the other less formal way of speaking (which Bernstein called the *restricted code*), working-class children tend to prefer the latter, putting them at an initial disadvantage in school. (See *language codes.*)

electability: the calculation of a candidate's chance of attracting votes according to his or her social characteristics. For example, candidates are deemed to be more electable if they are male, married with children, good-looking and so on.

elective affinity: a term used by Weber to describe the causal relationship between the ideas of ascetic Calvinism and the *spirit of capitalism.* The two meaning-systems were therefore congruent and through a variety of stages the ideas translated into the practices of *capitalism*. (See *asceticism*.)

electoral register: the list of those eligible to vote, which runs for one year without change. Its importance is that firstly it does not cover all of those eligible to vote, as some fail to register and secondly, that it is already out-of-date before it is used, as some electors die and others move away. The electoral register however, constitutes a prime *sampling frame* for sociologists, as it does encompass a significant number of those over 17.

elite: a small group at the top of an area of social life. It is often used to refer to the *power elite*, but elites can exist in any walk of life. For example, an important elite in post-modern societies would be the entertainment elite, who have the capacity to generate total devotion amongst fans. There are also elites within elites so that the Hollywood elite would be seen as the apex of cinematic elites.

elite theory: see *unitary elite theory*

embourgeoisement: the argument that the affluent working class are becoming like the middle class in economic standing, life style and attitudes, while the middle class are accepting them as their social equals. The theory first arose in the 1950s with the victories of the Conservative Party, and the notion that the very success of the Conservative Party in bringing *affluence* to a significant section of the working class would doom the Labour Party to permanent opposition, as their better-off working-class supporters turned to the Conservatives. The hypothesis was tested by Goldthorpe, Lockwood et al., who found little evidence that embourgeoisement was taking place. While the weekly wages of the affluent workers and *white-collar workers* were similar, life-time earnings were much in favour of the white-collar worker. Also, the affluent workers were becoming privatised, but beyond this, there was little similarity in life-style between them and the white-collar worker. Lastly, there was little evidence that affluent workers were seen as socially equal by white-collar workers. (See *socially aspiring worker*.)

emigration: see *migration*

emotions: feelings such as hate and love, which constitute the affective dimension of social life and which the *rationality* of sociology is often accused of neglecting. Emotions are an important factor in motivation, which *interactionism* in particular sees as the basis of social life.

empathy: the ability to understand the attitudes and behaviour of another person by relating these to one's own experiences. Interactionists in particular believe that the use of *qualitative methods* of research allows the researcher to benefit from such an understanding of those being studied. Weber used the word '*verstehen*', meaning to understand, to express the same idea. However critics of qualitative research methods argue that empathy between the researcher and those being studied leads to loss of *objectivity*.

empirical studies: those studies which are based on research yielding actual data, such as statistics, or transcripts of interviews, rather than works of theory.

empiricism: an approach to *knowledge* which argues that the only basis for knowing anything is experience itself. It is an approach which rejects the idea that sociology for example, can proceed through untested theorising, maintaining that progress can be made only through the collection of empirical observations. This approach has been criticised for denying the importance of *theory* in sociological work and relying on the collection of a vast number of often unrelated facts.

employment: the exchange of labour for wages or a salary, which is unequal in both economic and power terms. It is thus a logically distinct category to the wider concept of *work*.

empowerment: a term originally associated with the *New Right*, but now widely used. It concerns the dispersion of *power* to individuals, so that they begin to take responsibility for their own decisions and their own lives. It began as an attempt to roll back the power of the *State* by taking areas of decision-making traditionally associated with government and giving them to groups or individuals. Elements of empowering political programmes were the sale of council houses, the formation of housing associations, the introduction of *Local Management of Schools* etc. There is a much wider use of the term in, for example, education, where students are empowered through taking responsibility for charting and planning their own routes through courses, by the 'individual action planning' process.

empty bucket theory: a crude type of explanation of the effects of the mass media, which assumes that people approach media content with no prior beliefs or opinions, but just wait to be filled up with the ideas which the media put across. It tends to rely on a *conspiracy theory* of the media, where those in power seek to control subordinates in society by using the media to control what they think. Critics point out that the *audience* for media content are not 'empty' but approach media messages with the ability to choose and interpret material intelligently and with their own predispositions. (See *selective interpretation*.)

empty-nest families: families in which the offspring have grown up and moved out of the parental home, leaving the adult partners as a couple. The rise in *life expectancy* and the tendency for young adults to establish their own household as soon as possible has resulted in the creation of a large and growing group of middle-aged couples with few family responsibilities and, in many cases, relatively high incomes, particularly if both of them are in employment. The rise in the average age at which women bear their first child also means that, for many of these 'empty-nest couples', their services as grandparents will not be needed for some time after their last child has left home. There is considerable interest in this group by advertisers, who increasingly target such couples as potential buyers of a wide range of leisure and financial products. (See *household structure*.)

empty-shell marriages: where a married couple continue to live together but are only going through the motions of married life, often for the sake of the children. In all other respects the marriage has broken down. (See *marital break-down*.)

enclave development: a concept suggesting how *third world* countries are developed through the activities of *first world* agencies, such as the *trans-national companies*. The idea of enclave development was put forward by opponents of *under-development theory* which, it was argued, took far too negative a view of the first world. The process involves the creation of areas of high technology in countries of the third world, which then act as spurs to the development of the rest of the third world country's economy, as skills and *capital* are transferred from these pockets to the less-developed sectors.

encoding: how producers of media texts weave their messages into the images or words that they use. Producers' intentions are important here because they wish to get across particular messages to their *audience*. However, audiences do not necessarily decode the messages in the same way that the producer intended. (See *polysemic; text.*)

enculturation: a type of *socialisation* in which the young absorb the *culture* of a society holistically, through experiencing it directly. There are thus no specific mechanisms such as the *family* which engage in socialisation. (See *role-training; impulse control.*)

end of history: the idea that with the collapse of the communist regimes of Europe and the Soviet Union, the motor of history, which was competition between the two great ideological blocs of *capitalism* and *communism*, has stopped with the complete victory of capitalism. This suggests that there is now no serious alternative to capitalism as a way of achieving the 'good life'. Critics of the idea argue that this is to ignore a whole number of other possible motors, such the rise of *fundamentalism*, the rise of *Islam* or the competition between first and third worlds. (See *Cold War.*)

end of ideology: an approach associated with Daniel Bell, who argued that as societies become *mass societies*, there develops a *value-consensus* about what constitutes the 'good life', so that competing *ideologies* die out in the face of this agreement. Bell was writing in a time of optimism during the 1950s in the United States and has been criticised for being time-bound. Ideologies continued to be powerful during the Cold War period. (See *end of history.*)

endogamy: literally means 'marrying inside' and refers to rules which prevent a person from marrying outside his or her designated group. In Africa it used to be the rule among many tribes to marry from within one's own tribe, and Indians under the caste system had to marry someone from the same caste as themselves. Under the apartheid system in South Africa, the Prohibition of Mixed Marriages Act of 1949 meant that marriage could not legally take place between a white and a 'non-white' person. Endogamy is sometimes used by a group as an attempt to keep itself 'pure' by preventing children born of 'mixed blood'. However, there may also be economic reasons such as helping to keep the *wealth* of a tribe or clan within the group. (See *exogamy.*)

English as a second language: a reference to the fact that many children of recent immigrants to Britain will not have English as their mother-tongue, and English may not be the language spoken in the home. These children therefore face particular difficulties in the education system. While extra support is provided, cutbacks in education lead some teachers and educationalists to claim that such support is increasingly insufficient to enable the children to make the progress of which they are capable.

Enlightenment: the period leading up to the French Revolution, which was characterised by a belief in progress and with the challenge to traditional modes of thought posed by *rationality*. The Enlightenment is associated with *modernity* and the project associated with it is challenged in its turn by *post-modernism*, which denies the possibility of a teleological progress to a better society.

enterprise culture: a term developed by *New Right* theorists to describe a society in which individuals are encouraged by the social arrangements to enter business for themselves. The idea is that the *dependency culture* has reduced the capacity of the British population to control their own destinies. The future should be concerned with creating the conditions, especially over taxation and *welfare*, that encourage many citizens to take entrepreneurial risks and so increase employment opportunities for others.

enterprise zones: areas of deprivation defined in the 1980s as localities where private enterprise was to be given a free hand. There was a minimum of *bureaucracy* in these areas, rent and costs were kept low and a range of tax concessions granted. Enterprise zones were criticised for encouraging a 'grab-and-go' mentality, with short-term benefits to companies being the main motive force for moving to the enterprise zone. (See *community development programmes.*)

environment: originally meaning surroundings, with the growth of interest in green issues, the term has gained a new emphasis in sociology by being associated with the natural world which human societies inhabit. The impact of human activity, especially productive activity, on the natural world has been enormous and issues such as pollution, loss of green belt and the invasion of the motorway have become objects of sociological investigation.

environmentalism: a *new social movement*, which concerns itself with the protection of the natural and built surroundings which form the back-drop for human society. It is multi-faceted in its concerns and ranges from projects to clean up canals to the heritage movement, which aims to protect ancient monuments and buildings. Issues such as pollution and preservation have been brought to the top of the political agenda by environmentalists and altered the political programmes of all the major parties in Britain. The success of environmentalist movements such as Greenpeace has spawned a whole range of copy-cat organisations each seeking to emulate its success. Members of these range from anti-motorway protesters to animal rights activists. While main-stream environmentalists focus on peaceful and lawful process, there is a wing of the movement which is involved in more direct action and which can sometimes move into unlawful activity. The membership and organisational structures of the environmentalists are often fluid and changing.

epidemiology: the study of the nature, amount and spread of disease as a way of understanding the causes of particular diseases in order to develop an appropriate approach to prevention and cure. One of the earliest applications of epidemiology was the discovery in the 19th century of the link between cholera and infected drinking water, while one of the most recent is the attempt to understand *AIDS*.

episodic characterisation: used as a contrast to the idea of historical progress which sees history as one continuous story of improvement. It is the idea of *social change* as discontinuous, that is, comprised of events which are forged in their own circumstances rather than in response to an over-arching *meta-narrative*. The chief British exponent is *Giddens* who rejects all ideas such as *historical materialism* and argues that social change must be studied taking due account of accidental and contingent factors.

episteme: used by Foucault to indicate the way in which *knowledge* is structured or organised and which influences the way in which we view the world around us. It is therefore similar to a *paradigm*, but with a wider application to any *discourse* not just scientific ones.

epistemology: theories about the nature of *knowledge*. For sociologists, the term is used to refer to the sociology of knowledge.

epoché: a method in which the sociologist suspends the natural attitude, suggested by Husserl as a means of understanding the social world. That is, epoché involves putting the world 'in brackets' and approaching the *durée* or the stream of experience which constitutes our life as if it were an alien culture. The sociologist therefore treats the world as if they had never seen it before, putting aside all previous beliefs and understandings.

equality: the state of being the same in some respect, the concept has been attached to several factors which have formed the basis of sociological investigation. It is part of the *nature versus nurture debate* in the sense that there are clear biological differences between individuals, but also social differences which do not flow from these biological differences.

equality of opportunity: the principle that all people should be provided with an equal opportunity to succeed, irrespective of their sex, age, ethnic or religious group, physical abilities and sexual orientation. The principle is often used in the context of education, but has a much wider application, including in the workplace. (See *positive discrimination*.)

equality of outcome: a measure of *under-achievement* which compares different groups in terms of their qualifications gained, percentage of University entrants etc. Inequality of outcome can co-exist with *equality of opportunity* for a variety of reasons.

equilibrium: a state of balance between parts of the *social system*. Particularly associated with *functionalism*, the structures in society are said to tend towards a state of equilibrium, that is, where there is a change in the social environment which alters the balance between the sub-systems, there is an automatic process which seeks to restore the lost equilibrium. The notion is especially associated with those who adopt the *biological* or *mechanical analogy* in their depictions of society. (See *homeostasis*.)

ERA: see *Educational Reform Act 1988*

erklären: literally 'explanation', this is used as a contrast to *verstehen*, and is associated with the mode of studying the external objective world by employing the principles of science. As an objective methodology it is sufficient for explaining the external phenomena of society, but cannot access the subjective dimension.

eros: the erotic instinct identified by Marcuse as the object of *surplus repression*.

eroticism: the different social constructions which appear in every age associated with sexual desire. Foucault in particular investigated the changes in erotic formulations which have political as well as personal implications. For example, Foucault documented the ways in which the medicalisation of sexuality shaped definitions of acceptable eroticism.

Essex University Class Project: an analysis of data on *social class* from a sample of 1770 men and women. An interesting feature of the project is that the authors used its data to provide two descriptions of the *class structure*, one including, and one excluding, female employees. These showed that, because of the unequal spread of males and females throughout the *occupational structure*, classifications based only on male occupations tend to inflate the proportions of employees in the top and bottom categories, and to grossly underestimate the proportion of workers in the middle category, as shown by the table below. (See *Registrar-General's scale; Surrey Occupational Scale.*)

		Men and Women	Men Only
Higher-grade professionals	1	9.4	13.1
Lower-grade professionals	2	17.9	17.1
Routine non-manual	3	19.5	6.0
Small proprietors etc.	4	8.7	11.4
Lower-grade technicians	5	8.1	11.4
Skilled manual workers	6	12.5	17.4
Other manual workers	7	23.9	23.6

Source: H. Newby, G. Marshall, D. Rose and C. Vogler, 'Social Classes in Modern Britain', 1988

A comparison of occupational class: including and excluding female employees

established church: a *church* which is likely to have national *status* in a society, e.g. the Church of England, the Roman Catholic Church, the Greek Orthodox Church.

establishment: a general term for the ruling stratum in British society, it encompasses a number of *elites*, from the political rulers to the social elite, for example surrounding the Royal Family. There is a sense in which the establishment is used to describe the traditional sources of *prestige* and *power* in society and reflects a deferential attitude towards these.

estate stratification: found in *feudal* societies which are hierarchically organised according to an individual's inheritance and ownership of land, with the landless occupying the lowest stratum in society. Such societies are 'closed' in that it is very difficult for an individual to change the estate into which he or she has been born. The crucial *social status* in estate societies is that of the monarch, who owns all of the land under his or her control. It is the granting of land by the monarch to feudal lords which creates obligations of duty by those below to those above.

esteem: see *social status*

ethical constraints: factors which prevent a particular method or research study being used because of a belief that it would be morally wrong. Ethical constraints provide one of the main reasons why very few *laboratory experiments* are carried out in sociological research. Some would argue that certain kinds of *covert participant observation* are unethical, as with this method, the sociologist always has to deceive those who are being studied.

ethical issues: issues which have a moral dimension, such as the debates over euthanasia and *abortion*.

ethnic groups: people who share common history, customs and identity, as well as, in most cases, language and *religion*, and who see themselves as a distinct unit. It is thus an identity which members hold and which forms a basis for social action. Members usually seek to preserve their identity through a variety of closure tactics, for example, with regard to *marriage* which tends to be *endogamous*. Where they form a minority within the population, increased emphasis on tradition and custom help to maintain boundaries.

ethnic minorities: groups of people in a population who are from a different ethnic group from the indigenous population. It is an imprecise term, and in Britain is often used to refer only to people whose origin or family origin is Africa, the Caribbean, India, Pakistan or Bangladesh. The question on ethnic origin in the 1991 *census* showed that slightly over 3 million people, or 5.5% of the population, described themselves as belonging to an ethnic minority group.

ethnic plurality: a term used to describe the condition of post-modern societies which have more than one cultural group within them. This fracturing of society is associated with the dissolving of traditional national boundaries and the appearance of significant minorities in most societies.

ethnic under-achievement: the relatively low educational attainments of pupils from some ethnic minority groups when compared with average results of children from the indigenous population. Note that children from different ethnic minority groups perform at different levels. (In the U.K. children from Indian families tend to do well, while those from families of Afro-Caribbean and Pakistani/Bangladeshi origin do relatively badly). Some sociologists, such as Mabey, argue that the focus on ethnic group obscures the real underlying factor, namely that of *social class*. Children from Indian families are often from middle-class families, with parents in professional occupations, while children from Afro-Caribbean and Pakistani/Bangladeshi families are overwhelmingly the children of manual workers. Research by Tizzard *et al.* showed that the educational under-achievement of many black children could not be attributed to lack of *parental aspirations*. The majority of black parents took a keen interest in their children's education and wanted them to do well. In many areas, Afro-Caribbean parents have started 'Saturday schools' with additional tuition to help their sons and daughters do better at school. It is likely that a number of factors adversely affect the performance of children from some ethnic minority groups, particularly *racism*, both in and out of school, and *poverty*. (See *Swann Report*.)

ethnic vote: the concentrated electoral power of the ethnic minorities which gives them political influence in certain urban areas. The ethnic vote is high in the inner-city and any candidates in these constituencies, if not from the ethnic minorities themselves, must take account of their interests if they wish to be elected. The power of the ethnic vote has according to some sociologists been exaggerated because:

- independent candidates claiming to directly represent ethnic minorities have been unsuccessful in attracting votes
- ethnic minorities are themselves divided according to *religion, caste* and politics and therefore do not represent a bloc vote

ethnicity: a characteristic of social groups, which relies upon a shared *identity*, whether this is perceived or real, based on common cultural, religious or traditional factors. Ethnicity can involve a racial dimension, although this is not strictly necessary, as ethnic groups are usually based on narrower characteristics than those attributed to racial groupings.

ethnocentric: looking at an issue from the view-point of a particular cultural background and therefore obtaining a biased opinion of it. In sociology it is largely white sociologists who are said to be ethnocentric, though the term can be applied to any sociologist steeped in a particular cultural tradition.

ethnography: the study of the *culture* and way of life (or aspects of these) of a group of people by direct observation. The term is particularly used with reference to studies in anthropology, but ethnography is of course widely practised by sociologists. *Participant observation* studies form the most common type of ethnographic study in sociological research.

ethnomethodology: developed by Garfinkel as a challenge to orthodox sociology, the ethnomethodologist's fundamental approach is to stress the infinite ambiguity of *language* and *action*. Rather than assume that we understand what another person means when they say or do something, 'ethnos' argue that we have to struggle for their meaning, and that every situation is characterised by the search for common understandings. The social world is therefore built up of arbitrary rules, made up of a dense and often contradictory set of tacit understandings about what is going on. (See *practical theorists; indexicality; glossing.*)

ethos: the particular social and cultural characteristics and norms of a group, organisation or society. Being socialised into accepting and adopting the prevailing ethos is usually an important part of becoming a member of a group or institution, such as a religious group or public school.

eugenics: the science of breeding, it has become associated with plans for racial purity put forward by the Nazis in inter-War Germany. It is based on the far from proven links between genetic inheritance and various social and personal characteristics.

Euro-centric: examining phenomena from a European view-point. It is associated with *bias* which tends to exaggerate the importance of Europe in global affairs.

evangelism: an activity characteristic of some Christian religious organisations, particularly *denominations* and *sects*, which place an emphasis on preaching, particularly with messages derived from the Bible, and on the notion of salvation through personal conversion.

evangelistic bureaucrats: a concept devised by Davies to describe the attitude which many planners had about their role in local communities, in that they believed they could reform society through their work. They used their expertise to re-design the environment and saw themselves as consequently changing human behaviour. These planners tended to overcome the resistance of local councillors by deploying 'feel-good' words such as 'community' in putting forward their plans.

everyday knowledge: a phenomenological term which describes the commonsense that exists in society. It is the knowledge that we employ in our everyday, routine lives in order to effect social actions. Schutz argued that we build up our stock of everyday knowledge from our unique biographies. The contrast is with theoretical knowledge which is rational and thought-out. Everyday knowledge is the taken-for-granted knowledge which underlies our normal way of thinking. (See *commonsense world.*)

evolutionary theories: explanations in sociology which were heavily influenced by the theory of evolution put forward by the biologist Darwin. The implication of evolutionary theory is that societies have been constantly progressing from a primitive past to a sophisticated future, not as a result of planned change, but as a natural order of things. The assumption was that societies followed much the same evolutionary rules as biological species and that there was a 'natural selection' at work, in which successful societies displaced unsuccessful ones. Critics of these theories argue that they are ideological justifications for the developed world's exploitation of the undeveloped world, because such thinking allows this exploitation to be seen as a superior culture displacing an inferior one.

exchange theory: a sociological approach which stresses that the basis of social life is calculation by individuals. The idea is that social action is carried out where the individual has worked out the likely consequence of the action and what he or she may be likely to obtain from it. Relationships between individuals are therefore based on an exchange of benefits, with each calculating the best way of achieving what they want with a minimum cost in terms of what the other in the relationship needs. It is a concept drawn from economics and has been criticised for assigning too much *rationality* and deviousness to individuals in their everyday lives.

exclusion: a tactic of *social closure* in which an occupational group seeks to prevent other groups from obtaining the same rewards. This has the effect of emphasising the uniqueness of the occupational group, usually through some form of *credentialism*. (See *solidarism; credentialism*.)

exclusivist definitions of religion: those which define *religion* as a system of beliefs which focus on the *supernatural,* and rely on faith. (See *inclusivist definitions of religion*.)

existential sociology: rejecting most other sociology as too concerned with *rationality,* existential sociology starts from the idea that individuals are fundamentally situational (or existential). That is, people are like the world they inhabit, which is chaotic, uncertain, arbitrary and changing. People can only survive in this world by becoming like the world itself. They are therefore, at bottom, varied, changeable, contradictory and most of all, irrational. To the existentialists then, sociology must concern itself with the irrational – the emotional and affective side of motivation and action – because this is the ultimately real. (See *brute being*.)

exogamy: literally means 'marrying outside' and refers to the rules which exist in every society regarding the categories of people (usually kin) which a person may not marry. In modern Britain, this covers a fairly narrow range of relatives, but in many African societies whole *clans* are exogamous, that is, a person has to marry someone from a different clan. Exogamy is seen as a way of reducing conflict between groups, as a group is less likely to engage in hostilities with another group if it contains members of one's own family. (See *endogamy; incest*.)

expectancy theory: argues that work behaviour can be predicted on the basis of what individuals will subjectively expect they will achieve in taking up particular modes of behaviour in an occupation. The implication of the theory was that an individual will be motivated to work where the expectancy of work balances with the monetary values and *work satisfaction* actually received. As a *work motivation theory* it was criticised for assigning too much *rationality* to the individual in approaching work.

expectation of life: see *life expectancy*

experiential teaching: a style of teaching which provides the framework for pupils to become actively involved in what they learn and how they learn it, rather than being the passive recipients of knowledge handed down by the teacher. With experiential teaching, the teacher is viewed as one of a number of classroom resources, rather than as the sole repository of knowledge. (See *chalk-and-talk; discovery learning.*)

experiment: see *hypothetico-deductive method; laboratory experiment*

experimental group: a group within an *experiment* matched as closely as possible to another group, the *control group*. The main difference between the two groups is that only the experimental group is exposed to the *independent variable*, i.e. that which is controlled by the researcher and thought to be the cause of whatever changes are being investigated.

experimental method: see *hypothetico-deductive method*

expert society: see *post-industrial society*

explanation: an account of a phenomenon which is made understandable by identification of its causes. The search for explanations of social phenomena is a central feature of sociology, yet it is fraught with difficulty because of the complexity of social life and the capability of humans to exercise their free will to change the causes of things.

exploitation: see *appropriation*

expressive deviants: used by new deviancy theorists (NDTs) to describe those deviant groups at the margins of society, such as gays, drug-takers, prostitutes, who were the focus of much of their work. They were seen by NDTs as representing goodness at the margins, in contrast to mainstream society where the real criminals were located.

expressive role: the role which Parsons suggested is played by females within a *marriage*. The expressive role is the caring, nurturing, supportive role which many functionalists believe women perform 'naturally', as a result of 'biology'. The expressive role complements the *instrumental role* of the male breadwinner. Parsons suggested that children needed to grow up in a family in which these roles are performed by the respective parents if the children were to develop 'stable adult personalities'. Feminists disagree that 'expressive' tasks performed by women are somehow 'natural' to them. Eichler accuses Parsons of *androcentricity*, and says that men are able to interpret the housewife role in this way because they are rarely present when *housework* and *childcare* tasks are being performed. (See *instrumental role; dual role.*)

extended family: see *family structure*

extension leisure: a situation where leisure is seen as linked to work, or leisure activities function to support work relationships. In the case of the former, an example would be teachers reading around their subject. The latter is usually found amongst higher executives, such as playing golf with clients or entertaining colleagues. (See *complementary leisure; oppositional leisure.*)

external labour market: refers to jobs where the pay is low and working conditions poor, with the characteristic of part-time, temporary contracts. There is both little chance of advancement and a high turnover of the labour force. The members of the external labour market move in and out of the *internal labour market*, according to supply and demand. (See *dual labour market*.)

extrinsic satisfaction: in work, this is achieved through the monetary rewards which the employee receives. Workers who are interested only in extrinsic satisfaction are said to have a very *instrumental* attitude to their work, with home more likely to be their *central life interest*. (See *intrinsic satisfaction*.)

F

factory system: the process of production which emerged during the *Industrial Revolution*, when larger and larger groups of workers were brought under a single roof to carry out their work activities. The development of the factory system meant great changes for the way that people lived their lives, for example, introducing the concept of 'going to work'. It also allowed a huge increase in production, which eventually brought material benefits to many in capitalist societies, not just in terms of wages but also in terms of the products which became available to people. However, factory production has also been identified as a cause of increased *alienation* in society.

fallacy of misplaced concreteness: see *reification*

false consciousness: used by Marxists to mean ways of thinking which are the product not of the real material conditions the thinker inhabits, but of the ideological forces of other social groups. It is usually associated with the *working class*, who are said to be falsely consciousness when their thoughts are alienated from their real social being. Marxists use false consciousness to explain why the working class do not revolt against their subordination, but accept the legitimacy of the power structures which oppress them.

falsely accused: defined by Becker as 'one who does not engage in rule-breaking behaviour but who has been publicly perceived or labelled as a deviant'. Such people therefore suffer the consequences of being known as deviant without having committed any action which would warrant this. (See *pure deviant; secret deviant.*)

falsification: a principle of scientific procedure, whereby the scientist should attempt to disprove a hypothesis rather than seek to verify it. The logic behind this principle is that as scientists are human beings, there is a temptation for them to find support for their hypothesis and ignore results which disprove it. By concentrating on the falsification of hypotheses, scientists can work on the assumption that their theories are provisionally true until disproved. (See *verifiability.*)

family: commonsensically it is all the people we are related to by blood or marriage, but sociologically the definition is less obvious, with ambiguities surrounding the differences between family, kinship and *household*. There is a difference between the family living together in the same household at any one moment in time and those whom we think of as our families in the wider sense. The family is also intimately connected to moral issues, because the family is a biological as well as a social formation. (See *core functions of the family; family structure.*)

family credit: a social benefit in the U.K. which 'tops up' the income of low-paid workers with children. In 1993–4, an average of 513,000 people were in receipt of family credit.

family fit: a functionalist belief that the dominant *family structure* of a society will take that form because it best meets the needs of that society at that particular time. Thus functionalists such as Parsons claim that the *nuclear family* replaced the *extended family* as the dominant form in industrial societies because it provided a better 'fit' than the extended family, which was better suited to the needs of a predominantly agricultural society. It is suggested that the nuclear family, being small, allowed its members to be geographically mobile and more easily able to move to where work could be found, such as in the new factories. The research of the social historians Peter Laslett and Michael Anderson, however, showed that this was an overly simplistic view not entirely supported by historical evidence. Laslett found that in pre-industrial Britain, nuclear family households were quite common, one reason being that relatively short life expectancy made it difficult for many families to reach the three-generation stage. Similarly Anderson's research on households in the northern textile towns showed that in the mid-nineteenth century when industrialisation was at its height in Britain many families had relatives living with them, as kin were an important source of help, both in finding work and providing assistance in times of hardship. Although this co-residence of families declined in the first part of the twentieth century, other social changes have resulted in a growing diversity of family structure.

family of origin: used to describe the family into which an individual is born. (See *family of procreation.*)

family of procreation: used to describe the family in which an individual is a parent. (See *family of origin.*)

family reconstitution: a method used by Laslett in his study of *family structure* in pre-industrial England. It involves the painstaking 'reconstitution' of family trees using parish registers and other *documents* such as wills and ecclesiastical censuses. It requires a community which had both very little internal *migration* over a long period of time and, obviously, for which the relevant documents are still available. Using this method, Laslett was able to show that, contrary to functionalist ideas, the *extended family* was not the statistical norm in pre-industrial England. The method has also shown that the age at which couples married was closely linked to prosperity, which in turn was linked to the harvest. In periods of good harvests, the average age of marriage went down; in lean times and periods of famine, it rose sharply, as couples could not afford to set up an independent household.

family size: usually refers to the number of children born to a couple. Apart from a couple of 'baby booms' in the late 1940s and early 1960s, the overall trend in Britain has been towards smaller families. Family size is affected not only by the availability of reliable and affordable contraception, but by social *norms* governing the 'ideal' family size and by economic decisions regarding the cost of rearing children against an improved standard of living for the family. (See *birth rate.*)

family structure: the composition of a group of people living together as a family. The two basic family structures are nuclear and extended. A nuclear family is regarded as an adult couple and their dependent children. An extended family is one in which the basic nuclear structure has been added to, or extended, either vertically (e.g. grandparents, parents, children) or horizontally (e.g. two or more brothers living together with their respective spouses and children). While there have always been variations on these basic structures a number of social changes in Britain have resulted in a growing diversity of family structures. (See *lone-parent families; reconstituted families; empty-nest families.*)

fascism: a political movement of the right, which draws strongly on military imagery and organisation to represent the will of the nation. It demands absolute obedience from subordinates to superiors and has a tendency to militaristic expansion against neighbouring countries. As an authoritarian movement, fascism appeals to national-istic sentiment and is anti-democratic. It also tends to racial exclusion in its definition of the nation.

fatalism: an attitude whereby the holder believes that there is nothing they can do about their circumstances. Fatalistic attitudes are usually associated with the *working class* and express a certain pessimism about life-chances. Fatalism tends to lead to political inactivity, as the holders accept their present position as the only possible one.

fatalistic suicide: self-destruction which stems from over-regulation of the individ-ual by the collectivity. The classic example is the concentration camp prisoner who throws him or herself on the electrified fence rather than continue to suffer the total control of the camp guards.

favelas: an alternative term for the rather old-fashioned 'shanty town' and is used to describe those areas of *third world* cities where the conditions of life are harsh and basic amenities lacking. The use of 'shanty town' fell into disrepute because it sug-gested an unorganised and haphazard urban development. While there are haphazard features in any urban development, research in Latin America suggested that the people of the 'barrios' or favelas were more organised than was immediate-ly obvious. They banded together to protect their homes and arranged what few services could be provided. The favelas were therefore poor areas of third world cities, often with the inhabitants squatting illegally on other people's land, with lim-ited employment opportunities and poor housing materials. There were also vibrant political and cultural features of the favelas, with a culture of resistance and improve-ment predominating.

fecundity: the ability to give birth to live-born children. (See *fertility*.)

female conservatism: the idea put forward by psephologists that women show a greater tendency to vote Conservative than men do. While statistically accurate in the main there is no inevitability about this, and sociologists have been critical of those ideas which see this conservatism as somehow natural. Rather, they suggest that women's domestic role tends to limit their work opportunities, so that they are less likely to come into contact with Labour-minded influences in the workplace such as *trade unions*. The 1992 *general election* revealed some differences in the voting patterns of men and women, but these were not very great.

	Con %	Lab %	Lib/Dem %	Other %
All voters	43	35	18	5
Men	42	37	17	5
Women	43	34	19	3

(Source: N.O.P.)

Voting in the 1992 general election by gender

female crime: law-breaking by women; it has been an increasing focus for sociological investigation after having been neglected for many years. Early sociological approaches to female crime tended to see women who broke the law as somehow like men, or engaging in 'typically' feminine crimes such as shop-lifting or child-battering. More recent work has focused on female criminals in their own right and the emergence of 'untypical' activity such as female gangs.

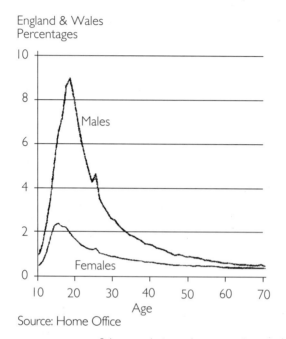

England & Wales
Percentages

Source: Home Office

Known offenders as a percentage of the population – by age and gender, 1993

female gaze: in the sociology of culture, the way in which visual texts are viewed from the standpoint of a woman, which contrasts with the usually dominant 'male gaze' associated with Western culture generally employed to objectify women as sex objects.

female under-achievement: a tendency for girls to perform less well at school than boys, particularly in Maths and the sciences, and to be less likely to enter higher education. However, although there is still evidence of gendered subjects, girls now out-perform boys at all levels of education up to and including 'A' levels, giving rise to concern about male under-achievement.

·1 or more A levels (or SCE highers)		GCSEs or SCE O/standard only (no A levels or SCE highers)		No graded result		All leavers (100%) (thousands)	
Males	Females	Males	Females	Males	Females	Males	Females
27.8%	31.4%	65.2%	62.6%	7.1%	6.0%	323.9	312.0

(Source: Social Trends 25, 1995)

School leavers' examination achievements by gender 1991–2 (United Kingdom)

femininity: those characteristics which are associated with being a woman. There is a traditional conception of being feminine which has been under attack by the feminist movement as acting to limit the possibilities of women, constraining them to act out defenceless and helpless roles. Conceptions of femininity are constantly being negotiated and re-negotiated as women take more and more control over their own lives and seek to find ways of expressing themselves in traditional and non-traditional ways. Femininity according to sociologists is therefore socially negotiated.

feminisation of poverty: the fact that a growing proportion of those in *poverty* are women. Reasons for this include:

- Most heads of *lone-parent families* are women, and such families are at risk from poverty.
- Women have a longer average life expectancy than men, and the elderly are at risk from poverty.
- Women's average earnings are less than those of men and many women are in very low-paid jobs.

(See *black feminism; liberal feminism; Marxist feminism; radical feminism.*)

feminisation of work: the process whereby certain categories of work, especially clerical work, have become dominated by female workers. The process is accentuated by the fragmentation of clerical work, which has reduced the skill levels of these occupations and made them susceptible to *colonisation* by female workers.

United Kingdom
Percentages

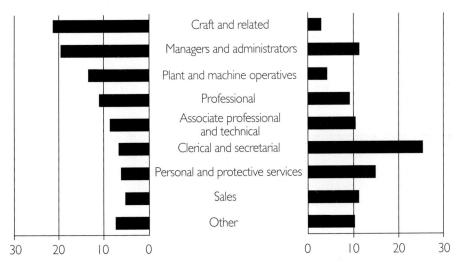

Source: Employment Department

Employees and self-employed by gender and occupation, spring 1994

feminism: the sociological (and philosophical) perspective which examines social phenomena from the view-point of women. Feminist critiques of the *classical sociologists* argued that they viewed social processes only from the viewpoint of males and the traditional invisibility of women in society was reproduced in sociology. The feminist movement in sociology therefore had two main aims:

- To redress the balance and examine society sociologically from a female point of view, laying bare the ways in which men dominate social relationships and restrict the opportunities of women.
- To explore women's lives, which had been neglected by traditional sociology, and open up the lives of females to sociological scrutiny.

(See *black feminism; liberal feminism; Marxist feminism; radical feminism.*)

fertility: a reference to the number of children born to a woman. (See fertility rate.)

fertility rate: the number of live births in a population per 1000 women of child-bearing age (usually reckoned as 15–50 years). The figure is often broken down still further into an age-specific fertility rate. The 1991 *Census* showed that in England and Wales, women aged 25–29 showed the highest fertility with an age-specific fertility rate of 120 births per 1000. The older age groups (women aged between 30–39) have shown a consistent rise in fertility rates since the early 1980s, reflecting both the rise in the average age at marriage and women's control of their own fertility. Many women now choose to develop a career before they start a family. Another measure of fertility is the Total Period Fertility Rate (TPFR), which measures the number of children a woman would have if she experienced the relevant age-specific fertility rates throughout her child-bearing life. The World Health Organisation estimates that a TPFR of 2.1 is necessary to keep population levels in a society stable (ignoring any possible effects of *migration*). The TPFR for the UK in 1992 was 1.8, well below the post-war peak of 2.95 in 1964. However, due to longer *life expectancy*, the number of births in the UK is expected to remain higher than the number of deaths for some time, leading to a natural increase in the population despite the lower-than-necessary TPFR. The Office of Population Censuses and Surveys estimates that the population of the UK will start to fall from the year 2028, when the number of deaths will start to exceed the number of births. (See *crude birth rate; death rate; fecundity.*)

fetish: an object which is worshipped or venerated because it is believed to have magical powers. Such objects often form an important part of religious or magical *rituals*.

feudal society: a society in which people are ordered in a strict *hierarchy*, depending on their relationship to the possession or non-possession of land. In theory, all land is owned by the monarch, who gives grants to the nobles or *aristocracy*, who, in their turn, rent or lease land to others further down the hierarchy. The landless have very limited rights in society, but owe loyalty to their feudal lords. Relationships in a feudal society are therefore based on obligations to superiors in the hierarchy. Feudal societies tend to be closed, with little chance of *social mobility*. Production in feudal societies is largely agricultural, with *wealth* being made from the farming of land. Feudalism broke down in western Europe under the impact of the growth in the commercial class located in towns and the rise in *capitalist relations of production*.

field experiment: an experiment carried out in a natural setting rather than in a laboratory. The method is not widely used in sociology owing to the difficulty of controlling the *variables*. (See *comparative method.*)

fieldwork: a general term used to cover a variety of sociological research activities in which the sociologist is actively engaged in the real social world in a direct way. It stands in contrast to work which is carried in a laboratory or a library. (See *laboratory experiments.*)

finance capitalists: members of a group within the capitalist class, who are concerned with banking and the movement of money around the *global market.* Aaronovitch identifies the finance capitalists as the new *ruling class* in late capitalist societies. Critics argue that members of this smaller group within the capitalist class have competing interests and do not act in concert. Moreover, individual finance capitalists are subject to the same impersonal forces of *capitalism* and can just as easily fall prey as make a great deal of wealth from them.

first world: that section of the globe which is most highly developed industrially. The first world usually includes the economies and societies of western Europe, the United States and Canada, Australia, New Zealand and Japan. The criteria for inclusion in the category first world include technological sophistication, an advanced service sector and a commitment to free enterprise. (See *second world; third world.*)

first-past-the-post: elections in which the candidate with the largest number of votes wins the seat, regardless of whether he or she wins a majority of the votes in the constituency. The system is argued to be unfair to the smaller parties, because the largest party's votes are concentrated in particular geographical areas while the votes of smaller parties are more evenly spread. This concentration ensures that the major parties gain a much larger number of seats in parliament than their aggregated vote would suggest. (See *proportional representation.*)

fiscal crisis: the result of the contradiction in *late capitalism* between the need to reduce state expenditure to maintain profitability in a global economy and the need to increase expenditure of welfare benefits to maintain legitimacy for the capitalist system. The fiscal crisis is discussed politically between those advocating a minimalist state and therefore a reduction in *direct taxation* and those who argue for an interventionist state and therefore continued public expenditure.

five giant ills: see *Beveridge Report*

five stages of economic growth: an idea developed by Rostow to describe the steps which undeveloped countries needed to go through to achieve a developed state:

1 Traditional society, characterised by agricultural dominance and a low technological state.
2 Pre-conditions for Take-off, where agriculture is re-organised to produce surplus food and national transport systems are developed.
3 Take-off, where society is transformed through increasing investment in advanced technology in the leading sectors of the economy.
4 Maturity, where industry is diversified into many areas of activity and investment increases to produce a dynamic industrial sector.
5 Developed status, where there is a growth of the *tertiary sector,* combined with high national consumption.

fixation: when a worker experiences frustration in work, one reaction may be for him/her to develop a compulsion to act in a certain way. The worker then becomes resistant to any change which might threaten the fixation.

flexible production methods: the ability of a firm to switch from manufacturing one product to another with little disruption of the production line and utilising much the same sophisticated machinery. This is a key element of post-Fordist production, which seeks to meet the consumer needs of *niche markets*. The ability to respond to rapid changes in demand is important for the survival of industrial organisations in the situation of post-modernity.

floating voters: those who are not fixed in their voting habits, but exhibit change in their political preferences. However, floating voters may be voluntary or involuntary. Voluntary floating voters make a choice to change their support, either because they are fickle, or out of principle, or because their usual party is not putting a candidate in their ward or constituency. Involuntary floating voters are the young who are voting for the first time and therefore have to record an 'abstention' for the last election and those who have died since the last election, but who remain on the *Electoral Register*.

folk devils: where a group with a particular common interest or activity becomes stigmatised by society at large and the target for adverse comment and activity. For example, New Age travellers have become folk devils in the 1990s, being subject to legislation and police activity designed to prevent their gatherings, and vilification in the press and television. (See *moral panics*.)

folk society: a term devised by the *Chicago School* to denote rural societies in which everyone knows everyone else. Such societies have a number of folk characteristics, such as oral traditions, their own style of music and dance and a tendency to keep themselves to themselves, while preserving traditions of hospitality. (See *Gemeinschaft*.)

food: substances eaten to maintain life, in sociology food is more than this, having symbolic as well as physical significance. The sociology of food examines the ways in which food is produced and marketed, the ways in which it is used as a medium of *status* and exchange and the ways in which there are class and ethnic differences in the attitudes towards and use of food products.

football hooliganism: the violent activities of football supporters, both organised and disorganised. Sociological interest has focused on the way that the violence is real or symbolic and the infiltration of ideologies such as *racism* amongst football hooligans. There is also a *social policy* interest in the success of various public order and social manipulation measures to combat the incidence of football hooligans. Another focus of concern has been the way in which football hooliganism is connected to images of masculinity and the traditions of football as a working-class male phenomenon.

forced mobility: where movement in the *class structure* is the result of changes in the *occupational structure* rather than an increase in the choices of individuals. The major cause of forced mobility in recent times has been the decline in manufacturing jobs and the increase in white-collar and service occupations. This has resulted in enforced upward mobility.

forces of production: a Marxist term which describes the raw materials needed to manufacture goods, the tools and machinery needed to work those materials and the *detailed division of labour* which is organised around that production. It is similar to the *means of production*, which includes division of labour under its umbrella. (See *relations of production*.)

Fordism: a type of industrial production associated with modernity, it is based on a strict *division of labour*, with workers performing low-skill repetitive tasks to produce mass standardised goods for undifferentiated markets. Fordist production is associated with Taylorist methods of management, where the crucial issue is control over the minute-by-minute actions of the workers to maximise production. Sociologists have argued that Fordist conditions are likely to lead to an alienated or at least instrumental workforce. (See *post-Fordism.*)

formal economy: the part of the economy composed of paid jobs, either in manufacturing, extraction or the service industries. A feature of jobs in the formal economy is that they are recorded by the *State* and therefore taxable. (See *informal economy; black economy.*)

formal interviews: see *standardised interviews*

formal organisations: used to describe the *structure* of an *organisation* and the ways that communication, decision-making and control are supposed to flow within it. Most formal organisations are hierarchical in nature, that is, the formal structure concentrates *power* and decision-making at the top of a pyramid of organisational positions. Those at the top control the activities of those below them, while those at the bottom are expected to obey the orders. Therefore, most formal organisations are 'top-down' organisations. (See *informal organisations.*)

formal rationality: associated with economic actions, this is the quantitative calculation of the effects of particular actions in strictly logical terms and often expressed as 'maximum production at minimum cost'.

formalisation: the process whereby enthusiastic *sects* adopt more ritualistic and routinised practices as members age and settle down. It is contrasted with inspirational forces within sects.

formalism: applied to organisational behaviour, it means an over-adherence to the formal procedures of the organisation, often at the expense of overall goals. By focusing on the fulfilment of formal procedures, bureaucrats are said to produce organisations which are rigid and unresponsive to *clients'* needs. (See *displacement of goals.*)

fourth world: a term sometimes used in the sociology of development to indicate those countries in Africa and Asia which are the poorest in the world and which stand out from the rest of the *third world* through their lack of *development.*

foxes: a term used by Machiavelli to describe those who gain and maintain *power* in society through cunning and deviousness. (See *lions.*)

fragmentation theories: explanations of the development in class structures which argue that the traditional classes of working and middle class have split into a larger number of fractions of class, which disrupt the formation of class solidarity The factors involved in fragmentation are:

- Growth in affluence, reducing external differences between the classes.
- Growth in occupational specialisation has resulted in the proliferation of middle-class occupations.
- *Social mobility* results in members of the fast-growing middle-class sector being recruited from diverse backgrounds.

Fragmentation theories suggest that all classes are split, with the modern *upper class* divided into four segments of the *elite,* the old professional class, *organisation men* and the *intelligentsia.* The *intermediate class* is highly fragmented through low-level non-manual workers, independent artisans to supervisors. The traditional working class has also contracted and fragmented into various levels of skill and particularly the employed and unemployed. (See *persistence theories; realignment theories.*)

frame of reference: used to indicate a particular way in which an individual comes to view the world, built up through his or her own experience of it. In looking at social phenomena, individuals do not do so objectively, but through the filter of their own experiences and understandings. The basic assumptions and pre-existing attitudes of the individual constitute a frame of reference through which individuals will view new events as they seek to establish their meaning. Though highly variable, frames of reference do have a collective existence as members of, for example, the same social class are likely to have similar experiences. They tend to be built up as images of other social groups and experiences, which may or may not be accurate accounts.

Frankfurt school: a group of radical sociologists who moved away from the Marxist assumptions of its founders to develop critical theory, which was critical of western *capitalism* and Soviet-style *socialism.* Though it has many variations within it, the Frankfurt school tended to view most progress as illusory, with science and Reason seen as tools for the perfection of tyranny rather than liberating society. In particular, their concern with society's relationship with nature preceded much ecologically-minded sociology.

free will: see *voluntarism*

free-floating intelligentsia: a concept used by Mannheim to indicate the social group he believed could stand outside their own social interests when carrying out their work on ideas and thus avoid ideologies such as *fascism* or *communism.* The intelligentsia could therefore avoid the pitfalls of *relativism* and put forward ideas which were more truthful than ideological.

friendship: the relation between two people which is based on mutual respect and liking, and which encompasses relationships of trust and loyalty between them. Though a central part of many people's lives, the importance of friendship in society has been little investigated by mainstream sociology.

fringe benefits: the wider monetary and non-monetary rewards that are given to workers outside of the main wage or salary. These may cover overtime payments, holiday entitlements, flexibility of work hours and other perks. Sociologists have been interested in the way that fringe benefits systematically differ between various groups of workers, with non-manual workers usually gaining greater fringe benefits than manual workers.

frustrated instrumentalism: a condition where voters increasingly vote against the party of government because of the decline in the material welfare that its policies has brought them. It is thus the lack of economic success which leads the electorate to register a protest vote against the government party. It is a feature of much democratic politics in the post-modern world.

frustration: where incentives other than money are not offered in work, sociologists argue that a psychological feeling of frustration may build up, which may be released in aggression, but which can also have other outlets, such as regression. (See *resignation; fixation.*)

frustration-aggression theory: drawn from the psychological work of Dollard, it was used in the sociology of *deviance* to suggest that aggressive behaviour is a result of the frustration of individual needs. For example, in the sociology of *suicide*, Henry and Short suggested that the frustration of blocked *goals* in times of business depression could lead to increased aggression against the self and therefore higher rates of suicide.

function: the job that an activity or institution does for wider *social structures*, and in particular its contribution to the maintenance and continuation of social arrangements. (See *latent functions; manifest functions.*)

functional equivalent: a structure in society that can carry out the same job as a different structure in another society with equal efficiency.

functional indispensability: the principle in *functionalism* that existing institutions are essential for society to continue to exist. This was criticised because it leads to inherent conservatism, with change being seen as somehow threatening to the continuation of society. Merton also showed that there were functional alternatives.

functional prerequisites: these are the basic needs that *society* must have fulfilled if it is to continue to exist. The assumption of the functionalists was that existing social arrangements meet some functional prerequisite, otherwise society would not exist. Parsons argued that societies had four basic needs, *Adaptation*, *Goal-attainment*, *Integration* and *Latency* (the *AGIL* or *GAIL* needs). (See *functionalism.*)

functional rationality: a term deployed by Mannheim to indicate a situation where the *division of labour* resulted in efficient production. Mannheim argued that functional rationality was often achieved at the expense of *substantial rationality*, with a consequent increase in the *alienation* of workers.

functional rebel: an individual who, according to *Durkheim*, protests that the existing social arrangements as unjust, because they do not accord with the distribution of talents. While the functional rebels oppose the existing political realities, they are called deviant by those who benefit from them.

functional unity: the principle in *functionalism* that everything that exists in society contributes to the maintenance of everything else. It was criticised because social institutions could be shown to have a high degree of *autonomy*.

functionalism: that approach in sociology which seeks to explain the existence of *social structures* by the role they perform for *society* as a whole. It is thus a structural theory, beginning its analysis at the level of society rather than the individual. The focus of analysis is the inter-relationship of interdependent parts and how the functioning of the parts is essential for the well-being of the whole. However, critics suggest that it:

- is a conservative approach, stressing order at the expense of conflict,
- ignores individuals in focusing only on the structural elements,
- is ahistorical, focusing on the present without any sense of the past.

functionaries: in Althusserian terms, these are the people who staff the *ideological* and *repressive state apparatus* and act as agents of capital, sometimes consciously, sometimes unwittingly.

fundamentalism: a religious belief (and any practices following from it) that there is a need to return to and follow the basic texts of that religion in order to gain salvation. Fundamentalist groups and movements exist in *Christianity, Judaism* and *Islam.* While it is an essentially religious belief, fundamentalism is often involved with overtly political issues, as its views can bring it into conflict with the *state* over how society should be run.

funding: the source of money required for sociologists to carry out research. Not only the amount of funding, but its source is of great importance to the nature of sociological research. Funding is usually obtained by a research grant, obtained from government-sponsored organisations such as the Economic and Social Research Council, from private bodies such as the Joseph Rowntree foundation, or from academic committees in universities or colleges. The researcher has to obtain the approval of the appropriate body before the grant is made. Funding may also be provided by a body such as a local authority or a charity who wish a particular piece of research to be carried out, in which case there will usually be certain conditions and restrictions on the subject matter, scope and possibly the methods of the research. It is often easier to obtain funding for research which can be used directly to shape or inform a particular policy than for 'pure' academic research.

fusionism: a theory in the sociology of *leisure,* which argues that work and leisure are becoming increasingly similar. Work takes on many of the attributes of leisure, such as piped music on the shop-floor and leisure takes on some of the organisational aspects of work. (See *leisure industry.*)

future indebtedness: where students are funded through loans rather than grants, it describes the putting off of debt payment until earning begins. The importance of future indebtedness is that it is claimed it can deter some working class students from pursuing their studies.

G

GAIL: see *AGIL*

gambles with death: a term used by Taylor to denote that most *suicidal acts* are Janus-faced, that is oriented towards both death and life. Taylor argues that there is a continuum of suicidal acts from the trivial to the deadly serious. Most however are gambles with death in which the *actor* creates situations in which the suicidal act is more or less likely to be detected and stopped. The less likely the detection, the more serious the attempt to die. (See *attempted suicides*.)

games theory: developed from economics, it attempts to apply mathematical values to decision-making situations, where there are limited choices and participants have different interests in outcomes, which might be expressed numerically. It has been criticised for attaching mathematical values to what are essentially non-mathematical, complex social situations.

gang: any grouping (usually youthful, urban and male) which seeks to control a 'territory' and operates on the margins of legality. Gangs have been a particular focus for sociologists of *deviance* who are interested in the way that they have sub-cultural rules and *status* systems and in the relationship between members of gangs and 'normal' society. Though often associated with violence, a distinguishing characteristic of youthful gangs is boredom. More organised and older gangs can move into more criminal activities, with an associated rise in disorderly behaviour.

garden cities: a housing innovation associated with Ebenezer Howard, which attempted to bring the countryside into urban areas. The development of garden cities demanded that each house should have sufficient garden for the occupiers to grow their own vegetables and flowers. The aim was to improve the housing stock, reduce overcrowding and preserve agricultural areas around the cities. This was in contrast to inner-city developments of the *urban renewal programmes*, which produced much higher density housing, with few private garden areas.

gated communities: middle class residential areas surrounded by physical barriers to prevent unauthorised access, and usually monitored and patrolled by security guards. Gated communities are increasingly found in the USA, and are a response to their inhabitants' fear of rising levels of crime. Charles Murray predicts that such communities will increasingly spread to Britain. (See *underclass*.)

gatekeepers: sociologically, those who control access to a valuable resource or outlet, by virtue of occupying a particular position. In the sociology of the media, gatekeeper refers to editors of journals and newspapers, whose decisions control what does and does not get published. They are therefore in powerful positions to shape what the public thinks about particular issues. The influence of the gatekeepers' *ideology* and interests is thus promoted through their ability to deny access to alternative ideas. In urban sociology, the *urban managers* act as gatekeepers, having the ability to open or close doors to valuable resources such as public housing, social security benefits etc. (See *agenda-setting*.)

gay rights: part of the *New Social Movements,* it refers to the campaign for equal treatment for lesbians and homosexual men. The focus of much gay rights agitation concerns the age of consent and the discrimination which gays experience in society, such as homophobic violence.

GCE (General Certificate of Education): a qualification which now exists at *Advanced* and *Advanced Supplementary (AS) level* only, and is traditionally the main external examination qualification taken by 18+ students in England and Wales. However an increasing number of 18-year-olds are taking courses leading to advanced level *GNVQ.* (See *gold standard.*)

GCSE (General Certificate in Secondary Education): the main external examination qualification taken by pupils aged 16+ in England and Wales. It was introduced in the 1980s to replace the existing dual system of 16+ examinations, the GCE O level and the *CSE.*

Geisteswissenschaften: used by Dilthey to indicate the social sciences as distinct from the natural sciences. The crucial difference is that the social sciences have to be explored internally, in terms of the mind or spirit as well as externally. (See *naturwissenschaften.*)

Gemeinschaft: developed by Tönnies to describe the types of relationship which are found in *communities,* and in particular, rural communities of the pre-industrial age. These sorts of relationship were close and intimate, because each individual understood where he or she was in relation to all others with whom they interacted. There is therefore a strong sense of position associated with *Gemeinschaft* relationships. *Gemeinschaft* relationships are *holistic,* that is, they involve the whole of a person's being, and are likely to be intimate and face-to-face. (See *Gesellschaft.*)

gender: used by sociologists to describe the cultural and social attributes of men and women, which are manifested in appropriate masculinity and femininity. Sociologists use gender as distinct from the anatomical divisions of sex because although the two are connected, they are not necessarily coterminous. For example, the anatomically male can adopt feminine behaviour patterns. In the case of transsexuals, gender behaviour can be transformed into an anatomical reality through surgery. Post-modernists suggest that this illustrates the way in which individuals can reconstruct very basic aspects of their identity in fundamental ways. The relationship between anatomical sex and gendered behaviour is thus complex and varied. (See *sex.*)

gender codes: hidden, unspoken assumptions about the proper roles of men and women which are transmitted through the *socialisation* process and which are negotiated by each new *generation.* Gender codes are not uniform but vary with location. Traditional gender codes tend to be stronger in the *working class* than the *middle class,* but all people have access to both conservative and radical gender codes and negotiate their way through to their own balance.

gender regime: used to describe the ways in which an institution is enveloped in messages concerning what is appropriate or inappropriate masculine or feminine behaviour. For example, it has been used in the study of schooling to examine the *hidden curriculum* messages about male and female behaviour.

gender stereotyping: see *masculinity; femininity; stereotyping*

genderquake: used by Wilkinson to describe the fundamental change in attitudes towards women's role in society that has taken place since the impact of modern *feminism*. Crucial to this genderquake is a change in female attitudes towards education and work. Women are now more likely to see themselves in terms of career than they are in terms of housewife and therefore have much more positive attitudes towards education as a means of achieving a good career.

general election: where the parties compete for the people's vote in order to form the national Government. The occurrence of general elections is fixed by law and forms the major focus for political activity in democratic societies. General elections are also carried out under different conditions such as *first-past-the post* and *proportional representation*.

general unions: trade union organisations of workers which include many different types of occupation across many industries. General unions tend to grow very large, either through recruitment in new and expanding industries, or through merging with other unions. (See *craft unions; industrial unions*.)

generalisations: propositions derived from studying a *sample* of people with specific characteristics which are applied to all people who have those characteristics. The ability to generalise is based on the representativeness of the sample being studied. It is important because it allows the cost-effective study of society as a whole.

generalised other: in *symbolic interactionism*, the ability of an individual to place themselves in the position of other people involved in a situation and calculate the effects of an action upon them. The capacity for *action* in society rests upon the ability to envisage the generalised other.

generation: all members of a society born in the same period and regarded as a collectivity, such as the 'pre-war generation', or the 'sixties generation'. It can also mean the members of a family descended by the same number of degrees from a common ancestor, or the time span between a group of contemporaries and the birth of their children, usually thought to be 30 years. It is often assumed that the generations in a society, having shared similar experiences, also share similar views and feelings.

generational unit: developed by Mannheim to describe those fractions of a *generation* which share something substantial in common with each other, as against all members of the generation, who may share little except age. Generational units are likely to be identified through class, *gender* or *ethnicity*.

genetics: the study of biological inheritance, it is an important counter-foil to the sociological enterprise. In part genetics explores the extent to which individuals are the product of their parental DNA and therefore the extent to which we are determined as individuals. Sociologists, while accepting that we are to an extent determined are more interested in the way that *culture* pre-disposes individuals to particular courses of action. Both genetics and sociology accept that there is a limited area of free will operating in society, though they both may differ over the extent of this. The contradiction between genetics and sociology is sometimes expressed as the *nature versus nurture debate*.

genre: in the sociology of culture, a type of *text*, such as detective fiction or science fiction, which has associated informal rules and literary conventions. Sociologists have widened the definition to include all types of text not just written ones.

gentrification: the process whereby upper-middle and middle-class families buy up cheap, large (often Victorian) houses in the inner city and other working-class areas. This was largely a product of the housing boom of the 1980s, when house prices rose sharply. The effect of gentrification is to produce islands of *wealth* in areas of relative *poverty*.

geographical mobility: the movement of people around the country, usually in pursuit of jobs. In sociology, the importance of geographical mobility is linked to the degree of openness of a society. Societies with very limited geographical mobility tend to have closed *social stratification* systems, with little movement between *social classes*. Geographically mobile societies also tend to be socially mobile.

germ theory of disease: a view that disease occurs through the action of invisible micro-organisms. The work of Pasteur in France and Koch in Germany in the late nineteenth century led to an understanding of the nature of infection. The implication of viewing disease in this way is that the emphasis tends to be on drugs-related treatment, with a corresponding lack of emphasis on disease prevention, and the focus is on the site of the disease in the patient, rather than a wider view encompassing the patient's subjective feelings and whole environment. A criticism of the germ theory of disease is its failure to explain why although many people are exposed to infectious organisms, relatively few develop the disease. For example, most of the population of Britain in the last century was exposed to the tuberculosis bacillus, while only some people developed tuberculosis, suggesting that other factors were at work. (See *bio-mechanical model of health*.)

gerontocracy: a society in which the old have *power* and are the rulers. Such social arrangements are often associated with *traditional societies* and in particular with those societies where the social stratification system is one of *age-sets*.

gerontology: the study of the old and the ageing process, which has become a contemporary focus for much sociological research. Sociologists are interested in the way that different categories of old people have different experiences of ageing and the way that the old have different *status* in different societies.

Gesellschaft: meaning 'association', the concept was developed by Tönnies to describe those relationships most likely to be found in urban areas. These were impersonal and calculative, based on the inter-relationship between one segment of a person's being with that of another person. An example might be the fleeting contact between shopper and sales assistant during the purchase of goods. Such relationships are superficial and based on a lack of knowledge of the respondent's background and social standing. (See *Gemeinschaft*.)

Gestalt: the idea that the whole is greater than the sum of the parts. Sometimes referred to as the group mind, gestalt theory implies that individuals, when grouped together, create an entity which has an existence of its own. The criticism of this is that it is very difficult to show the existence of the gestalt without a leap of faith. (See *reification*.)

ghettos: in sociology, an American term used to describe those areas of cities which are characterised by very poor housing, few amenities and often a high concentration of African-Americans. The term was originally applied to areas of European cities in which the Jewish population was segregated from the rest of the population.

ghost dancers: members of a *millenarian movement* which existed among the Teton native American tribe towards the end of the 19th century. Members believed that performing a 'ghost dance' would reverse the social and economic upheavals which had afflicted the tribe since the coming of the white settlers. The movement died out after a massacre of ghost dancers by American troops.

Giddens: the foremost contemporary British sociologist, who has been responsible for the development of *structuration* theory as an original theoretical contribution. He began his career as a re-interpreter of the classical sociologists and then as a contributor to the debate concerning the importance of class in contemporary capitalism. He has most recently been concerned to develop an understanding of the relationship between the global and the local.

gift: focused on by Bell and Newby as an important aspect of the *hegemony* of men over women in marriage. The giving of gifts by husbands to wives is seen symbolically as a means of establishing the superiority of the male in marriage. It also has the effect of creating obligation and dependence from the woman to the man

girl-friendly science: attempts to devise ways of teaching and presenting science to girls to enable them to overcome their traditional reluctance to study areas such as physics and to improve their achievements in science. Various methods have been used, including girls-only teaching groups, lunchtime sessions to enable girls to acquire confidence in handling particular kinds of equipment in advance of the lessons in which they will be used, the use of textbooks which use examples likely to be meaningful and interesting to girls, and using female role-models to persuade girls to take up careers in science and engineering.

Glasgow University Media Group: an influential school of research into the media, members focus on the *agenda-setting* activities of the media, especially television, and argue that there is an implicit ideological *bias* towards the *status quo*, in which news coverage presents certain groups such as *trade unions* in stereotypical terms.

glasnost: or openness, this was an attempt by President Gorbachev to open up the political system of the Soviet Union to fresh, non-communist influences and which ultimately led to the collapse of the Soviet system.(See *perestroika*.)

glass ceiling: a reference to the difficulty experienced by women at work in achieving promotion to a higher level. It is suggested that, above a certain level, there exists an invisible barrier which acts to prevent women from easily achieving the same levels of authority as their male colleagues. (See *feminisation of work; glass walls*.)

glass walls: invisible barriers which have the effect of segregating men and women into different types of employment, i.e. vertical segregation. For example, women form the greater proportion of nurses, school cooks, secretaries, primary school teachers and bar staff, while men with the same respective educational qualifications needed for these jobs are more likely to be found in different types of employment. (See *feminisation of work; glass ceiling*.)

global markets: a term expressing the belief that the demand and supply of goods is now a worldwide undertaking in which the level of trade between countries has dramatically increased. The existence of a global market for goods and services is based on the information revolution which computer technology has delivered. The implications are enormous, as developments in industrial production in one part of the world can have effects in widely separated and completely different countries. The global market is so vast that it cannot be controlled by any individual nation, nor, some would argue, by any international agencies. The global market is serviced by vast *conglomerates* of *trans-national companies*. Some sociologists have argued that the idea of a global market is exaggerated and that there has been a small increase in world trade which does not justify the idea of a revolution in the way the world operates.

global village: the idea that *mass communications*, particularly film and television, have been able to transcend national boundaries to the extent that the world has become like one village. It is argued that particularly with the rise of *media conglomerates* and the development of cable and satellite television, people around the world are exposed to the same messages. Many are concerned at the potential for the misuse of such *power*.

globalisation: the process of the increasing *interdependence* of societies on a worldwide scale. This interdependence can take a variety of forms, but sociologists have focused mainly on the globalisation of the economy and the globalisation of *culture*.

- In terms of the economy, the activities of the *trans-national companies* are seen as central to the globalisation of production. Decisions about where to locate industry are taken with the whole world as a possibility, rather than within the confines of the *nation-state*. The financial markets of the world are now connected through fast *information technology*, so that *capital* and resources can be switched around the world constantly, without any limits of time or space. Much of this type of globalisation is invisible to the individual, but the consequences are very real. Individuals may lose or gain jobs as a consequence of decisions reached by others thousands of miles away, who are operating with a global perspective. The implication of this view is that the nation-state is no longer the most important unit in the world's economy.
- More visible is the globalisation of culture, as the media images, increasingly drawn from a world-wide arena are transmitted into people's homes, through satellite or cable. Cultural products are increasingly dominated by media companies whose activities are spread throughout the world.

Critics of the concept of globalisation have argued that the process has been much exaggerated. It assumes that some individuals at the head of trans-national companies have almost superhuman powers of control and *rationality* which, in reality, individuals do not have. Sociologists such as Paul Hirst argue that, rather than a withering away of the national state as globalisation theorists have argued, there has been an internationalisation of the economy and of culture, based on the increased relationships between national states, which continue to be the most important source of *identity* in the world.

glossing: used by ethnomethodologists to suggest that everyone, in conversation and action, ignores possible misunderstandings by filling in understanding, without exploring it deeply. The need to gloss arises from the *indexicality* of language, which can only be understood in its context. As teasing out the context would be enormously time-consuming, people gloss in order to create meanings in the situations in which they find themselves. (See *ethnomethodology*.)

GNVQs: General National Vocational Qualifications are vocationally-based courses offered since 1992 to post-16 students in schools and colleges. The courses are offered at Foundation, Intermediate and Advanced levels and aim to give students broad knowledge and understanding of a chosen vocational area, and also to develop competence in the three core skills of communication, application of number, and *information technology*. GNVQs have proved very popular with students, and have helped to increase the *participation rate* of post-16 year olds in sixth forms and colleges. GNVQ courses are also being piloted with 14–16 year old pupils. (See *New Vocationalism.*)

go-slow: a tactic in *industrial conflict,* in which workers carry out their tasks as slowly as possible in order to cut production. The trick is to go slow enough to disrupt without going so slowly that the supervisor can legitimately complain about the pace the worker is setting. Safety procedures are often called upon by workers to justify the speed they adopt.

goal: an aim or target, usually associated with an *organisation*. Organisations are set up to achieve particular goals and therefore these are important motivators for members of the organisation. (See *goal-model.*)

goal-attainment: one of Parsons's *functional prerequisites*, this relates to the achieving of the system's aims, and in practical terms refers to political institutions. Parliament would therefore be an institution which would contribute to goal-attainment. (See *adaptation; latency; integration.*)

goal-model: a traditional way of conceiving *organisations* as devices for achieving aims. The importance of the goals in the goal-model is that they provide a measure of the *effectiveness* of any organisation, that is, how far it achieves its goals.

gaol displacement: see *displacement of goals*

gods of the gaps: used to describe the ideas which exist beyond formal religions, but which fulfil the spiritual and mystical needs of people in a secular society. Belief in astrology is usually found to be the main god of the gap.

going native: a state sometimes experienced by sociologists carrying out *participant observation*, particularly covert, in which they so identify with the group under study that they lose their academic detachment and *objectivity*.

gold standard: a supposed standard of academic quality, usually applied, particularly by certain government ministers, to A levels. This idea of a known quality has been used to resist recommendations to replace the traditional 'three-A level' pattern with a broader range of subjects, including vocationally-based courses of the same standard. (See *Dearing Report.*)

golden age of religion: an era presumed to have existed at some time in the past when members of society were far more 'religious' than they are today. This era is used to represent a stage from which we have since declined. However, writers such as Hill call the whole concept into question, arguing that historical evidence shows that the clergy always found it difficult to persuade the mass of the population to attend church regularly and to follow the various religious observances on 'holy days'. In other words, it is argued by some that the golden age of religion is a myth.

golden age of senescence: a mythical time in the past, when all old people were cared for by their families and were not placed in homes. It is mythical because not everyone lived in extended families or had the resources to care for the old in the family. Yet it is a powerful idea that contemporary society has somehow lost its capacity to look after its old people in the caring environment of the family. On the one hand, old people in the past were not immune from abuse and distress within the family, and on the other, the neglect by the modern family of its elderly relatives is exaggerated.

golden age of the village community: an assumed time when most people lived in small villages as part of stable communities, in which everyone was happy because they knew their rightful place in society. Critics of the golden age suggest that it is part of a conservative myth, which has an ideological importance in focusing attention backwards to a time when people were supposed to be happier. A recent example of this was John Major harking back to cricket on the village green. Critics argue that there never was a golden age, and that village life had many unappealing aspects, to the extent that many people were happy enough to migrate to the towns and cities in search of a better life.

golden age of tranquillity: a presumed time in the past when the young were respectful to their elders and did not engage in *juvenile delinquency*. This was a mythical time, as in each *generation* the old see younger people as threatening the old order and a peaceful way of life. In each generation, there is created a *folk devil* (from skinhead to bicyclist) who represents the freedom and the threat of youth. The threat of the young is therefore not in reality new but appears new in every generation.

government: the political and administrative organs of the *State,* it is composed in Britain of the Cabinet, Ministers and those MPs of the majority party who support them, together with the Civil Service who act as administrators.

GP fundholders: doctors in medical practices which have successfully applied to control their budget to purchase healthcare and use staffing resources as they see fit. It is argued that by allowing doctors to make these decisions they can meet the needs of their patients in the most effective and efficient way, for example by sending a patient to the hospital with the shortest waiting list for that particular treatment. Critics of the scheme point out that patients may be sent to hospitals many miles from their home, and fear that there will be growing pressure for doctors to prescribe the cheapest, rather than the most suitable, treatment. Nevertheless, by April 1996 more than half the population of England is expected to be registered with a fundholding GP.

grammar schools: under the 1944 *Butler Education Act,* these were selective schools which were intended for the most able 20% of children. Entry was officially by success in the so-called 'eleven-plus' examination, but a number of sociological studies, including that by Douglas, showed that there were a variety of other factors at work. Relatively few grammar schools now remain in the *maintained sector,* but some schools which have been awarded grant-maintained status are considering applying to become selective grammar schools. (See *tri-partite system.*)

grand theory: see *high theory*

grant-maintained schools: schools which under the 1988 Education Act have been allowed, following a successful ballot of parents, to opt out of local authority control and receive funding directly from central government. Initially, there were consider-able financial advantages to schools in 'opting out', although additional funding is no longer quite as generous. Out of some 24,000 *maintained sector* schools in Britain, just over 1,000 in England, 16 in Wales and 1 in Scotland had become grant-maintained by the middle of 1995. The biggest number to opt out occurred in the academic year after the 1992 *general election*, when 555 schools became grant-maintained. Since then, the number applying has fallen considerably, with only 50 schools opting out in 1994. The Conservative government which introduced the scheme argued that schools should be more independent, should be freed from the *bureaucracy* of local authority administration, and should be directly accountable to governors and parents. Critics argue that the different funding levels are unfair, and also express concern over pro-posals to allow grant-maintained schools to introduce selection.

great debate: a reference to a 1978 speech at Ruskin College, Oxford, by the then Prime Minister, James Callaghan, in which he called for a 'great debate' on the role of education and training in the economy. Callaghan was speaking at a time of reces-sion and rising *unemployment*, and argued that sustained economic growth would only be achieved and maintained if the education system produced sufficient numbers of suitably skilled and motivated workers. This emphasis on the link between education and the economy, and the policies which have since stemmed from it, is known as the *new vocationalism*.

green belt: areas within or around cities which are designated as open spaces and protected from development. The policy of creating green belts was an attempt to keep aspects of the countryside in the cities. By protecting open spaces from devel-opment, the hope was that the quality of life of city-dwellers would be enhanced. Green belts are under constant pressure from developers, as they are often in prime sites within cities. Government policies towards green belts vary, though there is a general commitment to preserve them.

Green party: a political organisation which places the *environment* at the top of its priorities. Though relatively minor in Britain, the greens have managed to place issues such as pollution, animal rights and the environment onto the political agen-da of all parties. They are a significant part of the *third force*, especially in Germany.

green revolution: the scientific advances in agriculture made since the Second World War which have changed the way that crops are grown. Scientific progress in agriculture at this time had two main elements. Firstly, selective breeding produced higher yielding crops, which were more resistant to disease and therefore more like-ly to end up as food. Secondly, the use of more sophisticated fertilisers and more effective pesticides reduced damage to crops and encouraged strong growth. The immediate results of the Green Revolution have been to stimulate food production throughout the world. However, sociologists have also examined the social conse-quences of this revolution, looking for both positive and negative, intended and *unintended consequences*.

- The first and major social consequence is that starvation has been reduced throughout the world. This at first may seem strange, given the high pro-file of famine in the media's reporting of events in the *third world*. However, the Green Revolution has allowed the sustenance of larger populations than was previously possible.

- Some sociologists have suggested that the Green Revolution has led to enormous *social dislocation,* by encouraging peasant farmers in the third world to take on credit they could not afford to buy the expensive fertilisers on which higher yields depended. One bad year often meant that the indebted farmers were forced to sell their land and migrate to already overcrowded cities in search of scarce work. The result of this was increased poverty for the migrant workers.
- Environmental sociologists highlight the increased toxins which enter the food chain through the intensive use of fertilisers and pesticides. The long-term effects of toxin build-up are not yet known.

It is also suggested that we are entering a period of New Green Revolution, as bioengineering manipulates the genes of food crops to produce vegetables and fruit with all kinds of desirable (and perhaps some undesirable) characteristics.

gross national product: a measure of the value of the production of a country. While economists are interested in the calculation of GNP, sociologists are more interested in the way that it represents the prosperity of a country and whether such a country is getting richer or poorer. It also provides a measure, when expressed as an amount per head of population, of the relative wealth of different countries.

gross volatility: is the total amount of vote-switching between one election and the next, both voluntarily and involuntarily. Therefore some of the gross volatility will occur because of the death of registered electors before the Electoral register runs out. (See *net volatility.*)

group: a collection of individuals who interact with each other on the basis of formal or informal contexts. For example, a friendship group would have informal rules for meeting and for carrying out activities, while an organised group of enthusiasts would have formal ways of coming together and interacting with each other. The concept stands in contrast to a category of people, such as 'working class' who may have limited interaction.

group theory of democracy: the idea that a functioning *democracy* is one in which natural collectivities, such as the family or the workplace stand between the state and the individual. The interests of individuals are protected from the *power* of the *state* by these intervening groups, who form the natural focus of *identity* for the individual. Representations to the state are made through these groups rather than individuals' futile attempts to make the state notice.

guest workers: a term drawn from the German *Gastarbeiter,* which defines immigrant workers as temporary residents rather than granting them full rights of *citizenship.* Members of the Turkish immigrant community in Germany were the original recipients of the concept, but as they have settled and had children who know little else except Germany, they have begun to agitate for more permanent rights. The term also distinguishes those non-German workers in Germany who have European Union rights from those who do not.

H

Halévy thesis: the argument that the hold of Methodism over the *working class* in eighteenth- and nineteenth-century Britain prevented the revolutionary upheavals that the rest of Europe experienced. It was the opportunity for independent organisation which Methodism provided, which channelled the energies of the leaders of the working class into agitation for peaceful change rather than violent *revolution*.

Hall-Jones scale: a method of classifying occupations into seven main groups, with professionals and senior managers at the top and unskilled manual workers at the bottom. A modified version of this scale was used by Goldthorpe in the *Oxford Mobility Study*. (See *Registrar-General's scale*.)

halo effect: where the *respondent* gives the answer that he or she thinks that the researcher wants to hear rather than what she or he really thinks. The phrase is also used to refer to the tendency to reward those of whom we approve in an overly positive manner. For example, pupils perceived as 'bright' may be awarded higher marks than those perceived as 'less bright' for similar pieces of work. (See *Hawthorne effect; self-fulfilling prophecy*.)

handicap: as distinct from *disability*, this describes the difficulties a disabled person faces which arise from the social reaction to their disability.

hara-kiri: ritual disembowelling as a form of *suicide* among Japanese. It is often used to demonstrate that actions such as suicide can have different social meanings in different contexts. So, rather than being a shameful, sinful act as suicide is seen in Catholic countries, hara-kiri is an honourable way of wiping out social shame.

hard statistics: those statistics relatively immune to the processes of *subjectivity* and manipulation in their collection. Examples are demographic statistics, such as those relating to births, marriages, deaths and divorce, and those detailing the number of school-leavers with particular qualifications. (See *soft statistics*.)

Hawthorne effect: the unintended effects of the researcher's presence, or the knowledge that the subjects of sociological research are taking part in a research study, which may lead them to alter their behaviour or responses. While particularly applicable to most kinds of *experiment*, the Hawthorne effect may also be present in all methods of *primary data* collection. (See *Hawthorne experiments*.)

Hawthorne experiments: research carried out for the Western Electric Company of Chicago between 1927 and 1932, interpreted and publicised by Elton Mayo. The experiments, into factors influencing employee productivity, are important for two main reasons. One is that they were one of the earliest attempts to investigate employees using the *human relations*, rather than the *scientific management*, theory of work, and the other is their conclusion that both the presence of researchers, and the involvement of subjects in the research process, can influence the results. (See *Hawthorne effect*.)

Headmasters' Conference: a group of the headteachers of 240 of the most prestigious independent boys' and co-educational schools, including the major *public schools*. The sexism apparent in the title reflects the overwhelming tendency of these headteachers to be male, and also the fact that it is only recently that girls have been allowed into some of these schools, usually at sixth form level. (See *independent sector*.)

headlining: where the media give prominence to a particular news story, thus ensuring that it becomes a matter of public debate. (See *agenda-setting*.)

health: 'not merely the absence of disease and infirmity, but complete physical, mental and social well-being' (World Health Organisation). Sociologists recognise the problematic nature of the concepts of both health and *illness*, and emphasise that these are socially and culturally defined. In Britain there are still significant variations in health and healthcare between *social classes* and between males and females. (See *inverse care law; bio-mechanical model of health*.)

health gap: the difference in health between members of different *social classes*. Health statistics show this gap clearly, as there are measurable class differences in virtually every indicator of health, including *life expectancy*. Concern is being expressed at the way in which the health gap has widened through the 1980s and the current decade. (See *Black Report*.)

health targets: national and local targets aimed at improving the overall health of the population. The 'Health of the Nation' campaign is an example of a national health target, while a community action programme aimed at reducing smoking among schoolchildren would be a local health target.

hedonism: often put forward as a value held by the *working class*, it is the belief that a person should live for today, gaining present pleasure as against future gain. (See *deferred gratification*.)

hegemony: the 'spontaneous' consent given by the masses to the type of society imposed upon them by the dominant group in society. It is the agreement of the masses to a set of *values* which are not theirs, but arise from the material interests of the *ruling class*. Though this may appear to be similar to *value-consensus*, it is different, because hegemony is never absolute like the value-consensus; it is economically determined and not genuinely spontaneous, but the result of a pervasive effort by the ruling class and its functionaries.

heredity: the genetic transmission of physiological characteristics from one generation to another. The concept is often discussed in the context of the *nature versus nurture debate* regarding *intelligence*. It also appears in discussions regarding the reasons for antisocial behaviour or criminal activity. Originally associated with Lombroso, ideas that a propensity to criminal behaviour can be predicted by an examination of characteristics such as skull size have recently resurfaced, e.g. in Rushton's work in Canada. (See *eugenics*.)

hermeneutics: a way of understanding *action* by the analyst understanding the text (or action) within the larger framework of the world-view which produced it. The method was derived from attempts to understand the authentic biblical texts, which had become distorted in translation. The true meaning was obtained by looking at the context in which the text was written. Similarly with social actions, the sociologist needs to place the event in its overall context and interpret the meaning of the event from this. It has been criticised because it is difficult to authenticate any one reading of an event compared to another person's reading.

Herrschaft: literally 'power over man', it was a concept used by Weber to indicate domination, that is the probability that orders, once given, will actually be carried out. Weber was concerned to describe the different types of domination associated with pre-modern and modern societies because he believed that there had been a fundamental change in typical types of *action* between the two forms of society.

heterogeneity: differences in many or all of the characteristics of a group. For example, a group of people present at any one time in a department store or an underground train are likely to have so many differences from one another that they would form a heterogeneous population. Depending on the nature of their research, sociologists may or may not wish their subjects to form a heterogeneous group. (See *homogeneity*.)

heterosexuality: where an individual's sexual drive is oriented towards the opposite sex. The forms which heterosexuality may take are immensely varied, but the officially sanctioned arena for heterosexual activity is marriage. (See *homosexuality*.)

heuristic device: a model or an idea which aids our understanding. Though usually applied to concepts such as the *ideal type*, Giddens argues that sociology itself acts as an heuristic device, because it aids our understanding of the social world.

hidden curriculum: all those things taught and learned in education which do not form part of the overt programme of subjects and courses. In particular, the hidden curriculum refers to the *values, beliefs* and attitudes which pupils learn alongside the knowledge and skills of the formal, *overt curriculum*. The messages derived from the hidden curriculum have a powerful influence on pupils' behaviour and their progress, or lack of it, at school. (See *ethos; labelling*.)

hidden economy: a term used to describe those economic activities which never come to the attention of the taxation agencies of the *State*. (See *informal economy*.)

hierarchies of credibility: a concept developed by Becker which suggests that in stratified societies, those at the top of society are in a position to ensure that their version of reality is accepted by society as a whole. Those in subordinate positions are less likely to be believed when struggling to put across their point of view to others. This led Becker to argue for a *sociology of the underdog* to redress the balance for the disadvantaged.

hierarchies of oppression: the process whereby different groups experience different levels of *discrimination* depending on the mix of characteristics they might have. So, while white middle-class women face gender discrimination, their black counterparts experience further discrimination on account of their ethnicity. Black lesbian women experience yet another hierarchy of oppression on account of their sexuality.

hierarchy: a central concept in *stratification*, signifying the ordering of social positions in a structure of superiority and inferiority. Most hierarchies can be depicted as a triangle, with fewer superior positions at the top of the hierarchy than subordinate positions at the bottom (see diagram overleaf).

Most *organisations* are hierarchical, with management, or sometimes just an individual, at the top of the command triangle. There can be more or fewer middle management positions, depending on how hierarchical the organisation is.

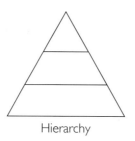

Hierarchy

hierarchy fetishism: a Marxist term, used to describe the splitting up of social groups into more and more levels of subordination and superordination, and the obsession with *status* and position which emerges from this. It is seen as a factor in the *false consciousness* of the *proletariat*, who, rather than uniting to combat the power of the *bourgeoisie* are distracted by petty squabbles over positions much lower down society's hierarchy. The subdivision of levels thus acts to create the illusion of movement upwards for individual members of the working class while leaving intact the monopoly of *power* enjoyed by the bourgeoisie.

hierarchy of needs: identified by Maslow as the rank order of the individual's needs, from the very basic to the more sophisticated. They are:

- physiological needs, such as food and shelter
- safety and security
- love, companionship and affection
- self-esteem and the esteem of others
- self-actualisation, (i.e. realising one's potential to the fullest)

The hierarchy was criticised as representing the hierarchy of needs for the academics who developed it rather than representing all people. In particular, the hierarchy does not represent the needs of women, for whom social needs may be more important than the self-esteem needs suggested by Maslow.

hierarchy of the sciences: associated with *Comte,* this was the belief that the natural and social sciences could be placed in a relationship of superiority and inferiority according to the complexity of their subject matter. Comte placed sociology at the top as the 'queen of the sciences'.

high culture: a term describing the arts usually patronised by the elite in society, such as opera, ballet, sculpture etc. It stands in contrast to *popular culture.* Sociologists use the concept when examining the media and in particular the policies adopted by broadcasters to reach different *audiences.*

high-tech: a term used to describe cutting-edge technologies, which are innovative and revolutionary. They usually involve a great deal of investment capital to be developed, are computer-based and ever more complex. The development of high-tech industries such as bio-engineering has led to a questioning of the moral implications of such power being used in society and on individuals. High-tech industries can be leisure-based and trivial or deal with fundamental issues concerned with life and death. (See *reproductive technologies.*)

high theory: attempts at explaining the large questions in sociology, such as 'why do societies persist?' Thus high theory is aimed beyond the merely empirical towards more philosophical areas. (See *theories of the middle-range.*)

Hinduism: a polytheistic *religion* which pre-dates *Christianity* by some three thousand years and forms the main religious belief system in India. One of the fundamental features of Hinduism is the belief in reincarnation, which views a person as having an unbroken succession of lives, not all human. The *caste* system provides the social embodiment of the main beliefs of Hinduism.

hinterland: the area in developing countries which provides the surplus wealth for the *metropolis* to exploit and appropriate. The hinterland is normally the least developed part of a *third world* country and receives the least benefits from the *development* process.

historical documents: a wide range of *documents* from the recent or distant past, the study of which provides information for sociologists. Historical documents such as parish registers have been used in the study of populations and population movements, wills have provided information on the extent of personal wealth of certain groups of people and medical records have been used to trace the nature, extent and treatment of disease at particular periods. There is a vast range of historical documents available to sociologists although, as with all forms of *secondary data*, they have to be used with care.

historical materialism: the basic concept of Marxism, this is where societies progress through history by the operation of economic forces. The motor of social change in historical materialism is the class conflict between the owners of the *means of production* in any society and the non-owning class. The fundamental conflict of interests between these two groups ensures that out of their struggle, new economic conditions emerge. This can be seen in the view of history put forward by Marx:

	Asiatic stage	Slave stage	Feudal stage	Capitalist stage
Owners	State	Slave-masters	Land-owners	Bourgeoisie
Non-owners	Villagers	Slaves	Landless	Proletariat
Mode of production	Self-sufficiency, reliant on irrigation	Slavery	Agriculture	Industry

holism: used in sociology when referring to the whole of a thing. Theories which stress the importance of *social structures* are said to be holistic in their approach, in that they focus on the whole of the social structure as the most important area of study for sociologists.

holistic leisure: a theory in the sociology of *leisure* which argues that work and leisure should be seen as subject to the same forces in modern societies. Holists argue that both work and leisure are subject to the same growing exploitation of human resources, so that the problems of work are the problems of leisure.(See *segmentalism; fusionism.*)

home background: one of the explanations put forward by some sociologists and politicians to explain the different levels of achievement in education by different groups of pupils, particularly differences based on *social class* and *ethnic group.* A number of sociological studies have revealed aspects of a child's home background which appear to influence the level of academic achievement. J.W.B. Douglas' *longitudinal study* showed the importance both of *parental aspirations* and the educational background of the parents to whether or not a child was offered a *grammar school* place, while Bernstein argued that progress was affected by the *language codes* learned in the home. Bourdieu developed the concept of *cultural capital* to explain the relative success of middle-class children. Critics have argued that too much emphasis on home background diverts attention away from other explanations, such as inequalities in *wealth* and *income* and the structure and organisation of schools. (See *compensatory education.*)

home ownership: a term which covers both those people who own their family residence outright and those who are paying off a mortgage in order to buy their property. In Britain home ownership has an ideological dimension in that it is seen as a desirable thing in itself. Conservatives in particular promote a high level of home ownership, to give individuals a stake in a society through being a member of a property-owning democracy.

homelessness: the lack of either a fixed address or adequate shelter. Homelessness is a growing problem in Britain, and accurate statistics are difficult to obtain. Under the Housing Act of 1985, local authorities are required to help those homeless people falling into the category of 'priority need'. These are families with young children, pregnant women, the elderly and those suffering from physical disability or mental handicap or illness. In 1993, nearly 340,000 households in Great Britain applied to be accepted as homeless; around half of these were deemed to be in 'priority need'.

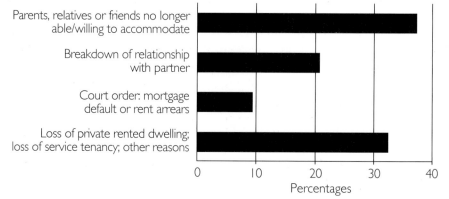

Source: Department of the Environment; Welsh Office; The Scottish Office; Department of the Environment, Northern Ireland

UK households found accommodation by local authorities by reason of homelessness, 1993

Many of these were placed in temporary accommodation, including bed and breakfast hostels. A growing number of people, many of them young teenagers, now live in 'cardboard cities' or sleep rough on the streets of Britain. Figures from the charity 'Shelter' indicate that the number of those sleeping rough rose from 683 in 1966 to 2,703 in 1990/91.

homeopathic medicine: treatment of disease and illness based on a belief that effective treatment should be based on the administering of minute doses of substances (usually plant extracts) which mimic or reproduce the same symptoms as the disease or illness. While frequently used in many countries of the world, until recently this type of treatment has been largely ignored or even ridiculed by the medical profession in western countries. However, growing concerns about the side effects of some drugs, or about the effects of their long-term use, have led to a renewed interest in homeopathic medicine, which is now available under the *National Health Service* for certain complaints. (See *allopathic medicine.*)

homeostasis: the tendency for interdependent elements to move towards a state of relatively stable equilibrium. While the concept originates from the sciences, it is used by some functionalist sociologists to refer to their belief that the 'natural' state of societies is one of harmony and *equilibrium,* and that conflict is therefore pathological, or abnormal. They argue that when this natural harmony is disturbed, mechanisms come into play to restore the equilibrium.

homeworking: the carrying out of occupational tasks by employees at home, not usually as additional to, but instead of, working in a workplace. Traditionally this kind of work has been low-status, low-paid work carried out by women, such as finishing garments, labelling envelopes or performing simple assembly tasks. However the advent of the computer has meant that increasing numbers of white-collar and professional workers are also spending some or all of their time working from home. While some people focus on the benefits of this (such as flexible working hours, the ability to combine paid work with *childcare,* reducing the number of commuters and the time spent commuting) others are concerned about the isolation which homeworking brings. (See *out-working.*)

homogeneity: the presence of a range of common characteristics within a group. A group of people of the same sex, age, social class, ethnic group, educational and occupational background and political views would form a homogeneous group. Depending on the nature of their research, sociologists may or may not wish their subjects to form a homogeneous group. (See *heterogeneity.*)

homosexuality: where an individual's sexual drive is oriented towards a person of the same sex. The term encompasses both lesbianism and gay male orientation. Sociologists such as Foucault have focused on the ways in which homosexuality has come to be seen as a distinctive attribute of certain individuals, associated with a particular life style and capable of 'treatment'. The creation of a medical *discourse* for homosexuality had the effect of marginalising and criminalising certain homosexual activities, which had previously not been sanctioned.

honest broker: a view of the *state* held by pluralists, which sees the role of the *government* as neutral between competing *interests groups.* Because the state is a referee between opposing ideas, it can make decisions in the best interests of all. The idea has been criticised for offering an idealistic view of the workings of the state, which not only favours certain groups systematically, but has its own interests to promote in its decision-making.

honour: a term denoting the standing of an individual in society and the subjective feelings of esteem which stem from that standing. Social honour has been an important dimension in most societies. It is bound up with ideas concerning proper behaviour and the regard that the group has for the individual. It has been of interest to sociologists of suicide as one cause of *altruistic suicide*, in which individuals are compelled by the duty of honour to kill themselves for the sake of their good name in the community.

House of Lords: the upper legislative chamber in the U.K., it is composed of the peers of the realm, both hereditary and life, and the Bishops of the Established Church. The power of the Lords has been curtailed during the course of this century, as the elected Commons has taken more powers to itself.

household: a person living alone or a group of people who have the same address and share one meal a day and/or the living accommodation. This differs from a *family*, which is defined as a married or cohabiting couple, with or without children, or a lone parent with children. Thus, most families live in households, but not all households are families. A group of students sharing a flat, for example, comprise a household but not a family. Since 1961 there has been a significant increase in the number of one-person households. People living alone formed 3.9% of all households in Britain in 1961, but 11.1% in 1992. (See *family structure*.)

household economy: a term used generally to describe the circulation of goods and services within the *household* and more specifically the jobs done by the members of the household which might otherwise have been done by workers in the *formal economy*. The term became prominent in the 1980s when DIY became an important element in the economy as a whole. This was demonstrated by the rise in the 'DIY Superstore'. Though home improvement has always gone on, it was the scale of DIY in the 1980s which began to displace workers in the formal economy, who would have otherwise been engaged in home improvements. The rise of DIY was related to the increased leisure time available in the post-war period.

housework: work undertaken to support the running of a *household*. It includes a wide range of domestic chores and is often extended to include childcare and out-of-home activities such as shopping. It tends to be seen as 'women's work', and of relatively low status. However, anthropological studies have shown that a wide variation exists regarding which sex should perform what type of domestic task, and in some cultures what we regard as housework tasks are shared or done interchangeably by men and women. In pre-industrial Britain domestic tasks were not the exclusive responsibility of women, nor was housework seen as a woman's main role. Records from medieval guilds show women engaged in a wide range of crafts and trades. In addition, housework enjoyed high status, as it was seen as a form of production rather than service. Both men and women were responsible for the production of many essential items required by the household, and as a result in many households women had to organise and oversee the work of what could be a considerable number of servants. An important factor was that the 'workplace' and the 'home' were not separate. This changed with the *industrial revolution*, at the end of which work was separate from family life, and this distinction eventually led to a separation of roles within the family which has persisted until today. Housework was not a topic which received much interest from sociologists (an aspect of *'malestream' sociology*) until Oakley's 1971 study of 40 working-class and middle-class housewives. This showed that the women spent an average of 77 hours a week on domestic tasks. They also reported feelings of isolation, boredom, loneliness and frustration, and described their work in terms similar to those used by male assembly-line workers, such as monotony, fragmentation, repetition and pressure from working at excessive speed. The women got little pleasure from their work, 70% being 'dissatisfied' with the role. Medical evidence shows that full-time housewives are more prone to physical and mental illness, including depression, than women in paid employment or men. Although it was widely believed that labour-saving domestic appliances would free women from housework, evidence shows that women still spend between 40 and 70 hours per week (depending on their circumstances) in domestic and childcare tasks. (See *dual role; housewife.*)

housing action areas: set up in the 1970s in *inner city* areas, these are areas in which government gave grants to householders to improve their houses. The policy came under attack during the 1970s because action areas were restricted to the inner city, whereas poor housing was not, leading to criticism that they missed their targets, which were the deprived. (See *Community Development Programmes.*)

housing classes: a term devised by Rex and Moore to describe those groups in the *housing market* who struggle with each other for access to different types of housing. They argued that housing classes were important in determining with whom a person associated, their interests and life styles. Housing classes were distinguished by their ability to satisfy the rules of the Council for waiting lists and the Building Societies for mortgages, which were biased towards the middle class and *respectable working class.* Rex and Moore identified seven housing classes.

1 outright owners of large houses in desirable areas
2 mortgage payers who own large houses in desirable areas
3 council tenants in houses built by the authority
4 council tenants in slums awaiting demolition
5 tenants of private house-owners
6 house-owners who take in lodgers to meet repayments
7 lodgers in rooms

Critics argue that Rex and Moore take the concept of 'desirable' for granted and that the seven classes are open to constant amendment and refinement. Moreover, it hides the most basic distinction in the housing market which is between public and private housing provision. This in itself has become blurred through the sale of council houses to tenants from the 1980s onwards. (See *council housing.*)

housing markets: a concept used to describe the supply and demand of different types of accommodation in society. The major focus of recent sociological interest in housing markets has been two-fold:

• The change in types of housing available, as publicly built council housing has declined, as well as the decline in the council house stock through the sale of previously rented council properties. There has also been a decline in privately rented accommodation. There has been a consequent rise in private owners.

- With the collapse of the housing boom of the 1980s and the consequent fall in house prices, sociologists have been interested in the appearance of negative equity, in which thousands of people own houses for which they paid much more than their current worth. This has consequences for the outlook that individuals have on their futures.

housing segregation: a concept developed by Rex and Moore to describe the separation of different ethnic minorities into particular residential areas and in particular, how black immigrants end up in the old, run-down housing of the *zone of transition*. While *racism* and low incomes play their part, the rules of the *housing market* also operated against ethnic minorities. For example, ethnic minorities found it more difficult to obtain mortgages, or gain priority on housing lists. The result of the operation of the housing market was that different ethnic groups were to be found in separate residential areas. Though the segregation was never total, it was sufficient to produce concentrations of ethnic minorities in the worst housing in the city. (See *substandard housing*.)

human capital theory: a theory of education which sees schooling for individuals as an investment in the future of society. The idea focuses on the way in which individuals can be trained through education, and society reaps the rewards later on in the development of technological applications. The idea was developed in the 1950s and has had a resurgence in the 1990s with the establishment of various training schemes.

human ecology theory: developed by Park and Burgess of the *Chicago School*, it likened the city to a social organism, with a life of its own. The city was made alive by the constant tension between the individual's need for freedom and society's need for social control. Heavily influenced by *evolutionary theory*, human ecology argued that there was a constant struggle for existence in the city, where the richest and strongest seized the most favourable urban locations and resisted attempts by other groups to displace them. Each urban area developed a distinctive life style which characterised the location. Critics of the theory argue that too much of this was taken for granted, such as what made a particular urban area attractive, what was the process whereby one social group was displaced by another, what was the nature of the power used to seize the best locations, etc.

human relations school: developed in reaction to *scientific management*, the human relations school emphasised the human dimension of work and tried to manage workers by recognising their need to be involved in their work, rather than just seeing workers as interested only in money. Originally, the Human Relations School was associated with Elton Mayo and the experiments carried out at the Hawthorne factory of Western Electric. The Human Relations School was often held as a contrast to the impersonality of scientific management and was presented as a less exploitative form of management, or 'management with a human face'. However, critics of Human Relations dismiss it as *cow sociology*, and argue that it represents just a different way of intensifying the *exploitation* of workers. Post-modernists have been interested in human relations as one of the ways in which post-modern workers become accepting of their own exploitation and actively involve themselves in self-surveillance, that is increasing their workrate as they accept responsibility for their own work.

hustlers: a term used by Pryce to describe black working-class youths who are unemployed. The implication of the term is that they have to make their living hustling on the street, as they are unable to obtain employment in the *formal economy*. (See *saints.*)

hydraulic society: ancient culture where power was related to the control over access to water. Hydraulic societies were identified in Egypt and in the Tigris-Euphrates basin, where survival depended on appropriate irrigation. Such societies tended to develop bureaucratic or theocratic control of the waterways.

hypergamy: marriage to a person of higher *social status* than oneself. In practice most marriages occur between people of broadly similar social status.

hyperreality: used by Baudrillard to suggest that our knowledge of the world is drawn from media images of reality rather than direct experience of it. The signs contained in media images constitute hyperreality and in the post-modern world are our main source of knowledge.

hypodermic syringe approach: an early approach to the study of the effects of the media on behaviour, it took the view that the media 'injected' its content into the audience's lives in a fairly direct way and subsequently influenced their behaviour. It has therefore been criticised for seeing individuals as passive in the process. (See *empty bucket theory.*)

hypothesis: one of the steps in the scientific method, it is the unverified assumptions which might possibly explain an observed phenomenon. In short, an hypothesis is an untested *theory*, or a possible explanation. The hypothesis is important to the scientific method because it provides direction for the research and shapes the experiments which the scientist designs. The hypothesis is also an exercise in creativity, because scientists must use their imaginations in devising possible explanations of events. (See *hypothetico-deductive method; laboratory experiment.*)

hypothetico-deductive method: the process involved in *positivism*, in which certain logical steps are taken in order to try to arrive at the truth. The method is usually conceptualised as consisting a series of stages :

1 observation: the researcher observes a phenomenon considered worthy of investigation
2 conjecture: the researcher thinks of a plausible explanation
3 hypothesis formation: the conjecture is put in the form of a predictive statement which can be empirically tested
4 testing: a rigorous empiral test is designed and carried out under controlled conditions, with all observations and measurements accurately recorded
5 data analysis: the resulting data are carefully analysed, using applied logical reasoning
6 final stage: in the light of the results, the researcher decides whether the hypothesis is confirmed, rejected or is in need of modification and further testing

IQ: a measure of a person's *intelligence* based on their performance in *IQ tests* and expressed as a number. The average (mean) is 100, and 95% of the population have an IQ which falls between 70 and 130.

I Q tests: cognitive tests which attempt to measure and define a person's *intelligence*. The first tests were devised by the French psychologist Binet at the start of the 20th century, when he was looking into the education of 'retarded' children. The process was taken a stage further by dividing a child's mental age (as measured by the tests) by her/his chronological age and multiplying by 100 to give the IQ. Considerable controversy surrounds the issue of IQ tests, with disagreement over what is actually being measured. Many argue that the tests are not neutral, and have an inbuilt cultural *bias* which favours white middle-class children, while others claim that a gender bias also exists. The psychologist Arthur Jensen has argued that the poorer performance of black Americans in IQ tests when compared with white Americans is evidence of the intellectual inferiority of black people, a view which has sparked considerable debate and controversy. Sociologists tend to focus on the tests as social constructs and look at how they have been used to categorise certain groups as intellectually inferior, rather than accepting the tests as objective measurements.

iatrogenesis: a concept meaning doctor-induced illness, it is used by sociologists to indicate that medical intervention can at times lead to negative outcomes.

icons: in sociology these are *signs*, usually pictures, whose meanings are transmitted through their similarity to the thing being represented, such as the Cross standing for Christianity. (See *index; signs proper.*)

ideal type: a typification of a phenomenon built up by extracting the essential characteristics of many empirical examples of it. The purpose of an ideal type is not to produce a perfect example, but to provide a measure against which real examples may be compared. For example, the most famous ideal type is Weber's *bureaucracy*, which is used to answer the question: 'How bureaucratic is this or that organisation?' Ideal types do not therefore exist in the real world, but are a sociological construction.

identity: the sense of *self* which develops as a child grows up and establishes him or herself as an independent individual. More recently, identity has come to be an important concept in sociology, under the influence of post-modern ideas. It has come to mean the sense of self associated with the identification the individual has with certain social formations. Post-modernists therefore see identity as a shifting situational aspect of the individual, in which an individual may have a certain identity as a woman and may identify with others because of a similar ethnic background, or whose identity is influenced by particular religious ideas. The importance of the concept of identity is that it allows a person some element of choice, freed from the determinism of, for example, much class-based analysis.

identity construction: the ways in which conceptions of the *self* are forged in relationships with others and with regard to existing notions of the self. For example, the construction of a sexual identity such as masculinity is carried out in terms of relationships with females and with current notions of what it is to be a man. Identity construction can lead to the reinforcement of traditional conceptions or to negotiated versions of them.

ideological form of incorporation: the way that oppositional *sub-cultures* are neutralised by capitalist society through the re-definition of deviant behaviour by the police or media. This is done either through *trivialisation* or *domestication*. (See *commodity form of incorporation*.)

Ideological State Apparatus (ISA): an Althusserian term used to describe those agencies of the *State* whose prime function is to secure the compliance of subordinates with the established capitalist order. Thus ideological *hegemony* is the result of pervasive effort by the State to establish legitimacy. The term has been criticised because it assumes something of a conspiracy amongst the functionaries of the ISA. The major ISA in modern societies is the education system.

ideology: though used in several different ways, it is a systematic set of beliefs, which serve the interest of some social group in society. Developed in particular by Marxist sociologists, ideologies are associated with *power* and the ability of those at the top of society to put forward their own ideas as right and natural for everyone in society. In some senses, ideology is also used to indicate the falseness of a set of ideas or at the least, a distortion of the truth. There is a distinction drawn here between 'ideology', which as the ideas of a particular social group, is necessarily partial, and 'truth', which is universally applicable. Perhaps the best way of describing ideology is as ideas that are put forward for a purpose – to fulfil the aims of a social group in society and which may or may not be true in some more fundamental sense.

illegitimacy: see *births outside marriage*.

illness: a physical or mental state which is seen as abnormal and undesirable and in need of 'treatment'. Sociologists emphasise the culturally-defined nature of the concept, and how illness is defined and treated differently in different societies and contexts. (See *aetiology; epidemiology; health; mental illness*.)

immigration: see *migration*

immigration controls: rules which are applied to define who (and often more importantly, who has not) the right of settlement in a country. Concern in some quarters about the number of immigrants to Britain, particularly those from the Indian sub-continent, Africa and the West Indies has led Britain in the last two decades to impose ever stricter controls on immigration. The issue is occasionally fuelled by stories in tabloid newspapers about the supposedly large number of 'illegal' immigrants in Britain. Controls are also imposed on those seeking not to migrate to Britain but to obtain political asylum. (See *migration*.)

immiseration: the process whereby the *proletariat* become poorer and more miserable, as their *exploitation* by the *bourgeoisie* is intensified. Marxists argued that this process is inevitable under a capitalist *mode of production* and would lead to widespread *poverty* and discontent. Critics point out that for many sections of society, including large parts of the *working class, capitalism* has produced a higher standard living than previously and therefore immiseration has not occurred. (See *polarisation*.)

imperialism: the process of empire-building associated particularly with the western powers in the nineteenth century.

impersonality: the requirement in an *organisation* that *clients* should be dealt with impartially, without fear or favour. Merton argued that the pressure to deal with clients impersonally could be harmful to the interests of clients seeking help from the *bureaucracy*, as they were reduced to a number or a cipher. (See *particularism; universalism.*)

impression management: according to Goffman, the manipulation of image by the social *actor* in order to convey particular messages to the *audience* of the action. The idea is that in interaction, individuals seek to convey favourable impressions to others, as part of a dramaturgical role. (See *dramaturgy.*)

imprisonment: the incarceration of those convicted of certain types of crime. Also in prison are those held 'on remand', i.e. accused of a serious crime and awaiting a trial. Different societies hold different views regarding the purpose of imprisonment, with the result that the proportion of the population in prison at any one time varies widely between societies. The UK has one of the highest rates of prison population in Europe (See *universities of crime.*)

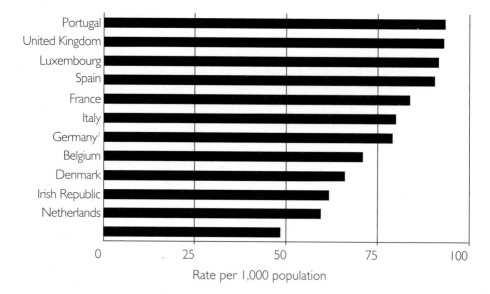

Notes: All data relate to period up to 1 September 1991. [1]As constituted since 3 October 1990. Source: Council of Europe; Home Office

Prison population – EC comparison, 1992

impulse control: a type of *socialisation*, in which the antisocial drives of children are limited and controlled, either through the application of restraint or through their sublimation into other legitimate activities. For example, violent tendencies may be channelled into soldiering. It is thus a control theory of socialisation. (See *role-training; enculturation.*)

incentive theory: a *work motivation theory* which argues that individuals will work harder when faced with a specific reward for doing so. It was the basis for piecework schemes in which individuals were paid more the more they produced in any specific time scale. *Taylorism* took up incentive theory and made it into a whole scheme of management.

inclusivist definitions of religion: those which define *religion* as any system of thought which attempts to make sense of the world and form a 'universe of meaning'. This kind of definition, used by Berger and Luckman, is much broader than that conventionally used to define 'religion', and could include, for example, ideologies such as *Marxism*. (See *exclusivist definitions of religion*.)

income: an inward flow of money over time. Many people's main income is wages from employment, but other sources of income include benefits, pensions, interest on savings and dividends from shares. Figures for the distribution of net income after housing costs, show that the share of income of the poorest fifth of individuals in the UK fell from 10% in 1979 to 6% in 1990–91, while that of the richest fifth of individuals rose from 35% to 43% over the same period. (See *wealth*.)

income support: a *means-tested benefit* payment for the unemployed, *lone parents*, the disabled and all those whose *income*, from whatever source, is defined as 'inadequate'. In 1993–4, there were 5,791,000 recipients. In 1995, claimants represented some 10% of the population, with nearly twice this number living in *households* dependent on income support, (for example the children of claimants). The unemployed make up almost half of claimants. (See *jobseeker's allowance*.)

incorporation of post-16 education: the process by which in 1993 colleges of further education were removed from local authority control and became independent institutions run by a board of governors and responsible for their own budget. College budgets are now set according to a formula decided by the Further Education Funding Council. College lecturers and managers were asked to accept new contracts with changed conditions of service and a new salary structure, which many thought led to a deterioration in the quality of their working life. One result of incorporation in many areas has been increased competition for students, both between colleges and between colleges and schools or Sixth Form colleges.

incorporation of the working class: the way in which the *working class* are wedded to *capitalism* and come to accept their position within it. The incorporation of the working class is the result of effort by the *State* to engage the working class in the material and ideological arrangements of capitalism. The *welfare state* is seen as one of the major ways in which incorporation is achieved, as it provides the working class with security and a stake in the system. Incorporation is not a permanent state and consent once given can also be withdrawn. The crucial factor in ensuring incorporation is the establishment of sufficient material welfare for the working class that they have too much to lose in changing the system.

independent sector: an educational term used to refer to fee-paying schools. (See *maintained sector*.)

independent variable: the variable chosen by a researcher to be controlled or manipulated during an *experiment* to observe its effects on other variables. In sociological research, where it is often difficult or impossible to control variables, the effects of an independent variable are often gauged by a retrospective examination of the available evidence. For example, a study of the effects of youth unemployment on the staying-on rate in schools and colleges would need to look at the possible correlation between the two. In this case, the level of youth unemployment would be the independent variable, and the participation rate of 16-year olds the *dependent variable.*

index: signs which carry their meaning from some causal relationship associated with them. For example, dark clouds can signify rain. (See *icons; signs proper.*)

index of deprivation: a list of aspects of material and social life the lack of which was used by Townsend as an indication of social deprivation. Townsend compiled the index for his 1979 research study 'Poverty in the United Kingdom'. Using the concept of *relative poverty,* he attempted to define a style of living which met with people's general approval. The index of deprivation covered material goods (e.g. lack of a refrigerator), household amenities (e.g. no flush toilet, bath or shower), social activities (e.g. no afternoon or evening out for entertainment in the previous two weeks) and nutrition (e.g. one or more days in the previous fortnight without a cooked meal). Using this index, Townsend showed that the lower the household *income,* the greater the extent of the deprivation. He found that for *households* with incomes at or below 150% of the current Supplementary Benefit levels, the rate of increase of deprivation accelerated. There were many criticisms of this way of measuring poverty. (See *consensual view of need.*)

indexicality: used by ethnomethodologists to indicate that all events, whether physical actions or the spoken word, are dependent on the context in which they occur for their meaning. Events can only be understood by reference to context, so the actual event is only a pointer to the meaning of the situation. In order to understand what is going on, actors need to grasp the context through *glossing,* or explore the indexicality of the event through further interaction. (See *ethnomethodology.*)

indicators of class: because *social class* is a very complex phenomenon, sociologists use various pointers to a person's position in the *hierarchy* of unequal rewards to establish his or her likely place. The concept of class combines a whole range of elements, both objective and subjective, so that it is difficult to pinpoint an individual's exact class position. However in research sociologists need to be able to use accessible clues to a person's class position. These indicators are not chosen arbitrarily, but are related to the distribution of rewards in society, which is an important element in the class structure. The most commonly used indicator of class is occupation. (See *Registrar general; Hall-Jones scale.*)

indirect taxation: taxes levied on the purchase of goods and services, (e.g. VAT). Unlike *direct taxation,* indirect taxation is regressive, that is, it takes a greater proportion of the income of poorer than of wealthier people. (See *progressive taxation.*)

individual action plans: plans drawn up by pupils, students and trainees which set desired targets and plan the sequence of actions which will allow those targets to be achieved. Such action plans are increasingly used, both in *GNVQ* courses and for career planning. The plans are meant to remain active documents until the target or targets are achieved, that is, users are expected to monitor, evaluate and, if necessary, modify the sequence of steps leading to the desired outcome.

individualised learning: a type of *pedagogy* where the tasks set in the classroom are geared towards the individual child's needs and abilities, rather than to a whole class.

individuality: the condition of the individual's uniqueness in the social world. Individuality constitutes one half of the central dichotomy of sociology, that is the relationship between the individual on one hand and *society* on the other. Sociologists are interested in the way that individuality is affected by *social forces,* and in many respects, *socially constructed.*

individuation: the process whereby religious institutions become less important in the individual's search for meaning. As industrial societies have developed so has the proliferation of religious forms, as groups and individuals reject traditional forms of religious experience and search out their own salvation.

inducement-contribution equilibrium: developed by Simon to describe the calculation that an individual makes before deciding to join an organisation or not. The inducement aspect is the rewards that the individual is offered, which are then balanced against the contribution, or effort the individual will have to give in return. Where the rewards (not just money) are balanced by the contribution, the individual is likely to participate in the organisation effectively

industrial conflict: a term which encompasses a number of strategies whereby workers may seek to pursue their own interests against management. This might include *work-to-rules, go-slows, strikes, sabotage* and *absenteeism.*

industrial democracy: a variety of situations where workers have some *power* in the workplace and therefore some control over working practices. There are a number of different ways in which industrial democracy can be accomplished, from direct control, trade unionists in the boardroom, or shareholding by the workers. The European Community's Social Chapter guarantees to workers in signatory countries the right to be consulted through works councils.

industrial relations: the network of rules which govern how managers and workers respond to each other in situations of *conflict.* Industrial relations have been a main focus for sociologists of industry, who have often taken a remedial approach, that is, studying industrial relations in order to resolve industrial conflict problems.

industrial relations systems theory: an approach to *industrial conflict* which focuses on the industrial firm as a unified system binding managers and workers. It emphasises the fundamental community of interest between management and workers and therefore any conflict should be resolved through negotiation. Industrial conflict is seen as *pathological* to the *equilibrium* of the system. Sociologists who concentrate on industrial relations systems have been criticised for taking a conservative approach, assuming that all problems can be resolved through appropriate rule-making. They are also criticised for assuming that managers and workers have identical interests in the success of the firm. Workers have their own separate interests from management and cannot be assumed to share common values with them.

industrial revolution: that period of time in the eighteenth and nineteenth centuries in Western Europe when societies were transformed from being agricultural to ones in which production was based on the factory system. (See *industrialisation.*)

industrial sabotage: usually where workers cause a breakdown in production, by damaging machinery. This is exemplified by the classic 'spanner in the works'. Industrial sabotage is sometimes caused by the pace of work being so high that workers take matters into their own hands, to force a rest period. At other times it may be the result of individual disgruntlement with conditions in the factory or a sense of grievance against the firm. As lost production means less profits industrial sabotage is taken very seriously by management and usually leads to dismissal if the perpetrator is caught.

industrial societies: where the goods and services needed for social living are produced primarily in factories, and where the majority of the population is engaged in servicing the needs of industry and manufacturing. The contrast here is with those societies which are mainly agricultural. The *wealth* of an industrial society is therefore found in the *secondary* and *tertiary sectors* rather than the *primary sector.*

industrial unions: trade union organisations of manual workers in a single industry regardless of skill or grade differences. An example might be the National Union of Mineworkers. These have been in decline over the 1980s as their membership has fallen, or the need for industrial strength has persuaded the members to amalgamate with other unions. (See *craft unions; general unions.*)

industrialisation: the process whereby a society moves from a predominantly agricultural base to one where the economy is dominated by manufacturing. Industrialisation is associated with dislocation as a society adapts to the massive social changes which industrialisation creates. *Urbanisation* and the growth in standards of living are just two of the consequences of industrialisation, which transform the way that people live their lives. Features of early industrialisation were the development of transport systems in canals, road and rail, the emergence of a banking system and the concentration of production in factories, working with industrial technologies. In one sense, industrialisation created sociology, as the *classical sociologists* were primarily motivated by seeking to understand the huge transformation which had occurred as western Europe industrialised. (See *industrial revolution.*)

inequality: see *social inequality*

infant mortality rate: the number of deaths in a population of infants under one year of age per thousand births. The Infant Mortality Rate (IMR) of a society is often

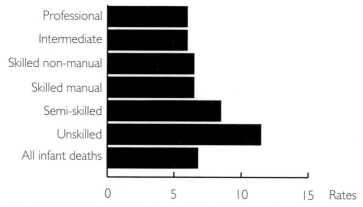

Notes: Data for births within marriage, deaths of infants under one year of age per thousand live births; Source: *Social Trends 1993*

Infant mortality rates by social class of father, 1990

taken as an indicator of general prosperity, and there are wide variations between different countries and different regions in the same country. The fall in the U.K. IMR before the second World War was due almost entirely to rising living standards rather than improvements in medical techniques. The IMR for England and Wales in 1992 was 6.5, but this figure conceals social class differences, with higher rates for babies from the semi-skilled and unskilled working classes. (See *death rate; neo-natal mortality rate; perinatal mortality rate.*)

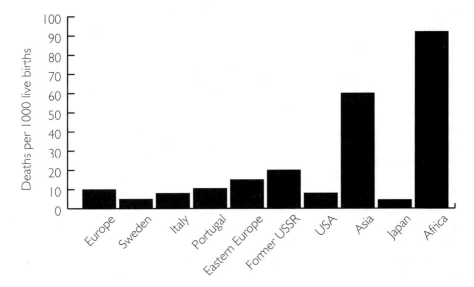

Infant mortality rates in selected countries/areas 1990–1995

infantilisation: the process whereby *childhood* gets longer and longer, as adolescents are forced to remain at home, usually for economic reasons. Thus, the development of training schemes for young people has prolonged the time of dependence on parents. (See *youth training schemes.*)

inflation: the increase in prices over the course of the year. As a central target of economic policy, the control of inflation also has social effects in which sociologists are interested. In particular the relationship of inflation to the wage demands of the trade unions has been a source of sociological investigation.

informal carers: those who take responsibility for the care of others (often relatives) who are unable through disability to care for themselves. The term 'informal' is used to show that these carers, though providing a crucially important service, are operating outside the formal system of care. Most informal carers are women, but a significant number of children provide vital care for disabled parents. (See *care in the community.*)

informal economy: the term is used in contrast to the *formal economy* to indicate economic activity, more or less legal, which is carried out using cash-based transactions. Many self-employed workers and the unemployed may engage in the informal economy at times. While the cash earned in the informal economy is legally obtained, it is easier to avoid taxation, such as VAT, in a situation where records of transactions may not be rigorously kept.

informal interviews: see *unstructured interviews*

informal organisations: used to describe the actual workings of an organisation, as opposed to the way the *formal organisation* describes what is supposed to go on. Informal organisations grow up within the constraints of the formal *structure* of the *organisation*, but they operate partially independent of it. Whereas formal organisations take no account of the human aspects of members, informal organisations show how members of an organisation work together outside of the formal rules to pursue their own interests, to protect each other from management, or to gain some control over the activities they have to carry out within the formal organisation. Thus, informal organisations represent the human dimension of participants in organisations and are a more valid description of what actually happens than the formal organisation.

information overload: the situation in the modern world where individuals are bombarded with opinions and facts about the world, which are often contradictory. It arises as a consequence of the *globalisation* of the media, which means that we can be subjected to enormous amounts of news and views at a fast rate. The pace of this information revolution is such that we cannot hope to deal with the amount of information we receive in any rational way. (See *babble of experts.*)

information technology (IT): the use of computers to store, manipulate and transfer knowledge. In post-modern societies, the employment of information technology is a central part of the economy and constitutes an information revolution in which the manipulation of information creates *wealth* in itself. (See *information over-load.*)

inheritance: the process whereby *wealth* is transferred from one *generation* to the next, upon the death of the older members. Systems of inheritance vary and are sociologically important for the distribution of wealth in society.

initiation: a *ritual* which allows and defines the passage of a person or group into membership of a defined group. Some societies mark the passage from one age group to another by initiation rituals, such as from youth to adulthood, while other initiation ceremonies are associated with particular occupations (e.g. military 'passing out' parades), religious groups (e.g. becoming a nun or a priest) or special societies (e.g. fraternities, the Freemasons).

inner city: as the name suggests, the inner city is usually to be found near the centre of large towns, but is also associated with poor housing, deprivation, high *unemployment* and in some cities a high concentration of ethnic minorities. In London the inner city can be found in several parts of the capital, not just the centre. Therefore, the inner city is a geographical, social and economic concept. The inner city is often the target of urban programmes, aimed at solving the associated long-term problems. Inner cities are thus often a *site of struggle* between national government, the local council and the inner city community.

innovation: according to Merton, this form of *deviance* occurs when individuals continue to accept the cultural *goals* of society but are denied the legitimated ways in which to achieve them. Innovation often takes the form of property crime, as individuals seek to achieve material wealth through illegitimate activity. However, innovation may also take the form of cheating in examinations for example. (See *retreatism; rebellion; ritualistic deviance.*)

insight: the sociological ability to see into the workings of social life in a creative and revelatory way. The *sociological imagination* relies on insight for its most penetrating observations.

institution: used in a variety of ways in sociology, it refers to established patterns of behaviour, which make up a rule-constrained order within which individuals can act.

institutional barriers: these are obstacles to involvement in, for example, political activity, which are a consequence of the operation of *organisations*. For example, selection committees of political parties often form an institutional barrier to women who are seen by the members as being less electable than men. Women are therefore less likely to be selected than men. (See *electability*.)

institutional power: the ability to get things done which emerges from holding a particular position in an *organisation*. It is usually associated with the top decision-makers in large organisations, whose occupation of key positions legitimises their ability to get their own way against opposition. The important feature about institutional power is that it is only given to an individual for as long as she or he occupies that position. It is therefore not personal but a feature of the organisational role itself. (See *political power; economic power.*)

institutional shareholding: where a company rather than an individual holds shares in another company's stock. The main institutional shareholders are the pension funds, whose managers tend to be conservative and short-termist in their approach to company policies. Sociological interest has focused on three aspects of institutional shareholding:

- the way that links between companies are developed as the same people appear on the Board of Directors of several firms, because the institutional shareholder has nominated them
- the way that institutional shareholding makes the control of large companies invisible
- the way that the institutions represented in Annual General Meetings can act as a block to what individual, small shareholders may desire

institutionalisation of conflict: refers to the process whereby *industrial conflict* between management and workers becomes governed by rules and therefore managed. Institutionalisation requires the organisation of opposing sides into *trade unions* and employers' federations and the establishment of negotiating procedures between them. Further institutionalisation takes place if procedures for *arbitration* are also established.

institutionalised means: used by Merton to describe the legitimate ways in which individuals may seek to fulfil their *goals* in society. For example, if an individual has a goal of a comfortable standard of living, then a job would be an institutionalised means, while stealing would not. (See *culture structure.*)

instrumental collectivism: put forward by Goldthorpe and Lockwood as the dominant consciousness of the *affluent worker*, it is an attitude towards work in which only the wages count, and any *trade union* involvement is on the basis of improving wages. It stands in contrast to more *class conscious* modes of thought, which are associated with the *traditional working class*. (See *trade union consciousness.*)

instrumental voting: individuals voting for the party which they calculate will financially benefit them the most, rather than considering any other political or ideological reasons for supporting a particular party. (See *chequebook voting.*)

instrumentalists: working-class voters who vote Labour because they believe that they will be financially better off as a result. They are achievement-oriented, but unlike *secularists*, they calculate that the Labour Party will give them a better deal financially. The difference between the instrumentalists and secularists is that the former are integrated into strong working-class communities who have an alternative value-system, strong enough to resist the dominant values of the *middle class*. (See *deferentials; pragmatists.*)

integration: one of Parsons' *functional prerequisites*, it relates to the ways in which the system needs to bind its members together as a unified whole. The *Church* is a good example of an integrating institution. (See *adaptation; goal-attainment; latency.*)

integrative race relations: an approach to immigrant communities which aims to involve and encourage 'immigrant' children through the inclusion of elements of their *culture* in the *curriculum*. Summarised as 'saris, samosas and steel drums', it was criticised for being tokenist and being included on a piece-meal basis. (See *assimilation; cultural pluralism.*)

intelligence: a problematic concept usually associated with the ability to acquire and retain knowledge, to learn from experience and to adapt behaviour to respond to changing circumstances. There is considerable controversy over whether human intelligence is hereditary and fixed at birth, or is much more flexible and capable of being developed with appropriate intellectual challenges and stimulation. This is often referred to as the '*nature versus nurture debate*', and the evidence is still inconclusive.

intelligence quotient : see *I Q*

intelligentsia: a term encompassing the *elites* of the arts, broadcasting, the universities etc., which made up the old liberal professions. The intelligentsia are seen by *fragmentation theory* to be an important component of the *modern upper class*. They are distinguished from other fragments of the modern upper class by their relative lack of remuneration and the distinctive *style of life* they pursue. They also tend to be more radical in their approach to politics than the other segments.

interdependence: where two individuals or social formations rely on each other for their basic *needs*. Interdependence is a feature of all societies, because even where there is only a basic *division of labour*, any one participant needs others to guarantee the fundamental means of life. For sociologists, the consequences of this interdependence create much of their field of study, as they examine the ways in which societies resolve the contradictions of personal desires and the desires of others locked into *reciprocity*.

interdependency: used by sociologists to describe the reliance of one social formation on another. It is particularly associated with *functionalism*, where it is seen as a central feature of social structures. Thus, for example, the social structures of the family and education would be seen as inter-dependent, with schools relying on parental support for children's learning and families needing schools to educate the children in all the ways that families could not possibly do.

inter-generational mobility: where movement in the *class structure* is measured by comparing the position of fathers (and occasionally mothers) against sons (and sometimes daughters). The opportunities for movement given to each *generation* are different and therefore the degree of mobility is likely to change. However it is difficult to measure this form of mobility accurately because the sons or daughters may not have reached the climax of their careers at the time of the study. (See *intra-generational mobility*.)

interlock: the degree of connectedness between companies, through the same Directors appearing on the Boards of different firms. Sociologists are interested in the degree of interlock in Britain, because it is used as an indicator of the existence of a *ruling class*. The idea is that the greater the interlock the more likely the members of Company Boards will act together to pursue their own interest. The problem with this approach is that it is difficult to show that, just because some people know each other and appear in the same arena, that they then act together in this particular way. Interlock can be illustrated in the following way:

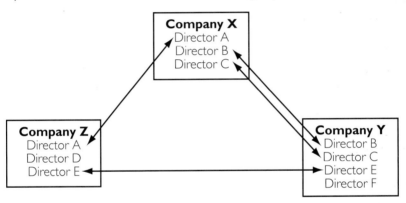

An illustration of the degree of connectedness between companies' Directors

inter-subjectivity: used by Schutz to describe how we have conceptions of the world and therefore how we understand each other. It is a central concept of the sociology of the everyday world and suggests that we each have a unique stock of knowledge, some of which overlaps with those with whom we interact. This overlap constitutes our inter-subjectivity. (See *everyday knowledge*.)

interactionism: a term covering a wide range of different perspectives within sociology, which share the feature that they begin their analysis of society from the level of the individual and work up to *society*. The focus of interactionist analysis is therefore the day-to-day activities of millions of individuals, who, through the way that they act together, make up what we call society. Interactionists agree that there is no such thing as 'society', apart from the individuals who constitute it and therefore their research is based on the small-scale interactions of everyday life.

interest groups: see *pressure groups*

intermediate class: used by sociologists of *stratification* to describe the mass of occupations between the *modern upper class* and the *working class*. The intermediate class is very amorphous, being a staging-post for those on their way up the stratification system and those on the way down. It also contains many individuals who will remain in the intermediate class for most of their careers. A fragmented location, encompassing such diverse occupations as clerks and skilled artisans, its members exhibit little solidarity or ability to combine to pursue their own interests. (See *new middle class.*)

intermediate groups: see *group theory of democracy*

intermediate technology: technological processes based not on the capital-intensive technology of the developed nations, but on processes which, though efficient, still make use of human labour. Intermediate technology is thought particularly appropriate for use in developing countries, which need the application of technology to make production more efficient, but which have limited *capital* and a large labour force to employ. Many of the systems which have been developed ensure that they are sufficiently simple to be repaired quickly and easily, using readily available materials. As most of the applications of intermediate technology cause far less damage to the environment than much advanced technology it is increasingly suggested that intermediate technology is just as relevant in the *first world* as the *third world*.

internal labour market: those employed on permanent lifelong career terms, with high pay, good working conditions and chances for promotion. It is white males who have traditionally dominated the internal labour market. (See *dual labour market; external labour market.*)

internalisation: the process whereby *values* and ideas are taken in by individuals as their own, so that they accept them as natural and normal. The *socialisation* process is said to result in the internalisation of values. However, some sociologists criticise the idea, suggesting that it is not an automatic process such as internalisation implies.

international division of labour: see *New International Division of Labour*

interpretative sociology: see *interactionism*

interviewer bias: unrepresentative, inaccurate or biased information given by a *respondent* to an interviewer. Such *bias* may be conscious, but is usually unconscious, and may arise from reactions to different features of the interviewer – appearance, manner, sex, age, perceived class, accent, tone of voice, gestures, etc. For these reasons, many sociologists using *structured interviews* employ trained interviewers to lessen the amount of bias. The bias can also derive from the actions of the interviewer him or herself rather than the respondent. Interviewers may misunderstand or fail to follow instructions, use probes and prompts in an inconsistent manner and make selective recording of responses. Attempts are sometimes made to distinguish between random errors and systematic errors in interviewing, but these distinctions are very difficult to make.

interview: a series of oral questions put by an interviewer (the questioner) to the *respondent.* Interviews are widely used in social research and are of two main types, *structured* and *unstructured interviews,* sometimes known as formal and informal interviews, or standardised and depth interviews. Questions used in an interview may be *closed* or *open-ended*, and interviews can produce *qualitative* or *quantitative* data.

intra-generational mobility: where movement in the class structure is measured by comparing the first job of an individual with the current job. The advantage of this measurement is that it charts real individual movement. The problem with this approach is that, of necessity, it omits young people from the process.

intrinsic satisfaction: the pleasure obtained from work which comes from doing the work itself. It is a central concept in *self-actualisation theories*, which argue that individuals would work harder if the job itself were interesting and not reduced to boring, specialised routine. (See *job-enrichment*.)

intuition: one basis of truth, the flash of insight which illuminates an issue or problem. Intuition is not a firm basis for truth, but it is a very powerful one. It is a useful technique in history, where the ability to visualise the *zeitgeist* of another age is crucial.

inverse care law: a relationship suggested by J. Tudor Hart in which the need for good medical care varies inversely with its availability. In other words those groups at or towards the bottom of the *class structure*, with generally poorer health than those in higher social groups, have less access, or less easy access, to appropriate medical resources. The concept may also be applied to make comparisons between people in the developed and the developing world.

inverted-U curve: devised by Blauner to explain the relationship between types of technology and levels of *alienation*. The argument was that, as technology developed away from its craft origins towards *assembly-line* production, alienation increased. However, as continuous process and automated technologies were developed, the level of alienation fell off. It is often illustrated in the following way:

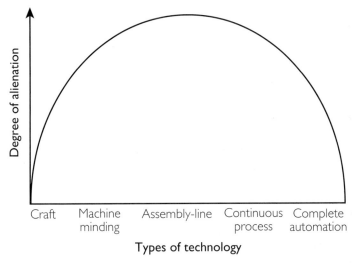

Inverted U-curve

invisible religion: a view particularly associated with Luckmann that certain features in contemporary society, while not obviously 'religious', nevertheless contain elements of *religion* in that they give everyday life meaning and significance. These features, or 'themes', are mainly concerned with individualism. Luckmann argues that the pursuit of individuality through self-expression and self-realisation can be seen in *social mobility*, achievement motivation, sexuality and the privatised family. Together, these form part of a 'sacred cosmos' through which the individual constructs a sense of 'self'. Luckmann suggests that a new form of religion, based on consumerism, is emerging, so that what appears to some to be religious decline is in fact a shift from one form of religion to another, reflecting a different type of society.

invisibility of women: referring to the ways in which women's lives and female concerns have usually been neglected in traditional academic research, so that for example our notions of women's history are thin and *androcentric*. Sociology has to the same extent as other subjects treated women as invisible and has until recently, been concerned mainly with men and male experiences. The growth of feminist sociology has to some extent redressed this imbalance. (See *malestream sociology*.)

involuntary minorities: developed by Gibson and Ogbu to describe those offspring of immigrants who are born in the host country and have already experienced a history of discrimination and exploitation there. Their *marginalisation* in the host country produces a strong reaction and rejection of the educational system which discriminates against them (See *voluntary minorities*.)

iron cage: a term used by Weber to describe the condition of modern societies, in which *bureaucracies* control the actions of individuals, so that freedom is curtailed.

iron law of oligarchy: a principle developed by Michels, which stated that all *organisations* eventually end up being ruled by a few individuals. His argument was that however democratic the intention of the founders of organisations, as these grow larger there is an inevitable tendency for *power* to be concentrated in the hands of fewer and fewer people. By virtue of their smaller numbers, those at the top of organisations are able to monopolise information and therefore power in their own hands. This pessimistic view of the possibility of *democracy* has been attacked from various positions:

- Some sociologists argue that Michels underestimates the democratic forces in organisations, and that for every concentration of power there are others struggling to bring power back to the ordinary members of an organisation.
- Others argue that there are empirical examples of long-standing democratic organisations which have defied Michels' 'iron law'.
- Still others argue that oligarchic organisations are unstable, as *autocracy* leads to resistance by those subject to arbitrary power.

Islam: a monotheistic religion dating from the seventh century A.D. based on the teachings of the prophet Mohammed. Moses and Jesus are recognised by Muslims as prophets, but Mohammed is seen as God's supreme prophet. Islam is one of the great world religions, with at least one billion followers worldwide. The followers of Islam can be divided into those who wish to see it co-existing in harmony with Western social and political values and those who believe that there is a need for Muslims to return to what they see as the basic teachings of the 7th century. These latter are often referred to as 'Islamic fundamentalists'. One of the areas of disagreement between the two groups concerns the role and status of women, as the fundamentalists have views concerning the status and clothing of women which are at variance with modern western ideas.

isolation: a condition of alienation identified by Blauner to indicate the worker's lack of membership of any industrial community. This results in the worker having no commitment to work and being subject to administration by impersonal management. (See *self-estrangement; powerlessness; meaninglessness*.)

J

job-enlargement: a reversal of *specialisation*, in which workers are given more tasks to do, so that they have varied work experiences rather than boring repetitive routines. Job-enlargement is claimed to interest workers much more in their work and thus increase their productivity.

job enrichment: see *work enrichment programmes*

jobseeker's allowance: a social benefit payment for the unemployed which will merge unemployment benefit and *income support* from April 1996. Unemployed claimants will be eligible for benefit for only six months instead of twelve and will have to prove that they are both serious in their intention to work and are actively seeking employment. If people are still without work at the end of six months they will receive *means-tested* payments in line with the rates for income support. Partners' earnings will also be taken into account. Supporters of the scheme claim that it is more efficient to administer, as Job Centres will make all payments, cutting the *bureaucracy*, and that its emphasis on the need to show the active search for work will weed out the work-shy and 'welfare scroungers'. Critics argue that the main reason for its introduction is just to save money (an estimated £200 million per year) and that it will further stigmatise the unemployed. Research shows that the newly unemployed in particular are very keen to find work.

joint conjugal roles: role relationships between spouses in which there is relatively little *domestic division of labour* by sex, and in which household tasks, *childcare* and *leisure* activities are likely to be shared. (See *conjugal roles; new man; segregated conjugal roles.*)

joking relationship: a relationship between two people or two groups in which one is permitted, or even obliged, to tease or make fun of the other, who must not take offence. Joking relationships are often found in situations containing the possibility of *conflict*, but where both sides are anxious that conflict should not occur. Under such conditions, the joking relationship thus becomes a ritualised form of the expression of antagonism under controlled conditions.

Judaism: a monotheistic *religion* of the Jewish people. It is the root religion of both Christianity and Islam.

just-in-time system: a type of production associated with *post-Fordism*, it uses computer control of stock to avoid the need for large-scale stockpiling of parts in warehouses, but instead delivers parts to the appropriate place in the production process just as they are needed. It is an example of the way that the control afforded by computer technology can assist industries to reduce their costs considerably.

justice: a term synonymous with fairness. Sociologists are interested in the way that the concept is translated into a system which dispenses judgement, punishes wrong-doers and protects those in need. The term is a contested one, in that what might seem to be an accepted definition of justice is open to challenge from different parts of the social structure. Because justice often concerns the resolution of *conflict*, it is argued that it is a basic requirement of a civilised society.

juvenile crime: argued to be a distinctive feature of urban living, this is law-breaking by the young. The existence of juvenile crime is supposed to develop with urbanisation, where the lack of *community* loosens the social controls that society has over the young, with the result that they exploit the increased opportunities for law-breaking which urban areas present. (See *juvenile delinquency.*)

juvenile delinquency: a wider term than *juvenile crime*, this is the disorder and disruption caused by the young in society and which is the focus for much of the policing activity of the *State*. While the term includes much serious activity, such as urban rioting and burglary, it encompasses less serious crimes such as graffiti, drunkenness, public disorder, etc. It also includes non-criminal activity such as being cheeky, truanting and so on. Young people have always been the focus of *social control* activity, as they are responsible for much of the high spirits of society as well as much of the crime. However, there is usually a sense amongst non-young society that things are getting worse than when they were themselves young. (See *golden age of tranquillity.*)

K

karma: the effects of all the actions of a person's current and previous existences, which will influence all future existence. Karma is allied to the Hindu belief in reincarnation. The term is also used more generally to mean 'fate'. (See *dharma.*)

kinship networks: people related by blood or marriage who provide a support system for members of the group. The extent to which these networks are formalised, acknowledged and used varies from society to society and over time. In Britain, particularly before the need for formal qualifications to obtain work and the introduction of the *welfare state*, kinship networks were very important, especially to the *working class*. Even today, when it is argued that the importance of networks has declined, many people find them an invaluable source of support. Despite the importance of formal qualifications, some members of the upper social classes still rely on these networks for career opportunities and advancement.

knowledge: the body of beliefs which is thought to be true. In sociology, knowledge is a multi-faceted concept, encompassing a number of issues. In epistemology, sociologists examine the grounds for believing that specific items of knowledge are true or false. Sociological interest in knowledge has also been focused on the relationship between the *social structure* and the form of knowledge in a society. For example, sociologists have examined the ability of those in power to define what passes for knowledge in society. In the sociology of education, sociologists are interested in what is passed on as knowledge in schools and colleges. In the sociology of religion, sociologists have focused on the nature of religious belief and its status as knowledge or otherwise. (See *knowledge-as-fact; knowledge-as-practice.*)

knowledgeability: the idea that human agents can draw upon different types of knowledge in carrying out their actions. (See *discursive consciousness; practical consciousness; unconscious motivation.*)

knowledgeable society: see *post-industrial society*

knowledge-as-fact: where what is learned in schools is presented as the objective truth, waiting 'out there' and being revealed to the students by the expert teacher. This recognises that there is a canon of wisdom and knowledge to which all members of a society should have access. (See *knowledge-as-practice.*)

knowledge-as-practice: where what is learned in schools is the result of exploration by the pupils, who discover knowledge through their own educational activities, guided by the facilitating teacher. This recognises that knowledge is a social product created through human activity and without an objective existence. (See *experiential teaching; knowledge-as-fact.*)

L

labelling theory: an approach in the sociology of education and the sociology of *deviance* which focuses on the ways in which the agents of *social control* attach stigmatising *stereotypes* to particular groups and the ways in which the stigmatised change their behaviour, once labelled. Labelling theory is associated with the work of Becker and is a reaction to sociological theories which examined only the characteristics of the deviants or under-achievers, rather than the agencies which controlled them. The central feature of the labelling theory is the *self-fulfilling prophecy*, in which the labelled correspond to the label, either in terms of delinquent behaviour or educational achievement. It has been criticised for ignoring the capacity of the individual to resist labelling and assuming that it is an automatic process.

laboratory control: the ability of a researcher, in a laboratory environment, to control all the *variables* in an experiment. This ability is regarded as one of the main advantages of the experimental method, but critics argue that such control is far less absolute than is often thought. (See *hypothetico-deductive method; laboratory experiment.*)

laboratory experiments: the classic method of research in the *natural sciences*, laboratory experiments are very seldom used by sociologists, although sometimes by psychologists. The main constraints on sociologists' use of experiments are both practical and ethical. (See *field experiments; hypothetico-deductive method.*)

labour aristocracy: see *aristocracy of labour*

labour market: the supply and demand of workers in the economy. The existence of a highly competitive labour market, in which more workers are seeking jobs than there are jobs available has been a feature of the 1980s and 1990s, as the *automation* of productive and clerical processes has occurred. This has led to high levels of *unemployment.* However, a generally competitive labour market can co-exist with sectors where there is a shortage of labour with the appropriate *skills*. This has led to various forms of training scheme which have sought to plug the skills gap. (See *training.*)

Labour Party: a British political organisation of the left, which includes a range of tendencies from democratic socialism to social democracy. The Labour Party is traditionally associated with the *working class* and financially supported by the *trade unions*. In the 1990s, the Labour Party rejuvenated itself in the form of 'New Labour' in response to four consecutive election defeats between 1979 and the early 1990s.

labour power: a concept used to denote the productive capacity of a worker's work. In Marxist terminology, workers are employed by the capitalist, not for their whole personality, but purely for their labour power, which is the capacity they have for making profit through their effort.

labour process: the means by which products are manufactured to satisfy human *needs*, through the application of *labour power*. The elements of the labour process consist of the work of the labourer, the tools of production and raw materials which are transformed by the labour process.

labour relations: see *industrial relations*

labour theory of value: the argument that the worth of a good is calculated by the labour that is put into its creation, and that the price should therefore be determined by the amount of work on the good and not by other considerations. The term is associated with *Marxism*, which privileges labour over all other components of production. Thus *capital* is seen by Marxists as only the outcome of past labour.

labour turnover: the rate at which workers leave employment with a specific firm. The majority of labour turnover is accounted for by retirement or redundancy, which is involuntary turnover. However, increases in voluntary turnover are argued to indicate dissatisfaction with the firm. (See *industrial action.*)

lads: a group of 12 working-class boys from the Midlands studied by Paul Willis in their last 18 months at school and first few months at work. Willis examined how the lads formed their own counter-school *sub-culture*, which was both racist and sexist, rejected the *values* and *ethos* of the school and consisted mainly of avoiding work and 'having a laff'. Willis is at pains to show that, rather than demonstrating the passive and uncritical acceptance of dominant capitalist values suggested by some Marxist writers as the usual response of working-class pupils in the education system, the lads actively created their own anti-education sub-culture and chose to enter manual work. Critics of Willis' study focus particularly on the very small *sample*, and question whether the lads had any real opportunities to change their life. (See *anti-school culture; delinquescent sub-culture; lobes.*)

laicisation: the process by which *organisations* once controlled by religious groups pass to the control of secular (non-religious) authorities. An example would be the national education system of France since the revolution. (See *disengagement; secularisation.*)

laissez-faire: literally meaning, 'leave to do', the concept is used as a shorthand for a particular philosophy of society, in which *government* has only a minimal role. Most recently associated with *New Right* sociology, laissez-faire suggests that the most efficient and free society is one in which the *State* provides only the most basic of society's *needs,* in the form of law and the defence of the nation. In particular, it is applied to the economic system, where the New Right argue that governments should not interfere in the market at all, but allow the free market to produce the fairest form of society.

language: a way of communication which involves symbolic representation. Language is possibly the distinguishing characteristic of humanity and enables the transmission of *culture* from one generation to another. It exists as an objective reality, in a structural form which individuals draw upon to make sense of each other. Language is therefore not just descriptive, but is in itself *action.*

language codes: patterns of speech identified by Bernstein, who argued that children from different social classes were socialised into using language in different ways. Bernstein argued that there were two main speech codes, the *'elaborated'* and the *'restricted'*. He believed that as education is delivered in the elaborated code used mainly by the middle class, this gave middle-class children an advantage over their working-class counterparts at school. Bernstein's ideas have been criticised, often by those who mistakenly thought him to have been claiming that middle-class speech patterns are somehow superior to those of the working class.

latch-key children: a journalistic term referring to the children of *working mothers* left unsupervised after school until their parents return from work. The term refers to the fact that many such children used to have their front-door key hung on a string round their neck. It was a widely-used term in the debate, sparked by the psychologist John Bowlby in the immediate post-Second World War period, surrounding the possible damage to children caused by the absence of their mother from the home. Bowlby firmly believed that mothers should stay at home, and linked what he saw as *maternal deprivation* to the development of *juvenile crime* and psychopathic personalities. These views led to many working mothers of the time experiencing strong guilt feelings, as well as social disapproval.

late capitalism: a term devised by Mandel to describe the situation developing in western societies in the latter part of the twentieth century. The features associated with late capitalism are increasing *automation* of production, increasing *exploitation* of workers and the development of larger but fewer worldwide firms. (See *contestation*.)

latency: also known as pattern-maintenance and tension-management, it is one of Parsons' *functional prerequisites* and relates to the ways societies seek to ensure commitment to the *values* of the system and to control those who might challenge those values. (See *adaptation; goal-attainment; integration*.)

latent functions: every *action* has unintended consequences and latent functions are the hidden or unacknowledged outcomes of people's actions. For example, while church-going may have the *manifest function* of worshipping God, it may have the latent function of integrating individuals into society.

law (of science): a statement usually derived from the results of a number of scientific experiments which attempts to be both universal (i.e. holds good for all similar situations) and predictive (i.e. can accurately state the outcome of a given set of circumstances). *Natural sciences* were based on the belief that a number of laws existed which governed matter (e.g. the law of gravity), and it was the task of the scientist, by experiment and logical reasoning, to discover these laws. As the equipment used in the natural sciences has become more sophisticated, allowing scientists to research phenomena hitherto impossible, such as sub-atomic particles, or far-away galaxies, the notion of universal laws has begun to be questioned, and many scientists now talk more cautiously of probabilities, rather than laws. Some scientists have developed the notion of 'chaos', which suggests that the universe does not, after all, conform to the previous theories of 'order', but rather that scientific events, including the development of life, occur randomly. (See *chaos theory*.)

law of the three stages: see *three stages of human development*

league tables: published tables of schools and colleges ranked in order of the number of examination passes gained by their students. First introduced in 1992, they are part of the Conservative Government's plan to make schools and colleges more publicly accountable, and to give parents the chance to compare different educational institutions. The league tables have been the focus of much controversy, as they take no account of other factors, such as the social intake of a school. Critics argue that the fairest way of showing the relative success of schools is by using the 'value-added' method, that is, comparing the level of attainment of pupils on entry with that reached on leaving.

leap of consciousness: when we move from the fundamental world of everyday *knowledge* to another reality, phenomenologists argue that we achieve this by jumping to a different way of thinking, which they describe as the leap of consciousness. (See *multiple realities.*)

Lebenswelt: the life-world, it stands for the everyday activities of people in society, in which individuals take the social world for granted as the natural order of things.

left idealism: an approach to *deviance* from the 1960s onwards, which focused on marginal groups in society, seeing them as the prototype of a new revolutionary movement against capitalist injustice. This approach saw protest against society's *norms* whether political or deviant as a rational response to the injustice within *capitalism,* and the coercion which is used to ensure *conformity.* This force was hidden within a velvet glove and pervasive efforts by many state agencies to ensure compliance. Deviance was therefore *voluntarism* breaking through the complacency of capitalist society. The idea was criticised because it played down the extent of working-class crime against the working class and the sheer anti-social nature of much deviant activity. It therefore represented a romantic view of deviant activity. (See *new left realism.*)

left-wing: in the political spectrum, those ideas and organisations which tend to be critical of existing social arrangements. These encompass democratic parties such as the British *Labour Party* and authoritarian anti-democratic parties such as the Communists. (See *right-wing, centre.*)

legal-rational organisation: an *organisation* based on strict rules limiting the *power* of superiors to order the lives of subordinates in the organisation. Legal-rational organisations have agreed procedures for carrying out tasks, which define each individual's role. The term is often used as a contrast to *charismatic* organisations, in which the whims of the leader determine the actions of subordinates. (See *bureaucracy.*)

legitimation: the process whereby control by the dominant group in society is consolidated with the acceptance of subordinate groups of the superordinate group's right to rule. Legitimation is important because societies based on *coercion* rather than consent are unstable. Legitimation is the result of effort, in which the dominant group uses state power to obtain the consent of those ruled through a variety of ideological agencies such as schools and the media. The ideological basis of legitimation varies from the *divine right of kings* to *meritocracy.* Legitimation is always conditional, in that changing circumstances can lead to the withdrawal of consent.

leisure: time when there is an element of freedom for the individual to choose what to do. Sociologists find it difficult to define exactly what leisure is, because different people will view similar activities carried out in similar circumstances in different ways. For example, two people watching a cricket match may have different views about the activity if one is a commentator and the other a spectator. As a result, sociologists such as Kelly, have broken down leisure into different categories:

	Freely chosen	Determined by work
Independent of work	Ideal or pure leisure	Complementary leisure
Related to work	Spillover leisure	Recuperative leisure

Types of leisure

leisure class: developed by Veblen to indicate that capitalist society had produced sufficient surplus *wealth* for some individuals never to need to work again. Within society they therefore formed a distinctive group, whose prime activity was to engage in the pursuit of leisure. The purpose of such activity was not to be idle but, in the absence of war and opportunities to plunder, allowed the leisure class to display their wealth in an ostentatious manner and thus establish their *honour* in society. (See *conspicuous consumption.*)

leisure industry: a term denoting the increasing tendency for *leisure* to be carried out in *organisations* where individuals pay for access to leisure facilities. In the past, leisure tended to be centred around the family and was not paid for. However, as *industrialisation* proceeded, leisure opportunities increasingly came to be provided by outside agencies. These organisations are not just providers of leisure, but are a major part of the modern capitalist system, with huge global interests. (See *globalisation.*)

leisure society: a vision of the future, in which the main focus of people's lives will be their pastimes and hobbies. The development of the leisure society is predicated on the advance of *automation,* which will not only reduce the necessity for everyone to carry out a 40 hour week at work, but will also produce enough surplus *wealth* to enable the majority of society to enjoy *leisure* activities as their *central life interest.* The idea has been criticised for ignoring the social inequality in society, which may produce increasing polarisation and the provision of leisure opportunities for a small minority of society, while the rest have more limited resources to pursue their interests.

Workers in the UK work, on average, longer hours than many of their counterparts in other European Union countries, as shown in the diagram below. (See *life style enhancement.*)

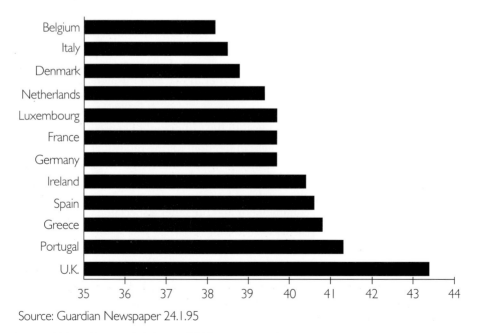

Source: Guardian Newspaper 24.1.95

Average EU working week in hours, 1992

leisure-poor: groups of people who, for a variety of reasons, are unable to take full advantage of *leisure* activities. They include those who have the time but not the money, such as the unemployed, the money but not the time, such as successful but over-worked business people and those with neither the time nor the money, such as mothers with young children from the lowest income groups.

leisure-rich: those people with both the time and the money to indulge in their preferred *leisure* activities.

lesbianism: where the *sexual orientation* of a woman is towards other women. It is to be distinguished from male *homosexual* orientations, which unlike lesbianism were criminalised in Britain until the 1960s. (See *heterosexuality*.)

letters: a form of personal *document* which may be used in sociological research. As with all *secondary sources*, letters have to be used cautiously. While some letters are intended only for the recipient, others are written with the expectation that, sooner or later, they will reach a wider audience (e.g. by politicians and authors). (See *diaries*.)

Liberal Democrat Party: a British political organisation of the centre, formed from an amalgamation of the Liberal Party and *Social Democratic Party*. While it has been the third party in elections, it is associated with Celtic fringe support and the distinctive tactic of *community politics*. It is pro-European and traditionally associated with individual liberty.

liberal feminism: a feminist perspective concerned to demonstrate that women suffer discrimination in many areas of life. It is sometimes referred to as reformist *feminism*. Liberal feminists actively campaign for equal rights for women. They are often criticised by other feminists, who argue that liberal feminists fail to challenge and to try to change the underlying social structure which leads to women's oppression in the first place. (See *black feminism; Marxist feminism; radical feminism*.)

liberation theology: a belief that people have a duty to free themselves from social, economic and political oppression in this world, rather than waiting for wrongs to be righted in the next. The doctrine of liberation theology is particularly associated with a number of radical groups which emerged within the *Roman Catholic Church* in South America in the 1960s.

life-chances: used in sociology to indicate the statistical chances of particular occurrences happening to different groups in society. For example, the life-chances of a member of the *working class* are very different from those of a member of the upper class. The working-class individual has statistically more chance of dying young than the upper-class person. If that upper-class person is also female their life expectancy is increased again. However, it is important to note that life-chances are group phenomena and cannot tell us what will happen to any specific individual. Other aspects of life-chances are issues such as education received, income earned, housing type, degrees of *health* and *illness* and so on.

life-cycle: a term denoting that most people in a society go through similar stages of development as they move from birth to death. A typical life-cycle might be as pictured overleaf. The concept is important in sociology, not just for the similarities it indicates, but also for the differences which might be examined. For example, women may have different life-cycles from men.

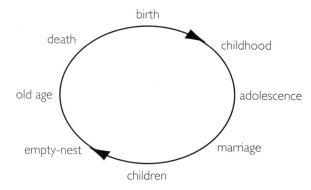

Example of a life-cycle

life-history: an autobiographical account usually obtained by *unstructured interviews* and often supplemented by personal *documents* such as letters and photographs. Life-histories can be used both to obtain an account of people's lives in the present, but also to obtain information about the past, such as from people who have lived through significant events such as the Great War, or mass emigration, or who represent a disappearing way of life, such as peasants in an industrialising economy. While providing very useful information which might be difficult to obtain by any other method, life-histories need, of course, to be treated with caution, as they are relying on people's memories and personal interpretations of the past.

life style: see *styles of life*

life style enhancement: associated with the idea of the *leisure society*, it is the provision of increased opportunities for individuals, usually in the area of leisure, which leads to greater enjoyment.

life expectancy: the average number of years a new-born baby can be expected to live. The correct term for this is actually 'expectation of life at birth', as life expectancy can be calculated at any age, e.g. 'expectation of life at 21'. During the period 1838–1854 the average expectation of life at birth in Britain was 39.9 for males and 41.8 for females. British babies born in 1994 can expect to live until almost 74 years of age if they are male and 79 if they are female. The expectation of life in Britain is currently rising by about two years every decade, though there are still significant variations between *social classes*. The increase in longevity is largely due to improvements in nutrition, housing and health care. The lack of such improvements in some countries leads to wide variations in life expectancy rates throughout the world. (See *ageing population; death rate*.)

life-world: see *Lebenswelt*

lineage: see *descent groups*

lions: a term used by Machiavelli to describe those who gain and maintain *power* in society through bold and courageous actions. (See *foxes*.)

lobes: a derogatory name given by the *lads* in Paul Willis' study to those pupils (also known to the lads as 'ear'oles') who worked hard at school, conformed to the school's expectations and were hoping for *white-collar work*.

local authorities: the political bodies which control towns, cities and rural areas, as distinct from national governments. Local authorities can come in different sizes, levels and with different compositions. For example, county local authorities have different functions and duties from district councils.

local elections: electoral events in which the parties compete for the vote of the electorate to gain control of communities in towns and counties, rather than nationally.

local labour market: the supply and demand for different types of worker within a locality. Each part of the country has its own labour profile, which is shaped by the type and variety of industry which is present within an area.

local management of schools (LMS): a system in which schools, under the direction of their governing body, have responsibility for managing their own budget, rather than having to accept the services provided by the local education authority. Some headteachers have complained that a great deal of their time is now taken up with financial matters, although many welcome the freedom the change has allowed to provide new resources. However, the limits set on school budgets in a period of cuts in public spending has forced some schools to make teachers redundant.

local opinion leaders: those who mediate information between the *mass media* and their contacts, and who concentrate on local affairs and issues. They are usually prominent members of the local community, well respected and asked for their opinions on a large number of local issues. (See *cosmopolitan political leaders.*)

locality: a term for a limited geographical or social area, which is much used in sociology to describe local space. A locality may for example be a village, or a defined area of a city, if it is being used geographically. However, it might also be used to describe a social position, such as 'factory worker'. The concept is therefore a flexible one, which can either unite those in a particular geography, or those dispersed geographically, but bound by similar social positions.

location: see *structural location*

logic of industrialism: a theory developed in the 1950s, which suggested that all industrialising countries would be forced by the needs of *industrialisation* to adopt similar social, political and economic arrangements. The 'imperatives' of industrialism are:

- a mobile work force
- an education system with a technological emphasis
- an urban society, with developed transport
- high levels of government intervention
- a complex *division of labour*

The logic of industrialism also suggested that *capitalism* provided the social arrangements which could best provide these imperatives and therefore alternative industrial societies such as *socialist societies* were *pathological* and would wither away. Critics of the theory argued that there were alternative ways that society could industrialise and that these imperatives could be met by social arrangements which were not capitalist. The critics also argued that the logic of industrialism ignored the very different histories and *cultures* of industrialising societies, which lead them to very different social arrangements. Although associated with *functionalism* and conservative sociologists, *New Right* sociologists are critical of the imperative which suggests that high levels of government intervention are necessary in an industrial society. The New Right argue that the workings of the market are the only imperatives for an efficient society. (See *convergence theory; three roads to modernity.*)

logics-in-use: used by Kaplan to describe the actual process of research, as against the account presented in the formal report of the work. There is a gap between the *reconstructed logics* and the logics-in-use, which represents the difference between the idealised account of science and the mistakes and false starts of the real process.

lone-parent families: families consisting of a dependent child or children living with only one parent, usually the mother. The proportion of lone-parent families in Britain has been growing since the end of the Second World War, and in 1992 they represented 10.1% of all *households,* compared with 2.5% in 1961. The 1992 figure represented over 1.3 million lone-parent families, containing approximately 2.2 million dependent children. While the media *stereotype* of the lone-parent family is often of the young, unmarried mother, lone-parent families are more likely to be created by the *divorce* or separation of the parents, or the death of a spouse. While some lone-parent families may enjoy a reasonable standard of living, as in families where the lone parent is a well-paid professional worker, many lone-parent families are in, or on the margins of, *poverty,* particularly where the main *income* is from state benefits. Lone parents make up around 15% of the bottom quintile (fifth) of the population in terms of income. Of the lone-parents in the bottom quintile in 1994, only 4% were in full-time work. In many cases, this is a result of the problems of finding and being able to afford suitable *childcare.* In an attempt to reduce the cost of benefits to the taxpayer, and make absent fathers pay what is deemed to be realistic maintenance, the *Child Support Agency* was set up.

lonely crowd: a term developed by Reisman to describe the conditions of modern living, in which individuals are crammed together in large *urban areas,* but have few intimate relationships with others. Thus, in the midst of plenty, individuals do not have interactions other than the transitory and superficial.

longitudinal studies: a research study of a *sample* of people who are investigated, usually by *questionnaires* or *interviews* or a combination of both, not only at the time of the original selection but also at regular intervals afterwards. While overcoming the problem of most sociological research as being a 'snapshot' taken at a particular time, the longitudinal study also has problems. One is persuading the original group to remain within the study over what is sometimes a long period of time, another is managing to keep track of the group, and a further concern is the extent to which the group remains representative. Simply being part of a study may make them more aware of aspects of their life which others might take for granted. This last point poses more or less of a problem depending on what kind of information is being gathered. (See *Hawthorne effect; panel studies.*)

longue durée: the passage of time measured by the fall and rise of institutions, which have a lifespan of their own.

looking glass Self: a suggestion by Cooley that we have an image of ourselves as a 'social self', which is built up by our reflections on the opinions that others have of us. It is to see ourselves as we think others see us. (See *symbolic interactionism; generalised other; Self.*)

loss of community thesis: the idea that in the transition from rural to urban living, people have lost the sense of identity of one with another, and with it, security and certainty. The assumption behind the idea is that *rural communities* were somehow more authentic ways of living than the soulessness of urban life. The contrast in the theory is between a lyrical and idyllic sense of place against crime and the loneliness of the old in urban environments. However, the loss of community thesis has been interpreted in different ways:

Emphasis on relationships	The loss of identity and affection, based on personal knowledge, and lost through the growth of scientific advances.
Emphasis on locality	The loss of the village as a locus for identity as it loses its economic self-sufficiency and becomes dependent on towns.
Emphasis on neighbourhood	The loss of local neighbourhoods in urban areas as developers destroy the traditional urban communities of the working class.

Versions of the loss of community thesis

Critics of the thesis argue that it is based on unsubstantiated views of rural living as somehow 'good' and urban living as 'bad'. It therefore simplifies what is a very complex process, relying on *stereotypes* of urban and rural life styles. For example, there is much research which suggests that *alienation* existed in rural communities and that communities existed in urban areas. (See *urbs in rure*.)

loss of family functions: the notion that, as institutions in society become more specialised, the *family* has lost many of its former functions, such as production. This view is particularly associated with Talcott Parsons, who argues that the loss of some functions does not, however, make the family less important to society. Other writers agree, claiming that the physical and emotional care and support provided by most families form an essential buffer against the increasingly impersonal and stressful world outside the home. (See *core functions of the family; death of the family*.)

loss of functions: part of the structural differentiation process, it is where a social structure has certain of its activities taken away from it, often by bureaucratic organisations.

loyalists: those groups in Northern Ireland who owe allegiance to the British Crown and are prepared to defend the British connection through force if necessary. They are therefore prepared to take up arms to defend the Union.

Lumpenproletariat: a term used by Marx to identify the unorganised working class who stood outside the *trade union* and political organisations which signified proletarian culture and politics. The lumpenproletariat have become associated with the *underclass,* the petty criminal, often unemployed, and the *culture* of the *inner city*. The Lumpenproletariat have little faith in political activity as a means of bettering their lot.

M

machine-minding technology: a form of technology developed during the *industrial revolution*, it consisted of mechanical devices, driven by some form of power in which the worker's main task was to ensure that the machines were running smoothly. The worker's function was to restart any machine which became stuck. This type of technology was usually associated with the textiles industries.

macro sociology: a focus on the large-scale and structural in society. Associated with *functionalism,* the emphasis is on the way that individuals are constrained by *social facts* and how society imposes particular courses of action onto individuals. (See *micro sociology.*)

madness: the disruption of 'normal' mental conditions, so that the individuals affected become unpredictable or *pathological* in their behaviour patterns. The study of madness has a sociological as well as a psychological aspect, as sociologists have examined the ways in which madness is socially negotiated and defined in different societies. (See *mental illness.*)

magic: the use of *ritual* to call upon *supernatural* powers to intervene in the natural world to effect a desired end. Sociologists have been interested in the way that magic is able to hold the faith of individuals even in a world which is supposed to be rational and secular. However, the manifestation of magic in the modern world tends to take less supernatural forms, such as astrology, belief in luck and so forth. (See *disenchantment.*)

magic bullet: an American term referring to the presumed relationship between the *mass media* and their *audiences,* i.e. that media messages were aimed at, and penetrated, an essentially passive audience who received these messages uncritically. (See *hypodermic syringe approach.*)

magnet schools: schools which have a considerable emphasis on one specialist area of the *curriculum,* and which attract the most able pupils in that particular field. Magnet schools have already been set up in the USA for curriculum areas such as the performing arts, literature and science. Some Conservative politicians have expressed an interest in creating magnet schools in Britain.

mailed questionnaires: see *postal questionnaires*

mainliners: a term used by Pryce to describe the conformist culture of black white-collar workers and their families. (See *saints.*)

maintained sector: an educational term which refers to schools maintained by public spending, either through local education authorities, or directly from central government, as in the case of grant-maintained schools. It is also often referred to as the 'state sector' in education. (See *independent sector.*)

majority control: used by managerial revolutionists to describe the situation in which a small group, usually from the same family, owns the majority of shares and controls a firm directly. (See *minority control.*)

male chauvinism: see *chauvinism*

male gaze: used in the sociology of *culture* to describe the way that films are often made with the viewpoint of men in mind, so that women are objectified as sex objects, rather than being represented as full human beings.

male under-achievement: a growing phenomenon in education, in which boys at all ages are showing poorer levels of achievement than girls. A number of reasons have been put forward to explain this, including that more examinations contain *coursework* elements, in which girls tend to do better than boys, and the fact that in some areas it is increasingly difficult for young males to find work, particularly those with relatively few qualifications. Such jobs as are available are increasingly aimed at females, as they are mainly shopwork, clerical work and jobs in catering and accommodation. It is suggested that the knowledge that there is little chance of employment acts as a de-motivating influence on boys. A problem with this explanation is that boys in areas with a more buoyant job market are also performing, on average, less well than girls. (See *female under-achievement.*)

malestream sociology: a concept developed by feminists to describe the origin and shaping of sociology by male sociologists and male concerns. Because the *classical sociologists* were all males living in patriarchal societies, the initial questions asked reflected male perspectives. Similarly the domination of sociology by males has also had the effect of marginalising female interests and areas of concern. Feminist sociology was developed partly in response to this situation.

management: the positions in an *organisation* which are concerned with the control of subordinates, so that co-ordination of activity is achieved for the efficient functioning of the organisation to achieve goals. Management has been treated as a distinct category within work organisations, with its own interests and social processes. (See *managerial revolution.*)

managerial revolution: developed by Burnham, amongst others, this view states that the individual control of industrial firms by capitalists in the nineteenth century has given way to control by teams of managers in the twentieth century. The important part of this separation of ownership from control is the development of joint stock companies, where shareholders buy a stake in a firm and thus dilute the control of the individual capitalist. Thus, the predominant ownership pattern has moved from the 'family firm' of the nineteenth century to the managerial control of the twentieth. The ideological impact of this development is that managers are able to take a more objective view of the firm and, for example, favour long-term investment over immediate profit. Critics of this theory have taken several positions:

- Some sociologists argue that the extent of shareholding has been exaggerated, with the majority of large firms still being controlled by a very small group of people.
- Others argue that wider share ownership allows the capitalist to control larger amounts of capital, while retaining individual control over the actions of the company.
- Another view is that while managers may have *operational control* over the day-to-day activities of the firm, the large shareholders still retain *allocative control*, in which decisions about where to invest and place resources in an industrial firm remain in the hands of the owners.

manifest functions: these are the intended consequences of *actions,* that is what the actions are intended to achieve. (See *latent functions.*)

Manpower Services Commission: now disbanded, the MSC was responsible in the 1980s for a whole series of *youth training schemes* and held an enormous budget to provide them.

manual unions: the representative organisations in the workplace of those who work with their hands. They are distinct from white-collar unions in two ways. Firstly, their *organisational goals* are different, with the manual unions more identified with the *Labour Party* and willing to pursue party political aims. Secondly, the behaviour of manual unions is much more likely to involve members in strike action. There are thus distinct *status* differences between manual unions and *white-collar unions,* which sociologists have tried to explore.

manual work: occupations which involve fairly hard physical effort, though it literally means work with the hands. Manual work is traditionally seen as *working class* and is part of one of the fundamental ways of classifying *social class* groupings.

margin of error: the range within which a given value is likely to fall. For example, it might be said in an opinion poll that 35% of people intend to vote Conservative at the next election, 'plus or minus 3%'. This means that the likely correct figure is between 32% and 38%. (See *sampling error.*)

marginal seat: a constituency where the share of the vote between the two top parties is so close that either could win in a general election. The amount of 'swing' needed for the seat to change hands is therefore small. (See *three-way marginal; straight fight.*)

marginalisation: the process by which certain individuals or groups are pushed to the periphery of, and sometimes excluded from, mainstream society. Disabled people are at risk of marginalisation, and so, it is argued, are the poor, whose *poverty* forces them to lead a *life style* increasingly at variance with that of the more fortunate.

marital breakdown: a situation in which one or both partners in a marriage believe that it has lost its meaning for them. Often, this breakdown will lead to *divorce,* but sometimes couples will continue to stay together 'for the sake of the children', and exist in an *empty-shell marriage.* Other couples actively seek help, by attending counselling sessions to try to repair the relationship. It indicates the end of a marriage, not legally, but in the reality of everyday living. It is claimed that the rate of marital breakdown is increasing, often due to the financial pressures of *unemployment* or low income.

market economy: where production and distribution are determined by the free activities of buyers and sellers, rather than there being any direction by the *State.* The market economy also functions as an ideological device for the *New Right.*

market forces: the balance of supply and demand for gods and services, unfettered by any artificial restraint. The *New Right* in sociology believe strongly that market forces should not be distorted by government intervention. By leaving the market free, they believe that the best of all possible societies will result. It is the exercise of individual choice in the market place that the New Right sees as the fundamental freedom. Critics of market forces argue that, left to themselves, they are unfair, in that all are not equal in the market place, with some having limited resources with which to make individual choices. (See *laissez-faire.*)

market research: research into the attitudes and buying and spending habits of consumers. While many of the methods used in market research are identical to those used in sociological research, its focus on the consumer market results in both the nature of the information gained and the use to which is put, being different from sociological research.

market situation: used by Lockwood to describe the degree of employment security of clerks and other occupational groups. In examining the *proletarianisation* thesis, the market situation of clerks was said to have changed from one of relative security to one of insecurity. The main reason for this change was the growth of universal literacy, which allowed the easy replacement of clerks. (See *work situation; status situation.*)

marketisation: the process in which market principles and practices are introduced into areas previously immune from the workings of a market. The prime example of marketisation has been education, where government policy has introduced a whole range of measures such as *league tables* and vouchers to introduce *market forces* into the system. The claim is that marketisation will produce a system more responsive to client needs. Critics have argued that it has more to do with saving money for tax cuts than any possible efficiency effects.

marriage: the legal union of a man and a woman. In Britain, as in many other industrialised countries, the institution of marriage is undergoing some radical changes, particularly in evidence since the end of the Second World War. Information from 'Social Trends 1994' shows that some of the main changes in evidence in Britain are that:

- between 1971 and 1991 marriages have fallen by almost 16%, while divorces have more than doubled over the same period
- in 1991 the numbers of people in the U.K. either marrying for the first time or marrying for a second or subsequent time, fell to 350,000, nearly 50,000 lower than in 1961
- over a third of all marriages in 1991 were remarriages, where either or both partners had been divorced; in 1961, this figure was less than one in ten
- for every two marriages in the U.K. in 1991 there was one divorce
- married women are starting their families later; in 1991, the mean age of mothers in England and Wales at the time of their first birth was 27.8 years – the highest age ever recorded
- nearly one in five unmarried men and women aged 16–59 were cohabiting in 1992
- almost one in three births in 1993 took place outside marriage, compared with an average of about one in twenty in the first 60 years of this century (apart from around the two World Wars)

Some people claim that the falling rate of marriage indicates a declining belief in the value of marriage as an institution. However, the number of cohabiting couples who are in stable, long-term relationships, together with changes in the law which give certain rights to 'partners' which were once available only to spouses, suggest that perhaps it is that what we mean by 'marriage' is changing, rather than it being in a state of decline. (See *cohabitation; divorce.*)

Year	Percentage remarriage
1961	9
1971	15
1981	31
1991	34

Source: Social Trends 1994

Remarriages for one or both partners as a percentage of all marriages in the UK

Marx: one of the classical sociologists, Karl Marx is distinguished from the others by the enormous influence he had on the world of politics, so that, from 1917, followers of his theory seized political power throughout a third of the world until the collapse of Soviet communism in the late 1980s. His influence on sociology has been to provide the methods of a critique of conventional sociology and capitalist society, by using the techniques of dialectical analysis. The main impact of his work in sociological terms has been in the areas of industrial sociology and class analysis. (See *Marxism; dialectic; historical materialism.*)

Marxism: a sociological perspective which emerged from the work of Karl Marx and which stressed the role of conflict in society. The key concepts associated with Marxism are the *dialectic, historical materialism, class struggle* and *revolution.* The basic argument of the Marxists is that economics is at the base of social life and progress is made through the struggle between different *social classes.* The *ruling class* in any society is based on the ownership of particular productive capacities and control of economic resources also gives the ruling class political and cultural control. Marxist sociologists have been influential across a number of areas of social life, particularly in the study of stratification, work and politics. There are different variations within Marxism, and they are often as divided from each other as they are from their political opponents. Critics of Marxism argue that:

- it is a determinist theory, giving little freedom to individuals
- it is wrong to give primacy to economics in the way that Marxists do
- emphasis on *conflict* denies the *social order* which is the characteristic of most societies

Marxist feminism: a branch of feminist thought which attempts to explain the particular place of women in capitalist societies. While recognising the inequalities between men and women, Marxist feminists focus their attention on the *class struggle,* seeing women's oppression not only arising from *patriarchy,* but primarily from *capitalism.* Women not only form part of the *reserve army of labour,* often being excluded from the *labour market,* but they also provide unpaid labour nurturing the current generation of workers and raising the next. The main source of their oppression, then, is seen as the capitalist system.

masculinity: those characteristics which are associated with being a man. There is a traditional conception of being masculine, which has been investigated by sociologists for its effects on male behaviour, both in regard to women and in the way that this limits the possibilities of men expressing themselves fully. Conceptions of masculinity are constantly being negotiated and re-negotiated as men seek to find other aspects to their character than the traditionally macho ones. There has been a resurgence in sociological interest in masculinity with the growth of *post-modernism* and its emphasis on the construction of identities. (See *femininity.*)

mass communication: the ability to transmit a message to a large number of people simultaneously. It is associated with the development of technologies which widen the reach of the communication device. The improvement in media technologies is a crucial part of the *globalisation* process.

mass culture: a collective term referring to cultural products and experiences aimed at a mass market. Many of these products and experiences are geared towards entertainment. Mass culture, also referred to as *popular culture*, is often contrasted with *high culture*, usually taken to mean those forms of *culture* appealing to a relatively small number of people, such as opera, classical music, 'serious' literature and art. Mass culture, on the other hand, is seen as designed to be accessible to a much larger group. It is traditional to view mass culture as somehow inferior to high culture, though sociologists have found that the study of mass culture yields a rich source of information about cultural forms and changing tastes.

mass leisure: a concept developed by Marxists to suggest that modern *leisure* is often provided for people in large numbers. A crucial part of mass leisure is provided by the media industries of newspapers, television and cinema which have grown into global conglomerations. (See *leisure industry*.)

mass media: those means of communication which reach large numbers of people at the same time. Sociologists have always been interested in the mass media, but as their importance in society has grown, so has sociological study of them. The mass media began with the development of newspapers and magazines in the eighteenth century. Modern mass media grew out of developments in the last part of the nineteenth century, such as the telegraph, and the early part of the twentieth century, such as radio and television. The term now includes a whole range of different technologies, including the computer, video and the telephone. Developments in the mass media are accelerating, with fibre technology, satellite television and the Internet, and the impact on individual lives is enormous. What that impact is, forms the object of study of sociologists of the media.

Mass Observation: see *diaries*

mass production: a process in which goods are manufactured in large numbers, usually through a form of *assembly line,* and supplied in a standardised form to the market. It is particularly associated with the first half of the twentieth century and is said to be a characteristic of *modernity*. (See *Fordism*.)

mass society: a concept developed by Kornhauser to describe a society where individuals were atomised, attached to hardly any intermediate groups which might stand between them and the power of the *state*. The idea has a negative moral connotation, in that it is used to describe a modern society which has lost the intimacy and authenticity of societies in the past. It is an expression of the fear of the totalitarianism which was experienced in the 1930s in Nazi Germany and Soviet Russia. The mass society developed as local traditions and culture dissolved under the impact of *mass media* influences, and the usual supports for individuals, in the form of families and local associations, were weakened. (See *mass media industries*.)

mass unemployment: where the numbers of the unemployed exist at high levels for a relatively long period of time. The classic period of mass unemployment was the 1930s, but it reappeared in the 1980s. Sociologists are interested in the effects of mass unemployment on individuals, their families and society as a whole. They recognise that there are differences between the 1930s and 1980s, in particular that the *welfare state* now provides a safety net for the long-term unemployed. However, changes in benefits during the 1990s has altered the nature of the safety net and led to increased pressure on the long-term unemployed.

material activity: economic actions in the widest sense – all the building, production, artistic and cultural artefacts which human beings produce. From a Marxist perspective, material activity leads to *consciousness*.

material control: a type of *power*, usually exercised in work *organisations*, in which money operates as an incentive and therefore a control over the activities of employees. (See *physical control; symbolic control*.)

material deprivation: in the sociology of education, under-achievement by the *working class* and some ethnic minorities has often been linked with the conditions of *poverty*. Factors such as poor diet, overcrowding and lack of homework facilities have been cited as factors which limit the achievement of deprived groups. However, it is difficult to show a direct causal relationship between material deprivation and educational attainment. (See *clash of cultures; cultural reproduction*.)

maternal deprivation: negative consequences allegedly resulting from the absence of full-time care by a mother for her young child or children. In the 1950s the British psychoanalyst John Bowlby argued that children denied such full-time care, as in the case of *'working mothers'*, might later suffer from *delinquency* or *mental illness*. Feminists in particular disagree with this viewpoint, arguing that it was used to persuade women to stay at home being full-time housewives and mothers at a time when women were not needed in large numbers in the labour force. Subsequent research has shown that, provided there are alternative stable care arrangements, young children actually benefit from short periods away from their mother. (See *child care; ideology of domesticity; latch-key children*.)

matriarchy: literally a form of society in which women are rulers and leaders. As there is little empirical evidence for the existence of such societies, the term is widely used to refer to situations in which the mother is, or is regarded as, the head of the household, and has authority over other family members, especially children. (See *patriarchy*.)

matrilineal: a form of kinship in which descent is traced only through females.

maturity: a stage at which physical development is complete. However, in many societies the term refers to the stage at which a young person is recognised as being able to take part in adult activities and *rituals*. The age at which this takes place shows considerable variation between societies.

McDonaldisation: a term used to describe the penetration of American cultural and economic products throughout the world. It is used symbolically and is drawn from the market and ideological success of the McDonalds Burgers franchises all over the world. It is a central process of the *globalisation* of *culture* and the economy and relies on the worldwide marketing of a recognisable logo and the provision of a standardised product. It is seen by some sociologists as an aspect of the neo-imperialism of United States *capitalism*. (See *coca-colonisation*.)

meaning: an important aspect of all *action theories*, it is the beliefs, intentions, purposes or motives which *actors* attach to their actions. In *phenomenology* meaning is created only by self-conscious thought, that is, when the *durée* is broken by reflection and the actor engages in looking back on or projecting forward about his/her actions.

meaninglessness: a condition of *alienation* identified by Blauner as the 'lack of a sense of purpose in work'. The feeling is connected to the worker's inability to see a link between his or her own work and the overall production process. (See *functional rationality; substantial rationality.*)

means of production: used in *Marxist* sociology to describe the factories, tools and machinery that are need to produce the goods and services which individuals need. According to the Marxists, it is the ownership or non-ownership of these which is the determinant of an individual's position in the *class structure*. (See *forces of production; relations of production.*)

means-tested benefits: *social benefits* which are delivered only when the claimant is able to show 'need', according to however this is defined. Supporters of means-tested benefits argue that the system allows benefits to be targeted towards those in greatest need. Others argue that the process by which a claimant must by definition prove to a bureaucrat that a genuine need exists, is unnecessarily demeaning, and that the complexity of the means-tested benefits system deters some of the genuinely needy from even applying. (See *universal benefits.*)

mechanical solidarity: the way in which traditional agricultural societies remain integrated, through individuals identifying with other people because they fundamentally experience the same things in life. This identity of sameness was argued by Durkheim to be the way that social life was made possible in stable rural societies. (See *organic solidarity.*)

mechanisation: the process whereby industrial production is no longer carried out through the manual skills of *craft* workers, but increasingly by machines. Mechanisation was a central process in *industrialisation,* which allowed the development of *mass production* techniques. More specifically, mechanisation has come to represent a particular era of industrial development, distinct from the era of *automation* which we are now going through. It is therefore associated with *Fordist* modes of production.

mechanistic organisation: a term used by Burns and Stalker to denote rigid, hierarchical, bureaucratic-like *organisations,* in which individuals have very specific and specialised tasks, co-ordinated by a dedicated management structure. Burns and Stalker argued that mechanistic organisations develop in a situation of industrial stability, where demand for mass-produced standardised goods is constant. Mechanistic organisations are therefore efficient at meeting this stable demand, through routinising manufacturing processes. (See *niche markets; organismic organisation.*)

media conglomerates: see *conglomerates*

media effects: a collective term referring to the different views which have been put forward to identify and explain the effects exerted by the mass media on their *audiences.* (See *hypodermic syringe approach; magic bullet; two-step flow model; uses and gratifications approach.*)

media industries: the centrality of media organisations in postmodern economies and the global and national companies which dominate the *mass media.* The importance of mass media industries can be defined in terms of the influence they have over patterns of behaviour which transcend national boundaries, and also in the wealth that they generate for those who own them. The economic importance of the mass media industries in society is therefore a focus for sociological investigation.

media representations: those images of our *culture* and society which are relayed by the *mass media*. Both sociologists and psychologists have studied media representations, and have particularly focused on those representations which lead to or draw on *stereotypes*. In this respect, women, blacks, homosexuals, lone mothers, striking miners, New Age travellers and members of various minority groups have provided good examples of negative media representations. It is, of course, possible for the reverse process to take place, and for positive representations to be used, such as sometimes in the case of leading politicians or members of the royal family who wish to improve their 'image' with the general public.

mediation: the process whereby individuals negotiate or alter their lived conditions of existence, so that they are transformed in some way into a different experience. In the media the mediation process is connected with the way that *ideologies* are transformed into news content through the operation of the news-values held by journalists. The argument is that *ruling-class* ideologies appear not in a raw form, but in a mediated way, so that they are absorbed without the recipients even knowing they have been exposed to them.

medical model of health: a view of *health* and *illness* which sees the body as primarily a machine, and the role of the medical profession to cure rather than to prevent illness, and to focus treatment on individuals, rather than exploring the relationship between individuals and their social and physical environment. (See *bio-mechanical model.*)

medical technology: the increasingly sophisticated and expensive equipment, including drugs, used by the medical profession. While some of this undoubtedly helps to save lives, concern is expressed over the fact that the equipment may be used simply because it is there, while other, less interventionist forms of treatment are ignored. Childbirth is often cited as a prime example of the use of medical technology, with childbirth increasingly treated as though it were an 'illness', rather than a natural process. Women wishing to have their babies at home using more 'natural' methods of childbirth have often faced strong opposition from the medical profession.

medicalisation: the tendency for an increasing number of areas of social life to become subject to medical classification and treatment. The classic example of this is the way that childbirth has increasingly become the province of male doctors as opposed to female midwives. Other areas which have become medicalised include sexuality, in its many different facets. This was an area of particular interest to Foucault, who saw the medicalisation of sexuality as part of a process of increasing *surveillance* in society, where the development of new *discourses* of power marginalised and stigmatised different groups. (See *de-medicalisation.*)

meltdown: a term devised to describe electoral disaster for a governing party, where the number of its MPs falls from a majority to a handful. The term emerged from the fall of the Conservative Government in Canada, who were left with only two MPs.

membership involvement ratio: an indicator of *strike* activity which calculates the sum of all workers involved in all strikes during a year divided by the average number of union members during that year. It was used by Ross and Hartman to compare the strike rates of different countries.

mental health: a state in which someone exhibits 'normal' patterns of thought and behaviour. The term is in a way very misleading, because it is often used in the context of exactly the reverse, i.e. mental illness. Therefore various 'mental health' acts are, in fact, dealing with 'mental illness'. It is important to note that what are considered 'normal' patterns of thought and, especially, behaviour are capable of a very wide interpretation, which differs over time, in different societies and according to the context in which the behaviour occurs, as well as the social characteristics of both the labelled person and the person doing the *labelling*.

mental illness: the supposed disturbance of 'normal' patterns of thought and behaviour. The concept is a very controversial one, as it rests on a definition of what is a 'normal' mental state. Sociologists such as Goffman have investigated mental illness in terms of *social control* and *labelling*, and it has also been studied in relation to *deviance*. The label can also be used as a form of *social control*. This was shown clearly in several of the show trials in the Soviet Union in the 1930s, when many intellectuals, especially those critical of the system, were deemed to be mentally ill and placed in psychiatric hospitals.

mercantilism: a belief that the economic prosperity of a society can only be secured by the state regulation of trade. (See *laissez-faire*.)

meritocracy: a social system in which rewards and occupational positions are allocated justly on the basis of merit, rather than on ascriptive factors such as class, gender, ethnic group or wealth. It is often claimed that modern *industrial societies* are more meritocratic than in the past, and that the education systems in such societies are also meritocratic. However, there is much evidence to show that ascriptive features such as those listed above exert a considerable influence on an individual's *life chances*. (See *ascription*.)

Mertonian functionalism: that branch of *functionalism* which does not accept that everything that exists in society has a positive function to perform within it, but that some existing structures have dysfunctional effects. That is, it is a type of functionalism which moves away from a conservative emphasis on order, towards an interest in *social change*. (See *dysfunction; structural-functionalism*.)

messianic movements: see *millenarian movements*

meta-narrative: developed by Lyotard to describe those theories and ideas which attempt to explain the whole of the social totality. Lyotard argues that these are *myths* or stories encompassing the whole of the natural and social worlds within their reach. Such meta-narratives may be religion, science, sociology itself or the idea of progress and Lyotard argues that, in a post-modern world, we no longer accept meta-narratives as being capable of explaining anything. Social life is so fractured and disjointed in post-modern conditions that no one theory can hope to explain everything. As a result, the project of the Enlightenment, which was to understand and control the world through the application of rational principles and the continuous progress of science, has been abandoned.

metaphysical stage: one of Comte's three stages of human development, this was where the *theological stage* was broken down as people speculated about the nature of the natural world, rather than taking religious authority for granted. (See *positive stage.*)

methodology: the study of the types of method used by sociologists, the reasons for their choice of method, and how they collect, select, interpret and analyse their data. The term is often used instead of 'method', e.g. a reference might be made to the 'methodology' of a particular piece of research, when what the writer/speaker is actually referring to is the method(s) used.

metropolis: a term used by *under-development theorists* to describe the position of large cities in the *third world*. These are seen as outposts of the *first world* in the *hinterlands* of underdeveloped societies. In the metropolis, local *elites* are dominant, both politically and economically. These local elites may be foreigners, the indigenous capitalist class, traditional feudal leaders or in some cases the military. The role of these elites is to act as the representatives of the first world in the third world, mediating between capitalist interests in the first world and their own populations. (See *enclave development.*)

micro sociology: a focus on the small scale and individual within society and usually associated with *interactionist* sociologists. The emphasis is on the way that millions of everyday events build up to make *society* and produce patterns of behaviour. (See *macro sociology.*)

middle class: the traditional *social class* grouping which stands between the upper and working classes, and which is usually associated with non-manual work, such as clerical work or the traditional *professions*. (See *working class.*)

middle-class radicals: a general term for those members of white-collar groups who support the *Labour Party*. They are radical because they are assumed to be voting against their own class interest and in favour of policies which will benefit those below them in the social *hierarchy*. (See *unionisation; colonisation.*)

migration: the movement of people to another region (internal migration) or another country (external migration). Migration is one of the factors, together with *birth rates* and *death rates*, which determine the population level of a country. Although much media attention is focused on the question of immigration to Britain, especially from the Commonwealth, each year Britain loses many thousands of people as emigrants, who move overseas. Over the period 1988–1992, the annual average number of emigrants from Britain was 227,900, while the corresponding figure for immigrants was 243,000, resulting in an annual net gain to the population of just 15,100. Over this period, 58% of immigrants to Britain were non-British citizens, nearly half of whom came from the European Community. Since the passing of the Immigration Act of 1971, there have been increasingly strict controls governing the right to settle in Britain. With regard to internal migration, 1992 showed a net loss of 10,000 people for England, with Scotland and Wales both gaining population. Within England, the South-East, the West Midlands and the North-West were net losers of population, while the South-West gained the greatest number of people. (See *immigration controls.*)

militancy: an attitude held by workers in which strong *trade union* positions are taken and which are associated with *industrial action* of various descriptions.

Sociologists are interested in why certain groups of workers are more militant than others, and what conditions encourage militant attitudes. *New Right* sociologists argued that militancy has been decreasing as the powers of the trade unions to create industrial strife have been diminished during the 1980s.

military-industrial complex: a term used by Mills to describe the domination of United States society in the 1960s by an alliance of manufacturers who supplied goods to the armed forces and the key personnel of the military, who wanted larger and larger budgets. Critics of the idea suggest that there are no formal or informal mechanisms by which such an alliance could be maintained and if there was a community of interest between them it was unconscious.

millenarian movements: religious movements which expect the world to be transformed by *supernatural* intervention in the near future. Many millenarian movements involve their members practising particular *rituals* which often borrow elements from other cultures or religions. It has been noted that millenarian movements often emerge among groups who are undergoing rapid *social change*, often accompanied by economic and/or political upheaval. (See *cargo cults; ghost dancers.*)

mind-body dualism: a belief that the mind and the body are independent of each other. It is a view associated with the 17th century French philosopher Descartes, whose views on mind/body dualism were counter to the prevailing Christian orthodoxy that the body and the soul were indivisible, and that unless the body were preserved intact the soul would be unable to ascend to heaven. Following the acceptance of Descartes' views in the West, it became possible to undertake the detailed study of human anatomy by dissection, opening the way for the development of medical science. (See *bio-mechanical model of health.*)

minority control: used by managerial revolutionists to describe the situation where between 20% and 50% of shares in a firm are owned by a small group of share-holders, which gives them great influence, because the rest of the shares are dispersed among a large number of others.

mixed economy: where there is no dominance by either the *public* or *private sector* in producing the goods and services that people need. The actual mix will vary from one society to another and political parties differ on how much of one or the other there should be. In the immediate post-war period, there was a move towards the public sector, but in the 1980s and 1990s successive Conservative governments moved back towards the private sector through their policy of privatisation.

mob: an unorganised, unruly mass of people, who are engaged on some type of public disorder. The mob was also symbolic in the nineteenth century of everything that the *upper class* feared – the first *folk devil*. Drawn from experiences in the French Revolution, the mob came to represent the disrespect of the lower orders for their upper class 'betters' and the fear of the upper class that their privileges could be taken away from them in an upsurge of violence.

mode of production: the way in which relations between the owners and non-owners of the means of production, as well as the *forces of production* themselves, are organised, which distinguishes one type of society from another. In Marxist terms, the mode of production is central to understanding the nature of a particular society. In feudal societies for example, the feudal aristocracy did not control the forces of production directly, which remained under the direction of the peasantry, but through their monopoly of physical force they were able to appropriate the produce of those forces of production and distribute them as the aristocracy saw fit. (See *relations of production.*)

models: intellectual devices which represent social phenomena in some way, usually through an *analogy*. There can also be diagrammatic models of the social and more recently mathematical models, where very complex relationships are manipulated by computers to depict patterns of social relationship.

modern apprenticeships: introduced in the 1990s to substitute for the traditional apprenticeships destroyed in the 1980s, they offer on-the-job training for a restricted period funded by central government and with guidelines built in for equal opportunities for applicants.

modern upper class: used by stratification sociologists to differentiate the traditional aristocratic *upper class* from the superordinate groups who dominate contemporary capitalist societies. The necessity for this concept arises from the growth of complex divisions at the top of society, in which the traditional upper class has been subsumed. The dominant sections of society which make up the modern upper class are the business *elite*, the professionals, the *intelligentsia* and the top management of large corporations.

modernisation: the process whereby societies move from being traditional to being characterised by rational action. Modernisation, as used by sociologists, has an ideological dimension, in that the process is imbued with positive feelings. The modern, in contrast to the traditional, is associated with being bright, exciting, up-to-date and attractive. In more recent times however, modernisation has come to have more negative connotations. Some sociologists see modernisation as destroying much of value in *traditional societies*. Other post-modernists see modernisation as producing soulless, uniform and ultimately inhuman social formations, such as tower blocks, urban squalor and increased crime.

modernisation theory: the dominant approach to *development* issues in the 1950s and 1960s, characterised by the search for those factors which undeveloped countries lacked and which were presumed the cause of their lack of development. This involved modernisation theorists such as Rostow in a comparison of developed countries with undeveloped countries to identify the differences between them. These differences were put forward as the reason for the *third world*'s lack of development. Different theorists put forward different factors as the main causes of undevelopment:

- a lack of technology
- a lack of capital
- over-population
- a lack of entrepreneurs
- inappropriate values for development

However, modernisation theories have been criticised for the following reasons:

- that they are 'Euro-centric', that is, they view the experiences of the third world from a western point of view
- that they lack an historical perspective, lumping all third world societies together, ignoring their individual *cultures* and histories

- that they assume that many of the features of third world societies which were imported by the colonial powers are 'native' to the third world
- that all the third world has to do to develop is to repeat the experience of the *first world*. This is difficult, because the first world developed without any competition from other societies, while the third world has now to compete with the first world.

(See *Five Stages of Economic Growth.*)

modernism: a movement in art, *culture* and architecture which accepts the progress of the *Enlightenment* project and is particularly concerned with functionality in form, where a preference for 'modern' functional design is always stated. It stands in contrast to post-modern forms of culture.

modernity: used to describe the condition of society from the *Enlightenment* of the seventeenth century to the middle of the twentieth. It encompasses a rational outlook on social issues and an attempt to shape social arrangements according to scientific and logical principles. Modernity can be seen as the belief in certainty and knowledge which is solid. There was little room for doubt in the modernist enterprise, as in various disciplines theorists tried to establish the rational principles by which subjects might be controlled and progress forged. (See *post-modernity.*)

modified extended family: used to denote the continuing importance of wider kinship networks, even when most people live in nuclear families or on their own. It is made possible by the development of modern communications, which have allowed families to keep in touch with each other even when they live at a distance. It implies that the wider family is still an important locus for *identity*, even where *geographical mobility* is high. (See *family structure.*)

monogamy: a pattern of *marriage* in which people may have only one legal spouse at a time. It is the form of marriage found in most western societies. The growing pattern in many industrial societies of marriage, *divorce* and remarriage (possibly continuing through more than one divorce/remarriage) is referred to as *serial monogamy*. (See *polygamy.*)

monotheism: a religious belief based on the notion of a single, omnipotent god. *Christianity, Judaism* and *Islam* are examples of monotheistic religions. (See *polytheism.*)

moral involvement: the way in which individuals are committed to a society if there is a *value-consensus*. Because individuals share common *values*, they are likely to be committed in a way which engages their moral senses. Such an involvement is likely to be deep-seated and lead to strong feelings of loyalty from individual members of society.

moral panic: a situation in which media reporting has created a *folk devil* of a particular social group, and the public demand of the authorities that something be done about it. This expression of concern is described as a moral panic, because it is based on an outraged sense of offence to public standards of behaviour, though the information which prompts it is often limited and inaccurate.

morbidity data: information relating to the nature and extent of *illness* in a population. It is usually measured by the number of hospital admissions and doctor-patient consultations, statistics relating to time off work as a result of sickness, and self-reported illness data from health surveys.

mores: (pronounced 'more-rays') preferred and socially sanctioned ways of behaving in any given society. These are a stronger form of *norms*, in which more fundamental habits of behaviour are involved.

mortality rate: the number of deaths per thousand of the population per year. These rates are often broken down to show differences by age, gender and social class. The *infant mortality rate* is considered a particularly important indicator of economic prosperity or the lack of it. (See *death rate*.)

mortification of self: the process in which, on entering a *total institution*, the individual is stripped of all social supports and individual *identity*. The process involves many different aspects:

- humiliation by staff
- abuse from staff and other inmates
- allocation of a number
- allocation of a uniform
- issue of standardised equipment
- cutting of career occupational contacts
- restriction of family access.

motivator-hygiene theory: developed by Herzberg, amongst others, to try and explain *work satisfaction* and work dissatisfaction. The theory suggests that the factors which lead to satisfaction in work are not the same as those which lead to dissatisfaction. Satisfaction factors were motivators and included achievement, recognition from superiors and responsibility. Dissatisfaction factors were more associated with 'hygiene' and included working conditions, as well as job security and type of supervision.

mugging: generally street robbery with violence, though the importance of the term sociologically is that there is actually no offence of mugging, just a vague and undefined category of offences. Sociologists have therefore been interested in mugging as a *social construction* and in particular in the way that the *mass media,* police and judiciary can shape public attitudes towards phenomena and create *moral panics*. It is the apparent appearance of a crime wave of mugging which set sociologists to investigate the reality behind the statistics. They were able to show that the statistics were less important in creating a moral panic than the official reaction to the statistics.

multi-cultural education: education which teaches pupils about the *culture* of other groups, particularly other *ethnic groups*. This has led to controversy, as some white parents have argued that they wish their children to learn only what they see as the indigenous British culture, rather than be taught about the food, customs and religious beliefs of other cultural groups, particularly immigrant ethnic groups. (See *anti-racist education*.)

multi-national companies: a term used to describe capitalist firms who carry out their business operations in more than one country. The concept was attacked for hiding the central issues of who owns these companies and in whose interest they operate. 'Multi-national' seems to imply that these companies are operating outside of national interests, and are not owned by individuals of any nation in particular. While there is some evidence of a dispersion of large companies' shares throughout the world, most of the large companies operating on a global level are still dominated by people from one particular country. It is thus possible to identify multi-national companies (MNCs) primarily owned by Japanese or American capitalists. For this reason, the concept fell into disuse. (See *trans-national companies.*)

multi-stage sampling: a *sampling* technique in which an initial (usually random) sample is selected, (for example of secondary schools in Britain) and then a further sample is drawn (say of groups of pupils within those schools). Multi-stage sampling can go through more than two stages, providing that the sample at the end of the process is large enough to generate useful data.

multiple realities: used by Schutz to suggest that every individual exists on a variety of levels, each of which is real for as long as we inhabit it. The basic reality is the *Lebenswelt*, the world of everyday knowledge, which exists at the level of the unconscious and which we inhabit without reflection. However other realities also exist when we pause in the everyday world and engage in other forms of thinking such as speculation, rational calculation, religious devotion, thinking sociologically. These other realities exist as long as we are thinking this way. To reach these states of thought, we perform a *leap of consciousness.*

multiple roles: as we move through different parts of our lives, we adopt different *roles* in different circumstances. For example, during the course of a day we may be parent, workmate, boss, customer, lover etc. We switch from one role to another with relative ease, though there is potential for *role conflict* within these multiple roles.

myth: a sacred tale which usually relates events of great significance to a particular society, such as the origin of its people, or tales about its gods or past heroes. This is the anthropological definition of myths, and they were studied by Malinowski, who used them to try to uncover the dominant *values* of a society, and by Levi-Strauss, who argued that all myths expressed ideas about certain fundamental 'binary oppositions', such as male/female, friend/enemy and nature/society. However, more recently Barthes has examined myths as a system of communication, namely the signs through which *culture* is expressed. For Barthes, myths could be found not only in oral or written *discourses*, but in all forms of *popular culture*, such as sport, cinema, fashion, advertising etc.

N

narcotisation: the process in which the *mass media* reduce individuals to a state of mindless existence. The process was developed as a contrast to the notion that the media provided an opportunity to educate and entertain the masses. The idea of narcotisation was a response to the power of the media in totalitarian societies, where absolute control over the radio and newspapers had seemed to ensure the domination of nations by particular ideologies. It was argued that, by being provided with endless diversions, the masses lose the capacity for independent political thought.

nation-state: the political unit which covers a particular geographical area, but more importantly, encompasses all those who identify with each other as sharing a common history, *culture* and language. The growth of the nation-state was characteristic of Europe in the nineteenth century, although the process is still continuing in the areas of the former Soviet Union and Yugoslavia. *Globalisation* theorists argue that the importance of the nation-state is in decline, under the impact of the twin processes of *globalisation* and localisation.

national curriculum: a *curriculum* introduced by the Education Reform Act of 1988 which, for the first time, laid down the content of the curriculum for pupils aged 5–16. As well as delivering the prescribed subjects and content, schools also had to prepare their pupils for standardised tests to be taken at ages 7, 11, 14 and 16. These ages were known as Key Stages 1, 2, 3 and 4, and were felt to represent crucial points in a child's education. The national curriculum proved very controversial, and was widely condemned by teachers and educationalists, who found it overly-bureaucratic and difficult to administer. It has undergone several revisions since it was first introduced, and now only English, Maths and Science remain as compulsory 'core' subjects which must be studied up to the age of 16. The results of the standardised tests have to be published and, in the secondary sector, are used to draw up '*league tables*' of schools, so that comparisons may be made between them. (See *Dearing Report.*)

National Deviancy Conference: a group of British sociologists who challenged the orthodoxies of criminology in the 1970s, by focusing on the deviants' own accounts of themselves and the political dimension of crime and criminality. The off-shoots of the NDC developed radical alternatives to conceptions of deviance, which shifted the focus away from the criminal and towards the forces of law and order. The increase in crime during the 1980s and the reality of violence as an aspect of criminal activity led several of the NDC theorists to turn to alternative ways of conceptualising crime, associated with a realist approach.

National Health Service: a system of delivering free healthcare to all citizens, which was set up in Britain in 1948, following the recommendations of the *Beveridge Report*. The NHS was initially of particular benefit to women and children, especially from the working class, as previously all treatment had to be paid for, and such health insurance as existed mainly covered employed men. Currently, as the number of elderly people in the population continues to rise, and the cost of drugs and *medical technology* becomes more expensive, some politicians and economists have begun to question whether Britain can continue to afford the NHS. Some health authorities have already banned certain operations deemed non-essential, and doctors and *NHS Trust* managers are pointing out that choices will increasingly need to be made regarding which patients may receive which treatment. Health care is the second highest area of government expenditure (almost 14% of the total) and costs approximately £35 billion per year. Despite this expenditure, there has been a significant reduction in the number of hospital beds, and cuts to the community care programme. The notion of a free health service has also been undermined, with many people now having to pay for dental and optical treatment and prescriptions. Some people are concerned that cuts in the NHS have a disproportionate effect on working-class people, as many middle-class people have private health insurance. There is also growing concern at the increasing *bureaucracy* of the service. Between 1989–1992, more than 2,000 extra managers and 18,000 clerks and administrators were employed by the NHS, while the number of nurses fell by 26,000 and the number of doctors rose by just 3,000. (See *care in the community; GP fundholders; inverse care law*.)

nationalisation: the policy and practice of taking industries into public ownership. Usually associated with socialist politics, it has fallen out of favour as the policy of *privatisation* has been implemented. The original nationalised industries were in areas seen as crucial for the operation of the economy such as mining, but the policy was extended to ailing industries such as aircraft and car manufacture, with the consequent drain on public finances.

nationalism: in general usage, it is the belief in the *nation-state* as the prime political unit, usually based on linguistic or cultural similarities. More specifically in Britain, it is connected with the impulse in the Celtic fringe towards independence from the English crown, as exhibited in Scotland, Wales and Northern Ireland.

natural history of professionalism: a concept developed by Wilensky which suggested that there were certain logical and historical steps through which an occupational group must go before it can become a *profession*. Critics of this approach to the professions are of two types:

- Some sociologists argue that the existing professions emerged at a particular historical time, when governments were infused with an *ideology* which was prepared to hand over powers to occupational groups. That time is now past and governments are unlikely to hand over any more power to non-professional groups.
- Other sociologists argue that history shows that the existing professions did not follow through a particular set of procedures in order to become a profession, but took a wide range of routes.

natural science: specifically, the disciplines of biology, chemistry and physics, but more generally, a way of looking at the natural world which is systematic, objective and capable of generating universal laws. The exact nature of natural science is in much dispute, with some philosophers of science arguing for only one strict way of doing natural science and others arguing that there is no one way of doing natural science. The latter argue that natural science, just like any human endeavour, is open to social construction. The term 'natural science' is misleading because it presumes that there is 'a' science. whereas in fact it is more accurate to talk about the natural sciences in the plural. Many of the assumptions regarding the methods and the degree of *objectivity* in science have been challenged, particularly by interactionist sociologists, and also by philosophers such as Popper and Kuhn. (See *falsification; hypothetico-deductive method; scientific revolution.*)

natural selection: see *evolutionary theory*

natural world: used as a contrast to the *social world*, this is the world that exists, regardless of human perception of it. It is the world of plants, animals, matter, atoms, stars and space etc. It is sometimes referred to as the objective world, because it would exist whether we subjectively experienced it or not. We do experience the natural world as external to us, but action theorists suggest that it only becomes meaningful when human beings impose their understanding onto it.

nature versus nurture debate: the controversy over whether human *intelligence* and behaviour is primarily determined by heredity and genetic make-up, or by the process of *socialisation*. The extreme positions in the debate are taken by those who argue in favour of the former view, such as Eysenck, and the cultural determinists, who support the latter. It is difficult to find really conclusive evidence either way, and many people adopt the position that both genetics and socialisation play their part in shaping human attitudes and behaviour; the question is one of emphasis. A concern expressed regarding the genetics view is that beliefs in the purely biological determinants of human character could be, and indeed have been, used to justify discriminatory treatment of particular groups, such as blacks. It also implies that there is little point in trying to 'cure' or 'rehabilitate' criminals, as it is in their 'nature' to offend.

Naturwissenschaften: a term used by Dilthey for the 'natural sciences' to distinguish them from the social sciences. (See *Geisteswissenschaften.*)

need-achievement: developed by McLelland to suggest that every individual, as a basic part of their human nature, has a basic desire to make something of themselves. However, the drive to achieve will vary from individual to individual, depending upon childhood experiences and the extent to which parental warmth supported competitive encouragement.

needs: what is required by individuals to survive. According to sociologists, definitions of need are socially constructed, so that they will vary from one society to another and at different times.

negative abstention: where electors fail to vote because they cannot be bothered to or have no interest in politics. Negative abstention is therefore a feature of indifference to politics. (See *positive abstainers.*)

negative correlation: see *correlation*

negative partisanship: voting against a party rather than voting for one. The increase in negative voting has been noticeable during bye-elections in the 1980s and 1990s, where electors chose to vote for the party most likely to defeat the candidate for the party in National Government, regardless of their own preferences. They tend to revert to their usual party in *general elections.* (See *tactical voting.*)

negotiated order: developed by Strauss as an alternative conceptualisation of society to the reified view of the functionalists, it suggests that society is constantly being worked and re-worked by those who live in it. Society does not therefore exist independently of the individuals who create it on a day-to-day basis, through their interactions with each other. This negotiation of the social order is not conscious, but an effect of the everyday activities of individuals.

neighbourhood: a term used to describe localities in *urban areas* which are characterised by a common sense of identity and usually a common life style. Neighbourhoods are usually class-based and particularly in working-class neighbourhoods they have a developed sense of *community*. To sociologists, the importance of neighbourhoods is that they demonstrate the existence of a sense of community in urban areas, contrary to the soulless stereotype often put forward. (See *loss of community thesis*.)

neo-colonialism: the situation in which the former colonial powers continue to dominate the affairs of the former colonies through a variety of means. Thus, while formal control of the colonies was given up at the time of political independence, the former colonisers tend to retain important influences over economic and even cultural affairs. Such ties between the former colonies and the former imperial power are partly the result of shared history, sentiment and a common language, but also operate through the dominance of trading and industrial organisations from the original colonial power. The terms of trade between former colonisers and colonised tend to operate in favour of the imperial power, which often controls crucial sectors of the former colony's economy. The former colonies often tried to break the dominance of the former coloniser's industrial giants through policies such as *nationalisation*, or restricting the amount of profits which might be patriated to the former imperial power. However, it is also argued that, with *globalisation*, the power of *trans-national companies* has grown so much that the interests of the former colonies and imperial powers can be ignored and we live in a post neo-colonial world.

neo-functionalism: sociological theory which draws upon and extends traditional functional analysis and seeks to apply its principles to the changed conditions of the late twentieth century. In particular, the neo-functionalist examines the problems of *integration* in an increasingly fractured world.

neo-Marxism: sociological approaches which update the insights of *Marx* and apply the basic principles of *Marxism* to the conditions of the second half of the twentieth century. In particular, the neo-Marxist perspective attempts to take into account the growth of sources of identity other than social class.

neo-natal mortality rate: the number of deaths of infants under four weeks of age per thousand live births. (See *infant mortality rate; perinatal mortality rate.*)

nepotism: a form of *power* in which key positions in *organisations*, whether political, administrative or economic, are allocated to relatives of those already in positions of power. The importance of nepotism is that it allows autocratic rulers to control societies through particularistic relationships. The regime of Saddam Hussein of Iraq would be an example of a nepotistic government.

nesting: where there are *hierarchies of oppression*, the way in which one level of oppression may be contained within another set of disadvantages associated with a different characteristic which is discriminated against. So, for example, for black women ethnic disadvantage may be nested within gender discrimination.

net volatility: the change in the proportion of the parties' votes between one election and the next. While net volatility may be low, in that the percentage change may be small, this may hide a high degree of *gross volatility*. The result may be very similar, but large numbers of people have changed their minds both ways. (See *volatility*.)

networking: the process by which people establish business and personal contacts which they believe will be useful to them. It is argued that, at least in the business world, this is easier for men than for women, as many of these contacts are made through membership of golf clubs and other clubs run mainly or exclusively for men. As many networking activities take place outside normal working hours, it is also difficult for those women who have *childcare* responsibilities.

neutralisation: an important part of the process of *drift*, where those committing deviant acts minimise the importance of their actions and provide justifications for them.

new Christian right: a term used to refer to those Christian groups which take a right-wing approach to matters of social policy. Such groups are exerting an increasingly strong influence in American politics in particular, where members of Christian right-wing groups form a numerically very strong group of voters. They are opposed to many actual and proposed social welfare policies, including the right to abortion, welfare payments to the poor, attempts at greater racial integration and the extension of certain *civil rights* to homosexuals, such as their acceptance in the armed forces. At the moment, the new Christian right is not such a powerful movement in Britain as it is in the United States.

new class: a concept developed by Djilas to describe the group of high communist officials who held *power* in the Soviet bloc and who used that power to further their own interests and those of their children. Djilas argued that this new class used their control of the *State* and also the industrial enterprises run by the State to establish their total control in society. They, to all intents and purposes, operated as a *ruling class*, just like the *bourgeoisie*.

new criminology: see *critical criminology*

new deviancy theory: an approach to *deviance* which wished to do away with assumptions about criminal types or criminal *sub-cultures*. It begins with the idea that everyone is potentially deviant, with deviant impulses, and the creation of a deviant is through the intolerance of the powerful who stigmatise and label the relatively powerless in society. The *working class* do not therefore have greater criminality per se they just have less *power* to resist the labels of the powerful forces of the social control agencies. True goodness therefore appears only on the margins of society amongst *expressive deviants*. This idea was criticised as representing a hopelessly romantic view of humankind, whose natural goodness is brutalised by official society. (See *National Deviancy Conference*.)

new international division of labour: the shake-up in the world's economy in which manufacturing jobs have been moved to the developing countries of the South and the North has retained high-tech industries. The move of manufacturing jobs to the *Pacific rim* has occurred because they are labour-intensive industries and the labour force is cheaper in the *third world*. High-tech industries employ relatively few workers who are mainly highly skilled and well paid. The consequence is increasing *unemployment* in the *first world*.

new left realism: a left-wing analysis of crime which acknowledges that inner-city crime is a reality, and cannot be explained away simply by reference to policing policies, a biased judiciary, media-led *moral panics* or the oppression of the *working class*, even if these are a factor. Writers such as Lea and Young view some Marxist writing on crime as over-romanticising the issue, and recognise that the victims of working-class crime are usually working-class people. They refer to themselves as left realists, rather than left idealists. Critics of the view argue that, by focusing on working-class crime, the new left realists are ignoring the *crimes of the powerful*, which pose a much greater threat to the working class.

new man: a term applied to those men who have allegedly moved away from the stereotyped image of the 'macho' male, who allow their natures to be more expressive, and who also take their share of domestic and *childcare* tasks. Despite many references to the new man in the media, and the increasing participation of many men in some domestic and childcare tasks, results of research by the Family Policy Studies Centre showed that reports of 'new manism' were greatly exaggerated. (See *domestic division of labour; symmetrical family*.)

new middle class: used to describe the post-war growth in certain non-manual occupations such as the salaried office workers, some managerial positions and professionals employed by large bureaucracies. The distinguishing characteristic of this group compared to the *old middle class* was that they were unpropertied.

new poor: groups of people in *poverty* who fall into groups other than the traditional groups of the sick, the disabled and the elderly. While these latter groups are still found among the poor, other categories now make up a growing proportion of those in poverty. They are low-paid workers, *lone-parent families* (especially those headed by a woman), the unemployed and the young homeless. Many of these groups receive all or part of their income from social benefits.

new professions: see *semi-professions; personal service professions*

new rabble: a term coined by Murray to describe members of the *underclass* inhabiting *inner-city* areas and causing businesses and the middle class to move out.

new religious movements (NRMs): a collective term applied to the numerous religious groups, not necessarily Christian, which have emerged in increasing numbers, particularly in western societies, in the last few decades. These groups are so diverse in character that Wallis has attempted to classify them with regard to their view on, and interaction with, mainstream society. Wallis suggests three main categories, as follows:

- World-rejecting – groups which expect their members to withdraw from the world, reject its values and live a life based on the principles of the group. Examples would be the Unification Church of Sun Myung Moon (the 'Moonies') and devotees of Hare Krishna.
- World-accommodating – groups which have relatively little impact on the way members live their lives; they are told to be more 'religious', according to how that is interpreted by the particular group. The main focus of religious experience tends to be in the acts of collective worship. Examples would be the house-church movement and Neo-Pentecostalism.

- World-affirming – groups whose values actively embrace the values of mainstream society, and claim to be able to make their members achieve greater success within it. Examples are Scientology and Transcendental Meditation.

Even apparently 'mainstream' religious groups, however, can display characteristics of new religious movements, such as the 'Nine o'Clock Service', with its particular appeal to young people, and its willingness to adopt methods more usually associated with mass youth culture in order to bring young people to the church. Many new religious movements are regarded with great suspicion, and even hostility on the part of the public at large, and it is interesting that the Anglican Church eventually felt that the Nine o'Clock Service was unacceptable in that particular form. (See *sects*.)

New Right: a perspective in sociology which draws upon conservative traditions and insists on the freedom of the individual and the primacy of the free market in all social and economic arrangements. Supporters of the New Right were influential in shaping social and economic policies in the 1980s and 1990s, introducing market principles into large areas of public life. There are various strands within the New Right, from the libertarians, who wish to reduce the power of the *State* to the bare minimum, to the traditionalists, who seek the return of a more respectful and deferential social order. New Right ideas and policies have been criticised for, amongst other things:

- overseeing a centralisation of *power* in the *State* while claiming to do the opposite
- replacing private monopolies with public monopolies
- for destroying any sense of *community* through the introduction of market relationships as the basis of social life.

new social movements: known as NSMs, this is an umbrella term for a whole range of organisations which are expressions of the *identity* of individuals in a post-modern world. They therefore are organised around interests and identities such as gender, ethnicity, sexuality, religious feeling etc. They may also express political identities in the broadest sense such as in the case of *environmentalism*. They stand in contrast to traditional political movements which were class-based.

new town: a post-war housing development in which designated green field sites were given new town status in order to produce housing for overspill populations of the large conurbations. The new towns were given specific advantages in attracting business to their locality and in planning permission to build houses. Though initially aimed at working-class city dwellers, sociologists showed that it was the middle class and skilled working class who took on the relatively low-cost housing in the new towns, leaving the unskilled behind in the new tower blocks of the *inner city*.

new vocationalism: a view of education which sees meeting the needs of the economy as one of its prime functions, and the series of educational initiatives since the late 1970s which have attempted to put this view into practice. Initiatives have included *TVEI, CPVE*, the *Diploma of Vocational Education* and *GNVQ* in schools and colleges, and the *Youth Training Scheme* (YTS) for school-leavers. (See *great debate*.)

new working class: a term which describes those manual workers who live in the south, work in the private sector and own their own homes. It is argued by Crewe amongst others, that this section of the working class can be attracted to Conservatism as a political force as it accords with their material interests. (See *old working class; sectoral cleavages.*)

	Old working class			New working class		
	Lives in North or Scotland	Council tenant	Union member	Lives in South	Owner-occupier	Non-union
Labour	52	57	45	36	39	43
Cons.	23	20	23	38	38	34
Lib/Dem.	13	12	16	22	18	16

Source: Daily Telegraph, 14 April 1992 © The Telegraph plc, London, 1992

Party support among old and new working class voters, 1992 (%)

newly industrialising countries (NICs): those nations in the southern hemisphere who do not easily fall into the category of third world, because they are relatively affluent or relatively developed. Firstly the oil-rich nations such as Saudi Arabia have a great deal of wealth, so that they cannot be seen as 'in poverty'. Secondly countries such as Brazil have high rates of growth and large *gross national products*, which makes it difficult to describe them as undeveloped. (See *tiger economies; Pacific rim.*)

news-values: the ideas and beliefs held by those involved in news-gathering regarding what constitutes good copy. It is argued that there is a professional *socialisation* process for new reporters which inducts them into these news-values and shapes the way that they go out to look for news. Typical news-values are the dramatic, the Royal Family, prominent personalities, and the closer to home the better.

NHS trust: a hospital or group of hospitals which have successfully applied for permission to become independent from district or regional management. Trust hospitals are allowed to raise their own funds, advertise their services and bid for contracts to treat patients. The first trusts were established in 1991, and by 1993 there were almost 300. Supporters of the scheme emphasise the greater freedom and independence it allows, and argue that the overall effect is to improve patient care. However, many medical staff claim that the need to attend meetings and become involved in fund-raising takes time away from the treatment of patients, while a growing concern is expressed that decisions are increasingly taken on financial, rather than medical, grounds. There has also been criticism of the very large salaries earned by some administrators and managers, particularly in the light of the relatively low pay of nurses and junior doctors. (See *National Health Service.*)

niche markets: a term used to describe markets where demand for particular goods is contained within identifiable and often small segments of the population, each requiring variations in a product. Niche markets can be defined by such social characteristics as age group, gender, class, ethnic origin, sexuality, or by considerations of style. Some sociologists would argue that niche markets are heavily influenced by the *advertising industry*, who constantly absorb, create and mould cultural and stylistic trends. (See *pink economy.*)

NIMBY: standing for 'not in my back yard', it is an attitude developed by those who in general approve of developments such as new housing or a home for disturbed children, except when they themselves are directly affected.

nomenclatura: the list of those in communist societies who were candidates for official positions through their membership of the Communist Party. They constituted a powerful block against reform, as their interests were tied up in the perpetuation of the bureaucratic communist system. The overthrow of the communist system in the late 1980s meant that many of the nomenclatura moved into positions of power in the newly privatised industries.

non zero-sum relationship: a situation of *power* between two individuals or social formations, in which all participants benefit from the outcome of the struggle. This view of power is interested in how parties to a struggle manoeuvre to attract support for their position and build up power through the consent of others. The aim of such relationships is the achievement of collective objectives, so that there are no outright winners or losers. Rather, all benefit to a greater or lesser extent. (See *zero-sum relationship*.)

non-manual work: occupations which do not involve heavy physical labour. It stands in contrast to *manual work*, and together these constitute a basic cleavage in industrial societies. Non-manual work is usually seen as *middle class* and would include both *white-collar work* and *professional* work.

non-response: the degree to which the members of a selected *sample* fail to participate fully in the research process. The term is usually applied to those who fail to complete *questionnaires*, particularly *postal questionnaires*. The degree of non-response has an important effect on the *reliability* of the final data, as the greater the degree of non-response, the less representative the sample.

non-statutory services: a range of services available to citizens, the provision of which is not laid down by law, and which are consequently provided largely by voluntary agencies. Examples of valuable but non-statutory services would be those provided by the Citizen's Advice Bureau, the NSPCC and the Samaritans. (See *statutory services*.)

non-voters: the widest category of those who do not cast their ballots in elections. It includes those who are registered to vote and do not and those who were never registered in the first place. Though it is a legal requirement that people register, certain groups are systematically omitted from the *electoral register*, such as the homeless, and those who object to voting on religious grounds such as the Jehovah's Witnesses. The rate of non-registration increased when the poll tax was in operation, as individuals resisted paying the tax and saw the register as one way of being traced.

non-work: a general term which covers all the different types of activity which an individual may engage in outside of *paid employment*. The concept is used because time out of work is not just *leisure* time, but can consist of *work-related time, obligated time* and so on. The area of pure leisure is not therefore equatable with non-work. (See *non-work obligations*.)

non-work obligations: these are the activities outside of work which individuals are under some pressure to carry out, but which retain an element of choice. For example, *housework* is a non-work obligation which is carried out to varying degrees by different individuals. (See *semi-leisure*.)

nonconformity: dissent from the practices of the established Anglican Church. It is applied particularly to Christian denominations such as Methodists and Baptists.

normal science: used by Kuhn to describe the position where science has a dominant *paradigm*, which privileges a particular way of looking at the world and suggests ways of looking for solutions to problems in science. (See *scientific revolution*.)

normative ambivalence: used to describe the usual state of the consciousness of the *proletariat*, where the workers accept the dominant middle-class values of society at one level, but do not operationalise them in any meaningful sense in their everyday work lives. This concept is used to explain the fact that many workers respond to opinion poll questions in terms of dominant values, such as rejecting strikes, but then act very differently in their own workplace, as they 'negotiate' their exception from the no-strike belief.

normative order: the system of rules of behaviour which operates in a given situation. These rules appear as normal to participants and become 'taken for granted'.

normative power: a type of control which relies on the giving or denial of *status* and acceptance to equals or subordinates. This is a very powerful form of control because it relies on the willing participation of those wishing to be accepted. (See *coercion; utilitarian power*.)

normative reference: the process whereby individuals or groups acknowledge a set of *values* as their source of inspiration for the way that they ought to behave. It is often the dominant value system which acts as a normative reference, but for the *working class* it might also be negotiated forms of it.

normlessness: see *anomie*

norms: social rules which define what is expected of individuals in certain situations. They are measures of what is seen as normal in society. Norms operate at several levels, from regulations concerning etiquette at the table to moral norms relating to the prior discharging of duties. (See *values*.)

north-south: an alternative term for the division of the world into rich and poor countries. It emerged out of the fact that the richest countries in the world tend to be concentrated in the northern hemisphere, while the poorest are to be found mainly in the South. Although this division has never been an absolute one, for example, Australia never fitted in easily, developments in the last part of the twentieth century have made the term virtually obsolete. In particular, the emergence of the *tiger economies* of South-east Asia have made such a neat division impossible to sustain.

noumenon: the 'thing-in-itself'; a presumed essence of a phenomenon which lies beneath the surface of reality. The search for the noumenon involves looking for deeper meanings and structures in society and is in contrast to *phenomenology*.

novices: young adolescents who are starting a career in *football hooliganism*, at around the ages of 10–12. They are usually at the front of stands and will usually graduate to become *rowdies*. (See *town boys*.)

nuclear family: a family unit consisting of an adult male and female and their dependent offspring. It is regarded by some sociologists (in particular functionalists) as the basic universal form of *family structure*. Functionalists such as Parsons also suggest that the nuclear family replaced the *extended family* as the dominant form in industrial societies because it provided a better fit, i.e. more closely matched the *needs* of society. The (white) nuclear family is sometimes referred to as the cereal packet family, because of its frequent portrayal by advertisers as the norm. Despite the fact that in 1992 less than four out of ten (39%) of all households consisted of nuclear family units, the notion of the nuclear family remains central to family *ideology*. Sociologists and particularly politicians of the *New Right* frequently express statements suggesting that many social problems in Britain stem from the fact that not enough children are being brought up in stable, two-parent families. The Conservative governments in office from 1979 emphasised their role as the party of the family, and their 'back to basics' campaign of the early 1990s (before it became discredited by a series of political embarrassments) was an attempt to re-establish what they believed were 'traditional family values' among the population.

NVQs (national vocational qualifications): a range of qualifications at different levels based on employment-led standards of competence in the workplace and which enable clear routes of progression. The awarding system is monitored and administered by the National Council for Vocational Qualifications. The aim of the introduction of NVQs was to provide a better-trained workforce and to improve the standard of vocational qualifications. Critics argue that the standards of NVQs still fall short of those applied in other European countries. (See *GNVQs.*)

object: see *subject-object dualism*

objective social class: position in the social *hierarchy* as indicated by some characteristic external to the individual, for example, occupation or income. Sociologists usually employ occupational scales to indicate objective social class. (See *Hall-Jones scale; Registrar-General.*)

objectivity: a lack of *bias*, preconceptions or prejudice. Objectivity is a central concept in the discussion about sociology and science, both in terms of whether sociology as a discipline and sociologists as researchers can be objective, and also the extent to which research in the *natural sciences* is as objective as is claimed. Scientists are not agreed over what it actually means to be objective. Some claim that by following the procedures of the scientific method, objectivity will follow. Others argue that as scientists are subject to values and prejudices as are all humans, it is very difficult to be objective, and therefore values and prejudices ought to be declared publicly. It is often argued that the replication of scientific work acts as a self-righting mechanism which eliminates experimental work which is subjectively tainted. Objectivity then can be applied both to the researcher, and the values and attitudes brought to the research process, and also to the method(s) used and the extent to which they are themselves neutral. (See *positivism.*)

obligated time: see *non-work obligations*

occupation: the job that a person does. Occupations are organised by sociologists into categories, based on their relationship to prestige, income and wealth. They are thus often used by sociologists as indicators of *social class.*

occupational scales: see *Hall-Jones scale; Registrar-General*

occupational structure: the distribution of different types of occupations in a society. The occupational structure is usually conceived in terms of three types of jobs, the primary sector, the secondary sector and the tertiary sector. Changes in the distribution of these have consequences for the stratification systems of modern societies. In particular, sociologists have focused on the decline of the primary and secondary sectors and the rise in the tertiary sector as influencing the class structure of society, so that the *middle class* is expanding and the *working class* declining. Two-thirds of all manual workers are men, while just over half of all non-manual workers are women (Please see the table overleaf.)

Occupation Group	All in employment (millions)
Managers and administrators	4.10
Professional occupations	2.61
Associated professional and technical	2.39
Clerical and secretarial	3.84
Craft and related	3.21
Personal and protective services	2.74
Selling	2.02
Plant and machine operators	2.47
Other occupations	2.16
Manual	10.32
Non-manual	15.08
Total	25.64

(Source: Labour Force Survey No. 14, December 1995)

Employment by occupations, Summer 1995 (not seasonally adjusted)

occupational transition: the change in *occupational structure* since the Second World War, which has involved the expansion of non-manual work and the contraction of manual jobs. The implications of the occupational transition are enormous and sociologists have been particularly interested in effects on *class structure*, with the development of a diamond shaped distribution rather than the traditional hierarchical structure.

Office of Standards in Education (OFSTED): an organisation set up by the Conservative Government to inspect, monitor, and report on the performance of schools. Inspections are carried out by teams of inspectors which include lay members (people who do not have a background in education). It is intended that schools should be inspected at least once every five years. Summaries of the reports must be published, and a copy sent to the parents of every child in the school. Since the first inspections in 1993, £380 million has been spent on OFSTED. Inspectors have the power to 'fail' schools and, if they are not satisfied that sufficient effort is being made to address the issues raised by the inspection, they also have the power to recommend the closure of a school. The first school to be closed under these powers was Hackney Downs, an inner-London boys' secondary school, which was closed at the end of 1995, and the pupils moved elsewhere.

official documents: *documents* produced by official bodies such as governments, local authorities, public commissions of enquiry, health authorities etc., and records such as those of court and Parliamentary proceedings and company records. While providing a rich source of information for sociologists, official documents can themselves be the object of research, i.e. can be examined as the products of various social processes to see the ways in which they reflect particular political or economic interests or viewpoints. As with all sources of *secondary data*, such documents need to be treated with caution.

official goals: the aims of an *organisation* set out in its founding charter, annual reports etc. These are usually vague and general, rather than describing the day-to-day goals of the organisation. (See *operative goals*.)

official statistics: statistical data produced by central and local governments and government agencies. Official statistics are produced in vast quantities, and provide a rich source of information for sociologists, much of it impossible for researchers to obtain themselves, e.g. statistics on the *birth rate*, or *census* data. The critical examination of official statistics as the product of social processes has played a significant part in much sociological writing, in particular statistics relating to crime, poverty and unemployment. (See *hard statistics; soft statistics*.)

old-boy network: a term which describes the continuation of friendship groupings made in the well-established *public schools* and *Oxbridge* into later careers. The existence of an old-boy network is argued to be a major factor in the perpetuation of traditional *elites* in society and the reason why *social mobility* into the top echelons of society is relatively rare. Whether the old-boy network exists or not is very difficult to prove. While clearly friendship does survive graduation from the public schools, there is limited evidence to suggest that these friendships operate to exclude non-public school graduates from important positions in later careers.

old middle class: a term encompassing members of the traditional *professions*, such as lawyers and doctors, and the owners of small and the managers of large businesses. The distinguishing characteristic of the old middle class was either property ownership or self-employment. The old middle class is now said by fragmentation theorists to be subsumed in the *modern upper class* and is distinguishable from the occupations which make up the *new middle class*.

old working class: a division of the *working class* proposed by Crewe. It is composed of manual workers who share certain characteristics, namely living in the North of England or Scotland, living in rented council accommodation, and belonging to a *trade union*. The significance of this group for Crewe was that it represented the traditional *Labour Party* supporters, unlike the members of the *new working class*, who were more disposed to vote Conservative. Given that the members of the old working class are declining in number, it has been suggested that the Labour Party may continue to win a declining share of the overall working-class vote. (See *traditional working class*.)

	Old working class			New working class		
	Lives in north or Scotland %	Council tenant %	Union member %	Lives in south %	Owner-occupier %	Non-union %
Labour	52	57	45	36	39	43
Cons.	23	20	23	38	38	34
Lib/Dem	13	12	16	22	18	16

Source: Daily Telegraph, 14 April 1992 © The Telegraph plc, London, 1992

Party support among old and new working class voters, 1992

oligarchy: see *iron law of oligarchy*

one-nation Tories: holders of a view within the Conservative party which is accepting of the post-war consensus concerning the necessity of a *welfare state* to ensure the wellbeing of all the citizens in society. It is opposed by those on the right of the Conservative party, who stress individualism and a minimalist role for the *State*.

one-parent families: see *lone-parent families*

one-party state: where political control rests in the hands of a single party, with all other political expressions of opinion, organised or unorganised, made illegal. The form of one-party states can take many guises from the apparent plurality of many communist societies, to attempts to force every individual into the ruling party.

one-way convergence: a type of *convergence theory* which argues that all industrialising societies will end up like the United States. One-way convergence has been boosted by the collapse of Soviet-style communism in eastern Europe and the acceptance of the free market in those societies.

ontological security: a term used by Giddens to describe the basic human need that the social and natural worlds which people inhabit exhibit some recognisable pattern which they understand and can operate within with some degree of confidence. It is thus the search for some sort of order and predictability in an uncertain and often changing world.

open enrolment: a system in which there are no formal restrictions on entry to a school or college, i.e. students of all abilities are accepted. It is also used to refer to the part of the *Education Reform Act 1988* which allows schools to recruit extra pupils if there is a demand, rather than having a limit imposed by the local education authorities. It is seen as a way of rewarding 'successful' schools, and encouraging or forcing less successful schools to bring about improvements.

open societies: those where there is a great deal of *social mobility* in the *class structure*. Openness is associated with modern, capitalist societies, which are said to be characterised by *meritocracy*. It is usually through education and certification that individuals can move upwards in the social structure. (See *closed societies*.)

open-ended questions: questions which allow the *respondent* to reply freely rather than providing a set of answers from which to choose. An example of an open-ended question is 'What are your views regarding the changes to your working-hours currently being considered by your management?'. While allowing the collection of much useful and interesting information, open-ended questions pose a problem in their analysis, particularly if a large amount of information has been gathered. One way of dealing with this is to construct broad categories, and to put answers into one or more of these, although if several researchers are involved in this process, there is considerable room for inconsistency, and therefore *bias*. (See *closed questions; coding; unstructured interviews*.)

operational control: power over the day-to-day running of a company. Associated with the managers of large companies, enough power is devolved to them to make decisions to ensure the smooth running of the organisation. However, the *goals* of the organisation, which all activities are tailored to meet, are set by those with *allocative control*. Therefore, while powerful in itself – for example, operational control would include the power to hire and fire workers – it is a secondary form of power.

operational definitions of suicide: the rules-of-thumb used by those with the power of deciding what is a *suicide*. In the case of Coroners, these are several verdicts open to them, and they need to use operational definitions when deciding which verdict to record for any individual case. The problem is that different Coroners are likely to use different operational definitions. Some might record suicide only if a note is left, others more readily might accept circumstantial evidence. This suggests that suicide statistics are *socially constructed* through these operational definitions.

operationalisation: the process whereby a theory or concept is translated into a practical instrument when the sociologist is carrying out research. For example, if sociologists ask people whether they are alienated or not, the sociologist could not guarantee that all *respondents* understood the same thing by this concept. Therefore, sociologists break the concept down into more understandable elements, in order to gain more meaningful data.

operative goals: what an organisation actually does and achieves, as opposed to what the *official goals* might say is the aim. Perrow argued that the operative goals are the more important ones and that they are shaped by the dominant group in the organisation. However, subordinate individuals and groups also bring their own operative goals into the organisation, which may undermine or support its effectiveness. (See *goal-model.*)

opiate of the people: a term used by Marx to describe *religion,* particularly in capitalist society, in which it is used by the oppressed classes to dull the pain of their exploitation. Religion forms part of the *ideological state apparatus,* and has, according to Marx, an important role in justifying the status quo and reducing the threat of revolution by making inequalities appear to be God-given.

opinion leaders: influential groups of people who access information from the *mass media,* digest it and pass it on to members of their circle. They are seen as a crucial part of the process of communication between the media and the mass of people in society. They expose themselves to mass media campaigns by the political parties and use media-supplied information to influence others around them. They are also opinion-formers, but are not in positions of power within the media itself. Rather they become leaders through the confidence of the group around them. (See *two-step hypothesis of the flow of information.*)

opinion poll: the collection of the public's attitudes through *questionnaires,* usually carried out by market organisations, from a carefully controlled *sample* of the population. The main use of opinion polls is to collect voting intentions. They are criticised because they are not always accurate and can therefore give a misleading impression of the state of political opinion.

oppositional leisure: a situation where there is sharp distinction made between work and *leisure.* It is usually associated with hard manual work such as mining and leads to leisure activities which are focused on the pub, sport or the home. The point of such leisure is to take participants' minds away from the arduous and sometimes dangerous nature of their work. (See *extension leisure; complementary leisure.*)

oppositional orientation: associated with the *working class,* these are attitudes opposed to the dominant bourgeois values in society. They have a physical manifestation in working-class organisations such as *trade unions* and the *Labour Party* and are composed of radical and socialist ideas, which stress collectivism against individualism and the importance of state provision of *welfare* for those least able to defend themselves.

opted-out schools: see *grant-maintained schools*

oral history: knowledge of the past gathered from information about a person's life obtained by direct questioning, usually by *unstructured interviews*. (See *life histories*.)

organic analogy: see *biological analogy*

organic solidarity: the way in which industrial societies integrate, i.e. through the inter-dependence of all individuals. This solidarity of difference operated, according to Durkheim, because of the complexity of industrial societies, in which no one individual could hope to provide everything needed for life. Individuals were therefore bound together by their need for each other. (See *mechanical solidarity*.)

organisation man: a term developed by Whyte to indicate that executives tend to develop similar personalities in their search for promotion. The features of organisation man were conformity, loyalty to the company, dedication to work and a preparedness to sacrifice family life for the good of the firm.

organisational culture: the *values, beliefs* and *norms* of a specific organisation which shape the ways in which individual members of the organisation interact with each other to achieve goals. The form of organisational culture varies and sociologists are interested in the ways in which these cultures affect the efficiency of the organisation.

organisational goals: the formal aims of an organisation when it is initially set up. Organisations have a purpose, expressed either formally in their charters, or more informally in the stated aims of members of the organisation. Therefore, organisations are devices for achieving goals. The importance of organisational goals for sociologists is that they represent one way in which the efficiency of an organisation can be measured, that is, by the extent to which it achieves its goals. However sociologists such as Etzioni argue that the formal goals of an organisation should not just be taken for granted. Organisations often have goals other than the formally stated ones. Individual members of the organisation may pursue their own goals at the expense of the formally stated ones. Other sociologists such as Simon argue that there is no such thing as 'the goal' of an organisation, but that goals represent a constraint on the actions of individuals in organisations, which may or may not be referred to when they are justifying a particular course of action they have undertaken.

organisational rules: the regulations which govern the behaviour of those who belong to an organisation. Sociologists have been interested in organisational rules because they were originally identified by Weber as one of the main instruments for ensuring the efficiency of organisations. In *legal-rational organisations*, there is a need for the co-ordination of activities to achieve maximum efficiency. Weber argued that one of the main ways co-ordination was achieved was through obedience to rules. However, this approach has been criticised by other sociologists:

- Blau suggests that rules can be *dysfunctional* for organisations, as well as functional. He argued that rules cannot cover all situations and the generation of new rules to meet challenges often creates contradictions and confusion. Moreover, rules can be employed by individuals in ways other than intended by those who created the rules and in pursuit of the individual's own gaols, rather than *organisational goals*.
- Perrow argues that, although rules are devised by *management* to control the actions of workers through co-ordination, the rules are double-edged

swords. While the rules may define what workers are supposed to do, they also create opportunities for workers not to do other things, which are beyond the remit of the rules. This allows for example, workers to disrupt an organisation by *working-to-rule* in a strict way.

- Ethnomethodologists, such as Zimmerman, argue that rules should be looked at situationally, that is, examined in the context in which they are actually employed. Only by so doing, will sociologists understand how the rules actually operate in an organisation. Rules are therefore a resource for members of an organisation to be employed or not employed as it suits their purposes.

(See *situational rules.*)

organisations: bodies of people, persisting over time, which are set up to achieve specific aims, and which are characterised by having a *structure* and a *culture*. The study of organisations is one of the central aspects of sociology, because individuals inhabit or deal with organisations throughout the whole of their life. Organisations differ from just random groups in various ways:

- Organisations survive the departure of individual members of the organisation. That is, organisations have a history which can precede an individual member.
- Organisations have goals, often written into their founding charters which guide the activities of members of the organisation.
- Organisations have decision-making and enforcement procedures, which seek to control the activities of members of the organisation.
- Organisations are characterised by the allocation of formal *roles* and duties to participating members.

Organisations have their *formal* and their *informal* aspects. There are also many different types of organisation. (See *bureaucracy, mechanistic organisation, organismic organisation.*)

organised crime: a concept used to describe the activities of groups which make their living from breaking the law. It is usually associated with extortion, drug-dealing and prostitution and the groups are run through the use of violence and are often in conflict with other organised criminals.

organised labour: see *trade unions*

organismic organisations: a term used by Burns and Stalker to describe flexible, responsive organisational structures. This type of organisation was in contrast to *mechanistic organisations*, and was distinguished by its ability to respond rapidly to conditions of change. The features which make such organisations responsive are said to be:

- a willingness by participants to contribute to solving problems according to their expertise
- a reflexive attitude by the organisation, whose members constantly review performance
- a commitment by members to achieve the overall *organisational goals*
- a network structure rather than a *hierarchy* of control
- a communication system in which information flows freely, not just from the top down.

Burns and Stalker saw organismic organisations developing whenever markets were no longer secure, and wherever the demand was for individualised, customised goods. They were therefore more appropriate to the production conditions of *post-modernity*. (See *niche markets*.)

ostracism: a sanction used by workers, in which offenders are ignored until they come into line with the wishes of the group.

other: developed by Foucault to indicate marginalised groups in society, who are characterised by mainstream society as somehow alien. This alienness is represented by the concept of the other. The other are pushed aside by powerful forces through processes such as *stigmatisation* and *marginalisation*.

other-worldly orientation: used by Pfautz to indicate individuals who focus on the after-life in dealing with the world around them. Social action is therefore shaped by belief in the *supernatural* and the continuation of life after death. (See *this-worldly orientation*.)

out-working: a system of production, where certain processes are given out to low-paid workers working from home. The system is symbiotic, if exploitative. The out-worker may be tied to the home because of *childcare* commitments, while the employer is relieved of the need to provide factory space for workers. There is also a strong element of the *black economy* operative in out-working. (See *homeworking*.)

outing: a strategy employed by some militant gay groups of making public the homosexuality of prominent figures, who would otherwise have preferred their gay-ness to remain private. The tactic is controversial and has split the gay community as to the ethics of forcing unwilling gays into the open. Those in favour of outing argue that they only 'out' those who have taken public stances against homosexuality.

over-representation of the poor: a reference to the fact that in the criminal sta-tistics, the *working class* appear disproportionately to the *middle class*. This is not because of their greater criminality, but because they are more likely to get caught, be processed and end up as a statistic.

over-urbanisation: the conditions of insecurity which affect many of the inhabi-tants of cities in the *third world*. The term does not mean over-population or over-crowding in these cities, although these may be aspects of insecurity. The inse-curity stems from the circumstances of *migration* to third world cities, where many peasants are forced off their land and have to seek work in urban areas. However, the economies of third world cities are geared to overseas, rather than local markets, with the result that there is 'growth without development', so that *unemployment* and *under-employment* in the cities is rife. As a consequence, adequate housing, sewerage and water supplies are absent from some areas as shanty towns or *favelas* develop.

overt curriculum: see *curriculum*

overt participant observation: see *participant observation*

overt research: research in which both the identity of the researcher and some-thing of the nature of the research are known to the objects of that research. The term is usually applied to overt *participant observation*.

ownership and control debate: see *separation of ownership and control*

Oxbridge: a word used to refer to two of the most prestigious universities in Britain, namely Oxford and Cambridge. While entry to Oxbridge has been widened, particularly since the end of the Second World War, and the proportion of undergraduates from state schools has increased, many Oxbridge students are still the products of the *public school* system. Oxbridge graduates make up a significant proportion of those in high positions in politics, business and the arts.

Oxford mobility study: a large-scale survey of *social mobility* carried out by Goldthorpe and the Nuffield team, who argued that they found a considerable increase in rates of social mobility since the Second World War. The increase was largely the result of changes in the *occupational structure* and was leaving a self-recruiting, more *homogeneous* working class behind, as occupational change slowed down. The major feature of social mobility according to the Oxford study was that it was *forced mobility*.

P

Pacific rim: a term describing the geographical location of the expanding and dynamic economies of the world, which heralds a shift in the global balance of *power*. The centre of world power has traditionally been Europe and the United States, with the 'centre' of the power bloc somewhere in the Atlantic. However, it is argued that production is shifting globally to produce a new centre of power somewhere in the Pacific, with the most dynamic economies of the world situated around the edge of the Pacific Ocean. This is partly to do with the move in United States production from the traditional north-east to the more dynamic west and south, partly to do with the predominance of Japan in the world economy and partly to do with the most rapidly developing countries in the world, such as Taiwan and South Korea, being situated there. The big unknown in this apparent development is what will happen to the enormous market represented by Communist China. If China opens up fully to trade, or develops an effective industrial sector itself, then the Pacific Rim is likely to form a powerful new focus for the world economy.

paid employment: used as a term to distinguish *work* in the *formal economy* from other types of work, such as domestic labour. One of the distinguishing characteristics of paid employment is the existence of an employer, although this does not take into account those who are self-employed.

panel studies: a form of *longitudinal study* usually associated with research into political attitudes and opinions. A selected group of people (the panel) is repeatedly tested for changes for changes in their political views and opinions, often to judge the impact of political broadcasts or campaigns.

panopticon: a type of prison building which enabled the warders to oversee every aspect of the prisoners' lives. It was associated with a view of prison which sought to survey the whole of the inmates' existence through organisational as well as architectural features. Foucault saw the panopticon as symptomatic of the increased *surveillance* in modern societies, aided by *rationality*.

paradigm: a set of ideas and beliefs (particularly in *natural science*) which provide a consensual framework or model within which practitioners operate. A paradigm defines existing knowledge, the nature of the problem or problems to be investigated, the appropriate methods of investigation, and the way in which the findings should be analysed and interpreted. Alternative views of the world are rejected by the dominant paradigm, whose *gate-keepers* obstruct the promotion of alternatives. An example of a paradigm might be the Newtonian or Einsteinian conception of the universe. The concept is particularly associated with Kuhn, who argued that scientific knowledge was neither objective nor cumulative, but developed through a series of paradigm shifts, during which existing paradigms were challenged and eventually replaced. Some sociologists argue that sociology as a discipline is in a pre-paradigmatic stage, as there is no consensus regarding the nature of society and how it operates, nor a generally accepted model of how sociological research should be conducted. The concept has been criticised because Kuhn uses it in many different ways and it ends up being a relativistic concept. (See *scientific revolution*.)

parasuicide: see *attempted suicide*

parent-teacher associations: organised groups in schools with representation of both parents and teachers, more likely to be found in primary and middle schools than secondary schools. These associations are often involved in fund-raising activities, but recently some have begun to take a more actively political role, with organised campaigns over issues such as class size, the *national curriculum*, the level of government funding in schools and proposals to close schools, especially village schools.

parental aspirations: the hopes and expectations of parents for their children, particularly in terms of educational achievement. Research by Douglas found that those children whose parents hoped that they would go to *grammar schools* and do well gained a higher proportion of grammar school places than children of the same measured ability whose parents did not have such high aspirations. It is often assumed that working-class parents have lower aspirations for their children than do middle-class parents, but a considerable number of working-class parents are extremely keen for their children to do well at school, seeing it as a way out of the working class and the chance to have a 'better life'.

parental attitudes to education: the views of parents concerning education and its value, and their view of the role of the school and the whole education process. It has been shown that parental attitudes can have a significant effect on the progress of the child.

parentocracy: both the increasing power given to parents within the education system, and their willingness to exercise it. The shift to parent power has come with the enhanced powers of governing bodies and the increased representation of parents upon them. Parental power is also claimed to emerge from the ability to choose which schools their children attend. Critics argue that governing bodies are limited in what they can do by central control of resources and that parental choice in effect leads to popular schools being able to choose which children to have, re-introducing selection by the back-door.

parity of esteem: a term from the Education Act of 1944 meaning equality of *status*. It was used with reference to the three types of secondary school created under the *tri-partite system*, arguing that the schools should be separate, but equal. In practice, *grammar schools* were regarded as having much higher status than either of the other types of school, particularly secondary modern schools.

Parliament: composed of two Houses, the Commons and Lords, this is the legislative body of the Government, charged with the passage of laws. It is dominated by the majority Party in the Commons and those who take the Conservative whip (generally support the Conservative Party) in the Lords. Members of Parliament are sent by the *electors* in constituencies to represent their interests in the House of Commons.

participant observation: a form of sociological research in which the researcher takes a *role* in the social situation under observation. The fact that the researcher is conducting research may be known to the other participants, in which case the participant observation is known as 'overt', or the role of the researcher may be such that her/his true identity and motive may be kept secret, in which case the method is known as 'covert participant observation'. Both methods have their advantages.

Overt research allows the researcher to ask questions, and no one would be surprised if s/he were seen taking notes. However, it can be argued that covert research allows the researcher even greater insight into the *values, meanings* and behaviour of those under study, as they are unaware that they are being studied. Participant observation also has its problems or, as critics would say, its weaknesses. Some of the main difficulties are:

- it is a relatively costly method, as most studies are conducted over a period of time
- it is impossible to say with certainty that members of the group studied are representative
- overt participant observation may lead to the *Hawthorne effect*
- covert participant observation leads to particular problems with regard to the keeping of accurate notes without being observed, and also of possibly having to remember lengthy conversations
- the stages of covert participant observation have been referred to as 'getting in, staying in and getting out', and all three of these can pose problems for the researcher
- the researcher may find it difficult to maintain *objectivity*, particularly after spending a considerable length of time with the group, i.e. may risk '*going native*'.

Despite these problems, the method is a valuable one, and has given particular insight into groups which would have been difficult, if not impossible, to study any other way, such as religious *sects,* teenage gangs, drug-users and *football hooligans.*

participation rate: a term usually applied to the proportion of 16-year-olds who remain in full-time education or training after the official school leaving age. The Government has been trying to increase the participation rate in Britain, as it is currently lower than that of many other industrial societies.

participative groups: a concept developed by Likert to denote a form of work organisation based on production by groups of workers rather than the individual on an *assembly-line.* Likert argued that organisations should be made up of interlocking work groups, who take responsibility for producing goods from start to finish, as opposed to the specialisation of the assembly-line. He argued that such organisation allows the self-actualisation of individuals, and thus increases efficiency. (See *job enlargement.*)

participative leadership: a form of *management* in which the managers are prepared to involve themselves in the everyday activities of the workers. While they continue to manage, it is with a 'hands-on' attitude, so that they know and understand the problems workers face. Similarly, workers are encouraged by participative leadership to become involved in the running of the firm. This stands in contrast to impersonal leadership, which is separated from the workers in time and space.

participatory democracy: see *direct democracy*

particularism: a situation where personal relationships are important in social actions. Particularism was a feature of traditional societies, where in particular family relationships formed the basis of public life. In particularistic societies, relatives and personal friends gain preferment over strangers. (See *universalism.*)

partisan alignment: the situation where support for the two major parties in Britain is stable and class-based, so that the *working class* largely support the *Labour Party* and the *middle class* support the *Conservative Party* in the main. It is important to note that, even in a situation of partisan alignment, significant fractions of a class will support a party which does not represent their supposed *class interest*. (See *duopoly*.)

Year	Conservative		Labour	
	Non-manual	Manual	Non-manual	Manual
1964	62	28	22	64
1966	60	25	26	69
1970	64	33	25	58
1974 Feb	53	24	22	57
1974 Oct	51	24	25	57
1979	60	35	23	50
1983	55	35	17	42
1987	54	35	20	45
1992	54	34	23	46

Voting by social class 1964–1992 (percentages)

partisan de-alignment: the process whereby electoral support for the two main parties, Conservative and Labour, diminishes and third parties increase their electoral basis. (See *class de-alignment; political identification*.)

party image: used to describe the way that voters see the different parties in stereotypical form. Party managers attempt to manipulate party images to create favourable views amongst the electorate and party images are argued by some psephologists to be powerful influences on the way people vote. A crucial aspect of a party's image is how united or divided it appears to be.

parvenus: meaning newcomers, it was often used as term of abuse for rising moneyed groups in society, who did not have the breeding of the *aristocracy*. It is therefore associated with the lack of *status* attached to money-making in societies dominated by traditional *elites*.

passing: a situation in which a sociologist undertaking covert *participant observation* is successfully able to adopt a *role* within the group, and keep her/his identity as a researcher secret from the other members.

paternalism: a system of social relationships which takes as its analogy the protective care which a father has for his children. It has both political and industrial forms. In the political manifestation, relationships between an authoritarian *elite* and subordinates are conceived as a type of 'father-knows-best' situation, in which decisions are removed from subordinates and concentrated in the authority figure, who then exercises this power in the interests of the subordinates. In the industrial form, employers take a wider interest in the welfare of their workers than just the wages they give them. In an advanced form, employer activity might extend to building workers' houses, providing education for their children and *leisure* opportunities for their families. Critics argue that even this benevolent form of paternalism is more about control than care, with only sanctioned leisure activities and particular forms of education being provided.

pathological: used to describe any feature of social life which may be fatal to society's survival in its consequences. The term was originally applied by functionalists for characteristics which undermined an assumed *value-consensus* in society. To functionalists, anything which did not contribute to the integration of society was likely to lead to disintegration and was therefore defined as pathological. For example, one-parent families were often seen by functionalists as pathological.

pathology: the study of the causes and symptoms of disease, both physical and mental. Durkheim also applied the term *'pathological'* to any form of deviant behaviour.

patriarchal ideology: a set of beliefs (and the practices which stem from them) which assumes that males are in some way superior to females, and that it is therefore natural and right that men should enjoy a more privileged position in society than women, particularly in terms of *power* and prestige. (See *patriarchy.*)

patriarchy: a form of society in which males are the rulers and leaders and exercise power, both at the level of society as a whole and within individual households. Feminists argue that the existence of a patriarchal system explains the multiple disadvantages experienced by women, as the supporting *ideology* leads to the assumption that male power and dominance are somehow 'natural'. Marxist feminists see patriarchy as inextricably linked with *capitalism,* because of the benefits it brings to the system. Women are used as a *reserve army of labour.* They produce the future workforce and, by their unpaid labour, nurture and support the male workers, a cost which would otherwise fall on *capital,* i.e. would need to be met in the form of higher wages.

patriation of profits: the process whereby profits made in the *third world* by *transnational companies* are transferred back to the TNC's country of origin. This is often achieved despite laws in the third world country which limit the amount of profits which might be sent back. Creative accounting processes, which are legal but against the spirit of laws prohibiting excessive patriation, are used to effect the transfer. Often, the dependence of a third world country on the activities of the trans-national companies ensures that patriation is achieved with little hindrance.

patrilineal: a form of kinship system in which descent is traced through males. It is argued that modern Britain has a basically patrilineal system as, although relatives are traced through both the male and the female lines, it is customary for married women to take their husband's surname, which is then passed on to the children. In the aristocracy, hereditary titles are passed through the male line, ignoring females, and in the succession to the throne, younger brothers take precedence over their sister(s).

pattern variables: a technique associated with comparative analysis, in which specific aspects of two societies are compared to see how similar or different they are. The way in which the similarities and differences pan out creates a pattern, which can be used to generalise about the effects of social changes, such as *industrialisation.* The technique is particularly associated with Parsonian *functionalism,* which attempted to establish the differences between traditional and modern societies through determining the pattern variables.

pattern-maintenance and tension-management: see *latency*

peasant economies: associated with pre-industrial and undeveloped societies, these economies are dominated by small-scale agricultural production, in which a significant proportion of the population gain their living from the land, mainly from small plots inherited through the family. The productive capacity of such economies is limited, but traditional agriculture such as this is often able to sustain large populations, because the people have worked out how to produce sufficient crops without causing long-term damage to the land.

pecuniary model: a *frame of reference* in which the holder sees society as differentiated into groups according to the money each possesses. Society is thus seen as a system of subordination and superordination in which money, rather than status or class is the defining characteristic. (See *power model; prestige model.*)

pedagogy: the science (or art) of teaching. Pedagogy is often divided into two broad types, traditional/conservative and progressive/liberal. The former has a view of teaching which has an emphasis on structure and control, with the teacher as the fount of knowledge, while the latter puts greater emphasis on the active involvement and participation of pupils, with the teacher seen more as one who creates a framework within which learning can take place. (See *chalk-and-talk; discovery learning; experiential teaching.*)

peer group: a group of people sharing common characteristics, usually age, but also possibly gender, occupation or ethnic group, who perceive themselves, and are perceived by others, as forming a distinct social group. In sociology the term is usually applied to adolescents and studies of peer groups have focused particularly on schools and leisure-based groups, including gangs. Peer groups can exercise considerable control over their members, and this *peer group pressure* is often much stronger than pressure exercised by other people, such as parents or teachers.

peer group pressure: the control exercised by a *peer group* over its members to achieve conformity. The most powerful form of peer pressure is usually the threat of exclusion from the group.

penology: the study of prisons. In sociology, prisons are seen as an interesting *case study* of a *total institution*, as well as an arena where ideological struggles over the role of penal institutions are carried through.

perestroika: or 'reconstruction', this was the part of the process of reform instituted by President Gorbachev in the Soviet Union during the 1980s, which ultimately led to the collapse of *communism*, and which focused on changing the economic principles which had governed Soviet industry since the 1917 revolution. (See *glasnost.*)

perinatal mortality rate: the number of still-births and deaths of infants under one week old per thousand births. (See *infant mortality rate.*)

periphery workers: in post-Fordist *modes of production*, those unskilled workers who are employed on a casual, often part-time basis to carry out non-essential parts of the production process. They might be involved for example in cleaning or catering work, often through a sub-contracting or *self-employment* arrangement. They are low paid and the firm has little obligation to them, so that they can be employed and dismissed easily. (See *core workers.*)

permeability: the extent to which the social distinctions which operate outside of an organisation are maintained within a *total institution*. For example, in a prison, gender does not permeate at all, while in an army camp, differences between men and women might be maintained in the allocation of tasks.

persistence theories: the arguments concerning *stratification,* which suggest that social changes such as *occupational structure* movements have not seriously altered the *class structure* of modern capitalist societies. In particular, these explanations suggest that the evidence concerning the distribution of *wealth, power* and opportunity shows that there has been no significant long-term movement towards a more equal society. Instead, the important divisions in society, such as between owners and non-owners, and between manual and non-manual workers, have continued to remain large. Indeed, the gap between the classes has arguably increased, because of the growth in *unemployment,* the reduction in *progressive taxation* and the decline in welfare services. (See *fragmentation; realignment theories.*)

personal documents: a term referring to a wide variety of papers and other documentary material which can be used as a valuable source of *secondary data.* Almost any personal document can be of interest to a sociologist, but among those most frequently used are letters, diaries, school reports, photographs, birth, marriage and death certificates, rent books or other *documents* relating to property, and wills. As with all secondary data, personal documents need to be treated with caution, but they can reveal significant insights, particularly into the past.

personal service professions: a term devised by Halmos to describe that group of occupations which deal with human beings and their social problems, in areas such as education, social work and mental health. This group aspired to professional status, but did not have that claim recognised by others and was not granted professional powers by the Government. The practitioners sustain a professional self-image, which separates them from other lower occupational groups, but which does not guarantee them entry into the ranks of the traditional professions. (See *new professions; aspiring professions.*)

perspectives: ways of looking at social phenomena from a particular view-point. A perspective is usually organised around a specific principle, which distinguishes it from other perspectives. Perspectives thus represent partial ways of looking at the social world. While perspectives are important in sociology, they are not all-encompassing because:

- it is frequently difficult to place an individual in a perspective, as sociologists often draw upon a number of perspectives in their work
- perspectives are continually changing as the world changes and as they are influenced by other perspectives
- individual sociologists can have long careers in which their view of the social world may change as they further develop their theories

pervasiveness: the extent to which an organisation seeks to control the lives of its participants. A *total institution* will be very pervasive, while a factory will be less pervasive. Some sociologists have argued that there are cultural differences between similar organisations throughout the world. For example, Japanese industrial organisations are more pervasive than their British equivalents.

petty bourgeoisie: in Marx's formulation of social classes, these are the self-employed, or those who employ very few labourers in their economic activity. They are associated with the shop-keeping and independent artisan class, who form a buffer between the *bourgeoisie* and the *proletariat.* Because of their intermediary position, they were seen as being pulled in both directions, sometimes taking a revolutionary role and sometimes a conservative stance in the political questions of the day. They were thus economically determined, but ideologically and politically fluid. (See *dominant level.*)

phenomenology: a *perspective* drawn from the work of Husserl and popularised by Schutz, it starts from the premise that sociology should be concerned with what appears to us on the surface of things and not with hidden depths to society. Our knowledge of the social world should therefore be based on things as they are, not things as we would like them to be. Schutz argued that each individual had a unique biographical situation, which constituted a stock of knowledge known only to the individual. So while we all know things different from anyone else, when we interact we assume that we can ignore these differences and act from our commonsense understandings – what we assume everybody knows. (See *everyday knowledge; multiple realities.*)

physical control: a type of *power* exercised by *organisations,* which includes force or the threat of coercion. In capitalist societies, it is government organisation which keeps a monopoly over physical control. (See *material control; symbolic control.*)

pillarisation: a term used to describe the division of a society vertically into, for example, different *ethnic groups.* Each section reproduces the usual social divisions to be found in society, but has an existence which is separate from other pillars. The classic example of a pillarised society is Belgium, which is divided into Flemish and Walloon sections, each having for example its own socialist and conservative parties.

pilot study: a small-scale test of a particular piece of research, particularly, but not exclusively, a *social survey,* in order to test its design and the nature and quality of the data generated. Particular emphasis is placed on testing the method of *sampling* and the questions used in the *questionnaire* or interview schedule, as flaws in the design of these are likely seriously to affect the quality of the research.

pink economy: a concept used to describe the spending power represented by the lesbian and gay populations in liberal Western democracies. With the emergence of a gay and lesbian community from the 1970s onwards, industry has become increasingly aware of the purchasing power of a group of people who are often to be found in well-paid occupations and who usually have few children to support. The existence of this group with a large disposable income has made them a target for industry, with the result that in the 1990s, positive gay and lesbian advertising images began to emerge. (See *niche markets.*)

Plaid Cymru: the Welsh Nationalist Party, which seeks self-government and eventually independence for Wales from the United Kingdom. Though committed to the democratic process, there is an extra-parliamentary nationalist group in Wales, which has been responsible for direct actions against English home-owners in Wales.

playing it cool: a reaction to being placed in a *total institution,* in which the inmate becomes indifferent to the organisation. It was developed by Goffman to describe the inmate who just stays out of trouble and 'does time'. (See *situational withdrawal.*)

Plowden Report: the 1967 report of the Plowden Committee, chaired by Lady Plowden, into primary schools in England and Wales. The report focused on the educational effects of social disadvantage, and recommended a policy of *compensatory education* for socially-disadvantaged children. The Report resulted in the creation of *Educational Priority Areas.*

plural societies: where there are distinct sections of the population in a society, distinguished by ethnic, linguistic or cultural features.

pluralism: the view of *power* in society, which sees it dispersed amongst many different groups and individuals. While there are several versions of pluralism, they are united by the rejection of any concentration of power in the hands of a single *elite*. Pluralists argue that decision-makers are acted upon by many different *interest groups*, whose activities often cancel each other out, but who are attempting to influence the political powers to make policy decisions in their favour. The *state* here acts as a referee between many different groups and makes decisions in the best interests of everyone in society rather than in the interests of any consistently favoured group. Pluralism has been criticised because:

- it has a very narrow definition of power, restricting it to political power
- it tends to see the operation of all interest groups as equally influential, when in reality some are more powerful than others
- it neglects the ability of powerful groups to prevent controversial issues being raised in the policy-making arena in the first place

(See *unitary elite theory.*)

pluralist theory of industrial relations: an approach which sees the firm as a miniature democratic state in which the opposing 'parties' of management and workers seek to pursue their own interests within the limits of the rules of *collective bargaining*. They argue that industrial relations are therefore typified by shifting alliances between different groups within the firm, who constantly manoeuvre for position in pursuing their own *goals*. Critics suggest that this is to ignore the historic imbalance between management and workers, in which the former can usually rely on the power of the *State* and the media to support their case.

polarisation: the process whereby opposites are driven further and further apart. It is particularly applied by Marxists to *social classes*, which they believe become more and more divided from each other by the logic of machine production. Marx believed that the owners of the *means of production* were forced by the logic of *capitalism* to increase the *exploitation* of the *proletariat* in order to maximise profits. The proletariat responds to this increase in *expropriation* by rejecting capitalism altogether and looking for revolutionary alternatives. (See *immiseration.*)

policing policies: the strategies adopted by the forces of the law to control the population, and in particular the criminal population. The two major alternatives in Britain are rapid response, where the police use fast vehicles to answer calls for help, and community policing, where a more preventative 'bobbies on the beat' stance is taken. The policing policy has political and social consequences which sociologists have been interested in investigating.

political correctness: a movement more mythical in the conception of its opponents than real, this is an attitude of mind which attempts to eliminate discrimination on the grounds of gender, ethnicity, ability or sexuality in word and deed. It is connected to the idea of *positive discrimination* and has led to the *whitelash* in the United States where the majority groups have reacted against attempts to privilege groups discriminated against.

political culture: the ideas and beliefs which underpin and inform the political system in a society. Sociologists have distinguished between different types of political culture, from the authoritarian to the democratic. The development of political cultures is processual often taking long periods to emerge and constantly changing. However, at certain times in a society's history, the political culture may change rapidly through revolutionary events.

political deference: an acceptance of the legitimacy of the Government whatever its political complexion. The most common example of this type of deference is towards the President of the United States, which has declined under the unprecedented personal attacks on President Clinton. (See *ascriptive socio-political deference; socio-cultural deference.*)

political identification: a concept used to describe the situation where individuals strongly support a particular *political party*. When the political identification of a social group is strong (for example, such as when the working class identify with the Labour Party and the middle class with the Conservative Party) alignment is said to take place. (See *class de-alignment; partisan de-alignment.*)

political immunisation: the theory that the older generation has been proportionately more Conservative, not simply because they are older but because of political influences when they were young. The theory suggests that political ideas formed in youth are held fairly constantly into old age, being immune to alternative influences. Therefore it is important in explaining any generation's political preferences to examine the situation which existed when they were young. (See *political senescence.*)

political participation: the involvement of individuals and groups in a number of electoral situations and organisations concerned with *power*. The level of participation is said to be lower amongst women and the young as measured by propensity to vote, to join and be active in political organisations and to stand for election. (See *female conservatism.*)

political party: an organisation of individuals united in a common purpose of electing Members of Parliament to form a *government* to introduce policies which the party supports. Political parties are therefore organised 'appetites for power' which encompass coalitions of individuals with different ideas, but who usually agree upon a principle of politics. These principles are often symbolic or encapsulated in vague concepts such as 'freedom' or 'socialism'.

political power: decision-making capacity which is held by those occupying positions in the machinery of *government,* either at the national or the local level. (See *institutional power; economic power.*)

political senescence: the theory that as people become older, they become more conservative. This drift to the right is associated with nostalgic longing for a golden age in the past, when the streets were safe. It is based on the calculation that the old vote Conservative proportionately more than the young. The idea has been criticised as a static analysis of voting, which sees a specific older generation, brought up at a time when the Labour Party was relatively new, and extrapolates this to include all old people. Analysis of voting behavious does, however, show different patterns among different age groups. (See *political immunisation.*)

Party	18–24	25–34	35–44	45–64	65+
Cons	37	36	37	42	49
Lab	34	39	37	34	31
Lib/Dem	21	17	20	17	13
(Source: N.O.P.)					

Voting by age in the 1992 general election (%)

political socialisation: the process whereby individuals are initiated into the dominant values and traditions of a society, including those values which define the legitimate processes of politics and the way that *power* is exercised. While the family is the main agent of political socialisation there is little overt indoctrination into political traditions. Rather, the traditions and *values* of a society are absorbed through the expression of general sentiments towards political symbols and personalities.

politics: is in a narrow sense the workings of the *State*, including the operation of national and local *government,* but in a wider sense politics is concerned with *power* and the ways in which individuals, groups and organisations are able to create history through the application of power.

polity: a political unit, usually the *State*. The term is taken from the Greek word for city-state, which was the important political unit in ancient Greece.

pollution: according to the Hindu laws of *dharma,* that which occurs when something of higher purity comes into contact with something of lower purity. Once pollution occurs, a cleansing ritual is needed. Notions of pollution, and therefore avoidance of those things likely to cause pollution, were important features of the *caste* system.

polyandry: a rare form of marriage in which women are legally permitted more than one husband at a time. (See *polygamy; polygyny.*)

polygamy: a pattern of marriage which allows more than one legal spouse at a time. (See *monogamy; polyandry; polygyny.*)

polygyny: a form of marriage in which men are legally allowed more than one wife at a time. This is the more usual form of *polygamy.* The balance between the sexes means that in polygynous societies few men have more than two wives and, of course, some men have none. (See *polyandry.*)

polysemic: used to denote that texts are open to many differing *audience* interpretations, and that their meaning also shifts over time. This is important, for example, where new producers re-interpret classic texts, such as the works of Shakespeare. Changing fashions and ideas constantly affect the *meanings* attached to the same words, for example the line between pornography and eroticism is constantly shifting. (See *encoding; decoding.*)

polytheism: a religious belief which accepts the notion that there is not one, but many gods. *Hinduism* is an example of a polytheistic religion.

popular culture: is used by sociologists to describe the mass features of the media in post-modern societies. The term was derived from the debate amongst broadcasters in the inter-war period over the relative merits of *high culture,* supported by the *elite* of which media controllers were then themselves a part, and developing programmes which would appeal to the taste of the masses. Popular culture has been adopted by post-modernists, who have detached it from the implication of being an inferior form and made it an important focus for sociological study in its own right.

population: the number of residents of a defined geographical area. In 1901, the population of the UK was 38.2 million. At the 1991 *Census*, the estimated population was 57.8 million, projected to rise to 62.1 million by 2031. The table below shows the distribution of the population of Great Britain (England, Scotland and Wales) by ethnic group. The data are obtained from the question in the 1991 Census on membership of ethnic group, the first time such a question has been included in the Census. (See *ageing population; migration; survey population.*)

Ethnic group	Number	Percentage
White	51,874,000	**94.5**
Indian/Pakistani/Bangladeshi	1,480,000	2.7
Black Caribbean, Black African and others	891,000	1.6
Other ethnic minority groups	645,000	1.2
All ethnic minority groups	3,016,000	**5.5**

(Source: Social Trends 1994)

Population of Great Britain by ethnic group 1991

population theory: identifies population growth as the main cause of *third world* poverty. Due to western medical advances, the *death rate* is falling in the third world, while the *birth rate* remains relatively high. As a result, population theorists argue that the increase in population in the third world hinders *development* as resources are channelled into *welfare* policies rather than development projects. Despite the diversion of resources into welfare, population growth it is argued outstrips the ability of the third world to produce enough food to feed its population, with the result that starvation and occasional famine result. The policy implications of this approach suggest that birth control measures are needed in the third world, regardless of the cultural or moral objections there may be to them. Critics of this theory come from the *New Right* and the Left. New Right theorists argue that population growth is, by itself, not the problem. They suggest that history tells us that development reduces the rate of population growth, and therefore there should be a de-regulation of *capitalism* in the third world to allow for rapid development. This would then solve the population problem. Such an approach is particularly to be found among the *New Christian Right*, who are hostile to *abortion* and, in some cases, suspicious of artificial birth control methods. From the Left, conflict theorists argue that it is not the size of the third world population which is the problem, because it consumes a minority of the world's resources. Rather, it is the consumption patterns of the developed world, with its emphasis on environmentally costly meat, which leads to periodic shortages in the third world.

populism: a political philosophy which appeals to the mass of the people as the source of all authority. Populist movements oppose the status quo and the governing *elite* and are often nostalgic and nationalistic in approach.

positive abstention: those who do not vote in elections because of a definite decision to withhold support. This may be because of dislike of a particular candidate, a protest against a particular policy or a simple disenchantment with the whole democratic process. (See *negative abstention.*)

positive correlation: see *correlation*

positive discrimination: these are measures designed to boost the prospects of disadvantaged groups by, for example, employing someone because of their membership of a particular social category rather than because they have the skills or qualifications for the job. Positive discrimination is illegal in Britain because of equal opportunities legislation. The most that is allowed under the law is 'positive action', whereby past discrimination is counter-balanced by non-discriminatory training programmes. (See *affirmative action.*)

positive stage: one of Comte's three stages of human development, this was the ultimate one, which was characterised by ideas that the natural and social worlds could be explained through rational thought and the application of scientific principles. Comte believed that by knowing things positively, the world could be controlled and shaped for the better. (See *theological stage; metaphysical stage.*)

positivism: the view that phenomena, of whatever description, should be studied in a scientific manner. The insistence on science stems from the attempt by thinkers to find out things for certain. The search for certainty comes from the desire to be able to change things for the better. Thus, sociological positivists argue that, by applying scientific principles of research to the study of society, sociologists will be able to put forward proposals for social change which will lead to a better society. Critics argue that this is untrue, because science cannot help with the moral choices that social change necessarily involves. Positivism has also been attacked from a number of other positions:

- that science itself is not as objective as it claims, and its 'truths' are as ideologically tainted as other systems of thought
- that positivism has not lived up to its promise in sociology, in that universal laws have not been developed
- that positivism is not an appropriate vehicle for the study of human society, because humans have free will and are not subject to invariate laws.

post-capitalism: an assumed development in the future in which a non-socialist state will emerge, in which the historic conflict between capital and labour is put to one side and a new sense of unity, based around the acceptance of the free market as the good society in action, will be the defining characteristic.

post-colonial pedagogy: the idea that those who are subject to racist practices and ideology should be developing in an active way the teaching challenges to racist patterns of behaviour in the classroom. This would empower disadvantaged groups by allowing them to speak with their own voice. It has been criticised for being at a high level of abstraction, with very little to offer in the way of practical strategies to challenge racist behaviour and ideas.

post-feminism: with the collapse of certainty in the post-modern world, this represents the fragmenting of the feminist movement into strands divided by particular identities, either political as with the socialist feminists or cultural as with the black feminists or sexual as with the lesbian feminists. Behind this fracturing is a rejection by the post-feminists that there is only one way to be a feminist woman in post-modern societies. Rather the emphasis in post-feminism is on the many different ways in which women can construct their identities drawing upon a whole range of *gender codes.*

post-Fordism: in contrast to Fordism, the organisation of production in a flexible and responsive way, so that constantly changing consumer demands can be met swiftly. Post-Fordism relies on computer technologies to produce and therefore there is a change in the type of worker needed by industry. Workers in a post-Fordist factory need to be flexible and multi-skilled, not resistant to changes in productive practice. (See *Fordism.*)

post-imperialism: the situation which emerged after the liberation of the colonies of the west, in which the exploitative relationships between coloniser and colonised were replaced by the beneficial development activities of the *multi-national companies.* Post-imperialism stands therefore in contrast to *dependency theory* which saw the continuation of exploitation by less direct means.

post-industrial society: a concept developed by Bell to suggest that a new type of society was emerging from industrial societies, which is characterised by the *professionalisation of everyone.* In Bell's view, industrial societies were changing under the impact of new technologies and a new society was developing which was predominantly *white-collar.* An implication of a post-industrial society is the end of class-based *conflict* and the emergence of a more unified, status-differentiated society. Other terms associated with the post-industrial society are Lane's *knowledgeable society* and Etzioni's *active society.* These convey the prominent position given to the *professions* in the post-industrial society, which Bell also characterised as the 'expert society'.

post-modernism: an approach in sociology, as well as other disciplines, which stresses the uncertain nature of societies, in which all certainties have been challenged and undermined, so that the conditions of lived existence occur in a global and fractured society in which there are no absolute rules or explanations. Post-modernism stands in contrast to most other sociological theories in that it rejects the Enlightenment project of seeking to understand and control society through the application of rational thought. To the post-modernist, societies cannot be understood in a rational way, because they are subject to constant change.

post-modernity: the condition of western society at present, it is represented by the dissolving of all certainty in *social structures,* as the temporal and spatial boundaries which define modernity break down and are replaced by fluid and fractured social relationships. The growth of a global economy and culture are central to the post-modern condition, where global events have local effects and vice versa. (See *modernity.*)

post-structuralism: theories which reject the idea that there are any underlying logics or structures in the social world. As far as the post-structuralists are concerned there is only the surface world, with no hidden depths. The proper study for sociology is therefore the world as it is experienced rather than some hypothetical underlying stratum. (See *structuralism.*)

postal questionnaires: printed *questionnaires* sent to *respondents* through the post rather than the questions being asked directly by an interviewer. Postal questionnaires have the obvious advantage of being relatively cheap, and provide a useful method where the *sample* may be distributed over a very wide geographical area. They are also helpful if the answers need reflection, or if the information needs to be looked up. As there is no one asking the questions, there can be no question of interviewer *bias*. However, postal questionnaires also have significant drawbacks. The main ones are:

- There is a generally low *response rate*, sometimes as low as 20%; this, of course, significantly affects the randomness, and therefore the *reliability*, of the sample.
- There is often a long timespan between the first and the last question-naires received back; this again can introduce bias, as those completing their forms later will have been exposed to information and events not experienced by the early returners.
- There is no guarantee that the questions have been answered by the select-ed respondent; s/he may have consulted with others, or even given the questionnaire to someone else to complete.

Nevertheless, postal questionnaires can form a useful method of research, particularly when conducting research among groups of people who may be difficult to reach by other methods, or who may not have the time to answer questions when an interviewer calls.

potlatch: a form of ritual and competitive gift-exchange found among indigenous people of the American Pacific which developed to the stage where huge quantities of possessions were ceremonially destroyed as a demonstration of wealth before rivals. These would then reciprocate with displays of their own. The economic value of possessions was therefore considered less important than the pursuit of social *status*. It has been suggested that potlatch was a response to a period of rapid social and economic change among the participating peoples.

poverty: a state in which, for an individual or a family, there is either a lack of resources sufficient to maintain a healthy existence (i.e. *absolute poverty*) or a lack of resources sufficient to achieve a standard of living considered acceptable in that particular society (i.e. *relative poverty*). Poverty is a very controversial concept and sociologists fail to agree on either its definition or on how it should be measured.

poverty cycle: an explanation of how *poverty* may be transmitted from one generation to the next, suggesting that one aspect of poverty leads to another, with the cycle repeating itself in succeeding generations.

Some critics of this view regard it as overly deterministic, and point out that it is possible for children from poor households to escape from poverty, often through educational success. However, few would disagree that the material deprivations of poverty make it more difficult for such children to succeed at school and in the job market than it is for their peers from more privileged backgrounds. Supporters of the view argue that it shows clearly the need for more generous benefits for impoverished households, particularly those with young children. (See *poverty trap*.)

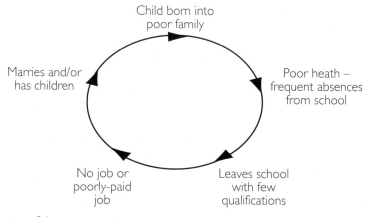

Representation of the poverty cycle

poverty line: a level of *income* below which an individual or household can be deemed to be in poverty. The concept is a controversial one, as it is almost impossible to achieve a consensus regarding what the chosen level of income should be. Within the member states of the European Union, the poverty line is usually drawn at 50% of the average income in that particular society. However, when Rowntree defined a poverty line for his 1901 study, he took the lowest possible level of income which would cover the minimum necessities for 'the maintenance of merely physical efficiency', or what we would call subsistence level. This notion of a very basic level of income was also used by Beveridge when he drew up National Assistance scales in the 1940s. Although he agreed that such a minimum does not by any means constitute a reasonable living wage, this approach has remained the standard in Britain for setting benefit levels. (See *consensual view of need; index of deprivation.*)

poverty of life style: a way of defining and measuring poverty which tries to take into account the actual quality of life possible on a certain level of *income*, rather than simply taking the amount of money available. (See *consensual view of need; index of deprivation; poverty line; relative poverty.*)

poverty trap: a situation in which a number of factors combine to prevent a person or household from escaping from poverty. Such factors include:

- low-paid workers obtaining a pay rise may discover that this raises them above the tax threshold, leaving them with the same income as before, if benefits are stopped
- the lack of any sizeable disposable income results in the poor buying goods in smaller quantities, losing the benefits of bulk-buying, and lack of transport often prevents their using cheaper out-of-town superstores
- it is very easy to fall into debt, and a fixed, low income makes it very difficult to clear the debt
- the poor often borrow their money from private 'loan sharks', who may charge an exorbitant rate of interest
- poverty leads to ill-health, making it more difficult to find and keep employment

- *means-tested benefits* can mean that an increase in income leads to loss of eligibility for some benefits or having benefits deducted pound for pound, making it very difficult to achieve a real increase in income

power: the ability of an individual or group to achieve their own aims against opposition. There are many different forms of power, but it is a basic dimension of social *stratification*. The distribution of power in society is a matter of debate amongst sociologists, with some arguing that there is a concentration of power at the top of society and others who argue that there is a widespread distribution in society. Power is not just confined to the formal political arrangements but exists wherever there are relationships between individuals, for example between a cohabiting couple.

power elite: the group believed by unitary *elite* theorists to dominate society, through their ability to control the important institutional positions in society. The elite is composed of those at the top of the great institutions of society, such as the *government,* the military, universities, industry etc. The power elite hold broadly similar views and share similar interests, so that policy decisions are made in their favour. They also have considerable influence over access to elite positions, so that they can pass on their privileges. The notion has been criticised by Marxists as denying the importance of economic power in society and by pluralists for assuming that there is some sort of gigantic conspiracy going on. (See *ruling-class; pluralism.*)

power model: a *frame of reference* in which the holder views society in terms of 'them' and 'us'. It is a dichotomous model of society often held by traditional proletarians in the *working class*. Oppositional in outlook, the power model views society as primarily a class-divided society. (See *prestige model; pecuniary model.*)

powerlessness: one of the conditions of *alienation* identified by Blauner as the inability to control one's own work. This has several dimensions, including the inability to influence management decisions, to determine the conditions of work and the pace of work. (See *meaningless; isolation; self-estrangement.*)

practical consciousness: our knowledge of social conventions and rules which we enact, even where we cannot articulate them. We thus speak grammatically without being able to explain the rules of grammar to one another, because of our practical consciousness. (See *discursive consciousness; unconscious motivation.*)

practical constraints: factors which may influence, or even prevent, the use of a particular sociological method. Practical constraints would include time, money, ease of access to those the researcher wishes to study, and the amount and source of funding. Gender and age can also act as constraints; in certain research situations a woman can go and ask questions in places a man could not, and *vice versa.* Some covert *participant observation*, such as that involving teenage gangs, would be difficult for an older sociologist to conduct, unless a suitable *role* could be found. (See *ethical constraints.*)

practical reasoning: used by ethnomethodologists in connection with scientific enquiry to suggest that scientists do not just produce theories separate from their everyday practices, but in the context of their specific social contexts. Scientists are therefore said by ethnomethodologists to be non-objective in their scientific work. Science is produced through the grounded experience of scientists and not as an objective process.

practical theorists: a concept used by ethnomethodologists which argues that everyone in society is essentially a sociologist in their everyday life, because they are constantly trying to understand and explain the social world that is going on around them. Because ethnomethodologists believe there are few if any common understandings between people, social life is a constant struggle to understand one another. It is this search for meaning which makes us all theorists of the practical world. (See *ethnomethodology; glossing; indexicality*.)

pragmatism theory: an explanation of *industrial relations* which looks for commonsense solutions to any problems. In identifying fair solutions to industrial problems it tends to draw upon management's perspectives, which are defined as:

- how to better utilise labour
- how to curb unofficial *strikes*
- how to control shop stewards

pragmatists: see *secularists*

praxis: in Marxist sociology, the unity of theory and practice. Marxists use praxis to describe the freedom of men and women to alter their real circumstances by the working through of ideas in the material world. Given the economic determinism of Marxism however, priority is given in praxis to the real material circumstances that people find themselves in rather than to the ideas they hold. Attempts to change economic circumstances therefore come out of those economic circumstances. Ideas about change are not 'free-floating' but socially constructed in the economic milieu that individuals inhabit.

pre-conditions for take-off: used by Rostow to define the situation which *undeveloped* societies needed to obtain before they could make the transformation to a developed state. The crucial elements of the pre-conditions are what happens in the agricultural sector, which must be re-organised to generate a surplus for investment in the industrial sector. In Britain, this took the form of the enclosure movement, where larger landowners took away common land and enclosed it with fences to form larger agricultural units. A transport system must also be developed, able to deal with the demands of an industrialising society. In Britain, this was the development of the canal system, but in other societies it might be roads, rail or river transport. (See *five stages of economic growth; take-off*.)

pre-industrial societies: used as a general term for those societies which have not undergone an *industrial revolution* and remain agriculturally based, it is more specifically used to refer to societies in the past rather than societies in the present-day. Sociologists argue that the transformation which *industrialisation* effected meant that there was a contrast between pre-industrial and industrial societies in many areas of social life which could be described by a series of dichotomies. Therefore the notion of a pre-industrial society is important for the contrast it provides with an industrial one, rather than in its own right.

pre-school education: this topic is the subject of much political debate regarding the degree to which this should be, and is, provided by government. Britain has fewer nursery school places, both state-provided and in the private sector, than most other European countries. The government has proposed that pre-school education for four-year-olds should be provided by offering the parents of these children vouchers, to be redeemed within the state or private sector. Critics argue that there are insufficient places available, and those local authorities who currently provide places will in effect lose money, as they will only receive additional funding for 'topping up'.

pressure group: an organisation formed for the purpose of influencing the political process either through the defence of members' interests or in the pursuit of particular policy. It thus represents sectional interests to the decision-making centres of government. The existence of pressure groups is a central part of the democratic process as they act as a channel of communication between the governed and the governors. The crucial difference between *political parties* and pressure groups is that the latter do not seek election. Rather they seek to influence the outcome of elections by supplying information to the electorate and then trying to influence those elected through lobbying.

prestige: in sociology this term is usually attached to occupations and is the honour attached by society to a particular job. Occupational prestige is associated with the functionalist perspective, which sees it as a basic dimension of *stratification* in highly specialised societies. The particular prestige attached to any job is determined by the *values* in society and its functional importance in contributing to the maintenance of society as a whole. In operational terms, prestige is usually ascertained by asking *representative samples* of the population to place a list of occupations in rank order of importance. Those which were ranked most highly are given the highest prestige and those at the bottom the least. Critics of the concept suggest three problems with it:

- Prestige scales usually end up as a defence of the *status quo*, because the sample already has the existing rank order in their heads. This is why different groups produce very similar rank orders. It is not because there is some inherent merit in these occupations, but because they are already defined as worthy.
- The use of prestige is often vague and encompasses many other indicators of class, such as *income*.
- In building a prestige scale individuals tend to privilege their own and similar occupations, so that any sample bias is inevitably exaggerating the importance of particular groups of jobs.

prestige model: a *frame of reference* in which the holder sees society as divided into many layers of differentiated *status groups*. It is usually associated with the *middle class* and the attitude that sees society as relatively open, with those at the top of society deserving their positions on account of their merit or *talent*. (See *meritocracy; pecuniary model; power model*.)

primary data: information collected by the sociologist at first hand, using any appropriate method.

primary deviance: identified by Lemert as the initial deviant act, which may or may not be noticed by others, and which may or may not be subsequently processed as a deviant act by the forces of formal or informal *social control*. (See *secondary deviance*.)

primary health care: health care delivered directly to the client in the community. The care could be delivered by a GP, a midwife or a community nurse.

primary labour market: see *internal labour market*

primary poverty: see *Rowntree*

primary sector: in the *occupational structure*, these are jobs in the extractive industries such as mining, farming and fishing. (See *secondary sector; tertiary sector.*)

primary socialisation: the learning of *values* and forms of behaviour in the front-line agency of the family. It is usually associated with the acquisition of basic attitudes and social skills, which form the foundation of civilised living.

primogeniture: a system of inheritance in which the eldest male inherits the family property and any title. It is largely associated with the Salic laws of western Europe which were dominant in pre-20th century Europe. More recent notions of inheritance have included all sons and daughters within their regulations.

private medicine: health care which is not directly funded by the *National Health Service* but which is purchased by the patient, often through a private health insurance scheme. Supporters of private medicine argue that it relieves pressure on NHS waiting lists, and that freedom of choice is a democratic right. Critics point to the fact that many private patients are treated by NHS-trained medical staff in beds or wards in NHS hospitals, thus benefiting from a hidden subsidy. As some doctors work partly for the NHS and partly in private practice, it is argued that this lengthens the waiting time for NHS patients. Another argument put forward against private medicine is that it helps to widen the *health gap* between rich and poor.

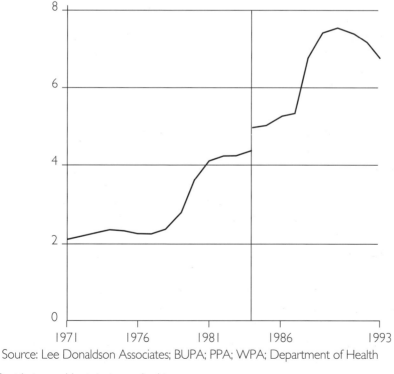

Source: Lee Donaldson Associates; BUPA; PPA; WPA; Department of Health

People insured by private medical insurance

private schools: see *independent schools*

private sector: those industrial and service activities which are funded for profit by private individuals or private organisations. The sector has grown enormously during the 1980s and 1990s as the government has sold previously nationalised industries and utilities to private ownership. (See *privatisation.*)

private sphere: used by many feminists to indicate the world of domesticity, with which women have ideologically been identified. Feminists have used the concept to show how women have been marginalised in society, through their association with the private rather than the public. Though neither the private nor the *public sphere* is the sole domain of either gender, it is the linkage ideologically which has led to the invisibility of women.

privatisation: a government policy which is concerned to reduce the *public sector* as much as possible, through the transfer of industries, activities and utilities into private hands. The aim of the policy is to reduce the burden on public finances and introduce the disciplines of private enterprise into what were seen as complacent industries. Critics have argued that it has resulted in the creation of private monopolies, with price rises beyond those which might have been expected if industries and utilities had remained in public hands, and without any efficiency gains for the consumer. Controversy has also ranged over the large remuneration which directors of previously publicly-owned utilities have been awarded. (See *nationalisation.*)

privatised working class: identified by Goldthorpe and Lockwood as a distinct section of the *working class* in post-war affluent Britain, members had withdrawn from public political activity into home and child-centred activities. As work had become less salient for the privatised working class, they had retreated into their homes and were less likely to spend leisure time with their workmates. This shift towards the home was accompanied by an increase in *DIY* activities and an increase in consumption of domestic goods. (See *affluent workers.*)

probability: a statistical term referring to the mathematically-calculated chance of a particular event occurring.

probability sampling: a sampling technique in which every unit in the *survey population* has a known chance of being selected.

problem of consciousness: in Marxist sociology, this is the gap between the objective material conditions of the class and the subjective manifestations in the minds of members of the class. Though members of the *working class* exist in a state of exploitation, in which they are denied their basic humanity, this does not lead inevitably to a revolutionary outlook. Marx argued that there were several reasons why there is no inevitability of revolutionary consciousness amongst the working class:

- Within the working class, there were differences in objective material conditions, from the large impersonal factory to the small workshop, in which the worker had personal contact with the capitalist.
- The chances of individual *upward social mobility* drain off the most able of the working class, defusing their revolutionary potential.
- The *ruling class* uses ideological power to consolidate its rule.
- The working class can wrest concessions from the ruling class, which allows an acceptance of the system through an alleviation of *exploitation.*

problem of order: a philosophical problem which asks the question why people obey the state when their natural instinct is to gratify their desires at any cost. The problem is that if individuals are interested only in themselves, why do they then form a society in which their individual passions are curbed by law and government force? (See *state of nature.*)

productivity: in economic terms, output produced per worker, but in sociological terms, productivity is a key *concept* underlying much of the work done in industrial sociology. Many industrial sociologists have been employed by industry to research ways of increasing productivity. For example, *work motivation theories* are based on the premise that if sociologists could uncover what makes workers happy, they could contribute to increasing productivity in the firm. (See *cow sociology.*)

profane: part of a dichotomy suggested by Durkheim, in which everything in a society can be viewed as either *sacred* or profane. Things which were deemed 'set apart and forbidden' were defined by Durkheim as 'sacred'; everything else in society was therefore profane. This distinction has been criticised as overly simplistic.

professional associations: the organisations which govern and control those occupational groups which have been granted professional *autonomy.* Though the professional associations have very similar attributes to the *trade unions*, in that they defend and promote their members' interests, Millerson argued that they were multi-functional compared to the single function of trade unions. In particular, professional associations have a different ideological basis from trade unions and adopt different tactics to pursue their aims. Thus, professional associations use *certification* to enhance prestige, while trade unions often use *industrial action* to achieve their goals. (See *social closure.*)

professional authority: the respect and acceptance which the public give to members of the *professions* on the basis of their superior knowledge and expertise in a particular area. Professional authority is the reason why professionals are listened to and their advice taken. Their knowledge-base is such that professional advice is more likely to be effective in solving problems than lay knowledge. This does not mean that professional authority is unchallengeable, but that professionals will usually be listened to with respect. *Clients* may challenge professional authority publicly through the professional body or by changing their practitioner.

professional crime: law-breaking committed by individuals and gangs for whom crime is a way of life. Professional crime is actually a small percentage of the total criminal activity, but represents one of the most visible and newsworthy aspects. (See *street crime.*)

professional employees: a concept developed to describe the position of those members of the traditional *professions* who are also employed in bureaucracies. Sociologists suggest that this position creates problems for the traditional professional. For example, the professional behaviour is theoretically governed by the code of ethics of the profession. Yet, in a *bureaucracy* the professional is also subject to the rules and discipline of the employer. These can sometimes be in conflict. A good example is the position of doctors in the National Health Service, where the ethic of service can conflict with the budgetary limitations imposed by health service managers.

professional referral: a situation in which a *client* is referred by one professional (e.g. a GP) to another (e.g. a consultant). (See *self-referral*.)

professionalisation: the process whereby an occupational group seeks to obtain professional powers for itself. Professionalisation is one of the ways in which *upward social mobility* is sought, and along with it, increased earnings and *status*. The process is particularly used by those occupational groups which have an individual skill to offer society, or esoteric knowledge supported by a theoretical framework. (See *social closure*.)

professionalisation of everyone: a concept developed to describe a hypothetical future for work, in which all workers would have the skills, training and rewards associated with today's *professions*. Friedman, for example, argued that as the manual labour force declined through *automation*, there would be a growth in knowledge-based service industries. Manufacturing itself would be dependent on skilled engineers and scientists, rather than routinised manual labour. Friedman argued that the large professionalised sector would be the new power in *organisations* and challenge *management*. Because of their knowledge, these professions would be able to resist *bureaucratisation* and would generate *organic solidarity*, ushering in a new era of prosperity and freedom. Critics argued that this was an optimistic view of the future and that *automation* does not leave the professions untouched. Indeed, the processes of *fragmentation* and *routinisation* affect all occupational groups and will change the traditional professions as much as *de-skilling* manual work. (See *de-professionalisation*.)

professions: types of occupation, such as law and medicine, which are self-governing, in that the representatives of the members of the occupation set the regulations which govern the behaviour of members. It is difficult to define a profession exactly as there is so much variation between different professions. However, most professions have the following characteristics:

- Their skills are supported by a systematic body of knowledge.
- Their possession of this knowledge gives them *authority* over clients, who do not possess the knowledge.
- The profession is given certain privileges by the community, such as the duty of confidentiality and the right to be judged only by other professionals.
- Their behaviour is regulated by a code of ethics.
- There is also a professional *culture* in which the professional is given certain *status* and symbols of authority.

A crucial aspect of a profession, as against other occupations, is that it is granted powers not usually given to other jobs, such as the power to regulate entry to the profession, and to carry out the long training needed to give practitioners the knowledge they need to practise effectively. (See *semi-professions*.)

progress: the movement towards a better existence in society. The idea of progress was a central feature of the *classical sociologists* and of the sociological project. Progress was seen as the outcome of sociological examination of the social world, as people came to understand and therefore control the forces at work in society. The concept has come under attack by post-modernists for being a particular ideological view of history and hopelessly optimistic.

progressive taxation: *direct taxation*, such as income tax, based on the principle that the more *income* or *wealth* one has, the more tax one pays. Progressive taxation is one of the ways in which a society may achieve a greater equality of distribution of income and wealth. (See *regressive taxation*.)

progressive teaching: see *discovery learning; experiential teaching; pedagogy*

Project Headstart: see *compensatory education*

proletarianisation: the process whereby *non-manual work* comes increasingly to resemble *manual work*, and non-manual workers adopt the attitudes of the *working class*. The concept is used across a wide range of white-collar and professional occupations, but has specifically been employed in considering the changes in clerical work since the nineteenth century. The evidence used to support proletarianisation includes the greater unionisation of *white-collar workers* and their willingness to employ the trade union tactics traditionally associated with manual workers. The causes of proletarianisation are many and varied, and include greater *bureaucratisation* of work, the *de-skilling* of work through computerisation and the emergence of universal literacy, which has destroyed the esoteric nature of clerical work. The concept of proletarianisation has been much criticised for over-simplifying social processes by equating changes in working conditions to changes in consciousness. It also denies the power of *status* considerations holding sway over white-collar workers.

proletarianisation of the professional: a concept developed by Oppenheimer, who argued that the *bureaucratisation* of work inevitably leads to a deterioration in working conditions for professionals, until they are subject to the same work discipline as manual workers. Features of bureaucracies which lead to proletarianisation are:

- the replication of factory conditions for professionals, such as the imposition of hierarchy, the establishment of bureaucratic rules and crucially, increased specialisation of tasks
- control over work is increasingly removed from the professional
- financial and status advantages are eroded as bureaucracies operate within strict budgets
- bureaucrats rather than professionals increasingly determine treatment

The main result of proletarianisation is the increasing *unionisation* of the professions. (See *de-professionalisation*.)

proletariat: one of Marx's major classes in capitalist societies, it technically includes all those who do not own the *means of production*. Because this definition would also include some members of what is seen as the traditional *middle class*, it has been criticised for providing a very crude division of society. It has therefore become used mainly to describe the *working class*, (that is manual workers) especially when it is used in a political sense. Marx believed that it would be members of the proletariat who would bring about revolutionary change in society, as they resolved the contradictions inherent in capitalist societies.

promotional pressure group: an organisation formed to promote a particular interest or cause through political lobbying and informing the general public about the issue. These groups tend to be pro-active and seek to effect a change which they see as being in favour of their particular cause. (See *protective pressure group*.)

proportional representation: an electoral system in which the ratio of Members of Parliament matches the percentage of the vote that each Party attracts. While this is said to be a fairer system than the *first-past-the-post*, it tends to lead to a proliferation of smaller parties and to potentially unstable coalition governments.

protective pressure group: an organisation formed to defend its members' interests in dealing with political organisations. Such groups would include *trade unions,* professional associations and the like. They tend to be defensive organisations reacting to events rather than promoting a particular course of action. (See *promotional pressure group.*)

protest vote: where the supporters of a particular political party register their dissent from current performance, either by abstaining or through voting for another party. Protest votes tend to appear most strongly in bye-elections when the Government is not going to be directly affected and protest voters tend to revert to their preferred party at the *general election.* This often means that large swings in bye-elections are not sustained in subsequent general elections.

Protestant ethic thesis: a term used by Weber to refer to a set of beliefs particularly associated with the Calvinist religious *sect* in the 17th century. Weber was interested in exploring the origins of the 'ethic' of *capitalism,* and suggested that these lay in the beliefs of the Calvinists. According to these, worldly work was seen as a 'calling', rather like a religious vocation, and it was therefore a duty to treat work as a way of honouring God. The Calvinists believed in predestination, that is, that from the point of creation, God had chosen those who would be 'saved'. As there was no way in which these decisions could be changed, and no way of knowing in this life whether or not one was among the chosen, Calvinists began to seek for signs of God's favour in their lives. Worldly success was seen as a sign of 'election' to the chosen. Emphasis was placed on a sober, thrifty life style, and on the 'stewardship' of goods rather than their use in displays of *conspicuous consumption,* and therefore a belief in *deferred gratification* in the form of the re-investment of profit rather than spending it on worldly goods. Weber argued that this particular set of beliefs, and the consequences which stemmed from them, provided the right social and economic climate for the development of what he called 'modern capitalism'. Weber used his argument about the relationship between the Protestant ethic and the '*spirit of capitalism*' to show that, under certain circumstances religious belief could be instrumental in bringing about *social change* and was not necessarily, as Marx had claimed, a conservative force in society. However, Weber's views have been criticised, and a 1959 study of the origins of Calvinism in the Zurich Reformation shows that modern capitalism appears to have already been in existence at the time. Nevertheless, Weber's views form an important part of the debate regarding the role of *religion* in society.

proto-typicality: a methodological term, suggesting that the *sample* under study by the sociologist points the way to how similar groups will behave in the future. The most famous proto-typical research was carried out in Luton on *affluent workers* by Goldthorpe and Lockwood. They argued that the workers in Luton were at the cutting edge of societal developments and the consciousness that they exhibited would be the consciousness that all affluent workers would eventually develop.

prudent sociability: the basis of morality according to Goffman, this is also known as 'tact' and implies a calculation of the most careful course of action before an *actor* acts.

prudential interest theory: an answer to the *problem of order*, this states that it is in people's self-interest to come into society for mutual protection against the cruelty of nature. It is thus a rational calculation of individuals to form social order. (See *competitive interest theory*.)

psephology: the study of voting behaviour.

pseudopressure group: an organisation which exerts political pressure on behalf of others, rather than in its own right. Political lobbying organisations are pseudo-pressure groups as they are paid by others to try and influence the outcome of decisions regardless of their own particular beliefs.

public ownership: see *nationalisation*

public schools: prestigious independent schools belonging to the *Headmasters' Conference*. Public schools have a long tradition in Britain, and while their intake may be slightly less exclusive than in the past, they continue to educate the sons (and latterly some of the daughters) of the wealthiest and most powerful families. Many prominent public figures in politics and business are the product of the public school system. (Note that in America, however, the term public school refers to schools within the *maintained sector*.)

public sector: those activities which are organised and funded by national and local governments. Apart from the direct activities of the *state* such as welfare benefit provision, it has included, in the past, large areas of nationalised industries and an important section of the housing industry. The public sector has traditionally been conceived as an area of support for the *Labour Party*, which is seen as more favourable to the provision of public services than the Conservatives. *Privatisation* of industries and utilities, the decline of council housing, and the tendering out of traditional State activities has led to a massive decline in the public sector in the 1980s and 1990s. (See *private sector*.)

public sphere: used by feminists to indicate the world beyond the home, of paid employment, politics, religion and other public activities. It is identified by feminists as a mainly gendered sphere, in which men dominate and in which women are tolerated at best. (See *private sphere*.)

pure deviant: defined by Becker as one who engages in rule-breaking activity and who is also publicly labelled as such. (See *falsely accused; secret deviance*.)

purposive action: doing something with an aim in mind, this is the distinguishing feature of *action*, as opposed to behaviour. Action theory defines action strictly in this way so that instinctive behaviour is not included. Interactionists believe that to understand action it is important to access the intentions of the person carrying out the action. (See *action*.)

Pygmalion effect: the way in which expectations and consistent behaviour by social actors can shape the behaviour of others in social relationships to produce a new situation. The name of the concept refers to the title of a play by G.B. Shaw, in which a cockney flower-seller is passed off as a duchess. Its use in education is taken from a study by Rosenthal and Jacobson of an American elementary school, entitled 'Pygmalion in the Classroom'. Having tested all the children's *IQ*, the researchers selected a *sample* of children at random, and informed the teachers that these were children of high academic potential. A year later, Rosenthal and Jacobsen returned and again tested the children's IQ, finding that those in the randomly-selected sample had, on average, made greater gains in IQ score than the non-sample children. A similar interpretation of the importance of teachers' expectations can be placed on findings from Douglas' longitudinal study, in which children of the same measured IQ at 8 years of age showed improved scores at age 11 if they had been taught in upper streams, and lower scores at age 11 if they had been taught in lower streams. It was also used by Barnard in the sociology of the family to describe the re-shaping of a woman's identity by the male, when she enters into marriage. She argued that this often leads to stress and depression as her aims are subordinated to those of her husband. (See *self-fulfilling prophecy.*)

Q

qualitative data: data which express, usually in words, information about feelings, *values* and attitudes. Such data are usually associated with qualitative research methods such as *participant observation, unstructured interviews* and the use of certain kinds of *personal document,* but qualitative data may also result from *open-ended questions* used in *structured interviews* and *questionnaires.* Interactionist sociologists in particular favour the collection of qualitative data. In practice, much research contains both qualitative and *quantitative data.*

qualitative research methods: methods which will result in mainly *qualitative data.* They include *observation, participant observation* and *unstructured interviews.* If using *secondary data,* the sociologist would be most likely to refer to *personal documents.* (See *quantitative research methods.*)

quality assurance systems: systems set up to ensure that certain agreed standards of quality are met throughout an organisation as a means of ensuring client satisfaction. Many such systems are now to international standards, e.g. ISO 9000.

quango: an acronym for 'quasi-autonomous non-government organisations'. These are bodies which are financed at least partly from public funds, and whose senior appointments are made by the government. The *Training and Enterprise Councils* are examples of quangos. Criticisms of such bodies stem from the fact that they often have a great deal of *power* and influence, receive public funding, yet are managed by non-elected officials. Many critics argue that quangos should be much more accountable for their decisions and actions than they are at present.

quantitative data: data which can be expressed in numerical form, e.g. numbers, percentages, tables. Positivist sociologists argue that the collection of quantitative data is less prone than qualitative data to *bias* arising from the subjective involvement or interpretation of the researcher. However, many interactionist sociologists claim that much quantitative data and the methods by which they are obtained, such as large-scale *social surveys* and *structured interviews,* contain both value judgements and subjective interpretations.

quantitative research methods: methods which will result in mainly *quantitative data.* They include *social surveys* and *structured interviews.* If using *secondary data,* the sociologist would be most likely to refer to *official statistics.* (See *qualitative research methods.*)

quantum theory of religion: the belief that everyone has religious feeling or a spiritual dimension which must be fulfilled by one means or another. The implication is that, if formal religions are rejected, then other *functional equivalents* are substituted. It allows no possibility that an individual might believe that no world other than the material one exists.

quasi-experimental method: see *comparative method*

questionnaire: a widely used tool in data collection, both in sociology and market research, which consists of lists of questions. The term is usually applied to formal, standardised questionnaires used in large-scale *social surveys.* The questions used may be *closed, open-ended* or a combination of both. Where a large number of *respondents* is involved, the closed questions are likely to be pre-coded, that is, each possible response is given a code number, which makes it easier and quicker to process and analyse the replies. (See *coding; sample survey.*)

quota sampling: a *sampling* method in which the researcher/interviewer has a list of characteristics required of *respondents,* and a given quota of each to select and interview. The usual characteristics include sex, age bands, marital status, occupation and/or social class, and may also include ethnic group. A researcher's quota, then, might be 50 males and 50 females; within each sex 20 manual workers, 20 white-collar workers and 10 professional workers, and within each occupational group a given number of people in particular age-bands. Quota sampling is not properly random, and is not as reliable as *probability sampling,* particularly if the sample size is small. It is quite widely used in market research, and less so in sociology.

QWL: quality of working life, this is an approach to organisational theory in which the experiences of all participants are examined to develop more productive ways of engaging participants in fulfilling the goals of the organisation. (See *job enrichment.*)

R

race: an imprecise term, the origins of which stemmed from a belief that it was possible to divide human populations into groups having distinct inherited physical characteristics. One view saw different racial populations as evidence of the process of evolution and natural selection, with some races being biologically more 'advanced' than others. These beliefs led to the idea that biological differences were accompanied by other innate differences, such as in *intelligence* and behaviour patterns. This view is now discredited, but sociologists are interested in how the concept of 'race' is often used to justify the oppression of one group by another, such as the treatment of the Jews by the Nazis, or the system of apartheid in South Africa. (See *ethnicity; eugenics; racism.*)

race relations: an approach to the study of ethnicity which dominated British sociology from the 1950s to 1970s, and which begins from the position of seeing ethnic minorities as strangers in a host country. The assumption behind this is the immigrant-host framework, in which there is a mythical view of a peaceful society, where existing race relations are harmonious. Any race relations problems can therefore be attributed to new immigrant groups failing to adapt to the host society. This position has been criticised for its assumption of a unified host society and for therefore blaming the victims of *racism* for their own disadvantage.

race spies: used by the *New Right* to criticise teachers who adopt anti-racist strategies in their classrooms and indicating a policing of thought and deed about racial issues which allows only the expression of *politically correct* ideas and behaviour. The implication is that anti-racist education is a totalitarian tool to impose a straightjacket of thought on young children.

racism: a belief in ideas about *race* which are often translated into negative feelings and discriminatory or hostile actions against members of the supposed 'racial group'. Racism can be expressed as individual racism, such as the use of negative and abusive language or even physical assault, or institutional racism, whereby members of a group may be discriminated against, such as in access to housing or employment on the grounds of their perceived 'race'. Another term for this is 'racial discrimination'. (See *race; ethnicity.*)

radical: a political position which presses for fundamental change in existing social arrangements. Though often associated with left-wing ideas, radicals can be also right-wing. The former tend to support change in favour of the lower classes in society, such as re-distribution measures, while the latter tend to be authoritarian and nationalistic favouring a strong uniform social order.

radical criminology: see *National Deviancy Conference*

radical feminism: a branch of *feminism* which holds the belief that men, and the patriarchal system they have established, are the origin and perpetuators of women's oppression. Men are also seen as the main beneficiaries of this oppression, primarily through the institutions of *marriage* and the *family*. There are differences within the radical feminist perspective, ranging from a belief that women can co-exist with men, provided that men are willing to overthrow *patriarchy*, to the belief that men are the 'enemy' and that women can, and should, exist without them. (See *black feminism, liberal feminism, socialist feminism.*)

radical value system: those sets of ideas associated with the *working class* which are oppositional to the capitalist system. The radical value system therefore seeks to change capitalism in fundamental ways and represents *class consciousness* in a traditional sense. (See *dominant value system; subordinate value system.*)

random sampling: a way of choosing a smaller number of 'subjects' from a larger population, with each member of the population having an equal chance of being chosen, through the use of an unbiased selection method. Each subject in the population is given a number and then the sample is chosen by a random method. The sample is usually generated using random number tables, though picking names from a hat would also be effective. The point of using a random method is that it usually generates a group which is representative of the population as a whole. (See *survey population.*)

ranking: the placing of phenomena in an order of superiority and inferiority; in sociology, most usually done with occupations. (See *prestige.*)

rapport: the feeling of identity between researcher and researched which allows the collection of appropriate data. The ease which rapport brings to the interviewee helps the sociologist to obtain the needed information.

Rastafarians: black followers of Ras Tafari Makonnen(the Emperor Haile Selassie of Ethiopia), who form an oppositional religious *sub-culture*, which rejects white-dominated power structures, including mainstream Christianity. The outward style they adopt is distinctive both for its dread-locks and for the use of 'ganga' (cannabis), which is of religious significance to Rastafarians.

rational action: see *Zweckrational*

rational choice model: a theory of voting in which support for a party is likened to a consumer decision. The theory suggests that electors are more open to rational argument than previously, and shop around for the policies that best fit their particular interests. Parties therefore have to compete for the individual elector's vote rather than take their class-based loyalty for granted. The theory has been criticised because:

- it over-emphasises the decline of class as a predictor of voting behaviour
- it over-emphasises the rationality of the electorate and under-estimates their affective loyalty
- it ignores the long-term forces which shape political preferences

(See *political participation.*)

rationalisation: the process whereby modern societies increasingly use logic and rationality to address and solve social problems. The development of *Zweckrational actions* was, according to Weber, one of the hallmarks of modern societies, in contrast to traditional ones. Some sociologists argue that rationalisation can be over-stressed and that modern societies are also characterised by the irrational and affective, not just the rational.

rationality: used by sociologists as a distinguishing characteristic of *modernity* which suggests that actions in modern societies are governed by logic and order. So, in modern rational societies, actions are said to be governed by logical thought, in contrast to the traditional societies of the past, where actions were controlled by what had always been done. Rationality has been particularly associated with bureaucratic organisations, where the actions of members of the organisation are co-ordinated and controlled through rules, to achieve *organisational goals* in a rational way. The analysis of rationality in sociology is particularly associated with the work of Max Weber, who distinguished between *Zweckrational action* and *Wertrational actions*.

re-aggregation of tasks: the process whereby *specialisation* is reversed and routine work tasks are put back together to give more *craft* skills to workers. A group of workers therefore produces a product from start to finish, each employing many different skills. (See *detailed division of labour.*)

re-alignment: a concept used by psephologists to indicate that there are fundamental changes occurring in patterns of voting behaviour. It is usually used in discussing the decline of class as a basis for voting for a particular party. In the 1950s and 1960s class was a good predictor of an individual's vote, with the manual *working class* largely supporting the Labour Party and the non-manual *middle class* largely voting Conservative. This situation is described as class being aligned with party. With changes in the occupational structure and the growth of the *'new' working class,* working class support for the Labour Party declined during the 1970s and 1980s, so that some psephologists were suggesting that new allegiances were emerging. The most common 're-alignment' suggested was the re-orientation of the skilled manual working class towards the Conservatives in general, and the ideas of Thatcherism in particular. The recession of the early 1990s and the emergence of 'new' Labour have undermined the idea of a fundamental re-alignment in British politics. However, evidence from the 1992 *general election* reveals that the skilled manual class (C2) gave slightly more of their votes to the Conservatives than to the Labour Party.

	Con	Lab	Lib/Dem	Other
Class A/B	59	20	19	2
Class C1	52	24	20	5
Class C2	41	38	17	5
Class D/E	29	50	17	4
(Source: N.O.P.)				

Voting by socio-economic class in the 1992 general election (%)

re-alignment theories: in stratification, these explanations argue that the old class divisions are disappearing and are being replaced by new and stable divisions. For example, Rex and Moore argue that new *'housing classes'* are emerging. Others argue that consumption patterns, or those who use public sector or private sector services, or regional divisions are now more important than class divisions. (See *fragmentation; persistence theories.*)

reaction formation: used by Albert Cohen to explain working-class *delinquency* as a rejection of middle-class standards and the adoption of the opposite as a status game that they can win. Thus, delinquency is a reaction to the respectability and academic standing of the *middle class,* which does not allow many working-class people to succeed in mainstream society.

real rate of suicide: a phrase used to indicate the actual number of suicides in a society rather than just the ones appearing in the *suicide* statistics. Given that we can never know whether an individual really intended to kill him or herself, the real rate of suicide is unknowable. However, it does highlight the gap between the statistics and actual events in the real world, raising questions about the *validity* of all statistics. (See *gambles with death*.)

realism: the general approach in sociology which argues that social phenomena such as structures and institutions have an existence beyond the lives of the individuals which make them up. The basic premise is that social structures pre-date the existence of any one individual member and continue after any individual's death.

reality construction: associated with the phenomenologists, this suggest that most arenas in social life are composed of individuals seeking to understand what is going on and who therefore come to different conclusions about what is actually happening. For example, the classroom has been explored as an arena of reality-construction, with the teachers giving one account of reality and the pupils giving various other accounts, none of which accord with the teachers'. Each participant in the *interaction* has therefore constructed their own reality about it. While phenomenologists accept that there is a basic understanding between all participants, ethnomethodologists argue that there is little constancy of meaning or sharing of the same reality from one classroom situation to the next, or in the same classroom from one day to the next.

rebellion: according to Merton, this form of *deviance* occurs when individuals reject either or both the cultural goals and *institutionalised means* in society. The focus of these deviants is the reconstruction of society on a different basis, substituting either new aims or means for the existing ones, or seeking to overthrow both means and goals. (See *retreatism; innovation; ritualism*.)

recession: a situation of deteriorating economic conditions, in which industrial production is in decline, *unemployment* is rising and the economy as a whole is shrinking. Recession plays an important part in the politics of a nation, as sociologists have shown how the fortunes of governments are bound up with the performance of business.

reciprocity: closely associated with *consensus* theory, this is the inter-relationship between two individuals or phenomena which involve the giving and taking of advantage and disadvantage. The classical example of reciprocity is the *gift*. Reciprocity is important in consensus theory because reciprocity involves mutual dependence, which helps to integrate individuals into the collectivity.

reconstituted family: a family in which one or both adults have been previously married, and therefore children are living with a step-parent and possibly step-brothers and step-sisters. The relatively high rates of *divorce* and re-marriage are leading to this kind of family becoming increasingly common.

reconstructed logics: used by Kaplan to describe the writing up of scientific research, in which real events are squeezed into a formulaic structure of reporting. The problem of reconstructed logics is that they do not tell the whole truth about the process of scientific experimentation. They tend to ignore the things that go wrong and present a sanitised version of *methodology*. Moreover, reconstructed logics also tend to conform to the dominant way of writing scientific work at the time and therefore may vary with time. (See *logics-in-use; paradigm*.)

recruitment policies: the application of particular policies by companies in the process of recruiting personnel. Such policies have recently come under scrutiny, as it is alleged that many companies have a hidden recruitment policy which discriminates against certain groups. The most common forms of *discrimination* are allegedly against women, particularly mothers of young children, members of ethnic minority groups, the disabled and those over a certain age, the last being referred to as '*ageism*'. Recently, however, one of the large supermarket chains actively pursued a policy of recruiting staff from the over-50s, arguing that these workers tended to be more highly motivated, reliable and with better skills than younger staff. Another area of concern regarding recruitment policies is the growing trend of recruiting only part-time workers. One of the problems in investigating this area is the difficulty of proving that a company is operating a discriminatory policy.

redistribution: the process in which *income* and *wealth* is either taken from the rich through *progressive taxation* and given to the poor in the form of benefits, or taken from the poor, in the form of *indirect taxation* and given to the rich, in the form of tax breaks. The issue of redistribution is a central political debate between the parties and lies at the heart of a fundamental philosophical division between those who believe in the *trickle-down effect* and those who argue for a welfare safety net.

reference group: the collectivity to which individuals or groups refer when making comparisons about their lives. Reference groups may be set up as models of behaviour or as representing goals for attainment. They may be positive or negative, encompassing respectively behaviour which is to be aspired to and behaviour which is rejected as inappropriate. (See *relative deprivation*.)

reflexivity: or self-reference, it is where a subject reflects on his/her own activities and knowledge. In sociology, reflexivity is used not just as a sociology of sociology, but also as the way in which individual *actors* in the social world are capable of reflecting on their own actions and ideas.

reformist feminism: see *liberal feminism*

refutation: the disproving of a *hypothesis* by the occurrence of a single event or piece of evidence. The term is closely associated with the philosopher Karl Popper, whose view of scientific knowledge was that it was always provisional, that is, could only be counted as 'true' until something occurred to show that it was not true, and it was the task of scientists to try to find evidence which would refute their hypotheses. In other words, we can only be sure of what is not true, rather than what is true. The example usually quoted in this context is that seeing one black swan refutes the hypothesis that all swans are white. (See *falsification; scientific revolution*.)

regional voting: an important feature of voting patterns, this shows that the support for the two main parties is concentrated in different areas of the country. Labour is strong in Scotland, Wales and the north of England, with pockets in the urban south. The Conservatives are strong in the south of England, with rural and suburban pockets elsewhere. It is this distribution which accounts for the two-party dominance which operates nationally in government, based on the *first-past-the-post* system patterns. The table overleaf demonstrates regional voting patterns.

	Con	Lab	Lib/Dem	Other
Voters in Scotland	25	39	11	24
Voters in the North	38	44	16	1
Voters in the Midlands	42	41	15	2
Voters in the South	50	26	23	2
(Source: N.O.P.)				

Voting in selected regions in the 1992 general election (%)

Registrar-General: a Government post, the holder of which heads the Office of Population Censuses and Services. The main usage in sociology is the Registrar-General's classification of occupations, which divides the population into five main groups. The groups are shown in the table below.

Social Class	Occupations
I	Professional and managerial
II	Intermediate
III (non-manual)	Skilled occupations, non-manual
III (manual)	Skilled occupations, manual
IV	Semi-skilled occupations
V	Unskilled occupations

The Registrar-General's classification has been much criticised. Criticisms include:

- the doubtful basis of placing different occupations into the various classes, which was done originally on the 'social status' of an occupation, and changed in 1981 to 'occupational skill'
- the problem of 'absentees'; members of the armed forces for example are left out
- the fact that the classification is based on mainly 'male' occupations, making it difficult to study the class position of women

Alternative classifications of *social class* which have been proposed include that developed by Goldthorpe in the *Oxford Mobility study,* the *Essex University Class Project* and the *Surrey Occupational Scale.*

regression: a situation in which, as a result of frustration in work, the worker reverts to childish forms of behaviour, such as pranks, to relieve the tension. On a more serious level, this can be expressed in temper tantrums or *industrial sabotage.* (See *resignation.*)

regressive taxation: taxation such as VAT which, being a flat rate independent of a person's *wealth* or *income*, takes a greater proportion of the income of the poor than of the rich. (See *progressive taxation.*)

regularities: in carrying out their everyday activities, people display patterns of activity, which are known as regularities. It is this patterned activity which is the basis of much social life and for example allows others to make assumptions about a person's behaviour in any given situation. The existence of regularities is thus an important aspect of *calculability.*

reification: treating an abstract concept as if it had a real concrete existence. This is a common criticism of functionalist notions of society, because they argue that society has an existence 'out there' beyond the sum of the individuals from which it is composed.

relations of production: these represent, in *Marxism*, the ways in which capitalists and workers interact with each other, in class terms. It is not usually used to describe how an individual capitalist deals with the workers he or she employs, but with the ways that, for example, the *working class* react to the conditions of work which the employers impose on them generally. According to the Marxists, the relations between the owners and non-owners are essentially antagonistic. (See *forces of production*.)

relativ-naturliche Weltanshauung: used by Scheler to indicate that the partial world-view each individual has is specific to them and also seems the natural way to view things. It therefore takes a leap of imagination to appreciate that another's point of view is equally natural to them. (See *Wissensociologie*.)

relative autonomy: developed by Althusser to describe the relationship between the base and superstructure in Marxist thought. This suggests that political and cultural forces have some degree of freedom from economic forces, although in the last analysis, politics and *culture* serve the long-term interests of the owners of the *means of production*. The problem of base-superstructure has been a central problem in Marxist sociology. Vulgar Marxism had assumed that the social totality was an expressive totality, in that all superstructural phenomena, such as politics or culture, were determined directly by economic forces. Althusser rejected this and argued that economic reality might dictate that the political and cultural spheres of society could be given real freedom to act, for example, to ensure the long-term survival of the capitalist system against the short-term economic interests of the capitalist class at any moment in time. However, the freedom of the political and cultural spheres was a qualified one. They were free to act, but only in the long-term interests of capitalism. The idea has been criticised for being contradictory, in that the freedom to act cannot be conditional upon acting in only one direction. Critics argue that this is not freedom at all, but just a more sophisticated version of *determinism*.

relative deprivation: a situation where, when people compare themselves with other imagined or real groups, they feel that they are less well-off than they ought to be. The importance of the concept is that feelings of deprivation are not always connected to absolute standards, but that comparatively well-off groups can still feel deprived if they compare their situation to other slightly better-off groups. For example, Glock and Stark suggest that feelings of relative deprivation may explain why some middle-class people join *sects*, and point out that feelings of relative deprivation are not necessarily confined to economic deprivation, but may also include social, ethical or psychic deprivation. (See *reference group*.)

relative isolation of the family: the argument that the weakening of wider *kinship* ties and increased *geographical mobility* have led to many contemporary families becoming both socially and geographically isolated. Talcott Parsons argued that the isolated *nuclear family* is the typical form in modern industrial societies. This is largely the result of the family losing many of its wider functions to other agencies, and specialising in the rearing and *socialisation* of children and the stabilisation of adult personalities through a close husband and wife relationship. Goldthorpe and

Lockwood, in their 1962 Affluent Worker study, noted that married couples spent most of their *leisure* time together, and that the husbands' activities were increasingly 'home-centred'. They referred to this type of family as *'privatised'*. It is suggested by some that the emotional stresses which may result from this isolation, particularly for mothers at home with young children, may be a factor in the breakdown of marriage. However, there are cultural variations in the relative strength of kinship ties, and it is also suggested that modern methods of communication enable family members to keep in contact even though they may live at a considerable distance. (See *kinship networks, loss of family functions.*)

relative poverty: the state of being poor with reference to a real, or perceived, standard of living in a society. It is very difficult to define relative poverty precisely, as standards of living vary over time and from place to place, and it is also difficult to agree on what should be the standard of living used as a reference point, and how it should be measured. In an attempt to measure the extent of relative poverty in Britain, Townsend, and then Mack and Lansley, using slightly different methods, compiled lists of items and activities which might be considered 'necessities' in modern Britain, and argued that those who lacked above a certain number of these should be viewed as being in poverty. Other sociologists, including those of the *New Right* such as Marsland, argue that this is too broad a definition of poverty, and therefore exaggerates the number of those deemed to be poor. (See *absolute poverty; index of deprivation; consensual view of need; poverty line.*)

relative rate of mobility: this is the amount of movement in the *class structure*, taking into account changes in the *occupational structure*, which might provide more or less opportunities in particular occupational groupings. Thus, while the *absolute rate of mobility* has been high since the Second World War, the shift from *primary* and *secondary sector* jobs to tertiary employment has meant that the relative chances of movement have remained much the same as before 1945.

relativism: a position in the sociology of knowledge which argues that all knowledge is partial and related to the position which the individual holds in the social structure. Therefore, there can be no such thing as 'the absolute truth'. Critics suggest that if that last statement is true, then relativism is by definition itself only partially true.

reliability: a term used in connection with research methods, particularly quantitative research. Research is said to be 'reliable' if, when repeated using exactly the same methods, it produces the same results. Positivist sociologists argue that methods such as large-scale sample surveys, yielding *quantitative data*, are more reliable than interpretative methods such as *unstructured interviews* and *participant observation*. (See *positivism; interpretative sociology.*)

religion: an organised expression of the perceived relationship between the *natural* and *supernatural* world, which usually refers to a god. In sociology, the definition of religion is not agreed upon, with different types of sociologist offering alternative views. A Durkheimian view suggests that a religion should be defined by the functions that it performs in society, in particular, the function of creating social solidarity amongst members of society. The problem with this definition is that as there is no reference to any god it could include many institutions which are not usually seen as religious, such as the Communist Party in the state socialist societies of eastern

Europe in the post-War period. A Weberian view suggests that religion should be defined by the belief in some other level of existence beyond the real world, and that religious ceremonies are therefore an expression of the relationships between the everyday world and this higher plane of existence. A problem with this definition is that it tends to exclude certain commonsense definitions of 'religions'. The Marxist definition of religion emphasises the role of religion as a 'cloak of respectability' for the *ruling class,* who use religion as a way of controlling subordinate groups in society, through the hope of a better life in the next world and fear of damnation if they rebel in this world. A problem with this approach is that it depends on religion being a conspiracy and ignores any real religious feeling.

religiosity: the sense of the religious in the individual. Functionalist sociologists see every individual as having this religious sensibility, which needs to be fulfilled in some way. Marxists tend to see religiosity as a 'false need', created by society as a means of *social control.* The importance of this difference is that, if religiosity is an essential part of the individual's make-up, then religion generally cannot decline, as there will always be a need for it. If, however, religious feeling is socially created, then theoretically societies could exist without religion.

religious observance: the observing of religious *rituals* and acts of worship. The decline of religious observance as measured by attendance at church has been cited as evidence in Britain that *secularisation* is taking place. (See *church attendance statistics.*)

reluctant militants: a term derived from Roberts to describe *white-collar workers* who go on strike. The concept conveys the fact that white-collar workers are often reluctant to strike, associating it with lower status *manual workers,* but that they can be driven to it by what they see as unfair treatment. This can be either a depression of salaries, as the economics of *recession* means that all sectors of the work-force have to accept sacrifices, or a deterioration in conditions, usually in comparison with other groups in the workforce.

remunerative power: see *utilitarian power*

replication: the exact repetition of an experiment by someone else. This shows that the results of the experiment are not just random or a fluke, but can be reproduced by other scientists. Replication is a central principle of the scientific method, because it establishes the *objectivity* of the experiments, in that they are untainted by personal pre-conceptions or biases. (See *hypothetico-deductive method.*)

representative democracy: a political system where the people elect someone who will represent them in political decision-making. The representative can be seen as having the right to express their own views about political policies or as being mandated by the electorate to carry out their collective will.

representative sample: a *sample* whose members are representative of the whole *survey population* in terms of the characteristics considered important by the researchers, (e.g. sex, age, social class, ethnic group, occupation, marital status). As a general principle, and provided that a suitable sampling method has been used, the larger the sample as a proportion of the population, the more representative it is likely to be. Thus, if the population under consideration contained 2500 people, a sample of 250 (1 person in 10) would be more likely to be representative than a sample of 50 (1 person in 50).

representativeness: the degree to which a research study is representative of other, similar kinds of group. In some studies great care is taken to ensure that the group is representative, for example by carefully drawing a *representative sample*. This is likely to be the case with a large-scale *social survey*. In other studies, greater emphasis is placed on the degree to which a whole group can be studied in depth, such as a group of school pupils, or a group of workers, or a tribe, or members of a religious sect. In such cases, even though the group studied may not be exactly typical of other such groups, the researcher believes that the depth of information gained is worth the possible loss of representativeness.

repressive state apparatus: a term used by the Marxist writer Althusser to refer to the army, the police and the judicial system in a capitalist state. Althusser argues that, under *capitalism*, the *bourgeoisie* will attempt to rule with the compliance of the *proletariat*, who are led to believe that capitalism is the 'best' system under which to live – indeed, they are discouraged from seriously considering any alternatives. The belief in capitalism as a system is spread by the institutions which make up what Althusser referred to as the *ideological state apparatus*, such as *education, religion* and the *mass media*. However, this *consensus* sometimes breaks down, and there is opposition to capitalism. At this point, the power of the repressive state apparatus will be used against the dissidents to maintain capitalist supremacy and the power of the *ruling class.*

reproductive technologies: a general term covering a whole range of developments in the area of birth and reproduction. These include *in vitro* fertilisation, fertility treatment and possible advances in cloning. While they have some importance for issues such as the genetic engineering of vegetables and animals, sociologists and particularly post-modernists are interested in the ways that these technologies intervene between nature and humanity, divorcing the reproductive act from the process of reproduction. Feminists are also interested in the way that male science has taken control of reproduction away from women and placed it in male hands through the development of reproductive technologies.

republicans: in Northern Ireland, those political movements whose long-term aim is merger with the Republic of Ireland. The republican movement encompasses democratic parties such as the Social Democratic and Labour Party and extra-Parliamentary groups such as the Irish Republican Army.

resacrilisation: a term adopted by Greely to refer to the resurgence of religious beliefs in many western societies, particularly the USA. Greely referred to this process as the 're-establishment of the sacred realm', and it is used as an argument to counter allegations that *secularisation* is taking place.

reserve army of labour: those groups in society who move into and out of the *labour market*, according to the demand in the economy for workers. The term was originally used by Marx to refer to a permanent pool of unemployed people which, he argued, *capitalism* needed to operate profitably. In contemporary usage, it is more likely to be used to refer to unskilled workers, often carrying out part-time, seasonal and temporary work as and when they are needed by companies. The most prominent component of the reserve army of labour is married women, who may or may not prefer to have a full-time occupation. Many feminists argue that the prominence of women in the reserve army of labour reflects society's *patriarchal ideology*, which sees women as only subsidiary wage-earners. Marxists draw attention to the usefulness of the reserve army of labour to the functioning of capitalism. It allows firms to recruit labour when they need to, but without any long-term commitment to them. The reserve army can also be used, according to Marxists, as a weapon to divide and rule the working class and to break strikes if necessary. *New Right* sociologists see the reserve army of labour as an important aspect of labour flexibility in a global economy, so that firms can respond swiftly to changes in demand by employing or sacking labour.

residential zone: one of Burgess's zones of the city, this was usually composed of high-class apartments, which were relatively close to the centre, but far enough away to be seen as a separate area. (See *urban zone theory*.)

resignation: a response to *frustration* in work, which consists of apathy and escapism. It is a consequence of the individual believing that their feelings of frustration are the result of their own inadequacy. (See *regression; fixation*.)

resistance: a term used by some sociologists of *youth culture* to explain the oppositional nature of many working-class youth cultures. It suggests that these *sub-cultures* are formed as an expression of working-class youth's rejection of the *alienation* of capitalist societies. The stress in this ideological opposition is not on political resistance, but on a resistance through *style*, in which dress, hostile behaviour patterns, music etc. are symbolic of their oppositional stance. Many youth culture theorists see this resistance as the post-war form of previous working-class attempts to create their own space, through the organisation of working-men's clubs, leek-growing, pigeon-fancying and the like. Critics of this idea argue that:

- It is a romantic view of working-class youth culture. Skinheads beating up members of ethnic minorities is not romantic.
- The resistance element is over-emphasised, with many stylistic features adopted by youth sub-cultures being adaptations of mainstream society.
- It ignores the fact that most working-class youths are conformist, not oppositional.

resistance theory: used in the sociology of education to explain the under-performance of male Afro-Caribbean students compared to other ethnic minority groupings, it argues that they are more likely to resist schooling as discriminatory rather than employ it to their own advantage as some other ethnic minority groups do. It has been criticised for assuming that resistance leads to the liberation of ethnic minorities from exploitation. Some sociologists argue that it leads to an anti-intellectual attitude which contributes to a further *marginalisation* of their position.

respectable working class: a group said to be found within the manual *working class*, who are set apart from other groups of workers by their habits and life styles. They are usually influenced by *religion* in some way and are keen to see themselves as separate from the *'rough' working class*. Their patterns of life often mimic middle-class life styles in certain ways, with an emphasis on good reputation in the community. (See *aristocracy of labour*.)

resondents: those who provide information for research purposes by answering questions. The term is usually applied to those taking part in *social surveys* and *interviews*. (See *response rate*.)

response rate: the proportion of responses obtained out of the *sample* in a piece of research. Different research methods vary in their likely response rates. Research using *questionnaires* conducted face-to-face by trained interviewers will have a fairly high response rate, while questionnaires sent by post characteristically have a low response rate (sometimes as low as 20%), even though follow-up letters are used. Low response rates indicate that the findings of the research may be biased, as those who reply might differ significantly in their views from those who do not. When looking at the results of *social surveys*, it is always advisable to look for the response rate. This is sometimes expressed as a percentage of the whole sample, and sometimes as the number of completed questionnaires or interviews. In this case, the number should be compared with the total number in the sample, which is usually expressed as N (e.g. N = 1500).

restricted code: a form of *language code* identified by Bernstein. It refers to a pattern of speech commonly used between close friends or members of a family, in which sentences are short and grammatically simple, and much of the meaning is implicit, i.e. understood by those taking part in the conversation without being expressed in words, or at least in detail. Bernstein argued that, while the restricted code is perfectly adequate for normal everyday conversations, another form of speech, which he called the *elaborated code*, is necessary to express more complex and abstract ideas, and is used extensively in education. While middle-class children learn both speech codes at home, working-class children tend to use only the restricted code, which puts them at a considerable disadvantage at school. Labov disagrees with Bernstein, arguing that the methods used to identify the two speech codes failed to recognise the richness and subtlety of working-class speech, which can and does express complex and abstract ideas.

restrictive practices: in industry, the use of particular modes of working by workers which limit the productive capacity of the firm. They are usually concerned with traditional ways of working which rely upon strict demarcation of workers' jobs, with no cross-over between different types of worker. They were evolved over many years by workers to provide themselves with some form of protection from the demands of employers and to increase the rewards they gained. The destruction of restrictive practices and the introduction of flexible working has been one of the main aims of the Thatcherite agenda of the 1980s.

retreatism: according to Merton, this form of *deviance* occurs when individuals reject both the accepted goals in society and the legitimate ways in which they may be obtained. As such, they become the 'drop-outs' of society, finding expression in alternative ways of living on the margins. This may take the form of drug-taking, wandering, squatting or alcoholism. (See *ritualism; rebellion; innovation.*)

revolution: used to describe any radical re-structuring, it is most often associated with the violent overthrow of an established political order by an opposing section of society. Sociologists are interested in revolution because it represents an extreme event in society, and sociological explanations have focused on the possible causes of revolutions and whether their outcomes involve any real change in the conditions of those for whom the revolution was intended. In a more general sense, revolution can refer to any social activity in which fundamental change occurs, usually swiftly, but also sometimes slowly. Thus, sociologists talk of the *industrial revolution* or *scientific revolution* in referring respectively to shifts in productive techniques and shifts in *paradigms*.

revolutionist sects: a type of *sect* identified by Wilson, the members of which believe that the world will be transformed by a single cataclysmic *supernatural* event, in which the existing order will be destroyed and a new divine order ushered in. Jehovah's Witnesses are an example of members of a revolutionist sect.

ribbon development: where towns and cities grow through housing being built along the major roads leading in and out of centres of population. Development therefore takes on the appearance of spokes:

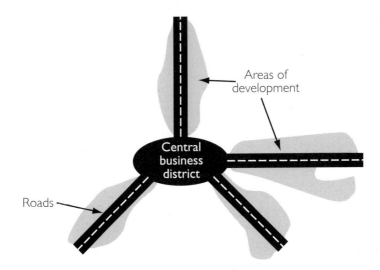

Representation of ribbon development

right to rule: the notion that the dominant group in society is naturally in charge of the political affairs of the *State*. It refers to some inherent quality, such as breeding, heredity or *intelligence*, which legitimates the power of the ruling group. (See *divine right of kings*.)

right-wing: along the political spectrum, the ideas and organisations which tend to favour the existing social arrangements and support traditional elitist values. The right encompasses democratic parties such as the British *Conservative Party* and authoritarian anti-democratic organisations such as the Fascist movement. (See *left-wing; centre*.)

risk society: a concept developed by Beck to indicate that in the postmodern world, life is experienced in many social areas as an increased sense of danger and challenge. Whereas the modern world offered some degree of certainty in social relations, with, for example, a class system to define an individual's social position, the postmodern world has seen the dissolving of such certainties, so that social life becomes more risky. (See *self-identity*.)

rites de passage: ceremonies or *rituals* which mark important transitions in an individual's life. Developed by anthropologists to describe in particular the traditions associated with becoming an adult, sociologists use the concept in connection with important points in a *life-cycle*, such as marriage, birth and death.

ritualism: where members of an organisation stick strictly to the rules, carrying them out as if they were the only justification for the existence of the *organisation*. Blau argues that ritualism stems from the insecurity of individuals in organisations, who find some sort of security in formally keeping to the rules, regardless of whether they are actually helping *clients* or not. This ritualism often leads clients to complain about the red tape which stifles the ability of organisations to respond effectively to need. (See *formalism.*)

ritualistic deviance: according to Merton, this form of *deviance* occurs when individuals reject the sanctioned cultural goals in society, but continue to follow the legitimised means of achieving them. The result is that these deviants continue to slavishly follow the rules to no apparent purpose. They may be often found in large *organisations,* insisting on a strict interpretation of the rules, regardless of whether goals are met or not. (See *retreatism; innovation; rebellion.*)

rituals: individual or collective actions, which are designed to achieve some social end and which have a repetitive element. Religious rituals, as expressed in ceremonies of all kinds, are perhaps the most obvious example. However, there are secular rituals as well, such as 'coming-of-age' celebrations. Rituals usually have a symbolic content, in which *meaning* is expressed through traditional actions, such as facing Mecca when praying, or crossing oneself. Durkheim argued that rituals were a way of expressing social solidarity, because taking part in a collective service reaffirms the individual's commitment to the collectivity of which he or she is a part.

Robbins Report 1961: a survey of the pattern of higher education in Britain, and an examination of the factors affecting the achievement of school children and their entry into higher education. The survey confirmed earlier findings regarding the link between academic achievement and parental occupation, and drew attention to the huge pool of untapped ability, particularly among the children of manual workers. The Report recommended that higher education should be available to all who wanted it, and suggested that there was likely to be a growing demand. Following the publication of the Robbins Report, the Government started on a programme of expansion in higher education, with the creation in the 1960s and 1970s of several new universities and polytechnics.

robotics: a term used to describe particular forms of new technologies. The usual representation of robotics is to be found in car assembly lines, where computer-controlled machines carry out the routine work of assembling the cars. Symbolically, therefore, robotics describes those new technologies which substitute for human labour in the production process. (See *new technology.*)

role: the expected pattern of behaviour associated with a particular social status under defined circumstances. The analogy is with roles in the theatre, but, unlike the theatre, these are not pretend roles. Roles allow individuals to predict how others will act in particular situations and to respond appropriately. They thus allow for a degree of *social order,* through their very predictability.

role conflict: a situation which arises when the demands of the different parts of our lives are contradictory. These demands can be trivial, such as needing to be in two places at the same time, or of a more fundamental nature, such as those associated with being a working mother. (See *role-set.*)

role diffuseness: where an individual engages in relationships on the basis of a number of aspects of their personality and functions. Role diffuseness is associated with traditional societies, where the activities of individuals are not specialised and therefore, when interaction occurs, it is on the basis of the whole person, not just one *role*.

role distance: the separation of an individual's deepest being from the *role* he or she is playing at the time. The concept is used to indicate the detachment or lack of engagement that many individuals feel in playing some of the roles they are required to act out.

role models: people whose behaviour and attitudes we try, consciously or unconsciously, to copy. Parents are often important role models, especially for ideas about *gender*. Teachers, bosses, pop and sporting stars and those of a higher *social status* are also often used as role models.

role specificity: where individuals engage in relationships for specific purposes and on the basis of a particular aspect of their social being. It is associated with modern societies, where roles are specialised and individuals relate to each other in a less holistic way than in traditional societies. The dualism (with *role diffuseness)* was developed by Parsons as one of the *pattern variables* between traditional and modern societies.

role-set: the total number of roles a person has to adopt when occupying a particular *social status*. As a worker, the individual may have a number of roles, e.g. employer, workmate, boss, trade union member, taxpayer etc.

role-training: a form of *socialisation* in which the young acquire the skills and attitudes necessary for the fulfilment of institutionalised positions in their adult life. It is usually associated with *secondary socialisation* agencies. (See *enculturation; impulse control.*)

Roman Catholic Church: the largest of the Christian Churches with a worldwide membership. The Roman Catholic Church has an authoritarian and hierarchical structure, and the conservative views of the Pope on issues such as divorce, contraception and abortion have caused controversy and the allegation that the church is out of touch with modern ways of thinking. The decision of the *Church of England* to allow women to join the priesthood has led some former Anglicans to join the Roman Catholic Church. However, not all the activities of the church can be labelled conservative. In South America, Roman Catholics have taken an active stand on issues of human rights, and the church was a powerful force in some eastern European countries, particularly Poland, during the overthrow of *communism.* (See *liberation theology.*)

romance, ideology of: used by sociologists to suggest that what might be seen as a 'natural' emotion is in fact a socially constructed *ideology.* The concept of romantic love has an historical origin, arising from notions such as 'courtly love' and has not been a universal feature of all societies. The development of the ideology of romance is said to be part of an increase in self-surveillance in modern and post-modern societies, in which individuals in society need fewer and fewer external controls such as force and punishment, but instead 'police' their own actions through accepting and acting upon dominant ideologies. The ideology of romance is therefore an important support for the structure of the *nuclear family.*

ROSLA (raising of the school leaving age): pupils whose 16th birthday fell in the academic year 1973/4, and all subsequent pupils, had to remain at school until they were 16+. The transition was not without its difficulties, as in the first few years schools had to retain and educate children who realised that, had it not been for the change, they might have been at work. Inevitably, the pattern soon became accepted as 'normal'. New programmes of study and examinations were developed for the so-called ROSLA children, among them the *CSE*. Recently, there has been discussion by some politicians regarding whether some children should be allowed to leave school at 14+, and enter a vocationally-based training programme.

rough working class: a fragment of the manual *working class*, distinguished by a particular life style. Associated with a 'drinking' culture and implicated in a criminal *sub-culture*, the 'rough' elements of the working class were often stigmatised as a dangerous group in society. They were often concentrated in particular occupations, such as mining or fishing and often had a 'public' culture, that is, one which was carried out outside the home, in public houses, race tracks and the like. There was also a tendency for the rough working class to be male-dominated, with women having a more domestic role. (See *respectable working class.*)

routinisation: the process whereby once-skilled jobs become repetitive and boring through the introduction of standardised procedures. It is usually associated with the introduction of *new technology* which effectively de-skills workers. Sociologists have used the concept with particular reference to office work, where the impact of firstly the typewriter and subsequently computer technology has allowed paperwork to become standardised, with low-level clerical grades of workers staffing the office. (See *de-skilling.*)

rowdies: 13–17-year-old football hooligans, who form the middle group in Marsh's *career hierarchy*. It is the rowdies who are responsible for much of the chanting and stylised violence at football grounds. Marsh has been criticised for under-estimating the amount of violence perpetuated by the rowdies and the *town boys*. (See *novices.*)

Rowntree, Benjamin Seebohm: a wealthy businessman and social researcher best known for his research into *poverty* in York in 1897, 1936 and 1950. Rowntree used a subsistence definition of poverty, based on the lowest cost of the basic necessities of life. He also grouped poor families into two categories. Those in *primary poverty* lacked the earnings sufficient to obtain even the minimum necessities, while those deemed to be in *secondary poverty* had earnings which would have been sufficient, had not some part been diverted to other expenditure, either 'useful' or 'wasteful. (See *poverty line.*)

rude boys: a term used by Pryce to describe black unemployed youths, whose class origins were not *working class*, but from the white-collar sector. Sometimes called rudies, there are many variations of the rude boy, with some turning towards drugs, others to crime.

ruling class: the group at the top of the social order who govern the rest of society, either directly or indirectly. The term is usually associated with Marxist theory, in which the ruling class plays a central part. Marxists define membership of the ruling class by ownership of the *means of production*. Through owning wealth-creating assets, Marxists argue that the ruling class are able to control much of what goes on in society, including *government*. Though the precise relationship between the owners of the means of production and politicians, administrators etc. is subject to much dispute, the Marxist view can be summarised in the phrase 'an owning class is a ruling class'. The power of the ruling class does not just control government, but also, according to Marxists, influences what is produced in the media, what is taught in schools, and also extends into many other areas of social life. Some Marxists argue that the ruling class directly control these other spheres of social life, while others suggest that institutions such as government are relatively autonomous. Non-Marxist sociologists deny that there is a ruling class in this sense at all. Their main point is that Marxists do not identify the precise ways in which the ruling class is supposed to rule. (See *economic determinism; relative autonomy.*)

rural areas: otherwise known as the countryside, in which the predominant economic activity is agriculture. Living is characterised by small residential areas, such as villages, in which individuals will know most of the other people in the same location.

rural community: an important concept for early sociologists such as Durkheim and Tönnies who believed that such communities played a vital part in instilling basic moral values in their members. They were concerned that the break-up of rural communities under *industrialisation*, and the subsequent process of urbanisation, would leave people rootless and unsatisfied, and lead to *anomie*. Tönnies used the term '*Gemeinschaft*' to refer to the notion of '*community*'. Empirical research by Wilmott and Young and Gans challenged the idea that 'communities' could exist only in rural areas. Pahl also showed that it was mistaken to believe that the populations of *rural areas* were necessarily close-knit communities, showing that marked social divisions could exist between different groups of residents. One of the current debates in the sociology of community concerns the extent to which there are real differences between rural and *urban areas*. (See *Gesellschaft.*)

rural-urban continuum: the idea that there are few stark differences between city and countryside, but rather a graduation between the big city on the one hand and isolated farmsteads on the other, with a huge range of size of community, styles of life and habitats in between. The idea was developed by Sorokin to counter simplistic dichotomies between the two types of location.

sacred: a term used by Durkheim to refer to those things in society which are regarded as set apart and forbidden, and not forming part of everyday life. All other phenomena could be labelled, according to Durkheim, as '*profane*'. He argued that every society makes the distinction between the sacred and the profane, and the study of religion should focus on those phenomena regarded as sacred.

saints: a term used by Pryce to describe the religious section of black, especially Afro-Caribbean, working-class people. (See *rude boys.*)

sample: the group selected from the wider population to take part in research. Choosing an appropriate sample is an important stage in the research process. (See *sampling; sampling frame.*)

sampling: the selection of a part of a *survey population* to be studied rather than the entire population. Sampling is a widely-used procedure both in sociological research and in industry, for example in checks on quality control. There are various methods which can be used to select a sample, but the overall aim is usually the same, i.e. to make the sample as representative of the whole population as possible. This allows any conclusions drawn about the sample to be broadly applicable to the whole population. (See *random sampling.*)

sampling error: the difference between data based on an entire *survey population* and data collected from a *sample* of that population. No sample can be relied on to be so representative that it is completely identical to the whole population. *Random sampling* methods can keep the sampling error to a small and calculable percentage.

sampling frame: the list of people (the *survey population*) from which a *sample* will be drawn. In sociological research, a common sampling frame is the *electoral register.* Others, depending on the nature of the research, could include school rolls, club or *pressure group* membership lists, a list of subscribers to a specialist magazine, or telephone directories. It is not always easy to ensure that the sampling frame is complete. For example, the advent of the community charge (poll tax) meant that some people did not register as electors, and telephone directories exclude not only those without telephones but those who have opted to have ex-directory numbers. The omission of certain people from a sampling frame can affect the degree to which the sample, and therefore the findings, are representative of the population as a whole.

sampling interval: the randomly chosen number between 1 and the number which represents the proportion of the population in the sample (e.g. 1 in 30) which is used to add to each selected name on the list from which a *systematic sample* is being drawn.

sampling unit: the level at which sampling takes place. While sampling units are usually the individual, if a sociologist is taking a sample of hospitals in Britain, then the sampling unit would be hospitals (not the individuals within the hospital).

sanction: the means whereby a social *norm* is enforced, either by a positive or negative device and either formally or informally. A formal negative sanction for example might be a law which leads to imprisonment of those who break it.

satellite towns: small *urban areas* located close to large cities, which constitute a major source of housing for workers in the city. The economy of satellite towns is intimately connected to the city, with workers dependent on the city for employment and shopping.

schooling: formal education delivered in specialist institutions.

science: see *natural science*

scientific management: a theory developed by F W Taylor which applied scientific principles to the management of workers in an industrial firm. (See *Taylorism*.)

scientific Marxism: that variant of *Marxism* which searches for the invariate laws of history which exist independently of human free will and deterministic of it. It thus denies the importance of the individual in the sweep of history. The scientific school includes Marxists such as Althusser, Poulantzas and Blackburn. (See *critical Marxism*.)

scientific revolution: a term given by Kuhn to the process in which a once dominant scientific *paradigm* is successfully challenged, overthrown and replaced by another. Kuhn's argument is that, at any time, in any branch of knowledge, including *natural science*, a particular set of ideas, beliefs and practices (paradigm) is used to explain natural or social phenomena. The paradigm is defended by academics and practitioners, and is taught to those newly entering the field. However, according to Kuhn, a paradigm, although it may be accepted for a very long time, is only temporary, as it will not be able to explain satisfactorily all the pheonomena in that discipline or branch of science. Alternative paradigms will begin to emerge to challenge the prevailing set of ideas, and eventually one will succeed and will replace the existing one, becoming, in its turn, the dominant paradigm. With the adoption of the new paradigm, a scientific revolution will have taken place, and the whole process will begin again. Kuhn is thus challenging the idea that 'science' is a set of *'laws'* which represent the 'truth'. Kuhn's views have been challenged by those who claim that there is no evidence that scientific knowledge has developed in this way. Interactionists make use of Kuhn's ideas to challenge the positivist view that interactionist sociology is not 'scientific', by arguing that positivists themselves have a mistaken view of the nature of science.

scientism: a term which suggests the dogmatic application of the principles of science to the social world, so that an inflexible and inappropriate sociology is developed.

scientist as human being: a concept developed by interactionists, to emphasise that science is not carried out by cold, objective, dispassionate robots, but by individuals with all the human foibles we might expect, such as pride, status and proneness to error. Thus, scientists operate in a situation of pressure, to publish, get results, bring in funds and gain the recognition of their peers. Interactionists argue that these pressures create a predisposition for scientists to privilege evidence which proves their hypothesis and to explain away or ignore results which do not. (See *objectivity*.)

scope: the number of activities in an institution which are carried out jointly by participants. The degree of scope will vary from one type of *total institution* to another, so that prisons will have a high degree of scope, and a hospital will have less scope. (See *pervasiveness*.)

Scottish National Party: the nationalist third party in Scotland which seeks independence from the United Kingdom, whilst staying within the European Union. The

SNP is divided between a socialist tendency which reflects the dominance of the *Labour Party* in central Scotland and a cultural tendency, which reflects the traditional 'tartan culture' of the Highlands.

second world: a term used in the sociology of development to distinguish the former socialist economies of eastern Europe and the Soviet Union from the capitalist economies of the *first world*. While second world economies contained highly developed sectors, such as the space programmes of the former Soviet Union, they also retained many out-of-date and unsophisticated technologies. They thus often had the surface appearance of advanced technological societies, while relying on an industrial base which was stagnant and undynamic. The collapse of *communism* in the second world at the end of the 1980s revealed the underlying weaknesses of their economies. One of the most startling revelations was the extent to which second world economies had ignored environmental and safety issues in the running of their economies. (See *third world*.)

secondary data: information used by sociologists but which has not been collected by them. Secondary data include *official statistics*, historical and personal *documents*, books and films. While providing a great deal of important information, all secondary data must be used with caution, as it is not always possible to know the criteria surrounding either the collection or the selection of the information.

secondary deviance: identified by Lemert as a deviant act which has been publicly processed as a deviant act so that the perpetrator becomes labelled a deviant. The importance of the distinction between this and *primary deviance* is that everyone commits primary deviant acts from time to time, with few social consequences. More serious social consequences arise from secondary deviance, where the stigmatising force of the label is likely to lead to changes in relationships between the labelled person and the people around her or him and perhaps a change in the attitude and behaviour of those so labelled. (See *labelling*.)

secondary health care: patient health care, usually curative in nature, provided in hospitals. (See *primary health care; tertiary health care*.)

secondary labour market: see *external labour market*

secondary organisations: *organisations* which depend for their existence on a previously existing organisation. *Trade unions* are the main type of secondary organisation that exists.

secondary poverty: see *Rowntree*

secondary sector: in the *occupational structure*, these are manufacturing jobs, usually located in factories, and construction work. (See *primary sector; tertiary sector*.)

secondary socialisation: the learning of skills and attitudes outside the main agency of the family. In modern societies, schools are the main agency for secondary socialisation and are associated with the learning of specific occupational skills as well as attitudes which contribute to work discipline. (See *primary socialisation*.)

secret deviant: defined by Becker as one who engages in rule-breaking behaviour but who has not been perceived or labelled publicly as a deviant. This is not just a question of a deviant who has not been caught, because the *labelling* process is not automatic. (See *falsely accused; pure deviant*.)

sect: a religious group with characteristics which distinguishes it from either a *church* or a *denomination*. It has been suggested that common characteristics of sects include:

- membership is by conversion
- there is usually a charismatic leader
- members are accepted only if they are thought suitable
- the claim is made that only the sect has the 'true' way to salvation

However, sociologists such as Wilson have argued that an attempt to define sects by reference to common characteristics is unhelpful and, indeed, impossible, as sects take so many different forms. Wilson proposed a typology based on the sect's views of, and relationship to, the *values* of mainstream society, namely whether a sect was world-rejecting, world-accommodating or world-affirming. Although precise figures are difficult to obtain, sect membership appears to be growing, casting doubt on the view that *secularisation* is taking place in many western industrial societies. (See *new religious movements; theodicy of disprivilege.*)

sectional interests: the divisions of society into groupings which have something in common. An individual may be a member of many sectional interests, ranging from class interest in the broadest sense, to occupational, religious, regional or ethnic groupings. In political terms, sectional interests represent the basic unit of political appeal. The successful politician is usually rooted in a sectional interest.

sectoral cleavages: in *psephology*, this is used to describe the different patterns of voting behaviour between those on opposite sides of important social characteristics beyond *social class*. Psephologists have identified home ownership/public housing, north/south and working in the private/public sector as important factors in the study of voting and these represent the sectoral faults along which either sides votes. Labour is therefore associated with those who rent council housing, live in the north and work for the state. Conservative voters appear on the other side of these sectoral cleavages. (See *new working class; old working class.*)

sectoral model of urban areas: developed by Hoyt as an alternative model to *urban zone theory*, the growth of cities is seen as occurring in wedges from the city centre, rather than concentric circles. This theory suggests that *ribbon development* is an important factor in the evolution of cities. This development looks like this:

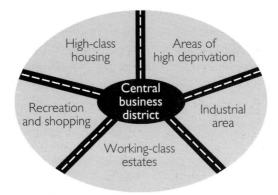

Sectoral model of urban areas as developed by Hoyt

secularisation: usually defined as the process in which religious thinking, practices and organisations lose their social significance. Weber argued that the development of scientific knowledge and rational thought would replace beliefs based on *magic*, superstition and the *supernatural*. Evidence of secularisation is usually presented as a decline in church attendance and religious observance, and the declining power of the church and religious leaders in everyday life. However, this evidence is contested. It is argued that much religious practice goes unrecorded in the kind of statistics which are presented to show evidence of secularisation, e.g. people worshipping in house churches, joining in religious programmes on television, and membership of *sects* tend to be ignored. It is also pointed out that, in many societies, the church remains a powerful political and economic, as well as religious influence, and that in some industrial societies (such as the USA) membership of religious groups is increasing, rather than decreasing. Surveys show that a majority of the population of Britain when asked still profess a belief in God or some kind of supernatural force. Weber's prediction of the decline of religion as a result of rational thought is questioned, using evidence of beliefs in magic, superstition and the supernatural. It is also pointed out that the '*golden age of religion*' is historically suspect. Parsons claimed that religious institutions, far from losing their influence, were becoming more highly specialised, and still had an important function. While membership of some churches in the UK appears to be declining, membership of other religious groups is showing an increase.(See *disenchantment; disengagement; differentiation.*)

	1970	1991
Trinitarian churches		
Anglican	2.55	1.81
Presbyterian	1.81	1.24
Methodist	0.69	0.46
Baptist	0.30	0.23
Other free churches	0.53	0.66
Roman Catholic	2.71	2.04
Orthodox	0.19	0.28
All trinitarian churches	8.78	6.72
Non-trinitarian churches		
Mormons	0.09	0.15
Jehovah's Witnesses	0.06	0.13
Spiritualists	0.05	0.04
Other non-trinitarian churches	0.08	0.14
All non-trinitarian churches	0.28	0.46
Other religions		
Muslims	0.25	0.52
Sikhs	0.08	0.27
Hindus	0.05	0.14
Jews	0.11	0.11
Others	0.05	0.08
All other religions	0.54	1.12

(Source: Social Trends 25, 1995)

Church membership (adult active members) in the UK (millions)

secularists: also known as *pragmatists*, those *working class Conservative* voters who support the Conservatives because they believe that they will be financially better off under them. The *achievement* orientation of these manual workers influences their voting decisions to the extent that they weigh up the financial implications of each party and plump for the Conservatives. However, there are also Labour voters who are achievement oriented. The difference between the two groups is that secularists tend to be integrated much more strongly into the dominant middle-class value consensus. (See *instrumentalists; deferential voters.*)

segmentalism: a theory in the sociology of *leisure* which argues that modern life is carried out in two distinct spheres, *work* and leisure, which are largely independent of each other. Individuals choose which of the spheres is to be their *central life interest.* (See *holism.*)

segmented labour market: the ways in which jobs are differentiated by levels of pay, skill and prospects in a structured way, so that similar jobs in different companies will exhibit similar conditions, and different jobs within the same company will have different conditions. Skill levels, pay and conditions are socially structured and tend to be occupied by people with different characteristics such as gender or ethnicity.

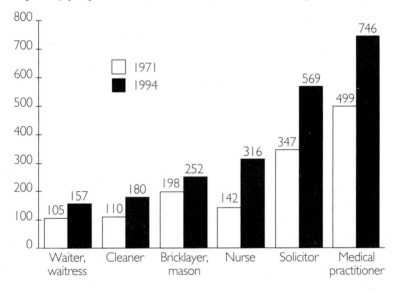

Source: Social Trends 25, 1995

Real gross earnings, £ per week, April 1994 prices

segregated conjugal roles: roles within a *marriage* in which the husband and wife perform separate and quite distinct tasks. Typically the male role is primarily defined as the 'breadwinner' and major decision-maker, while the wife's role is that of 'homemaker', with a sharp focus on *housework* and *childcare.* In her 1957 research, Bott found that couples with segregated domestic roles also tended to spend their *leisure* time in separate activities. (See *conjugal roles; joint conjugal roles.*)

segregation: the separation of one ethnic group from another, both geographically and socially, by means of law, customs and values. Segregation was an institutionalised system in the southern states of the United States, where the black population was separated from the dominant white majority through force, intimidation and ingrained habit. (See *bussing*.)

selective exposure: the idea that individuals do not use the mass media haphazardly, but with purpose. Katz and Lazarsfeld, for example, argue that people tend to look for media experiences which reinforce their existing *beliefs*. They therefore seek out media content which coincides with their views and turn away from those media experiences which contradict long-cherished beliefs. This view is supported by the trend towards theme television, for example, where channels are devoted to niche media markets, such as religious groups, sporting interests etc. People also seek out newspapers whose views tend to reinforce their existing political beliefs. In this context, it is interesting to compare the newspaper readership of Labour voters at the time of the 1992 *general election* with what *New Labour* voters read. (See *selective interpretation; selective retention*.)

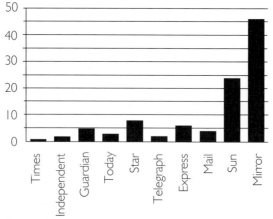

Source: Guardian Newspaper, 30.10.95

Labour voters newspaper readership – 1992 election

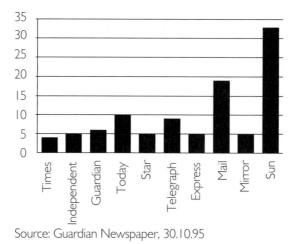

Source: Guardian Newspaper, 30.10.95

What New Labour voters read

selective interpretation: the way in which individuals see media images in a particular way, so that they are slotted into existing beliefs and attitudes, regardless of the intention of the producers of the media material. The classic example of this was the 'Mr Biggott' cartoon of Kendall and Wolfe's study. Although intended as a parody of bigoted views, the *audience* for the cartoon interpreted it in ways which fitted their existing prejudices. (See *selective exposure; selective retention.*)

selective retention: the way in which the *audience* for media content do not retain all the information they are given, but keep only those aspects which conform to their existing beliefs. (See *selective interpretation; selective exposure.*)

Self: in *symbolic interactionism,* the ability of an individual to see him or herself as an external object. That is, it is our ability to step outside ourselves and see the results of our actions as if we were someone else. It is the Self which allows us to anticipate the effects of our future actions and gauge the outcomes of alternative courses of action. It is therefore the basis of *calculability* in social life. (See *generalised other.*)

self-actualising theories: explanations of work motivation which assume that every individual has a *hierarchy of needs*, at the top of which is the need for individuals to fulfil their personal potential. Associated with Maslow and Argyris, such theories imply that a particular form of work organisation, that is one which offers opportunities for personal fulfilment, is the most efficient. Critics of these theories such as Silverman, argue that the need for self-actualisation is an assumption which cannot be proven. Rather, Silverman argued that needs are not unchanging and given, but vary according to the situation in which individuals find themselves. Therefore to base work organisation on the assumption that individuals need self-actualisation is mistaken. However, Argyris responded that Maslow had always recognised the changing nature of needs, and accepted that there was only a limited number of individuals for whom self-actualisation was a necessity. (See *job-enrichment.*)

self-assessed class: see *subjective social class*

self-employment: where workers work for themselves rather than for an employer. The self-employed sector is an important part of the economy constituting a block between capital and labour. The ranks of the self-employed are fragmented, including small entrepreneurs such as plumbers and low-paid casual workers such as *outworkers*. The role of self-employment is argued to be increasingly important in post-modern societies, where the costs of employment are likely to increase. Therefore, more and more people, it is argued, are likely to be self-employed by large-scale organisations as independent consultants, casual workers and the like, creating a *hidden economy*. (Please see table overleaf.)

Occupational group	Self-employed
Managers and administrators	19
Professional occupations	15
Associate professional and technical	15
Clerical and secretarial	3
Craft and related	29
Personal and protective services	4
Selling	6
Plant and machine operators	9
Other occupations	9
Manual workers	15
Non-manual workers	12
Total in self-employment	13
Total number of part-time male workers	1,139,000
Total number of part-time female workers	5,083,000
Total number of part-time workers	6,222,000

(Source: Labour Force Survey no. 14, December 1995)

Percentage of all who are self-employed, Summer 1995 (not seasonally adjusted)

self-estrangement: a condition of *alienation* identified by Blauner to indicate a feeling by workers of depersonalised detachment from work. It is the denial of *self-actualisation* in work. (See *isolation; powerlessness; meaninglessness.*)

self-fulfilling prophecy: a statement made about a predicted outcome which, by being made, helps to bring about that outcome. The concept is closely linked to that of *labelling*, and in sociology is used particularly in the contexts of *education* and *deviance*. It is argued that, by making a prediction, (e.g. these pupils will all do well because they are the brightest in the class) those in positions of influence will act as though the prediction were already true (i.e. in the case of the example, teachers would have high expectations of the pupils concerned). This also causes those about whom the prediction has been made to respond accordingly, and thus make the prediction come true. (See *pygmalion effect.*)

self-identity: used by postmodernists to describe the ways that the individual constantly creates an image of him or herself to present to the public world, in a reflexively self-conscious manner. Thus, individuals constantly re-create themselves through their everyday practice and re-write their own biographies by choosing life styles. The implication of this is that individuals no longer have a single *Self*, but re-construct themselves in a series of Selves throughout their lifetime. Giddens believes that the creation of self-identities empowers us, in that we can be who we want, when we want. Beck believes that this self-identity is uncomfortable, because if it is an unsuccessful Self, we have only ourselves to blame. (See *risk society.*)

self-orientation: one of Parsons' *pattern variables,* which argues that, in modern societies, *individualism* and personal success are more important than the interests of the collectivity. (See *collective orientation.*)

self-recruitment: the degree to which the sons and daughters of the members of a *social class* end up in the same social class themselves. The higher the degree of self-recruitment in a society, the more closed it is likely to be. Self-recruitment has been found to be highest amongst the top social class, as members use their privileges and position to ensure advantage for their own children. There is also a significant amount of self-recruitment amongst the *working class,* though this is mitigated by the *occupational transition.* (See *social mobility.*)

self-referral: a situation in which a *client* himself or herself seeks the services of a professional, e.g. a social worker or psychiatrist. (See *professional referral.*)

self-report studies: surveys of the population which ask them to confess to crime they have committed but for which they have not been caught. The studies are one of the ways in which the *dark figure* of crime can be shown. They have been criticised because there is no way of knowing how true the reports are, nor how representative they are of society as a whole. (See *victim surveys.*)

semi-autonomous employees: one of Wright's *contradictory class locations,* these are those non-owning occupational groups who sell their labour power, but who have some control over their own work processes because they have valued skills. An example often used is airline pilots, who have many of the features of the *proletariat* in their job, but also have some independence in the execution of their work.

semi-leisure: a concept developed by Dumazedier to indicate those activities carried out outside of work which have an element of compulsion attached to them. Though they may be done in a person's own time they are not necessarily pleasurable, e.g. *housework.* (See *leisure; non-work obligations.*)

semi-professions: a concept describing those occupations which aspire to professional status, the practitioners of which may call themselves professional, but who do not have the full range of professional powers. The semi-professions are associated with 'people-working' professions or what Bennet and Hokenstadt described as 'full-time people workers'. The knowledge base of the semi-professions is less theoretical than the traditional *professions,* and professional training is more concerned with the transmission of methodological skills than substantive knowledge. Teaching is a good example of a semi-profession. Another important difference between the traditional professions and semi-professions is that the latter tend to function largely in bureaucratic settings and are less likely to be found in private practice. (See *personal service professions.*)

semi-skilled labour: work where there are some basic capabilities needed by the worker to perform the task. Training is likely to be minimal and rewards relatively limited. (See *skilled labour; unskilled labour.*)

semiology: see *semiotics*

semiotics: the study of the system of *signs* in society. In the beginning semiotics was mainly concerned with *language,* but has been developed under Barthes into a powerful analysis of the symbols employed by the media and the *myths* that are deployed in modern societies. (See *signifiers.*)

separation of home and work: the process whereby, during the *industrial revolution,* the unity of family life and production was dissolved. Prior to *industrialisation,* most families worked together on the land and produced other goods they needed at home. Therefore the family unit was also a production unit. With the development of widespread factory production, economic life was transferred to locations outside the home and this was to have profound effects on *gender* roles. By converting the peasantry into wage-labourers, the female tasks of child-bearing and suckling could be less easily combined with productive work. Thus women were forced into a domestic role, with increased dependence on men. (See *cottage industry.*)

separation of ownership and control: developed as an idea by Berle and Means, it argued that with the emergence of the joint stock company, direct control of large corporations had, in the main, moved from the personal control of the owner to a situation in which the owners relinquished control of the firm to the managers. (See *managerial revolution.*)

serial monogamy: the recently developed pattern of *marriage* in which an individual can have several marriage partners over the course of his or her lifetime, with the majority of these marriages ending in *divorce.* The pattern is most apparent in the United States and is a consequence of increased *life expectancy* and the increased span of a lifetime marriage.

service class: used by Goldthorpe to describe those jobs at the top of the *occupational structure.* It is composed of the professional groups, administrators and managers and supervisors of non-manual employees. In following a Weberian schema, Goldthorpe was concerned to use styles of life rather than ownership as the distinguishing feature of classes.

setting: a form of dividing pupils into groups (sets) for particular subjects based on their ability in those subjects. Thus, a pupil might be in a top set for English, a middle set for French, and a bottom set for maths. The system is different from *streaming* in that children are divided for individual lessons, rather than across the *curriculum.* (See *banding.*)

sex: the biological divisions between males and females (and very occasionally hermaphrodites). Sex is argued by sociologists to be distinct from *gender.* Though the two are clearly connected, they are not necessarily directly related. Sociologists debate with members of other disciplines such as biologists the relative importance of biological forces such as sex, and social and cultural forces such as gender. Obviously, sociologists tend to give priority to social explanations in examining the differences between the sexes. However, there is some meeting of the disciplines of sociology and biology in this area, with various cross-cutting and complex interactions between them.

sex ratio: the balance between the numbers of men and women in a population. A balance between the sexes is usually reached around the age of 40, when the greater number of males born, and their propensity to die earlier than women, equalises. There are therefore more males in the population below the age of 40 and more females above the age of 40. In some societies, the practice of female infanticide and more recently selective *abortion* can lead to a greater imbalance in the sex ratio.

sex stereotyping: where ideas about the proper *roles* of men and women are given to over-simplification and near-caricature. The classic sex-stereotype is the distribution of paid work and domestic chores, in which women take prime responsibility for housework and men are the main breadwinners. This is stereotypical because there is a limited number of households which actually operate in this way, and yet it has a powerful ideological and political pull. The *mass media* provide a powerful source of sex stereotyping.

sexism: discrimination against a person or group on account of their biological sex. Most sexist practices have historically been aimed against women and they can either be deliberate or unconscious. Deliberate sexist practices and ideas are often drawn from fundamentalist interpretations of religion, in which women and men have clearly separate and unchallengeable roles, with women in the subordinate position. Though there are examples of overt sexism, sexism most frequently operates in western democracies through unconscious *sex-stereotyping*.

sexual division of labour: where work in its most general sense is divided between what is seen as women's work and what is men's. The most basic sexual division of labour is between paid employment and *domestic labour*, in which women have traditionally been allocated prime responsibility for the latter. In more recent times, the sexual division of labour has expressed itself in paid employment, where some jobs have come to be seen as primarily women's work. It is particularly in the lower levels of the caring occupations, such as nursing or cooking, that men and women have become occupationally segregated. (See *glass walls.*)

sexual harassment: the use of language or actions to denigrate and humiliate a person on account of their *gender*. The extent and importance of sexual harassment is a *site of ideological struggle* as different groups insist on its widespread prevalence or argue that it is much exaggerated. While sexual harassment undoubtedly does take place, sociologists have tried to establish its incidence in a variety of situations, most notably the classroom.

sexual orientation: used as a general term in sociology to describe the object of an individual's sexual drive. Though this is an individual characteristic, sociologists are interested in the way that groups develop around sexual orientations. While heterosexuals, whose orientation is towards the opposite sex, might be expected to form one group, there are obvious divisions within it, such as between men and women. Similarly, within the homosexual identity there are many divisions, the main one being between gay men and lesbians.

sexuality: see *sexual orientation*

shake-out: a term used to describe the loss of mainly manual labour from industries, due to automation of the production processes. The term substitutes as a neutral form of more negative concepts such as 'sacking people' or 'redundancies'. Since the 1980s a whole range of euphemisms has been developed to sanitise social developments with unpleasant consequences. (See *down-sizing*.)

shanty towns: an old and now little-used term for *favelas*, they are the unorganised housing areas which emerge in the *third world*, and which have few amenities such as running water or electricity. The term has fallen into disrepute as these areas become more established and serviced by the city councils of the area.

shift work: the organisation of labour, so that production is maintained round the clock, with the workers working in units of about eight hours. Workers usually have to take alternating turns at the different shifts, with the night shifts as the least popular. New computer technologies allow the intensive production associated with shift work and *high-tech* industries are often therefore associated with an intensification of shift work.

sick role: a social *role* legitimised by the medical profession which allows people to withdraw temporarily from their social duties and obligations. As a functionalist, Parsons believed that society would only work properly if everyone fulfilled their social obligations to the rest of society. Illness allows a legitimate, usually temporary, withdrawal from at least some of these obligations (e.g. going to work). Parsons suggested that by bringing sickness within the domain of doctors, people would be encouraged to 'become well' and take up their social duties again as soon as possible.

significant others: those who are given importance in a person's life, perhaps acting as *role-models*, but also those who constitute an important audience for a person in a particular role.

signification: the way that cultural *signs,* such as pictures and words, create meaning. For example, television images are not just windows on the world but are imbued with ideological meanings, which can be read like a *text.* Much of the signification of advertising is mythological, referring to an idealised past or setting, such as the use of pastoral scenes to sell factory-farmed produce.

signifiers: images, objects or words which bring to mind other ideas or meanings (the 'signified'). For example, a pastoral scene may be associated with freshness or pureness and therefore may be an important signifier for an advertising campaign for food.

sign: a symbol which stands for or represents something else. A sign indicates a relationship between a *signifier* and the signified. A sign may be a mark on a paper or a sound and is a central concept in *semiotics.* The meanings attached to signs may be direct and fairly obvious or they may be mediated, so that the meaning depends on social convention rather than direct symbolism. (See *semiotics.*)

signs proper: used by Saussure to indicate meanings derived from agreed conventions in society, such as red indicating 'stop'. (See *icons; index.*)

single parent families: see *lone-parent families*

sink estates: run-down council housing areas which have the highest concentration of people with problems, who are often allocated to the worst housing. As a product of the policy of some local councils, the sink estates tend to spiral into the most undesirable housing areas, from which people are desperate to escape and which themselves cause social problems, such as high levels of vandalism, drug-taking, suicide etc.

site of struggle: a term which describes any *location,* either geographical or social which is contested by different social groups. For example, housing is a site of struggle between different *housing classes* over access to various types of housing.

sites of ideological struggle: social locations in which the ideas of different social groups compete to establish precedence and domination. Schools are often cited as the prime site of ideological struggle in which advocates of different conceptions (of, for example, history) attempt to establish themselves as the legitimate holders of the subject. So traditional conceptions of history such as the exploits of great men, battle it out with those who argue for black history, women's history, social history and so on.

situatedness: used by post-modernists to describe where an individual stands in social formations. Our situatedness is concerned with our position in economic and social relationships, which groups we identify with or belong to etc. The importance of our situatedness is that it will affect the understanding we bring to bear on our experiences and create a partial knowledge of the world around us, distinct from (but no better than) other partial knowledge derived from the situatedness of others.

situational constraints: these are circumstances in which people find themselves which limit their course of action. For example, motherhood acts as a situational constraint to getting involved in political activity, though this does not usually apply to fatherhood. Situational constraints can be permanent or change as people move through their *life-cycle*. (See *institutional barriers*.)

situational constraints theory: an explanation of *poverty* which rejects the idea that it is the *culture* of the poor which is responsible, but argues that it is the circumstances in which the poor find themselves which are the cause of their poverty. In particular, it is the fact of low wages or *unemployment* which forces the poor to act the way they do. The poor therefore do not have a distinctive culture, but share that of mainstream society. They simply do not have the resources to finance the *life style* associated with mainstream culture.

situational rules: the guidelines to behaviour that actually operate in any given circumstance, as opposed to the formal rules which are supposed to be operating. The concept was developed by ethnomethodologists such as Bittner to explain how individuals made sense of their everyday activities. Bittner argued that individuals used or ignored formal rules according to the situation in which they found themselves and according to which best suited their intentions. The point that was important for the ethnomethodologists was that formal rules do not determine individuals' behaviour in *organisations*. Rather, they are used by individuals *reflexively* (referring to oneself and the position one is in) to justify any decision or course of action. Critics of this approach argue that it places too much emphasis on the *rationality* and spontaneous thought processes of social *actors*, while ignoring aspects of behaviour such as tradition or emotion.

situational withdrawal: a reaction to *total institutions*, in which the inmate withdraws attention from everything except the immediate events concerning the body and becomes a 'silent' and minimal participant in the everyday activities of the institution.

skewed deviants: according to Durkheim, these appear when society allows individual passions to have a free rein and the inappropriately socialised individual engages in deviant activity. Thus, the skewed deviant emerges in a society characterised by *anomie*.

skilled labour: work in which workers need a high level of training and specific capabilities in order to perform their tasks. Traditionally, skilled labour attracts higher wages and better conditions, although some highly skilled occupations may not be rewarded to the extent expected. (See *semi-skilled labour; unskilled labour*.)

skills: the abilities which individuals have and which occupations demand to varying degrees, so that effective performance can be achieved. There are many different types of skill, which exist in a *hierarchy* of *esteem*, and which can be concerned for example with manual manipulation, intellectual thought and design talent. Skills have been a focus for sociologists of education as vocationalists have argued for a greater emphasis on the skills needed for industry in a post-modern world. (See *new vocationalism*.)

skills crisis: a reference to the shortage of workers with the particular skills needed by employers. Despite the high number of workers who are unemployed, some employers find difficulty in filling vacancies as applicants lack the required skills. In order to try to overcome this, a number of initiatives have been launched, such as *NVQs* and Training for Skills.

slavery: an extreme form of *stratification* in which the enslaved have no rights or freedom, and are subject to the total control of their masters. Slaves are often drawn from a conquered people, and enslaved by the conquerors. Slavery appears to have existed before recorded history, and therefore is found in many different forms. An extreme form of slavery in which the slave is regarded as the property of the master, something to be bought and sold, is known as 'chattel slavery'.

sleeper effect: where the effects of media content are delayed, with the messages initially rejected, then accepted, as inhibiting factors are worn down by repetition of the message. (See *drip effect.*)

snowball sampling: a *sampling* method in which a researcher gains access to a group and then uses members of this group to make contact with others, and then in turn uses the new group to make further contacts, and so on. Although the method obviously does not result in a *random sample*, it is sometimes the only way to gain access to sufficient numbers of a particular kind of person, for example members of a religious *cult*, or people engaged in deviant activities.

social action: action affected by the existence of others, involving the understanding and interpreting of their behaviour. Social action therefore involves interaction, either directly or indirectly. An example of the direct form might be talking with another person. An example of indirect social action might be writing those same words in a letter, to be read by someone else later.

social benefits: a term usually referring to benefits, particularly financial ones, received through the *welfare state.* (See *means-tested benefits; universal benefits.*)

social change: the process whereby societies or aspects of society move from one state to another. The study of social change was central to the *classical sociologists,* because society was undergoing massive changes when the early sociologists were writing. Sociologists who emphasise social change at the expense of *social order,* tend to focus on *conflict* in society, and the contradictions that exist between social groups and interests. However, there is also a difference between those who stress social change through evolution and those who focus on revolutionary change. (See *consensus.*)

social class: the hierarchical divisions of a capitalist society, in which *wealth, income* and *occupation* form the defining characteristics of each group. The classic formulation of *social class* in Britain is of a three class society, upper, middle and working, in which the largest concentration of people is in the *working class.* As a rough rule-of-thumb, the distinction between manual and non-manual occupations can be seen as the dividing line between the middle and the working class. For the *upper class,* concentration of wealth, *power* and *status* are important as defining characteristics. Social class however is subject to change and some sociologists have suggested that there has developed a society in which the middle sector has grown so large that 'we are all *middle class* now'. Others argue that the significant development in social class during the 1980s has been the appearance of an *underclass,* with little prospect of full-time employment.

social closure: used by Weberians to indicate the attempts by social groups to monopolise privileges and rewards for themselves, by closing them off from other groups. Any social group can practise social closure, though the tactics employed tend to differ according to whether the group is at the top or bottom of the occupational *hierarchy*. The importance of the concept is that it helps to explain divisions within classes as well as between them and can take into account gender and ethnic complexities. (See *credentialism; exclusion; solidarism.*)

social construction: whereby a phenomenon is built up through social processes rather than being a natural occurrence. The use of the term social construction has become popular as sociologists have focused increasingly on *identity* as an organising principle of postmodern life. The term was originally used to describe the ways in which, for example, statistics did not always represent the real rate of what they were supposed to describe, but were the product of social processes involving many decisions by many individuals. In terms of identity, the concept is used to illustrate the view that an individual's character is not totally given, but is built up by the individual in terms of different conceptions of gender, ethnicity, sexuality etc., which are influenced by personal preference and the reactions of others.

social consumption: a term used to denote the use of goods and services beyond what is needed for basic subsistence. For example, consumption concerned with meeting religious or kinship obligations is social consumption, the demands of which can sometimes be met at the expense of individual consumption.

social contract: the agreement assumed by utilitarian theorists to exist between individuals when they come together to form a society. According to Hobbes, individuals in a *state of nature* are assumed to be anti-social, and liable to pursue their own selfish interests at the expense of others. However, this leaves individuals open to physical violence and threats. In order to avoid this, people form a society, in which they agree to respect the lives and property of others in return for being left in safety to pursue happiness, within limits. This does not mean that there is a real contract, but rather an implicit understanding that those who offend the social contract by engaging in crime should be punished in order to protect all the other members of society. (See *utilitarianism.*)

social control: the process whereby society seeks to ensure *conformity* to the dominant *values* and *norms* in that society. The processes may be informal, relying on the force of public or peer opinion to ensure compliance, or formal, employing specific social agencies to encourage or enforce conformity. The tactics adopted to establish social control may include a mixture of negative *sanctions*, which punish those who transgress the rules of society and positive policies which seek to persuade or encourage voluntary compliance with society's standards.

social democratic consensus: the post-war unspoken agreement which existed between the major political parties on the shape of social and political policies. The consensus focused on the *welfare state* as a way of redressing the disadvantages which certain sections of the population experienced and on promoting equal opportunity in a meritocratic society.

Social Democratic Party: a short-lived breakaway group from the *Labour Party* in the 1980s which stressed the importance of the social market, tempered by a concern for justice and social unity. It was opposed to the collectivist impulses of the Labour Party left and sought to break the two-party dominance of British politics. The majority eventually amalgamated with the Liberal party, apart from the Owenite tendency.

social disorganisation: describes the situation where there are conflicts in social codes and confusion about the proper way to behave. In such a situation, there is little stability in social relationships and the individual stands out as a separate entity, motivated by unregulated impulses and drives. The resulting loss of organisation, according to Cavan, can lead to increased *suicide* rates, as individuals become unable to cope with the instability. To Cavan, social disorganisation leads to personal disorganisation and increased suicide. (See *ecological fallacy*.)

social division of labour: a concept developed to describe occupational differences in society. It is used as a more sophisticated version of the idea of *specialisation* and in contrast to the *detailed division of labour*. In traditional societies there is only a limited social division of labour, with very little occupational specialisation. As societies become more complex they develop many more differences in occupations.

social engineering: planned social change brought about by the implementation of particular social policies. Some argue that social engineering is a legitimate and even desirable role of governments, while others are concerned at the potential for the abuse of such power, citing examples such as Nazi Germany as evidence. Education policies in particular are often viewed as social engineering, e.g. the *tri-partite system*, *comprehensivisation*, and the American policy of *'bussing'* children to achieve greater racial integration in schools.

social facts: phenomena which are external to the individual, but which act upon him or her in a constraining way A good example of a social fact is a law, as it exists independently of any individual yet shapes the way he or she acts. Durkheim argued that sociologists should 'treat social facts as things', that is, deal with them as if they were actually real, with an objective existence beyond individual subjectivity. (See *reification*.)

social forces: used by Durkheim to indicate aspects of society external to the individual, which act upon the individual. An example of a social force might be a wave of patriotism, which could sweep up the individual, who would then both contribute to it, but also be propelled by it.

social fund: a budget made available to Department of Social Security (DSS) offices to provide loans to the recipients of social security benefits. The loan system, introduced under the 1988 Social Security Act, replaced the system of grants for the provision of items of clothing and essential equipment such as beds, bedding and cookers. Only a very limited number of people are still eligible for grants. The intention was to create a sense of social responsibility amongst benefit claimants, by making them manage their financial affairs and repay the loans. However, social security officers have to keep within strict budget limits, which means that some people, although in need and eligible for a loan, are unable to receive one. Similarly, claimants who are in debt and who may be having repayments deducted at source from their benefits may be refused a loan on the grounds that they would be unable to repay it. One intention of the Conservative government which introduced the system was to encourage the voluntary sector, such as charities, to play a greater role in the provision of *welfare*.

social inequality: the skewed distribution of the scarce resources in society, which is reflected in an unequal distribution of prestige and feelings of superiority and inferiority amongst individuals.

social mobility: movement up and down the *class structure*. The study of social mobility is one of the central concerns of *social stratification* theorists. The amount of social mobility is a measure of how rigid a society is and how locked into traditional structures it is. A high degree of social mobility therefore makes the drawing of class boundaries difficult, because of the fluidity it engenders. It is also difficult to measure the extent of social mobility, because it relies on occupational scales (such as the *Registrar-General's*) with all the problems that these have. (See *inter-generational mobility; intra-generational mobility.*)

social order: the patterned *action* or regularities which people display in their social lives. It is social order which allows a degree of predictability in social life and therefore allows much social life to proceed. A focus on social order by sociologists tends to lead to conservative perspectives about the social world, emphasising integration and cohesion at the expense of *conflict* and change.

social policy: the actions of governments and their agents in relation to their citizens. While social policy is usually associated with the legislative activities of the *State* in the area of the *welfare state* (housing, health etc.) the term covers wider activities than these, such as taxation, pension policies and employment laws. In academic terms, social policy is the economic, sociological and political study of the impact of planned government activity. The relationship between social policy and sociology is seen differently by various sociologists:

- Some argue that there is a direct input into social policy by sociologists, especially those who are used by the government as consultants or employees.
- Others argue that the importance of sociology for social policy is in creating a climate of opinion which influences the development of policies.
- Yet others argue that sociology should have little or no effect on social policy, because sociologists should stand aside from government and be critical of its actions.

social problem: (as distinct from a sociological problem) this is a phenomenon which society identifies as being in need of remedial action, because of its negative effects on individuals or on society as a whole. Although social problems such as *poverty*, ill-health and hooliganism are often the focus for sociological study, sociologists do not confine their interest only to the problematic features of social life. They are equally interested in the positive aspects.

social science: a general term which covers subjects concerned with the workings of society in some respects and which seek to establish general propositions about them. The term usually covers sociology, psychology, economics and politics.

social security: the system of welfare support provided by the *State* to its citizens. It has two elements. There is a contributory aspect, in which unemployment benefits, old age pensions and sickness benefits are paid through National Insurance contributions. There is also a non-contributory element, which provides a safety net for those in most need.

social segregation: a feature of urban living, this refers to the separation of social groups into distinctive neighbourhoods and the lack of social interaction between them. Wirth argued that as cities grow the degree of social segregation increases, so that any relationships between different social groups in the city are composed of emotionally empty contacts, with only segmental and instrumental involvement.

social selection explanation: an explanation for the preponderance of ill-health among the lowest-paid which argues that their lack of selection for higher paid jobs is a result of their ill-health. The causal relationship is therefore from ill-health to low pay and not vice versa. (See *Black Report.*)

social status: the honour or prestige given by members of society to groups or individuals. This is based not just on economic standing, but on social standing as a whole and has a real manifestation in the life styles of the groups or individuals associated with a particular status. The concept is particularly associated with Weber, who used it to obtain a finer analysis of social differentiation than class analysis allowed. Moreover, Weber argued that social status was a firmer basis for the analysis of *social action* than class itself.

social structure: see *structure*

social surveys: the systematic collection of information about a given population. The term is commonly used in connection with surveys using standardised *questionnaires.* Social surveys usually result in *quantitative data* about the population studied, and are widely used, not only in sociological research but also by government departments and in market research. Although most social surveys gain their information from *sampling* the population, the largest social survey in Britain is the ten-yearly *census,* which attempts to include all members of society.

social system: patterned regularities and relationships between individual *actors* and collectivities, reproduced over time and space. They are thus relatively permanent features of society which individuals invest with an external existence, talking about them as if they were real.

Social Trends: an annual digest of statistics published by the Central Statistical Office, the government agency responsible for compiling and publishing a wide range of *official statistics* for the United Kingdom. Social Trends provides a wealth of *secondary data* for social scientists, covering many aspects of life in contemporary Britain. To celebrate the 25th anniversary of the publication, a CD-ROM was issued in 1995 with data from every edition of Social Trends from 1970–1995.

social world: used as contrast to the *natural world,* this is the world constructed by human beings and their activities. It includes physical artefacts which people manufacture, and also patterned regularities that we create through our interactions. The social world is therefore composed of buildings, *institutions, structures,* dyads, triads etc.

socialisation: the process whereby the young of a society learn the *values,* ideas, practices and *roles* of that society. The socialisation process is a semi-conscious one, in that the major agency for socialisation, the family, would not necessarily see itself in this role, while some *secondary socialisation* agencies such as *education* are deliberately set up for this purpose. The socialisation process is never total, as the young take on some of the lessons, but reject, adapt or expand on others. In this way, societies retain some continuity but also progress.

socialism: a political philosophy which stresses the communal ownership of the *means of production* and communitarian policies. It has many variations, ranging from the complete control of all productive processes to more utopian notions of communal living, in which individuals take responsibility for their own decisions within a *frame of reference* which includes the collective.

socially aspiring worker: a member of the *working class* who seeks to join the *middle class,* either economically or socially. The concept is used to distinguish workers who wish to be mobile (whether they are accepted by the middle class as equals or not) from those who are happy to remain working-class and have no ambitions to be socially mobile. (See *assimilated worker.*)

society: the social totality of all the relationships in a given space. The notion of a society exists at several different levels. In the main, it is used in conjunction with the *nation-state* as a society, in that within the boundaries of a nation-state, a distinctive society is likely to form. However, there is also a sense in which there is a human society, of all human relationships together. In the Durkheimian sense, society has a real existence outside of the individuals who form it. Sociologists may also use society in a non-nation-state sense, for example in defining 'Jewish society'.

sociobiology: an approach to social behaviour which argues that patterns of human conduct can be explained by biological imperatives such as the drive to spread genetic inheritance as widely as possible. It was developed from Darwinian notions, but goes much beyond these, seeking to explain social arrangements as the inevitable consequence of biological inheritance. It has been criticised by sociologists because:

- it is deterministic, in identifying patterns of behaviour which cannot be altered by free choice
- it ends up defending the status quo and traditional gender roles
- it does not explain the mechanisms whereby biological drives can only be satisfied in particular ways.

(See *genetics.*)

sociocultural deference: an acceptance of a traditional social and moral order, sometimes known as 'traditionalism'. (See *ascriptive socio-political deference; political deference.*)

socioeconomic group: broad collections of individuals who share similar occupational positions in the social hierarchy. They are thus wider than occupations but smaller than classes and constitute a sub-group within a *social class.* For example, skilled manual workers form a socioeconomic group distinct from unskilled manual workers.

sociotechnical system: a way of looking at productive *organisations* associated with the *Tavistock Institute,* in which human factors were taken into account as much as the physical requirements of the machines. The point about a sociotechnical system approach was that it repudiated a *technological determinist* approach, arguing that managers had choices when designing work-flow systems, which could take into account the need for workers to be satisfied in their work.

sociodrama: group role-playing which helps individuals to deal with problematic relationships and issues; developed by Moreno.

sociolinguistics: the study of *language* in its social and cultural context. Sociolinguistics has been particularly concerned to examine the class, ethnic and gendered forms of language which individuals create and develop and which are transmitted through everyday life and through *cultural reproduction.*

sociological imagination: the ability to link the experiences of individuals to the social processes and structures of the wider world. It is this ability to examine the ways that individuals construct the social world and how the social world impinges on the lives of individuals, which is at the heart of the sociological enterprise.

sociological myth: the belief held by some teachers and drawn from ill-digested lessons in sociology that all working-class children under-achieve. It is mythical because many working-class children are highly successful within the education system. However, this sociological myth plays an important part in the *labelling* and *self-fulfilling prophecy* processes, which may influence some working-class students to accept the label of 'failure' and act accordingly.

sociology: the study of individuals in groups and social formations in a systematic way, which grew out of the search for understanding associated with the industrial and scientific revolutions of the eighteenth and nineteenth centuries. It is now an established discipline in post-16 education and has offered generations of students insights into the social world they inhabit. Often accused by the right of being left-wing, it includes individuals of every political opinion, who are united by a commitment to search for knowledge and understanding, through providing evidence for the theories and insights they offer.

sociology as a science: one of the key theoretical debates in sociology, namely whether it should follow the principles and practices of the *natural sciences.* Those sociologists who argue that it should are called 'sociological *positivists*', while those who do not believe that sociology should be a science are generally called 'anti-positivists'. However, the terms positivist and anti-positivist hide a variety of positions. Positivists can be functionalist in their approach or Marxist. Anti-positivists include those who wish sociology could be a science, but feel that it is impossible because of the nature of the subject-matter, and those who believe that sociologists should never try to be scientific, because human beings are not able to be studied in a scientific way. The crucial difference between the two positions concerns their attitude towards their subject matter. Ultimately, positivists believe that there is sufficient regularity of behaviour amongst people to generate *laws* about them. Anti-positivists argue that human beings have *free will*, are awkward and contradictory, so that laws about them can never be generated.

sociology of the underdog: used by Becker to describe his taking the side of the powerless in society when doing sociology. Becker argued that, since *value-freedom* was impossible, it was imperative that all sociologists declare their allegiances. For him, this meant that he looked at social phenomena from the perspective of those most disadvantaged in society and his sociology was geared to bettering their position. Gouldner criticises this as not being a sociology of the underdog, but a sociology for the underdog by well-paid, well-meaning, middle-class sociologists. (See *hierarchies of credibility.*)

sociogram: see *sociometry*

sociometry: a method developed by Moreno of gaining information about how the members of a group feel about each other, in order to identify types of relationship within the wider group. It is widely used, particularly in the USA, in education and the workplace to study group dynamics. The method involves asking members of the group questions such as 'who are your best friends?' or 'whom do you least like to be with?'. The replies are plotted on a diagram, known as a sociogram, and individuals can be identified as 'stars' (those who receive lots of positive choices) and 'isolates' (those who receive few, if any, friendship choices). The sociogram also allows friendship groups or clusters to be identified, which can be useful when asking people to work collaboratively in teams.

soft statistics: statistics which are particularly prone to *subjectivity* in both their collection and presentation. These are usually statistics which describe aspects of society in which the potential for value judgements on the part of those who collect and those who interpret the data is very high, either because of the nature of the phenomenon under consideration, or as a result of political motivation. Examples of soft statistics are those on *crime, suicide, strikes* and *poverty*. (See *hard statistics; official statistics.*)

solidarism: a tactic of *social closure*, in which a social group acts collectively to gain increased rewards, usually from superordinate groups. It is mainly associated with the working-class *trade unions*. Solidaristic tactics include *collective bargaining*, striking and demarcation disputes. (See *exclusion; credentialism.*)

solidarity: the feelings of identification and mutual interest manifested by a group. It is usually associated with the proletarian fraction of the working class and has a real existence in the actions that they employ to defend their interests, such as trade unionism or political activities.

span of control theory: the span of control is the ratio of managers to workers in an organisation and the theory suggests that workers work best when the span is large and therefore supervision is light. Likert for example, showed that both morale and productivity were higher when control was carried out with a light touch. It is a contrast to *scientific management* which argued for a narrow span and tight control over the activities of workers. (See *Taylorism.*)

spatial boundaries: used by post-modernists to refer to the distinctions in location in which activities are carried out. Modernity is typified by boundedness in which different activities would have particular spaces given over to them. As an example, in schools this might be the science laboratory or the sociology department. It is argued that in post-modern societies these spatial boundaries dissolve so that rigid distinctions of location no longer exist. (See *temporal boundaries.*)

special needs: a term applied to those who, generally because of a disability, have needs additional to those of others without such disability. It also implies a duty on the relevant institution or organisation to try to meet those needs. The term is particularly used in the context of *education*, where it is correctly known as 'special educational needs', and is applied to pupils with either physical disabilities, learning difficulties or a combination of both.

specialisation: the splitting down of work tasks into their smallest constitutional parts. Though it is sometimes referred to as the *division of labour*, they are not quite the same thing. Specialisation is a central feature of *Taylorism*, and describes the ways in which any work task can be broken down into smaller tasks. This means that workers will specialise in a work activity which is less and less skilful, so that less training and financial reward for the worker is needed. Specialisation therefore contributes fundamentally to the profitability of firms who are mass producing standardised goods.

spiralists: identified by Watson as those who are upwardly mobile through climbing *hierarchies* in large-scale *organisations*. They tend also to be geographically mobile and rely on expert knowledge in making claim to a higher *status*. (See *burgesses*.)

spirit of capitalism: the ideas, values and typical modes of behaviour of Calvinistic Protestantism, which underlie the practices of *capitalism*. The ideas of thrift, self-discipline and a capacity for hard work were seen by Weber as the source of the patterns of behaviour which were appropriate for the development of the capitalist system of production. However, this idea has been criticised from a variety of positions:

- Some sociologists have argued that Weber does not show that the early capitalists, although Protestant, actually held these ideas in any depth.
- Others have argued that it was not the Calvinist ideas which were important for the Protestants' behaviour, but their marginality in a Catholic-dominated world which led them to capitalist practices.
- Still others have argued that the ideas came from the practices of capitalism and did not cause it.

spiritualism: a belief, and the practices arising from such belief, in the existence of the disembodied 'spirits' of people now dead, and the ability of certain people to communicate with them. While it is difficult to obtain figures, spiritualism appears to have a considerable number of believers in Britain. The medium Doris Stokes, although accused of being a fraud, was easily able to find audiences to fill very large theatres and auditoria when she 'performed' on stage. The belief in spiritualism is used by some to cast doubt on Weber's idea of *disenchantment*.

sponsored mobility: a form of *social mobility* which allows working-class children to achieve upward mobility by winning places at *grammar schools* and achieving good academic qualifications. The concept was used by R. Turner in the 1950s, when England and Wales had a *tri-partite system* of education, to make a comparison between the English and American education systems. (See *contest mobility*.)

spurious correlation: a situation in which there appears to be a correlation between two or more variables, but in fact no causal relationship exists. For example, it might well be shown that the rise in the number of cohabiting couples has been accompanied by a rise in the ownership of mobile telephones, but it would be most unwise to suggest that one was caused by the other.

stages of development: see *five stages of economic growth*

stages of the family: the argument made by Willmott and Young that *family structure* in Britain can be shown as passing through a number of historical stages. These, they suggest are:

- Stage 1 – the pre-industrial family. The family is primarily a unit of production. This type of family gradually died out with the spread of *industrialisation*.

- Stage 2 – the early industrial family. The family ceases to be a unit of production and members become individual wage-earners. The *extended family* and *kinship* networks provide important support. This type of family was typical of the late 18th, 19th, and early 20th centuries.
- Stage 3 – the *symmetrical family*. The family becomes smaller and more *privatised*. Conjugal roles become more 'symmetrical' (i.e. more egalitarian) even though not the same. This is partly a response to the increasing participation of married women in the labour force.
- Stage 4 – the asymmetrical family. This was perhaps a more tentative model, and was based on the family life of a *sample* of managing directors. The men become more work-oriented and less likely to spend most of their *leisure* time at home. Women take the major responsibility for the home and children. Wilmott and Young, referring to the notion of *stratified diffusion*, suggested that changes in technology would give more people interesting jobs, and the work-oriented life style of the managing directors in their sample would 'diffuse' downwards to other social groups.

Wilmott and Young point out that their model represents the dominant, rather than the only type of family structure in any one stage. Most of the attention which has been given to these arguments has focused on the stage 3 symmetrical family. Many sociologists, particularly feminists, argue that there is little evidence for the widespread existence of such families. There is also little evidence to suggest that technological changes are resulting in more people being engaged in interesting jobs. (See *domestic division of labour; new man.*)

standardised assessment tests (SATs): nationally-administered tests which form an important part of the *National Curriculum* and are administered to all children in *maintained sector* schools at the ages of 7, 11 and 14. The results are made public so that parents may compare the performance of different schools. The Conservative government which introduced the system wished to have a national standard of pupils' attainment, and hoped that the SATs would bring about more rigour, particularly in primary schools. Teachers have complained about the very heavy administrative load the SATs have produced, and some have been unhappy at the constraining effect they have had on the *curriculum*. Pupils in independent schools do not have to take the tests. (See *league tables.*)

standardised interview: see *structured interview*

state: a wider term than *government*, this includes all the organisations which are agencies of the governing institutions in society and their activities amongst the general populace. Thus, Parliament and the Royal family are obvious parts of the state, but so are the civil service, the military, the organisations which provide welfare and social security and the public education system. The growth of state activity in the twentieth century has been enormous and sociologists have been interested in the extension of state *power* and attempts to roll back the frontiers of the state. The political balance between the state and the individual has been a focus for sociological investigation, as well as being politically controversial in itself. (See *centralisation.*)

state capitalism: used by Barrington-Moore to denote the development of private industry in Japan, sponsored and guided for political reasons by state support. The political leadership of nineteenth-century Japan saw rapid *industrialisation* as the only way to avoid the imperialistic tendencies of the western powers and therefore grafted onto the traditional great houses of Japan a system of industrial development, which left large numbers of firms concentrated in private hands. However, plans for industrial development were determined centrally in the national interest, rather than occurring piecemeal as individual capitalists saw opportunities to profit. (See *state socialism.*)

state of nature: a hypothetical position which is used by philosophers to describe the condition in which there is no society. It is assumed that, as basic human nature is selfish, the state of nature is a war of all against all, in which unconstrained desire leads to a life which is 'nasty, selfish, brutish and short'. Society is therefore brought into being to avoid the state of nature. (See *utilitarianism.*)

state schools: see *maintained sector*

state socialism: used by Barrington-Moore to describe industrial development in which enterprises are sponsored and directly owned by the *State*. This leads to a centrally planned economy, in which the national development plan determines where resources should be placed, which sectors should be developed and which neglected. This centralisation allowed heavy industrial development to take place in the Soviet Union, but at the expense of consumer products and meeting the material needs of the population. (See *state capitalism.*)

state-dependent population: those who rely on public provision for their major services. For example, pensioners receiving only the old age pension are part of the state-dependent population. Benefit claimants, council house tenants and anyone else who needs state support for their main source of *income* are part of this group. (See *welfare dependency.*)

status: a position in society associated with particular *roles* and duties. It is not the same as *social status*, which is associated with Weberian sociology.

status consciousness: a belief that individuals can advance by their own actions, and achieve improvement in their lot by virtue of their own efforts. (See *trade union consciousness; class consciousness.*)

status frustration: where individuals have their aspirations to a particular position in the social *hierarchy* blocked by circumstances, such as a lack of qualifications, *social closure* by superior groups or even bad luck.

status group: a collectivity, distinguished from others by the amount of *prestige* or honour which is accorded to it. Social positions such as occupation or class position have negative or positive estimations of honour attached to them and these are grouped into a *hierarchy* of superior and subordinate status groups.

status inconsistency: where the estimation of *prestige* given to individuals does not accord with some other social position which they are also in. For example, status inconsistency is accorded to those black individuals who occupy high occupational positions in the *professions*.

status passage: a concept developed by the *Chicago School* to indicate the transformation of an individual into a 'professional'. The Chicago School argued that professionalism was a state of mind, into which individuals (both professionals and *clients*) had to be inducted. This was achieved with professionals through intensive training and socialisation into professional *culture* and ethics. It was this process which took the individual from a 'lay' frame of mind and gave them the status of professional.

status predicament: used by interactionists to describe the contradictions in consciousness experienced by those in middle-class occupations, who are subject to *proletarianisation* forces. For example, the traditional middle-class orientation of clerical workers has been challenged by changes in their objective circumstances, so that they have been pulled towards a working-class consciousness. The dilemma for them is how to reconcile their historical allegiances with their changed circumstances.

status situation: used by Lockwood to describe the identification of clerical workers and their relationship with their employers. Traditionally, clerks have been close to employers, both physically, in terms of their *work situation* and ideologically, in the sense that they identified their fortunes as resting with the employers. The status situation implied a sense of superiority in the consciousness of clerks over manual workers. The *proletarianisation* thesis suggested that this identification was being replaced by a solidarity of consciousness with the *working class*. (See *work situation; market situation*.)

statutory services: services which the *state* undertakes to provide for citizens as a right of *citizenship*. Examples of statutory services are education, health care and child benefit. (See *non-statutory services*.)

stereotyping: the process whereby groups or individuals are characterised in simplified and often pejorative terms, so that all members of the category are seen in one particular way. For example, popular stereotypes of gay people include some form of effeminate behaviour, so that all gays become seen as taking on female characteristics, whether they do or not.

stigmatisation: the process whereby individuals are labelled with some marginalising characteristic, such as 'deviant' 'mad' etc. Causes of stigma may vary from negative signs or names to some physical attribute, such as 'staring eyes'. The result of stigmatisation is usually that the stigmatised are prevented from being fully accepted by the rest of society. Where the stigma is accepted by the person being stigmatised it becomes an important part of the *self-fulfilling prophecy*.

straight fight: a constituency or ward where only the two main parties are competing for the electorate's vote. The proportion of constituencies in a *general election* in which there are straight fights has declined as third parties have increased in popularity. (See *marginal seat; three-way marginal*.)

stratification: the hierarchical division of societies on the basis of a social characteristic. Social differences are stratified in societies when the relative possession or non-possession of a social characteristic such as *wealth* or *status* becomes the distributing principle for individuals within a system of unequal rewards. Different societies use various organising principles for slotting individuals into the *hierarchy*. Traditional societies have often used hereditary characteristics as the basis for distribution, while more modern societies often use wealth or income. The importance of stratification is that those at the top of the system have greater access to scarce resources than those at the bottom.

stratified diffusion: the view that particular cultural beliefs and practices spread from the upper social groups down through the status *hierarchy* to lower groups. It is thus believed that many practices which are first observed in the middle classes will filter down to the working classes. Bott believed that the *joint conjugal roles* which she observed in middle-class couples would eventually replace the working-class *segregated conjugal roles*, and it is suggested that the '*new man*' will begin to emerge in working-class families. However, critics claim that the evidence shows that this is a grossly over-simplified view of the spread of cultural beliefs and practices, and it is by no means a simple one-way process.

stratified sampling: a form of *sampling* in which the *survey population* is first divided into mutually exclusive groups and then a *sample* is drawn from each, the size of the sample in each being proportionate to the number of members of that group in the survey population. For example, a survey of a college in which there were 2000 students, equally divided between males and females, might be conducted by drawing a simple random sample of 100 male and 100 female students. However, if the students were drawn from three distinct and very different neighbourhoods, in the proportion of 1000 students from neighbourhood A, 800 from neighbourhood B and 200 from neighbourhood C, the students could first be divided into three groups, A, B and C, reflecting their home neighbourhood. A sample could then be drawn from each group, with 100 from A, 80 from B and 20 from C, with equal numbers of male and female students in each, assuming that each group had a roughly equal balance of males and females. This arrangement is likely to be more *representative* than a *simple random sample*.

streaming: an organisational device used in some schools by which pupils are divided into separate streams according to their supposed ability. Streams are generally rigid, in that a pupil will remain in the same stream across all areas of the *curriculum*. Movement between streams is relatively rare, as pupils in different streams tend to be taught at different levels, and sometimes have access to different subjects, e.g. only top stream pupils being able to take Latin, or only bottom stream pupils doing woodwork. Research studies have shown that streaming is a powerful influence on the formation of pupil *sub-cultures* in school, sometimes with negative consequences for the pupils and the school. (See *banding; labelling; setting*.)

street crime: one of the most visible forms of crime and associated with degrees of violence, it includes activities such as mugging, robbery with violence and snatching, and is usually perpetrated by the working class on the working class. It is thus the most feared and despised type of crime.

streets-in-the-sky: a concept describing the high-rise developments in housing in the post-War period. Originally, tower blocks were seen as a solution to the chronic housing shortage. They offered high-density, low-cost housing which could be built quickly. Architects and planners were motivated to improve the lot of ordinary people by providing them with this kind of housing. However, the streets-in-the-sky quickly became unpopular with the people who lived in them for a variety of reasons. They were low-cost because many were not well-built, and for this reason beset with problems of damp, lifts continually breaking down, or deterioration in the concrete fabric. They also gave greater opportunities for criminals to operate, and the absence of gardens and safe play spaces for children led to a decline in communality.

strike duration ratio: an indicator of strike activity obtained by dividing the number of working days lost by the number of workers involved in strikes for a particular year. It was used by Ross and Hartman to show that there had been a gradual decline in the striking habit since the Second World War.

strike rates: the measurement of recorded withdrawals of labour which allows comparisons to be made between different firms in the same industry, different industries and different societies. Raw strike statistics tell sociologists very little about the propensity to strike and do not allow inter-industry or inter-societal comparisons. The production of strike rate statistics allow such comparisons to be made, through taking into consideration for example, the numbers of days lost per 1000 workers. (See *membership involvement ratio; strike duration ratio.*)

strike statistics: the number of stoppages of work reported to the government in any one year. The problem with strike statistics is that they are a *soft statistic*, with problems about the *reliability* of collection and therefore about their validity. For example, different governments use different definitions of what constitutes a reportable strike and it is therefore difficult to make cross-cultural comparisons of strike rates. Moreover, many strikes go unreported as the management neglects to inform the government. It is thought therefore that the total number of strikes is under-estimated. Some sociologists argue that the strike statistics are subject to *social negotiation* and are therefore not very valid. Most published statistics on strikes in the UK show an overall decline in the last 25 years, though the trend is far from even. However, a low rate of strike activity does not necessarily indicate worker satisfaction, as the ability to take legal strike action in Britain was severely curtailed during the years of the Thatcher government.

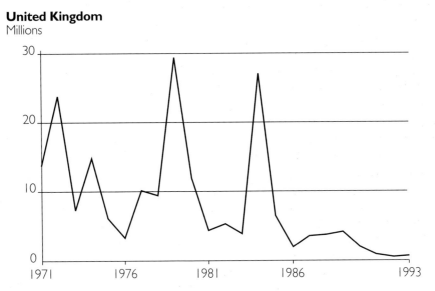

United Kingdom
Millions

Source: Employment Department

Labour disputes: working days lost

strike-proneness: the propensity of workers in a particular industry or country to go on strike. Industries associated with high strike-proneness are mining, ship-building and other heavy manufacturing occupations. Those with low strike-proneness are agriculture, and most types of office work. (See *cohesive mass segregation.*)

strikes: a form of *industrial conflict* in which workers withdraw their labour to achieve their goals. Strikes may be official, that is, held with the support of the *trade union,* or unofficial. Sociological interest in strikes is three-fold:

- as a measure of industrial discontent in a society
- in the causes of strike action
- in the experience of being on strike

(See *unofficial strike; wildcat strike.*)

structural differentiation: the historical process whereby social structures become increasingly specialised and segregated from each other. It was seen as an important part of the *modernisation* process by Parsons, who argued for example that as religious institutions withdrew from non-religious functions such as welfare, they became more effective institutions, focusing only on their core activities. Structural differentiation therefore produced purer more spiritual religious organisations.

structural location: the position of individuals in the social arrangements of a society. Structural location may include a whole range of factors ranging from the size of the workplace of the individual to whether a person lives in a rural or urban environment.

structural position: see *structural location*

structural-functionalism: the form of *functionalism* associated with Talcott Parsons, with an emphasis on the way that *structures* in society interact with each other to perform positive roles for society as a whole. The distinctive feature of structural-functionalism is the notion that everything that exists in society has a positive function to perform. This has been criticised, not least by other functionalists, as providing justification for the existence of such phenomena as the mafia, child abuse etc. (See *functionalism.*)

structuralism: theories in sociology which give priority to the analysis of social structures, rather than the individual. There are many variants of structuralism, but they all operate from the premise that there are underlying rationales or formations in society which are initially hidden from the individual, but which can be explored by sociologists and laid bare by them. The individual is thus unimportant except in so far as he or she carries out the *actions* dictated by their structural position. More recently, structuralism has become closely associated with the analysis of *language* through the work of Saussure and Barthes. Language is seen as the fundamental structure in society, with all human products being a form of language. So, while every sentence may be a 'speech act', it is drawn from an underlying structure of language, made up of the rules about the relationships of sounds to ideas. (See *icons; index; signs proper.*)

structuration: developed by Giddens to dissolve the structure-action dualism, it stresses the mutual inter-dependence of *structure* and *action,* in that structures are created by the patterned activities of individuals, who call upon structural forms in order to perform those actions.

structure: a term widely used in sociology to indicate a social formation which is more than just a collection of individuals or groups. Social structures are relatively permanent features of society which take on new characteristics different from the individuals who make up the social structure. So, a structure will survive the death of any individual member, will have a history of its own and has a role to play in society beyond that played by any individual life. Examples of structures are the *family*, the *education* system and language itself. *Language* is a structure because it is made up of words, which when placed together in sentences take on a meaning beyond the individual words which compose the sentence. Language changes over time (it has a history), it extends across *generations* (it survives the death of any individual member) and it is the means by which individuals are able to act together in society (it has a role to play). However, it is important to recognise that a structure is not a thing and does not have thing-like attributes. Structures are found in the continued activities of individuals across time and space.

structure-action dualism: this is one of the central debates in sociology, concerning whether it is the actions of individuals which are the prime social phenomena, or whether social structures are the more important aspect of social activity. Sociologists divide on this issue to become structuralists or interactionists. However, the distinction is in many senses a false one, with most sociologists dealing with both aspects in their work, even where they do focus their attention on one level at the expense of the other.

structured interviews: *interviews* typically used in large-scale *social surveys*, in which *respondents* are asked the same questions in the same order and their replies codified. It is argued that this type of interview helps to reduce significantly the degree of *interviewer bias*. However, structured interviews by their nature do not yield the kind of in-depth information which can be gained from an *unstructured interview*.

structured questionnaires: questionnaires which use closed, *pre-coded questions*.

style: in sociology, this is used to describe the features of *sub-cultures* in symbolic form. A style is composed of the dress, speech, behaviour and leisure interests of sub-cultural groups. When placed together they form a distinctive image, which identifies an individual immediately as a member of the sub-culture. The style adopted can also indicate the sub-culture's attitudes towards mainstream society, and whether this is *oppositional* or *conformist*. (See *resistance*.)

styles of life: associated with Weber, these are the patterns of consumption carried out by particular status groups in society. On a mundane level, the style of life is associated with the goods that people consume and the taste that they exhibit. At a deeper level, they are the standards of propriety, judgement and good taste which each group holds to. The problem with the concept is it is difficult to determine who decides what constitutes good taste.

sub-contracting: where a firm gives out parts of the production process to other independent firms, because it is cheaper for them to do it than the main firm carrying it out themselves. Non-essential processes, such as catering or cleaning are often sub-contracted, which has the effect of *down-sizing* the main firm's work-force. (See *periphery workers*.)

sub-cultural signs: these are symbols which denote membership of a specific group, which is separated from the rest of society. They are often symbols like dress, music, ways of behaving or a particular form of slang.

sub-culture: an identifiable group within a society, whose members share common *values* and have similar behaviour patterns. Sub-cultures can be based around social characteristics, such as ethnicity, or on *styles* generated by the individuals who make up the sub-culture, as in the case of punk. Sub-cultures usually share some features with the host culture, but may also be oppositional to it.

sub-employment: developed by Braverman to indicate those who are not in full employment, but who do not register as officially unemployed. These are:

- those long-term unemployed who have given up looking for work and therefore cease to register as unemployed. This group is particularly large amongst the black and Hispanic populations of the United States
- part-time workers, who are low-paid
- those paid below the minimum wage in the United States, often illegal immigrants.

sub-standard housing: housing in need of repair to make it fit for habitation. The Department of the Environment classifies the 'worst' housing as the 10% of dwellings with the highest repair costs to bring them up to fitness for habitation. A 1991 survey showed that the worst housing (as defined above) is found in urban areas, village centres and isolated rural areas, with inner London having the highest percentage (16%) of such dwellings. The survey also showed an ethnic bias to the occupancy of substandard housing, with white and Afro-Caribbean households less likely than average to be living in such housing, while one in five households headed by a Pakistani or a Bangladeshi lived in unsatisfactory housing, more than twice the average for all ethnic groups. Substandard housing is one of the major causes of ill health.

subject-object dualism: often written as S–O, it is the dilemma that the world (the external object) is only experienced by the individual (the internal mind of the subject). The problem is whether the categories of the social world would exist without the subject, or whether the subject imposes categories onto the external world in a way that is open to change and negotiation.

subjective poverty: the state of feeling poor by comparison with a particular *reference group*. Thus a family with a car might experience feelings of subjective poverty if they lived in a neighbourhood in which the majority of families had two or three cars.

subjective social class: a person's position in the social *hierarchy* as identified by the individual him or herself. The significance of subjective social class is that sociologists argue that it is the most important *indicator of class*, because the class people place themselves in is likely to affect their behaviour more than *objective social class*.

subjectivity: an individual's perspective or point of view about a thing. Subjectivity is also defined as a lack of *objectivity*, that is, where the individual's own view influences the approach taken to an issue. The position of subjectivity in sociology is ironically affected by the sociological position taken by the sociologist employing it. For positivistic sociologists, subjectivity is something to be looked down on, as tainting 'objective' social scientific research. It is thus to be avoided. For interactionists, the subject's subjectivity, or individual view-point is exactly what should be examined by the sociologist. It is only the subjectivity of the individual which gives meaning to the social world.

subordinate value-system: associated with the *working class*, this is the set of ideas which recognises that the system is unfair, but which also recognises the limitations of political action to change it. The subordinate value-system is therefore not oppositional, but is more concerned with community values and *solidarity*. (See *dominant value-system; radical value-system*.)

subsistence economy: see *peasant economy*

substantial rationality: a term deployed by Mannheim to indicate the comprehension of the individual of the whole work process. Where substantial rationality is lacking, *alienation* is likely to result.

substructure: the *'Unterbau'* of Marx, it is the economic base of society, which lies beneath and gives rise to all other social phenomena. The use of substructure as the cause of the social totality has led to the criticism that it is a deterministic concept, allowing no independence to other social and cultural structures such as the education system, architecture etc. (See *superstructure*.)

subterranean theologies: used by Pin to describe the existence of much magical and superstitious belief amongst the urban *working class*, who are otherwise unconcerned with formal religious beliefs. The survival of such non-rational beliefs amongst large numbers of people is problematic for those sociologists of *secularisation*, who argue that there is a decline in *supernatural* beliefs.

suburbanisation: the process whereby cities develop outlying districts, which are connected to the centre through employment and transport systems. Suburbanisation may occur through the specific development of housing on the outskirts of towns, or by the growth of cities so that they swallow up villages and hamlets which lie in their way.

suburbia: a term which describes the areas of cities in which the majority of the population live. Suburbia is associated with the lower-middle and middle class and contains the more desirable residential areas of the city. It is associated also with a particular style of life, which is home-centred and family-oriented. In American sociology, suburbia represents one aspect of the *American Dream*.

succession of goals: an explanation of what happens when an *organisation* achieves its *goals*, that is, new goals are devised so that the organisation can continue to exist.

suicidal act: a term used to denote that there are a variety of circumstances in which an individual may attempt to take his or her own life. The actual moment of *suicide* is surrounded by other events and circumstances, which give meaning to the suicidal act itself – for example, whether it is a serious attempt to take one's own life or whether the chances of detection are high. (See *gambles with death*.)

suicide: in Durkheim's classic definition, this is any case of death where the victim has acted, either directly or indirectly, positively or negatively to bring about the death. Durkheim was thus offering a wide definition of suicide, including events where the victim carried out the action him or herself, or where the actions of others might result in the victim's death. Actions which avoided life-saving action were also included. Durkheim's interest in suicide arose out of the very individual nature of the suicidal action. He wanted to show that, even with gun in hand, the individual was caught up in social processes. Types of suicide can be illustrated by the following diagram:

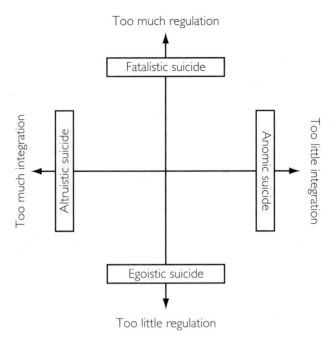

Types of suicide

suicide rate: the number of suicides per million population in a society. The suicide rate, rather than the total number of suicides in any society, is an important measure for sociologists for two reasons:

- it allows the comparison of societies in terms of how suicidal the population is. The result is that sociologists can identify high and low suicide countries
- it allows the comparison of the incidence of suicide in any one country over time to see if it is on the increase or decrease

The idea of a suicide rate has come under attack by many interactionist sociologists who argue that it is a *social construction,* made up of thousands of individual decisions by coroners who have different *operational definitions* of what is a suicide. It does not therefore count the *real rate of suicide.* However, though the statistics are socially constructed in this way, it is all the more impressive that, year in, year out, they stay remarkably stable in different societies. Suicide rates in many societies vary by gender and age. In England and Wales concern has been expressed regarding the rise in suicide rates among young men.

England & Wales
Rates per 100,000 population

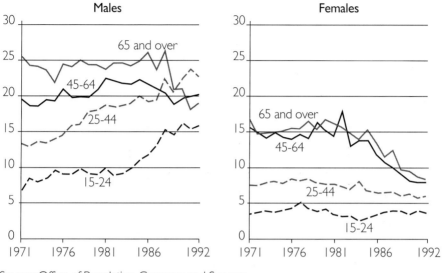

Source: Office of Population Censuses and Surveys

Death rates from suicide: by gender and age

suicidogenic impulses: used by Durkheim to describe the *social forces* in society which impel individuals toward *suicide*. These might be such forces as the degree of *integration* in a society, or the amount of regulation. To Durkheim, these social forces were real, not theoretical and were linked to the fundamental natures of different societies. They accounted for the different *suicide rates* in different societies.

sunrise industries: the industrial sector associated with computer technology and the development of new forms of production such as bio-engineering. Some sociologists argue that the sunrise industries constitute a new *industrial revolution* which will transform the way we live in the same way that the first one did. Others argue that the effects of the sunrise industries will to reinforce the divisions in society as more and more people are made unemployed by the development of automated processes.

supernatural: that which lies outside the 'laws of nature', and which can only be explained by reference to magical or divine forces.

superstructure: the 'Überbau' of Marx, it is all the social and cultural activity in society that arises from the economic activity of the *substructure*. In one sense, the superstructure is the social world, apart from economics, and is the product of labour in the widest sense.

surface reality: a concept used by post-modernists to describe the appearance of the world as it is presented through media images. They argue that it is impossible to penetrate this surface reality to find out what is really underneath, because there is nothing underneath these surface images. Things are as they appear in *hyperreality*.

surface world: a concept used to describe the kaleidoscope of everyday life, as it is experienced – chaotic and meaningless. The implication of the concept is that there is no structure to the social world, only life as it is lived. (See *post-structuralism.*)

surplus repression: an idea developed by Marcuse that capitalist society is engaged in keeping down the *proletariat,* above and beyond what is necessary for the continuation of the capitalist system. In particular, the capitalist system suppresses the erotic instinct in society. (See *eros.*)

surplus value: the difference between the worth of the *capital* employed at the beginning of the productive process and the worth of the goods produced at the end. The difference is accounted for by the purchase by capital of the labour power of the worker. Labour power is itself wealth-producing, as it accounts for the profits which accrue to the capitalist. Therefore, the difference between the price of purchasing labour power and the worth of the final commodities is the rate of appropriation of the worker's labour power. *Exploitation* can be intensified by increasing the length of the working day, thus expanding the time that labour power is operative without increasing the cost, or by increasing the productivity of the worker by, for example, changing the organisation of work or using new machines.

Surrey occupational scale: a way of classifying the *occupational structure* developed by a team of sociologists from Surrey University. An important feature of the scale is that occupations are classified in such a way that those occupied mainly by members of one sex are shown separately. The resulting data show clearly the predominance of men in the upper and lower groups, and that of women in the intermediate group. The occupational classes devised by the Surrey group are as follows:

1 Higher professionals
2 Employers and managers
3 Lower professionals
4 Secretarial and clerical
5 Foremen; self-employed manual
6 Sales and skilled manual
7 Semi-skilled
8 Unskilled.

(See *Essex University Class Project; Registrar-General's scale.*)

surrogate religiosity: where, for an individual, secular beliefs or *ideologies* take the place of religious beliefs in providing meaning and purpose to that individual's life.

surveillance: used by post-modernists to describe the type of social control exercised in post-modern societies, in which individuals police themselves through the operation of ways of thinking and behaving which define what is normal in society. The shaping of behaviour in post-modern societies is thus established through *discourses,* by which individuals channel their own activity into socially acceptable forms. This is in contrast to the *social control* by force used in pre-industrial societies and social control by the rule of law associated with *modernity.*

survey: see *social survey*

survey population: all the members of the group in whom a researcher is interested when conducting a *social survey*. The survey population will form the basis of the *sampling frame*, although not all members of the survey population will necessarily be in the sampling frame.

sustainable development: where the process of *industrialisation* does not result in damage to the environment or the loss of natural resources, so that progress can be maintained over a long period of time. It is particularly concerned with the rational exploitation of replaceable resources, especially in agriculture and fishing, so that a constant source of revenue can be sustained. However, it has also come to signify the sensible use of irreplaceable resources such as minerals and the search for alternatives to, for example, finite mineral oils.

suttee: a ritual in India, in which the widow of a recently deceased husband throws herself onto his funeral pyre, as a matter of honour. It is often used in the sociology of *suicide* as an example of how social pressures can overcome individual instincts.

Swann Report: the result of a government-sponsored investigation into the educational performance of children from *ethnic minority groups*. The Swann Report was published in 1985 and concluded that differences in educational achievement were largely the result of a variety of socio-economic factors, including *racism* and *poverty*. (See *ethnic under-achievement.*)

symbiosis: a concept developed by the *Chicago School* to describe city living, in which members of different cultures come to live together within the same habitat, or zone of the city. The idea is based on the assumption that natural areas grow up within the city.

symbol: see *sign*

symbolic control: a type of power, usually exercised in the higher parts of an *organisation*, in which *prestige*, acceptance and *status* operate as the incentives and therefore as a control. (See *material control; physical control.*)

symbolic interactionism: drawing its inspiration from Weber, this starts from the assumption that we inhabit a symbolic world, in which symbols have shared meanings. Language is one set of symbols which we share. The social world is therefore constructed by the *meanings* that individuals attach to events and phenomena and these are transmitted across the generations through the language. A central concept of symbolic interactionists is the *Self*, which allows us to calculate the effects of our actions. The perspective has been criticised because:

- it did not elaborate its methodology sufficiently
- it ignores the emotional side of the Self as a basis for social action
- it has no proper concept of the Self.

symbolic referent: these are ideas or *signs* to which individuals refer or give acknowledgement when they are negotiating courses of action. They help individuals to justify the decisions they make. For example, ethnomethodologists use symbolic referents in the sociology of organisations when examining goals. They argue that the goals of the organisation are employed as bargaining counters by participants when they are seeking to achieve particular outcomes, in negotiating with other individuals and groups.

symmetrical family: see *stages of the family*

system: see *social system*

systematic sampling: a sampling method frequently used when the *survey popula-tion* is on a list, such as a school roll or an electoral register. If the *sampling frame* contains 5000 names, and the sample size has been agreed as 200, then the sample will be 1 in 25 people on the list. A random number is selected between 1 and 25, say 14. The 14th name on the list is chosen, then 25 (which is known as the *sampling interval*) is added to this number, thus 14 + 25 = 39, therefore the 39th name is includ-ed in the sample, then 39 + 25 = 64, so the 64th name is included, and so on until 200 names have been drawn. This is a very quick and easy way of drawing a sample, but care must be taken if the sampling frame is ranked in any way or otherwise 'organised'. If one were drawing a sample from a very large school using school reg-isters, and it was the custom of the school to place boys' names first on the class register, and then girls' names (which is a fairly common practice), and if the sam-pling interval were so large that only one name would be drawn per class, the sample could end up containing only pupils of the same sex.

T

taboo: that which is forbidden by religious law or by custom.

tactical voting: a strategy in which individuals cast their vote not according to their own political preference, but in order to achieve the best result from their political point of view. This often takes the form of voting for the second party in a constituency, when the political preference is actually for the third party, in order to prevent the election of a more despised first candidate.

take-off: the crucial and middle stage of Rostow's five stages of economic development. The term described the transformation of an agricultural society into an industrial one. The crucial aspect of the transformation is increasing investment of between 5 and 10 per cent of *Gross National Product* in the developing sectors of the economy. Another feature of take-off is the rapid technological developments which happen in the leading sectors of the economy and the consequent development of supportive industries to service these leading sectors. (See *five stages of economic growth; pre-conditions for take-off.*)

taken-for-granted: that which is accepted by members of society without thought and on which much social *action* is based. It is a central concept of ethnomethodological thought because ethnomethodologists believe that social life is carried out on the basis of taken-for-granted assumptions. (See *glossing.*)

taking the natural attitude: used by Husserl to describe the situation where individuals take their everyday world for granted, seeing it as the natural order of things and not to be questioned or challenged. (See *Lebenswelt.*)

talent: the usually in-born abilities that an individual might have in a particular field. For example, musical talent or academic talent might be seen as gifts of nature. Sociologists argue that the idea of talent serves an ideological function also, in that it is used to internalise the failure of those who do not succeed. If a child does not succeed in a particular area, they come to see themselves as untalented in that field, therefore failure becomes the individual's fault, not the fault of the system.

target group: a group of people with particular characteristics which render them the focus of attention of another individual or group. The purpose of this attention might be to persuade the target group to accept advice or recommendations (e.g. persuading homosexuals to practise safe sex as a way of limiting the spread of AIDS) or to buy a product or service, or to obtain information from them (e.g. by means of a *social survey)* in which case the target group would be the population.

taste: associated with the idea of styles of life, the definition of what is stylish in a particular time. Taste is a very elusive concept, because it is socially constructed and therefore varies from time to time and place to place. In post-modern sociology, taste has become a very important concept as attention has switched to consumption rather than production. Therefore the arbiters of taste in a society have become the new capitalists in post-modern societies, as they define what is seen as worthy and worthwhile in terms of culture and art.

Tavistock Institute of Human Relations: this is an important British organisation which studies industrial productivity through a consideration of the relationship between technology and social and psychological aspects of production. They argue that there is organisational choice available as to how those relationships can be shaped and that the task of the sociologist is to investigate the optimum arrangements that can be made within the limits of the technology.

tax threshold: the level of income at which a person starts to pay tax. (See *income tax.*)

taxonomies: classifications of social life devised by sociologists from their studies. Taxonomies are one of the basic ways in which sociologists seek to place an order on the often chaotic social world and are a first step in the development of *theories.*

Taylorism: the name given to a *management* system developed by F W Taylor, in which the activities of workers are tightly controlled according to principles generated by the application of scientific observation to the workplace. Sometimes known as *Scientific Management,* Taylorism is associated with time-and-motion studies and increasing *specialisation* of tasks. Braverman argued that the most important consequence of Taylorism was the *de-skilling* of workers. Sociologists dispute the importance of Taylorism, with some arguing that the principles did not spread very far in British industry, and that where they were implemented, they were strongly resisted by workers.

teachers' expectations: see *pygmalion effect*

technicism: the sociological term for red tape, that is the abundance of rules and regulations in *organisations,* which often stifle the ability of the organisation to deliver its *goals* to its *clients.* (See *ritualism; formalism; displacement of goals.*)

technological determinism: the idea that similar machines, related to each other in similar ways, always produce similar types of work organisation and similar attitudes amongst the workers who operate them. The concept is built upon classifications of technology into *craft, machine-minding, assembly-line, continuous process* and *automated* technologies. Each of these is associated, according to technological determinists, with different organisational structures and worker *consciousness.* In the case of attitudinal effects, Blauner argued that *alienation* reaches its height in assembly-line technology and decreases with the introduction of automation. For organisational structure, Woodward argued that the more complex the technology (from craft to automation) the more complex the *management* structure needed. However, technological determinism has come under a great deal of criticism from various sociological positions:

- Some argue that the empirical findings of the technological determinists are mistaken, and that high levels of alienation are to be found in automated industries.
- Some argue that technological determinists ignore the importance of individuals and the way that they can choose to react to different technologies.
- Others argue that similar technologies in different societies lead to different management styles, that is, there is an element of managerial choice in deciding on structures.
- Yet others argue that technological determinism is a myth and that the process is the reverse of what the technological determinists say. That is, it

is technology which is determined by social and economic forces, rather than the other way around.

technology: the machines used both in production and in everyday life, and the way that they are organised. Sociologists have always been interested in the effects of technology on society, but they have difficulty in defining what exactly it is. A narrow definition focuses only on the machines themselves and usually their degree of complexity. This tends to be the definition taken by *technological determinists*. A more Marxist and/or interactionist definition tends to include the social and economic forces which shape the development of the machines. Other sociologists include a more ideological element in defining technology, arguing that technologies provide the justification for capitalists controlling workers, through the need for co-ordination and *efficiency*.

teenage economy: a term used by Abrams to describe the development in the post-War period of a market for goods specifically aimed at *adolescents*. It was the result of growing *affluence* in the economy and the emergence of a *youth culture* which had disposable income at its finger-tips. The teenage economy was particularly associated with the *media industries*, especially music.

teenage marriage: a marriage in which at least one of the partners is under 21 years of age. These have declined in number since the 1960s and in 1991 only 11% of brides and 4% of grooms were under 21. Part of the reason for this is the lessening of the *stigma* attached to unmarried mothers, as many teenage marriages in the past took place to legitimate a pregnancy. Social attitudes towards *cohabitation* have also relaxed.

teleological explanation: one which explains a phenomenon by reference to the end it serves. So functionalist theory is teleological in that it explains the existence of social customs through the purpose they serve for the maintenance of society as a whole. The problem with this is that it implies that all action is purposeful and deliberate. However, action is more complicated than seeing a problem, thinking up a solution and acting upon it. People do not always act purposively or from conscious motivation.

televangelism: the use of television to reach a mass *audience* for the preaching of evangelical or fundamental *Christianity*. The term is applied particularly to the United States, where so-called televangelists such as the Rev. Jerry Falwell, Jim Bakker, Oral Roberts, Pat Robertson and Jimmy Swaggert regularly broadcast on prime-time television. It has been estimated that about 25% of Americans are evangelical or fundamental Christians, so the potential audience is very large indeed. However, in the 1980s, when televangelism was at its height, figures showed that only about 8% of the total American viewing public (15 million people) were regular viewers of such programmes. This figure fell after both Jim Bakker and Jimmy Swaggert were involved in sex scandals towards the end of the 1980s. Research indicates that televangelism does not convert non-believers; rather it is watched by those who are already followers and who enjoy the particular mix of gospel music, home-spun philosophy and fiery preaching which forms the staple diet of such programmes. However, the members of the *New Christian Right* are now using religious-based programmes to 'cross over' into mainstream television, and are producing soap operas and game shows with a religious message which are proving increasingly popular with American audiences. With the advent of cable television to Britain, it is possible that 'God slot' programmes will appear on British television, but media researchers do not consider that they will prove as successful as in America, mainly because, under British laws, they cannot appeal for funds.

temporal boundaries: used by post-modernists in describing the division in time between different activities. Modernity is characterised by strict separation of activities into slots of time. For example, school subjects have distinct units of time (lessons) given over to them. In post-modern societies, these boundaries are dissolving as the distinctions between traditional subjects disappear. (See *spatial boundaries*.)

tender-minded: applied to a set of political attitudes which tend to be liberal in outlook. For example the tender-minded often see prisons as agencies of rehabilitation as well as punishment.

Tepoztlan: a village in Mexico which was studied by anthropologist Redfield in the 1930s and then studied again in the 1940s by Lewis. The village is therefore important because it provides one of the few cases of replication in sociology and the results found by both sociologists were different from each other. Critics argue that these differences were the result of the different expectations of the two researchers.

tertiary health care: long-term health care aimed at rehabilitation or maintaining the quality of life, e.g. care provided in nursing homes or residential homes for the elderly.

tertiary sector: in the *occupational structure* these are service jobs, usually carried out in offices. (See *secondary sector; primary sector*.)

text: used in sociological analysis of the media to denote any programme, book, magazine, film etc., which has to be 'read' by the *audience*. Texts in this sense are much wider than the traditional use of the word and imply that messages may be transmitted by a whole variety of media and are not just the written word. (See *encoding; decoding*.)

thaumaturgical sects: *sects* which promise their members a variety of personal benefits which will occur through *supernatural* or miraculous intervention.

theocracy: a society which is ruled by the priestly caste, who use religious ideas to control the population and establish their dominance through the manipulation of religious *symbols* and *rituals*.

theodicy: explanations of the contradiction between the existence of a just and benevolent god and the existence of evil and suffering in the world. The contradiction is at its most acute when the pain and suffering are inflicted on the innocent, particularly children.

theodicy of disprivilege: a concept used by Weber to refer to religious explanations which legitimate social inequalities. Weber argued that certain *sects* would have a particular attraction for the poor and socially deprived as they explained social deprivation as God's way of testing faith, and also promised a reversal of fortunes in the next life. Worldly suffering was thus endowed with a moral justification.

theological stage: the earliest of Comte's *three stages of human development*, distinguished by the explanation of phenomena by reference to the *supernatural* world. Religious authority was therefore the ultimate source of explanations of the social and natural worlds. (See *metaphysical stage, positive stage*.)

theories of the middle range: identified by Merton as explanations derived from empirical data in specific areas of social life. They are attempts to bridge the gap between *high theory* and *empiricism*.

theory: a systematic and general attempt to explain phenomena, and in the case of sociology, the social world around us. Theories are advanced to cover general areas of social life, yet they are often partial in that they are put forward by sociologists from a particular sociological perspective. There are different levels of theory in sociology from *high theory* to *taxonomies*.

theory x: developed by McGregor to denote those traditional *organisations* which ignored their workers' needs for *self-actualisation*. Such organisations tended to treat workers as rational economic beings, motivated by money and nothing else. (See *theory y*.)

theory y: the alternative to theory x, McGregor argued that organisations with theory y structure recognised their workers as more than just there for the money. Theory y organisations therefore rejected the *detailed division of labour*, in favour of *job-enlargement, participative leadership* and *de-centralisation* of responsibility.

third force: a concept used to describe the political forces and organisations which lie outside the two main parties of Labour and Conservative. The actual political complexion of the third force varies according to geographical location and the political issues resonant at any time. So, in Scotland, the third force is the Scottish National Party, in the south of England it is the Liberal Democrats. At one time the Green Party represented a third force in European elections.

third world: a popular term for the less developed areas of the globe, in which *poverty* and lack of *development* is predominant. The concept is usually applied to the poorer countries of Asia and Africa, which are heavily reliant on agriculture in their economies. The term third world has come under heavy criticism for its all-embracing nature. Critics argue that it is wrong to lump all African and Asian countries together in this way. Each country has its own history, *culture* and problems and to use an umbrella term like third world is likely to result in general solutions to poverty which do not fit the needs of individual countries. However, proponents of the concept argue that the major problem countries of the third world face is their relationship with the *first world* and it is therefore appropriate that they develop a common strategy in dealing with the richer nations. (See *second world*.)

thirty/thirty/forty society: a proposed new categorisation of British society which divides the population of working age into three groups. These are:

- an advantaged 40% with relatively secure jobs and therefore good prospects for future income
- a newly-insecure 30% who, though in work, are in forms of employment which are structurally insecure
- a disadvantaged 30% who are unemployed, economically inactive and increasingly marginalised.

this-worldly orientation: used by Pfautz to indicate individuals who focus on the present in dealing with the world around them. Social action is therefore shaped by a pragmatic ethic, in which satisfaction here and now is an important component. (See *other-worldly orientation*.)

three hundred and sixty degree appraisal: a system in which the performance of individuals in work is assessed by all those with whom they come into contact, whether superiors, subordinates or equals. The idea is drawn from *quality assurance* mechanisms, and argues that feedback is essential if performance in work is to be enhanced.

three roads to modernity: three suggested alternative ways in which a society could industrialise, i.e. *capitalism, state socialism* and *state capitalism.* Barrington-Moore argued that historical evidence suggested that these were the models which societies had adopted when industrialising. Britain and the United States were used as an example of capitalist development, Russia as an example of state socialist development and Japan as an example of state capitalism. They were therefore presented as 'roads to modernity' for undeveloped societies. Critics of this approach argue that all the models are inappropriate for modern times, because they describe situations where for one reason or another the industrialising society had little competition from more developed societies. In the case of the western capitalist societies, they industrialised early, whilst Japan and Soviet Russia remained relatively isolated from more developed societies and were able to industrialise with little exposure to competition. Critics also suggest that undeveloped societies were also trying to develop their own roads to modernity through such policies as *intermediate technology* development or third worldism. (See *development.*)

three stages of human development: used by Comte to explain the way that human societies have developed. He argued that it was the change in ideas which led to progress in the material world. In particular, it was the relationship of ideas about the control of the environment which were crucial for the social actions characteristic of each stage. (See *theological stage; metaphysical stage; positive stage.*)

three way marginal: a constituency where the three leading parties are all so close in proportion of votes that any of the three could win it at an election. (See *marginal seat.*)

tiger economies: those once-poor countries of the *third world* which have exhibited high rates of *development* in the 1980s and 1990s. Countries such as South Korea, Taiwan and Singapore have placed *industrialisation* at the forefront of their policies, with the result that they have 'roared' ahead of neighbouring countries in attracting foreign capital and investment. Some sociologists have argued that a common feature of these economies is an authoritarian state which has kept labour cheap and inhibited the development of independent *trade unions.* Others have suggested that it is the openness of these countries to capitalist penetration from *first world* companies which has led to successful development. (See *Pacific rim.*)

time: the measured passage of existence, sociologists have argued that time also has social dimensions. Time can be seen as the *durée,* which is the flow of everyday life and the *longue durée,* which is the rise and fall of social institutions. Time is also divided by humans into historical epochs such as the Modern Age, which are divisions of convenience, but which also encapsulate the *Zeitgeist.*

time-and-motion studies: the use of scientific observational techniques to study people working, in order to establish the most efficient and therefore profitable organisation for a production line or office. Time-and-motion studies are traditionally associated with *Scientific Management* techniques, where their purpose is to control the minute by minute actions of the worker. They have been met with great suspicion by workers who have been subject to them, who view them as eroding the traditional rights of workers to control the pace of their work.

time-budget studies: the investigation by sociologists of the *domestic division of labour* by asking spouses to record the amount of time they spend on particular domestic tasks during a set period of time. The results of such studies produce remarkably similar findings in which women, regardless of whether they work outside the home or not, take most of the burden of household tasks.

total institutions: organisations in which individuals spend their entire time, either permanently or temporarily. Organisations such as prisons, asylums or Army camps control the whole life of inmates while they are part of the institution. Though there are different types of total institution, they are similar in their all-encompassing nature and in particular because they have a residential aspect. Inmates therefore participate in such organisations as whole persons. Total institutions are usually divided into the following groups:

Type of total institution	Example
For the incapable and harmless	Home for the blind
For the incapable and unintentionally harmful	TB Sanatorium
For the capable and intentionally harmful	Prison
For the more efficient pursuit of tasks	Boarding school
Retreats from the world	Monasteries

Total Quality Management (TQM): an industrial principle transferred into education, which seeks to involve all members of the organisation in the production of a valuable product by making each individual responsible for their own part in the process. In education, this involves placing the learner at the centre of educational institutions' procedures and giving them ownership of their own learning. This is achieved through providing arrangements which allow students to adapt learning programmes to their own needs so that a quality education results.

totalitarianism: a situation in which absolute *power* is held by a group in society, which seeks to control as many activities and ideas of the citizens as possible. The totalitarian group may be an aristocracy, the military, a political party or a minority ethnic group. Totalitarian regimes take control of the media and other ideological agencies in an attempt to control the minds of the population.

totemic religions: see *totemism*

totemism: a system of beliefs and practices centred around the notion of a mystical relationship between the members of a social group such as a tribe or clan and an object or class of objects, usually a particular species of animal or plant. The totem is an object of *ritual* and worship for the group. Durkheim argued that the totem came to symbolise the whole group, and in worshipping the totem, the group was actually worshipping and revering itself, which he believed led to increased social solidarity.

tough-minded: applied to a set of political attitudes which tend to be authoritarian in outlook. For example the tough-minded tend to see prisons as primarily agencies of retribution as well as punishment.

town boys: these were the oldest of Marsh's groups of *football hooligans* and tended to be less involved in violence, however stylised, as they rested on their reputations and previous exploits as *rowdies*. (See *novices*.)

town planning: an attempt by local and national interests to create an environment in urban areas which meets the needs of different urban groups. It is a function of local councils to plan the development of urban spaces in a systematic way. Sociologists are interested in the way that the results of town planning affect individuals and groups within these spaces. The results of town planning decisions by *urban managers* can be the disruption of communities, the creation of pedestrian space, the death or re-vitalisation of city centre shopping areas etc. Castells argues that town planning is about, firstly *social control*, as it siphons working-class populations into specific areas of cities, and secondly, about creating an urban environment which is conducive to the creation of *wealth*, by building roads, communications etc.

traction: a concept developed by Baldamus to describe the feelings of pleasure which a worker could gain from the rhythm of work. Baldamus identified several types of traction:

Type of traction	Description
line-traction	where the rhythm is established by the product moving down the assembly-line
process-traction	where the rhythm is established by the nature of the physical changes going on
object-traction	where the rhythm is established by the picture of the work-object in the worker's mind
machine-traction	where the rhythm is established by a constantly running machine on which a worker is working

trade union consciousness: the awareness by individual workers in a factory, plant or industry of their common interests, and their joining together to form collectivities to promote them. This form of consciousness leads to trade union struggles. As a form of collective consciousness, it is to be distinguished from *class consciousness*. (See *status consciousness*.)

trade unions: organisations of workers set up to defend and promote their interests and improve the condition of their working life. Sociological interest in the trade unions has largely been focused on their expression of the consciousness of workers and their role in *industrial relations*. However, much of the work on trade unions in sociology has been criticised for taking a managerialist view, seeing them as problems for firms to deal with. Another important aspect of trade unions which has been studied is the extent to which they can truly be said to represent the interests of their members. Different types of occupation show differences in the extent of union membership. Trade union membership has fallen in the UK since the 1970s. (Please see the table opposite.)

	Males	Females	All persons
Managers and administrators	19.5	19.4	19.5
Professional	38.4	56.4	45.5
Associate professional and technical	33.6	52.9	43.1
Clerical and secretarial	35.9	24.7	27.4
Craft and related	28.7	27.8	28.6
Personal and protective services	39.6	22.2	27.9
Sales	11.9	11.2	11.5
Plant and machine operatives	42.5	33.1	40.6
Other	32.4	24.2	28.1
All in employment	30.7	28.0	29.5

(Source: Social Trends 25, 1995)

Trade union membership by gender and occupation, Great Britain, Autumn 1993 (%)

United Kingdom
Percentages

Source: Employment Department

Trade union membership as a percentage of the civilian workforce in employment

traditional action: a form of *action* from Weber's typology where behaviour is governed by customs and where beliefs are habitual rather than rational. Weber saw pre-modern societies as characterised by traditional action, with actions influenced by the way things have always been done. Such actions are often very resistant to change. (See *affective action*.)

traditional societies: those social arrangements where behaviour is governed by what has always been done. The important rules governing social behaviour have been passed down from generation to generation and are distinguished by a high degree of *ritual*. Such societies do not change very quickly and tend to be characterised by *mechanical solidarity*. Though there is a tendency for traditional societies to be seen as 'primitive', they have their own high culture and sophistications which can often be dismissed as old-fashioned, but which are efficient adaptations to natural conditions.

traditional teaching: see *chalk-and-talk; pedagogy*

traditional voters: those who vote consistently for the same Party. These are the strong supporters of each Party and though often associated with the class basis of the two main parties, can be found in all parties from all classes. Often traditions of voting extend across generations, with sons and daughters following their parents in voting habits. Traditional voters are in decline as *volatility* increases.

traditional working class: a concept applied to those manual workers in heavy manufacturing or extractive industries, who have historically exhibited high levels of solidarity. They have been the backbone of both *trade union* and *Labour Party* development and often distinguished by high levels of geographical segregation. (See *privatised working class*.)

traditionalists: those working-class voters who vote Labour because of their strong sense of identity with it as the party representing the interests of the working class. They are usually found in solidaristic working-class communities, especially in areas of heavy manufacturing or extractive industry. The traditionalists are often the most class-conscious of working-class support for the Labour Party and have a hold on the working-class organisations in the community such as the unions, the clubs and the local Labour Party itself.

trained incapacity: a term coined by Veblen to describe the situation where an individual's skills and abilities can lead to inadequate performance in an *organisation*. Veblen used the concept to explain how *actions*, while successful in the past, may become inappropriate in changed circumstances and lead to inefficiency rather than efficiency. An example might be that chickens can be trained to respond to a bell by offering food as a reward. The same bell can also be used to summon them to have their necks wrung.

training: a conception of education as a preparation for a life of work, which has traditionally appeared in the further education sector but which, during the 1980s and 1990s has increasingly penetrated secondary schools in the form of vocational education. The idea of training is to provide the next generation with the appropriate *skills* to function effectively in work. The appearance of training schemes to try and deal with the appearance of youth unemployment has been a significant development of the 1980s and 1990s. (See *Great Debate*.)

Training and Enterprise Councils: Government-funded regional organisations set up in 1990 to administer and develop youth and adult training schemes, to provide funding and advice to new businesses, and to liaise with employers regarding the training needs of the workforce.

trait theory: an approach to the sociology of the *professions* in which the characteristics of many professions are examined to produce an *ideal type.* The problem with the approach is that there are so many traits identifiable that it is difficult to know when to stop. Millerson, for example, identified 23 traits of the professions, taken from 21 different writers on profession .

trans-national companies: those firms which carry out their business on a global scale. This concept replaced *multi-national companies* because it was seen as a more accurate description of these firms. Trans-national companies (TNCs) therefore operate in a global market place, aided by the *information technology* revolution, and are able to switch resources and personnel to those areas of the world where the greatest profit beckons. Sociologists have tended to focus on the activities of the trans-national companies in the *third world*, though they have an impact on social life in the *first world* as well.

- Some sociologists argue that the role of the trans-national companies in the *third world* is an exploitative one. Susan George, for example, has suggested that the trans-national companies use the third world as a dumping ground for possibly unsafe products, which do not have permission to be sold in the *first world*. It is also suggested that trans-national companies pursue profit in the third world regardless of the harmful effects of their products on the people. Through the power of advertising, people in the third world are persuaded to buy products they do not need and cannot really afford, such as cigarettes, when the money would be better spent on local produce.

- Other sociologists see the activities of the trans-national companies as beneficial, because they provide third world economies with *capital* and *entrepreneurship*, so that they actively contribute to the development of third world countries. The model put forward here is one of reciprocal benefit, in which the trans-national companies gain a decent profit and the third world countries are helped to industrialise. The *Tiger economies* of the *Pacific rim* are said to have developed as a result of this relationship.

- A third aspect of trans-national companies in which sociologists have been interested, is their power. While most TNCs are controlled by individuals from one particular society, they are responsible to their shareholders rather than any particular national interest. They therefore have the power to affect the lives of millions through their investment decisions, such as where to locate industry, or to concentrate production. The result of such decisions is that thousands may be thrown out of work or gain new opportunities, depending on where investment is made. It is also argued that the global effect of such power is to depress the real incomes of workers as the TNCs switch investment round the world in pursuit of the lowest possible costs.

(See *coca-colonisation.*)

transcendental ego: identified by Husserl as that which all minds have in common – the essential properties of the mind. Husserl argued that it was the transcendental ego which led us to the truth about things – to knowledge itself. The transcendental ego is therefore the way in which our mind necessarily knows the world because of the way the mind is organised in all humans.

transferable skills: a central idea of *new vocationalism,* they are non-specific abilities which are carried by the worker from one job to another. Transferable skills are developed to meet the needs of post-modern industry, which requires flexible workers whose skills are not rooted in traditional work practices, but which can be employed in different work circumstances. Critics of the notion of transferable skills argue that they have the effect of *de-skilling* workers, because skills which can be used by anyone have little market value. Non-transferable skills are those from which workers derive their power and monetary rewards.

transformative capacity: the ability of something to effect social change in a large-scale fashion. Weber identified the ideas of *Calvinism* as having this transformative capacity, though other sociologists have argued for other social formations and ideas as the main cause of the change from *feudalism* to *capitalism.* (See *spirit of capitalism.*)

triangulation: the practice of using more than one, and usually at least three, different research methods when carrying out a piece of research, so that the different kinds of data will complement each other. Triangulation is also likely to increase the *validity* of the research.

trickle-down effect: an assumed process by which the *wealth* of the richer members of society filters down to the poorest. A belief in this process was used by Conservative governments from 1979 to justify cuts in *income tax*, particularly for very high earners. It was argued that by reducing very high levels of taxation, the wealthy would be encouraged to use their entrepreneurial skills to generate more wealth. This would trickle down to those below in the form of more jobs within a generally more prosperous society. There is little evidence to show that this process has taken place; in fact much evidence points to the contrary, i.e. the richer people have become more wealthy, while the poorest groups in society have become relatively poorer.

tripartite system: a system of selective secondary education in England and Wales introduced by the Education Act of 1944. Three types of secondary school were created, namely secondary grammar, secondary technical and secondary modern. As few technical schools were built, in most areas children went to either a grammar or a secondary modern school. The system was increasingly criticised for its bias in favour of middle-class children, and the corresponding wastage of ability, particularly among the working class. (See *comprehensive schools; parity of esteem.*)

trivialisation: the process whereby oppositional *sub-cultures* are neutralised through being made a spectacle or reduced to what Barthes calls the 'status of clown'. This often means the transformation of the sub-culture into an exotic form. (See *domestication.*)

truth: beliefs which are held to be correct. The issue of truth is a critical one in epistemology. There are different bases for what is held to be true, such as intuition, faith, tradition and most importantly for sociology, science. The attraction of science as a basis for truth, compared to faith for example, is that it is *verifiable*. By knowing something is true for certain, sociologists hope to understand and therefore control the social world. However, post-modernists argue that this dream of the *Enlightenment*, that human beings can know something for certain, is itself a fallacy. They argue that there are no *meta-narratives* which can explain the whole of the social world and that therefore there is no such thing as truth.

turn-out: the proportion of the registered *electorate* who vote in elections, expressed as a percentage. Turn-out is important because differential turn-out between the supporters of the parties can affect the outcome of elections.

TVEI (Technical and Vocational Educational Initiative): a government-funded scheme introduced into certain schools in the 1980s under which schools received generous amounts of extra funding for running new courses with a strong vocational bias for selected groups of pupils. (See *new vocationalism.*)

two faces of power: the idea that *power* can be exercised not only by getting your own way against opposition (the first face) but also by preventing an issue ever being raised as controversial in the first place (the second face of power). It is argued that this second face is more powerful because it ensures that society is run in favour of the dominant group without opposition, as policies which benefit that group are unchallenged and accepted as the normal running of society.

two-step hypothesis of the flow of information: the idea that media information does not have a direct effect on the whole of a media *audience,* but is mediated through *opinion leaders*, who absorb the information and pass it on to their immediate group. It stands in contrast to the idea that the media influence everyone directly and therefore that political media campaigns directly affect the way that people vote. The two-step hypothesis suggests that opinion leaders are the crucial conduit for political information. (See *hypodermic syringe model.*)

two-way convergence: a type of *convergence theory* which accepts that all industrial societies will end up being like each other, but suggests that there is a new synthesis to emerge, which takes elements from all existing societies. The result will be a new type of highly industrialised society, with its own distinctive characteristics.

typification: the organisation of *knowledge* in terms of the typical features of phenomena rather than their individual characteristics. It is a process which both sociologists and lay people engage in, as they seek to make sense of the social world in which they live. Typifications therefore cover a whole number of cases and seek to encapsulate what is common about them.

U

Überbau: see *superstructure*

unavoidable abstainers: those registered to vote but who do not cast their ballot for reasons which were compelling. The biggest group of unavoidable abstainers are those on the *electoral register* who have died since their name was included. Other unavoidable abstainers are those in hospital, or away on business on election day. (See *avoidable abstainers.*)

unconscious motivation: the reasons why we do what we do, which are hidden even from ourselves. These lie below the conscious rational motivations we employ, and Giddens argues that sociology has historically neglected this part of *action*. (See *discursive consciousness; practical consciousness.*)

under-achievement: the failure of a person or group of people, particularly in an educational context, to perform as well as expected or as well as indicated by their potential. Traditionally, the main groups of underachievers in the British education system have been females, working-class pupils and children from some *ethnic minority groups*. These are not, of course, mutually exclusive groups. Recently, however, the academic attainments of girls at school have outstripped those of boys, with the result that there is growing concern over male under-achievement. The relative under-achievement of children from the working class and some ethnic minority groups is still apparent, despite the existence of *comprehensive schools*. (See *ethnic under-achievement; female under-achievement.*)

under-development: the process whereby *third world* countries are exploited by the *first world*, and end up worse off than they were previously. The term was used by *under-development theorists* and *dependency theorists* to explain how, prior to colonisation by the first world, third world countries often had industrial sectors of their own. When third world countries became colonised, the laws governing trade between the two societies were altered to favour first world goods, with the consequent destruction of the indigenous third world industries. Dependency theorists therefore argue that the state of undevelopment characteristic of third world countries is not a 'natural' state, but is the result of relationships with the first world countries. (See *development; colonialism.*)

under-development theory: a view that it was in the interests of capitalist countries to keep their colonies, both former and current, in a state of submission. Arising directly from the *Marxist* tradition, the theory was developed in the 1950s by Paul Baran, who explored the strategies which the colonial powers used to exploit both those countries which were still directly ruled by a European power and those which had gained their independence. These strategies included the direct exploitation of the third world's natural resources and the use of 'clients' in the *third world*. The aim in either case was the 'patriation' or return to the *first world* of as much surplus profit as possible. (See *patriation of profit.*)

under-employment: the situation where people have jobs, but where these do not fully employ them. It often takes the form of low-paid part-time work and accounts for the emergence of a growing *informal economy*.

underclass: a highly controversial concept applied to a group or groups of people at the bottom of the class system. The concept is associated with the American writer Charles Murray, and first received wide public dissemination in Britain in an article by Murray in the Sunday Times newspaper in November 1989. Murray's ideas are based on the USA, where he has identified the life style of the underclass as characterised by high levels of *illegitimacy*, violent crime and drop-out from the labour force. He argues that it is what he refers to as the 'deterioration of the family' in the lower classes which has led to the creation and growth of the underclass. In further articles in 1994, Murray stated that, re-visiting Britain, he could see evidence of a growing underclass in Britain. Using data for England and Wales from 1992, he showed that, compared with 1987, property crime had increased by 42%, the violent crime rate by 40% and the number of *births outside marriage* had grown from 23% of all births to 31%. Murray claims that the growth of the underclass has profound implications for the class system and for society as a whole, arguing that the physical segregation of the classes will become more extreme, shops and other businesses in working class areas will become vacated, resulting in widespread 'squatting' and arson in these areas, and the middle classes will begin to move to '*gated communities*', i.e. residential areas surrounded by physical barriers to prevent unauthorised access. There are a number of criticisms of Murray's views, including the following:

- his arguments are based on moral, rather than scientific and logical reasoning
- 74% of births outside marriage in Britain are registered by both parents, indicating a stable relationship
- the majority of *lone parents* are separated or divorced, rather than unmarried
- he ignores the real constraints on some people, such as a lack of available jobs
- much of the squalor and blight of urban areas is a result of lack of investment
- it is unhelpful to describe such disparate groups of people as young unemployed males, female heads of lone-parent families, the chronically sick and disabled and the impoverished elderly as a 'class'. Their experiences and their goals are likely to be very different

undeveloped societies: a concept used to describe an assumed 'original state' for all societies, in which the potential of those societies is not realised. The term is associated with *modernisation theory*, which suggests that the development of societies from an agricultural basis into an industrialised state is central to societal progress. This perspective emerged from the *evolutionary theories* of early sociology, which under the impact of Darwin's theory of evolution saw societies following the same route of progress as had the human species. This theory therefore compared, usually unfavourably, the 'primitive' state of undeveloped societies with the sophistication of developed societies. Undeveloped societies were seen as primarily agricultural, with a large peasant sector and influenced by traditional religious beliefs. The natural resources of undeveloped societies are unexploited by the inhabitants, who are seen as being content to follow a subsistence life-style. (See *development*.)

unemployment: the state of being without work. Sociological interest in unemployment has grown as the proportion of the population out of work has grown.

Attention has been focused firstly on the *validity* of the unemployment statistics, as Government has continually changed the definition of being unemployed, and secondly, on the experience of being unemployed. Unemployment in Britain also has an ethnic dimension, with varying rates on unemployment between different ethnic groups, as shown in the table below.

	Unemployment rate
White	8.3
All ethnic minority groups	19.3
Black	24.7
Indian	11.9
Pakistani/Bangladeshi	29.8

(Source: Labour Force Survey No. 14, December 1995)

Unemployment rate by ethnic group, Summer 1995 (not seasonally adjusted) (%)

unintended consequences: the outcomes of *actions* which were not meant and usually unanticipated. Since Weber's work, most sociologists have viewed social actions as *rational*, that is, calculated to achieve particular effects. A course of action is therefore chosen to result in specific outcomes. However, all social actions also result in other outcomes which were not intended by the *actors* involved. Some of these outcomes may be the opposite of what the social actors meant to happen.

unionateness: a scale developed by Blackburn to measure how like a *trade union* an organisation was. The seven factors for deciding were:

1 willingness to take militant action
2 willingness to call itself a trade union
3 willingness to register as a trade union
4 the priority given to *collective bargaining*
5 the degree of independence from the employer
6 affiliation to the TUC
7 affiliation to the *Labour Party*

unionisation: the process whereby members of an occupational group join a *trade union* in such numbers that the occupation is said to be unionising. The concept is often used in reference to the *semi-professions*, which are located between the powers and high rewards of traditional *professions* and the industrial muscle of the *manual trade unions*, which can often produce affluence for their members. Unionisation is one of the tactics that members of the semi-professions may turn to in order to attempt to protect and improve their financial rewards and working conditions. It is also seen by sociologists as a major reason why some middle-class members vote Labour in elections, as an expression of their trade union membership. (See *density of membership.*)

unionists: though generally referring to those who believe in the union of England, Scotland, Northern Ireland and Wales, it is more specifically associated with members of a number of parties in Northern Ireland who defend the connection with the British Crown and who are opposed to absorption into the Irish republic. There is an extra-parliamentary dimension to unionism in the shape of, amongst others, the Ulster Volunteer Force.

unitary elite theory: an approach to the issue of *power* in society, which suggests that there is a single group which rules, whose members are to be found in the key institutional positions in society. The unitary *elite* theory rejects ownership as the distinguishing characteristic of the ruling group, and instead argues that *location* is the important dimension, thus allowing the possibility of meritocratic movement. However, in the main, the unitary elite theorists see the main interests of the ruling elite as defending their own power and passing on their privileges to their children. There are thus limitations to the amount of *meritocracy* in a society, although there are alternative ways of replacing and renewing elites. Unitary elite theory has been criticised because:

- it assumes that just because people know each other, they operate as an elite, which is not necessarily the case
- social change at the top occurs more than unitary elite theorists allow
- it denies the importance of the representative tradition in democratic societies

(See *circulation of elites; pluralism.*)

unitary theory: an approach to *industrial relations* which sees the firm as analogous to the family, in which any opposition to management is seen as hostile and unacceptable. The unitary theorists emphasise common purpose and unity in the firm and are antagonistic to the idea of workers linking up with each other in any way other than approved by management. *Trade unions* are only tolerated when they are 'moderate' and serve the interests of the firm.

universal benefits: welfare benefits which are available to everyone as a right of *citizenship*. Examples would be the state retirement pension and child allowances. (See *means-tested benefits.*)

universal church: see *ecclesia*

universal functionalism: a principle of *functionalism* that all activities in society positively contribute to society as a whole. It was criticised because non-functional patterns of behaviour can be shown to exist. (See *functionalism.*)

universal laws: statements of cause and effect which apply to all situations in which similar conditions exist. Laws at this level of generality exist as the outcome of the scientific method, which takes verified instances of specific knowledge and generalises them to all similar circumstances. Universal laws therefore allow the scientist to examine a situation previously unseen and to predict the outcome of the events. By so doing, the scientist can know things for certain and thus control the future. A classic example of a scientific universal law emerges from the consideration of what happens when sulphuric acid is mixed with sodium hydroxide and the result is sodium sulphate and water. By examining other situations in which an acid and a base are mixed together, the scientist might generalise to the universal law that any acid added to any base will always produce a salt and water. (See *generalisability.*)

universalism: where the rules of a society are applied equally to all, with no fear or favour. Personal relationships are given no advantage in public affairs, and individuals are dealt with in terms of the rules generated to ensure fair dealing. This, along with *particularism*, constituted one of Parsons' *pattern variables* for traditional and modern societies.

universality of the family: an argument put forward by the functionalist George Murdock that some form of family exists in every society. It is generally agreed that whether this argument is regarded as true or not depends on the definition of 'family'. While all societies have rules governing sexual relationships, the responsibility for rearing children and the inheritance of property, there are very wide variations in all of these arrangements. (See *core functions of the family*.)

universities of crime: a description of prisons which implies that one of their main, if unintended, functions is to teach inmates how to be better criminals. The concept is used in the debate between those who see prisons as vehicles of retribution and those who argue they should be for rehabilitation.

unobtrusive methods: methods of research which are used without the subjects being aware that they are bring studied. Unobtrusive methods usually form part of a *qualitative research* study, and include *observation* (provided that the observation is unnoticed) and *covert participant observation*. It is claimed that the main benefit of unobtrusive research methods is that they avoid possible changes in the subjects' behaviour or conversation which could arise if they knew they were being studied (i.e. the *Hawthorne effect*).

unofficial strikes: situations in which workers withdraw their labour without the support of their *trade union*. Interest in unofficial action has grown as, since the 1980s, government restrictions have limited the ability of trade unions to undertake official action. When because of these restrictions trade unions do not respond to the demands of their members, then unofficial action grows.

unskilled labour: work in which there is no training or talent needed by the worker. These are often the most lowly paid of occupations and are associated with the basic working class. (See *skilled labour; semi-skilled labour.*)

unstructured interview: an *interview* which usually has as its aim the probing of emotions and attitudes rather than the gathering of factual information. Unstructured interviews are usually tape-recorded, to allow the interview to resemble as much as possible a normal conversation and also to allow other researchers to listen later on. There is no interview schedule, rather the interviewer has a mental list of topics or headings around which s/he will try to direct the interview, as unobtrusively as possible. Skilled interviewers conducting unstructured interviews 'listen with the third ear', i.e. note not only what is being said, but how it is being said, and what is being omitted, and also take note of non-verbal information, such as facial expressions and other *body language.*

unstructured questionnaires: usually applied to *questionnaires* which contain all, or a large majority, of *open-ended questions*. The term is not really accurate, as a questionnaire by definition has a structure.

Unterbau: see *substructure*

upper class: a term used to denote the dominant social group in society, but more specifically employed to indicate the aristocratic *elite* which controlled capitalist societies until the Second World War, sometimes alone and sometimes in alliance with other classes.

upward social mobility: where an individual or group moves from a subordinate social position to a higher one. Upward mobility can occur for a number of reasons. In modern societies, education is the main vehicle for upward mobility, though marriage and enterprise can be alternative routes. There are also structural factors which affect the chances of mobility in a society. For example, change in *occupational structure,* when middle-class jobs expand, can create more openings for those in subordinate positions. (See *downward social mobility.*)

urban areas: localities characterised by high population *density,* in which large numbers of people co-exist who are likely to be engaged in manufacturing or service industries.

urban blight: a blanket term used to describe aspects of parts of large cities which render them ugly, inhospitable and even dangerous places in which to live, and where residents are poorly served in terms of employment opportunities and amenities such as transport, shopping and community facilities and play areas for children. The blight is often a result of a combination of bad planning, corruption, poor housing and low investment, and reflects the fact that many of the residents of these areas will be among the most poor and deprived in the population.

urban cowboys: used by Simmel to describe the street-wise successes of the city environment. In the fast-moving world of the city, the urban cowboy is able to manipulate the life of the street to his own advantage.

urban crisis: a term developed by Castells to suggest that the crises which *capitalism* periodically undergoes, are manifested most of all in the city areas of the nation. That is, the city is the main arena of modern *class struggle.* Castells argues that cities go into crisis when basic services are no longer met through *welfare,* and when *unemployment* rises fast. The crisis leads to disorder on the streets. In these circumstances, the State's response is repression, with riot shields and new forms of police weapons and tactics being used. Critics argues that this account is a very simplistic one, in which the *State* can do no right. However, Castells' view of the State is that, whether it is providing welfare or quelling urban riots, it is always in the interests of capitalism.

urban development programmes: an aspect of government policy towards areas of high deprivation, developed during the 1980s. It gave control of remedial programmes to government-appointed *quangos* called Development Corporations. In these programmes, red tape was done away with, land and premises were made available, and Corporations were given control over the whole range of community policies such as housing, transport etc. The London Docklands was a prime example of a Development Corporation. Such Corporations were criticised for being undemocratic and for ignoring the wishes of the local community. (See *enterprise zones.*)

urban dispersal: the process by which residents of urban areas leave the towns and cities and move to the suburbs or rural areas. The trend has been noticeable from the 1970s, and reflects the increasing tendency of businesses to relocate in rural, 'green field' sites. For the firms, it is suggested that one of the reasons was the pool of cheap labour available in these areas, much of it female. For many workers, it provided the opportunity to fulfil the dream of the 'rural idyll', in which there is a romanticised view of life in the countryside.

urban ecology: the sociological approach to a city, in which the social characteristics of an area are investigated; it is associated with the *Chicago School*. (See *concentric zone theory; symbiosis*.)

urban housing: an approach to town planning from a Marxist point of view, which sees housing policy and practice in the city as a means of social control. Having private and public housing divides workers from each other and the role of managers of council housing ensures uniformity and conformity. The managers of council housing are therefore social police officers according to Marxists. Critics of this approach argue that it is based on the notion of a huge conspiracy of all housing managers, which is highly unlikely, and say that many housing managers do not see themselves in this way.

urban managers: a term developed by Pahl to describe those people in positions of influence over the *housing market* in cities. Occupations like building society assessors, planners, architects, social workers etc. are all involved in the housing market and have their own goals and interests which they impose on the less powerful individuals in the housing marketplace. Pahl argued that sociologists need to examine the activities of such groups to see how they distort and manipulate the market.

urban renewal programmes: after the Second World War, most British cities planned to transform their housing stock by pulling down the terraced houses of the *inner city* and putting up modern housing, often in the shape of tower block developments. These were the urban renewal programmes of the 1950s and 1960s. The results of these programmes have been heavily criticised for destroying fundamentally sound housing, which needed renovation, for cheap and unpopular *streets in the sky* which in the 1990s are themselves having to be pulled down. Another consequence of these programmes was the destruction and dispersal of long-standing working-class communities in the cities. The members of these communities were often displaced to estate developments on the outskirts of cities.

urban riots: from the 1960s onwards, British cities have periodically been subject to disturbances by young people, who have taken to the streets and engaged in running battles with the police. Sociologically, these have been interesting with regard to the *alienation* of the young from society which is demonstrated by the disorder, and also for the policy initiatives which have been stimulated in response to urban unrest. Another interesting dimension has been the ethnic issue associated with urban riots, which have sometimes involved youngsters from the ethnic minorities.

urban social movements: a term developed by the Marxist writer Castells to refer to groups of urban dwellers who form groups to pursue a collective interest in an aspect of life in their *community* about which they feel concern. Areas of interest are typically transport, education, housing and concern over crime and vandalism. Urban social movements are essentially local *pressure groups,* and Castells considered them an important source of *social change*.

urban villagers: a term coined by Gans to describe the existence of communities in city environments. It emerged from a study of Boston and New York, where Gans found lively ethnic and working-class communities, very different from the isolated individuals that the *loss of community* thesis suggested. In Britain, urban villagers were found in a large number of *community studies* in the 1950s and 1960s.

urban zones theory: developed by Burgess to explain urban processes, the theory states that cities are spread out in successive zones, each occupied by a particular type of person. The theory, based on Chicago, suggested that cities developed in this way. However, other sociologists have tried to apply the theory to other cities with limited success. Even in the United States where most cities have been planned carefully, the concept of concentric ring development does not work uniformly. The theory has therefore been criticised for being over-simplified and for assuming that developments were natural rather than the result of the exercise of political and economic *power* by social groups in cities.

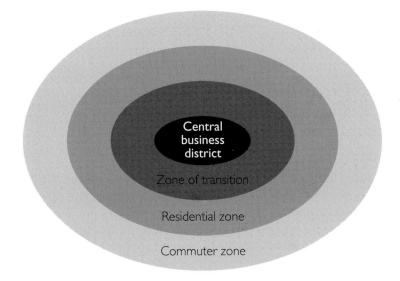

Central
business
district

Zone of transition

Residential zone

Commuter zone

A representation of urban zones theory

urbanisation: the process whereby populations increasingly live in towns and cities rather than in villages and the countryside. Urbanisation is arguably one of the greatest changes which has occurred during *industrialisation*. The process is enormous, creating a great deal of dislocation and causing many social problems. Urbanisation can occur in a planned fashion, but is more often than not unplanned, with towns growing rapidly into cities and cities into *conurbations*. The flight to the city can occur in any situation but is particularly associated with industrialisation. Nevertheless, cities attract people from the land because of the opportunities they represent, whether the society is industrialising or not. (See *urban dispersal*.)

urbanism: used by Wirth to emphasise that living in urban areas was a distinctive way of life, separated from rural living by a variety of factors. Urbanism was characterised by the collection of heterogeneous individuals in a large, dense and permanent settlement. These features, it was said, produced a distinct pattern of life, shown in its *impersonality* and *social segregation*. (See *density*.)

urbs in rure: literally 'the town in the countryside', a term developed by Gans to describe the invasion of the countryside by many of the alienating features of urban living. The crucial development for the urbs in rure is the opening up of villages to the city worker, so that in many villages the majority of the population no longer work in the locality but commute to the city. Gans also noted that there was conflict between the in-coming commuters and the original inhabitants of the villages, particularly over the way the local housing market is distorted by the commuters, raising prices to levels the original inhabitants are unable to afford.

uses and gratification approach: associated with the sociology of the media, this theory argued that individuals used the media to satisfy certain psychological and social needs in their life. It was an individualistic approach, which was criticised for ignoring the social context in which individuals used the media.

utilitarian power: a type of control in which money or material rewards are used to direct the activities of individuals. This type of *power* relies on the calculation of individuals that the money reward is worth giving up freedom of action. (See *coercion; normative power.*)

utilitarianism: a political philosophy which stresses the rational self-interest of individuals in coming together in society. Starting from the premise that people are naturally self-interested, the utilitarians argue that it is in the self-interest of all to form a society in which everyone might pursue their own happiness within certain constraints, rather than accepting the 'law of the jungle'. (See *state of nature.*)

utopian sects: *sects* which withdraw from the world in order to develop a new, ideal way of living, in the hope that the superiority of the new model will become so apparent to others that they also will seek to adopt it. (See *new religious movements.*)

V

validity: the ability of a test or research method to measure what it sets out to measure. For example, IQ tests are often contested with regard to their validity, as there is no consensus over what IQ tests are actually measuring – is it 'intelligence', or the ability to do well in IQ tests? Research into the motives of football hooligans carried out by *standardised questionnaires* would probably be less valid than research using in-depth *interviews,* or covert *participant observation.*

value-added: see *league tables*

value-consensus: a general agreement about what are the things of worth in society. To Parsons, the value-consensus was the basis of *social order,* as it integrated disparate individuals and reduced *conflict* between them. The value-consensus is not a conscious one, in that individuals do not have to think about what their *values* are, but it emerges from the past, as the best, most effective way of getting things done. The extent of a value-consensus in society has been challenged, with many sociologists denying that it exists at all:

- Some argue that values are imposed upon the rest of the population by those at the top.
- Others suggest that the value-consensus is a useful ideological device for keeping the compliance of those at the bottom of society.
- Post-modernists argue that in a society which is fragmented and composed of many different groups, there is little general agreement between the composite parts as to what constitutes the 'good life'.

value-freedom: the idea in sociology that research should be carried out without the researcher's beliefs and ideas intruding into the research and influencing the design and execution of the project. Value-freedom is a central characteristic of *positivism* but is influential right across the sociological spectrum. For positivists, value-freedom is a desirable aspect of research, and achieved by following objective procedures which emulate the *natural sciences.* For some anti-positivists, value-freedom is not possible, because of the human agency involved and therefore the best that can be obtained is for the sociologist to declare his or her values to allow others to decide if these have interfered with the work. Still others argue that value-freedom is impossible and therefore commitment should be substituted. As long as that commitment is made clear, the research can be checked and verified. (See *sociology of the underdog.*)

values: ideas or beliefs which are thought to be valuable by those who hold them. There is an ethical dimension to the concept of values, in that beliefs about goodness are often attached to them. In functionalist sociology, values have a central place, as they are thought to be crucial in forging social solidarity amongst disparate individuals. (See *value-consensus; norms.*)

variable: a characteristic which can be measured and thus subjected to numerical analysis. Common variables in sociological research include age, social class, educational qualifications, ethnic group, support for a political party, income and marital status. Variables are, by definition, not constant, but reflect differences within a given population. One of the important advantages claimed for *laboratory experiments* in natural science is the ability of the researcher to control and manipulate the variables, particularly the independent variable (that which is thought to be able to bring about changes in other variables, known as dependent variables). One of the objections put forward to sociology being regarded as a science is the inability of sociologists, when carrying out research, to control the variables in the situation. (See *hypothetico-deductive method.*)

verifiability: the process whereby an *hypothesis* can be shown to be true through experimentation. It is verifiability which is at the heart of the traditional view of *positivism.* This approach stresses the need for scientists to demonstrate that their hypotheses are true by designing experiments which verify them. (See *hypothetico-deductive method.*)

verstehen: literally 'to understand', in sociology it means to put oneself in the shoes of another in order to appreciate their particular experiences and perspectives. It is perhaps best understood as *empathy*, the feeling that one person can have for another's subjective being and objective circumstances. Verstehen was suggested by Dilthey as the way in which the sociologist can access the subjective world of the individual *actor*, and thus understand the intentions and meanings behind the things they do. It is thus a central concept in sociology, because, unlike the natural world, the social world exists both as an objective reality and in the subjective consciousness of the people who inhabit that world. (See *erklären.*)

victim-blaming: explanations of social phenomena which pin responsibility for their existence on the people who most suffer from them. Victim-blaming theories are often found in the sociology of *poverty*, where the poor are themselves seen as responsible for their own poverty. For example, explanations which argue that poverty is the result of individual fecklessness are said to be victim-blaming, because they see poverty emerging from the poor's own behaviour patterns and not as a result of structural causes.

victim studies: canvasses of the public which request them to report any crimes which they have experienced, whether or not they have reported them. This is one of the main ways in which the *dark figure* of crime is exposed, particularly in cases of rape. Such surveys usually show that the real rate of criminal activity is at least double that which appears in the official crime statistics. Victim surveys have been criticised because there is no way of verifying the information given by *respondents.* (See *self-report studies.*)

vital statistics: the official records of important demographic trends such as death and birth rates.

volatility: changes in voting behaviour between one election and the next. Increased volatility has been a feature of elections since the 1970s and is particularly noticeable in bye-elections. It is a symptom of a decline in *political identification.* (See *gross volatility; net volatility.*)

voluntarism: the belief that individuals are completely autonomous and able to exercise free will and choice. It was an attitude held by action theorists to show that what people did actually mattered in terms of the creation of history. It was developed by Parsons, who believed that the freedoms which *capitalism* gave could lead to the good society through the actions of autonomous individuals. (See *determinism.*)

voluntary associations: organisations, either political, recreational or social, where membership is optional rather than compulsory. They are seen by many sociologists as central to the operation of democratic societies, standing between the individual and the power of the *State*.

voluntary minorities: used by Gibson and Ogbu to describe those groups who have recently migrated into a host country and who tend to see education as a way of bettering their lot. Regardless of qualifications gained elsewhere, voluntary minorities tend to start in the *occupational structure* somewhere below where they should be and therefore see education as a ladder of *social mobility*. (See *involuntary minorities.*)

voucher schemes: proposals by the Conservative government of the mid-1990s to give parents of four-year-old children, and post-16 students, educational 'vouchers' with a nominal cash value which could be 'spent' to buy education. The parents of four-year-olds would use their vouchers to buy nursery education, while post-16 students would use their vouchers to enrol on education or training courses. The scheme to buy training is already in operation, with students being allocated 'training credits'.

vulgar Marxism: a term used to describe the most deterministic of the variants of *Marxism,* which put forward the idea that everything in society was directly influenced in the most fundamental way by economic circumstances. It has been attacked for reducing history to a conspiracy theory, in which the *ruling class* manipulate members of the subordinate class and exploit them in every sphere of social life.

wealth: the total value of the possessions held by an individual or a society. It is usually distinguished from *income,* because wealth can itself be income generating, for example where an individual owns a factory. Sociologists have mainly focused on the distribution of wealth in two ways:

- In a global sense, interest has been on the inequality in wealth held by countries of the *first world* compared to those in the *third world.*
- In a societal sense, the distribution of wealth in a country has been a constant focus of sociological interest, in particular whether the gap is increasing or decreasing. For most people, their single most valuable asset will be their house. Wealth in Britain is very unevenly divided among the population. If the value of dwellings is excluded from calculations of wealth, the wealthiest one per cent of the population of the UK in 1991 owned 28% of marketable wealth, and the wealthiest 50% owned 92%, leaving the bottom 50% of the population owning the remaining 8% of marketable wealth.

A major problem with examining the distribution of wealth is that there is no general agreement amongst sociologists and economists as to what constitutes wealth. Part of this problem is that wealth can actually be hidden from statisticians, in order to avoid taxation. The emergence of a global economy has allowed the transfer of wealth across national boundaries with ease.

Weber: one of the *classical sociologists,* his work is often seen as a counter-point to that of Marx, in that he sought to move away from the economic *determinism* of Marx's work to a more complete and voluntaristic approach to the investigation of society. He was also concerned to establish the importance of ideas rather than material forces as a vehicle for *social change.* To this end, he argued that religious ideas were important in shaping the practices which led to the development of capitalist society.

welfare: actions designed to promote or bring about well-being, whether for individuals, groups or entire populations. The term is closely linked to *social policy,* as at central or local government level, social policies are the instruments through which welfare is delivered.

welfare dependency: a situation in which personal or household income is solely from welfare payments, e.g. the state retirement pension or unemployment benefit. Such people are likely to be among the poorest in society. The term is particularly associated with the *New Right,* who argue that over-generous welfare benefits have made many people too reliant on the *welfare state.*

welfare state: a society in which the state, in the form of the government, accepts the responsibility of ensuring a minimum standard of living for all people as a right of *citizenship.* The modern welfare state in Britain was introduced just after the Second World War by a series of Acts of Parliament based on the recommendations of the *Beveridge Report.* Although particularly associated with the payment of welfare benefits to the needy, a welfare state delivers a range of services, including healthcare, education, housing and leisure services. LeGrand argues that although the welfare state is presumed to cater primarily for the poorer groups in society, the middle classes actually benefit more, through their greater use of health, education and transport services and tax subsidies on mortgages. The precise nature of the role of the welfare state is the focus of intense political debates and struggles, both between and within political parties. There are four main perspectives on the role of the welfare state:

- Liberal: the welfare state is there to provide a safety net for those in need, and to help redress the worst economic injustices and inequalities in society.
- Social Democratic: there are certain inalienable rights of citizenship in a modern democratic society which it is the duty of the state to provide. The welfare state should play a redistributive role with regard to *wealth* and *income*, with a view to moving towards greater equality.
- Marxist: the main function of the welfare state is an ideological one. By providing workers with a certain basic level of income and life style it encourages them to accept *capitalism*, and indeed gives them an incentive to help to make it work. It therefore reduces their revolutionary tendencies.
- New Right: the welfare state is over-protective and too generous in its benefits and has led to the formation of a *dependency culture*. People should be made to focus less on their 'rights' and more on their 'duties' to society. The welfare state should be greatly scaled down, with people made to turn to the private, rather than the public, sector for the majority of their welfare needs.

Weltanshauung: literally a world-view, used by Weber to describe the particular way of looking at things which was attached to a specific social group. Sociological interest has focused on the origins of different world views and their effects on the behaviour of those who hold them.

Wertrational: actions guided by logic which are aimed at achieving or promoting a particular value or idea. Defending the homeland by taking up arms is seen by Weber as the ultimate *Wertrational* action, as it may involve the death of the individual, but would be a rational death if it saved the thing which was valued. *Wertrational* was one of the two types of *action* which typified modern societies. (See *Zweckrational.*)

white-blouse workers: female workers in routine, lower-grade middle-class occupations, particularly clerical and secretarial work. Workers at this level of non-manual work have traditionally been known as *white-collar workers*, but as a high proportion of them are female, the term white-blouse workers is increasingly adopted, particularly in American literature on the subject.

white-collar crime: criminal acts committed by middle-class people in the course of their work and introduced by Sutherland in the 1940s as a contrast to working-class crime. He argued that the sharp business practice of many business people was often illegal. Thus, attention was drawn to such activities as price-fixing, back-handers and invisible crimes connected with shoddy goods and so on. Sutherland argued that white-collar crime was pervasive but did not appear in the criminal statistics because it was difficult to detect and to convict the perpetrators even if it was detected. (See *corporate crime; work crime.*)

white-collar unions: these are the representative organisations in the workplace of workers in clerical or professional occupations. They are historically latecomers to the *trade union* movement, of which they now constitute an important element. White-collar unions are important to sociologists because they seem to represent a move away from middle-class *consciousness* by those who join them. Traditionally trade unionism is associated with the *working class* and therefore any increase in the numbers of white-collar workers joining trade unions is seen as a significant development. Some sociologists argue that this indicates an increasing identification by many members of the *middle class* with the working class. Other sociologists argue that all it means is that more white-collar workers are seeking to improve their pay and conditions through collective action rather than individual bargaining. They still keep their consciousness of superiority over *manual workers.*

white-collar work: occupations which are situated in offices. These are also known as desk-jobs and are usually designated as middle-class, non-manual occupations. (See *manual work.*)

white-collar workers: as a group, these are usually conceived of as the lower middle class, representing the clerical work-force and occupying a crucial *structural location* between the *working class* and the traditional *professions* of the old middle class. More recent formulations of *class structure* tend to place white-collar workers in the intermediate class. (See *white-collar workers.*)

whitelash: shortened version of 'white backlash', it describes the reaction against *affirmative action* programmes in the United States which give preferential treatment in the labour market to members of minority groups. The whitelash has been criticised as being *racist,* but it accounts for the Republican domination of government in the early part of the 1990s, as many whites voted against the affirmative action programmes of the Clinton administration. (See *positive discrimination.*)

wildcat strike: when workers withdraw their labour suddenly and without taking notice of the usual rules for regulating *industrial action.* Most wildcat action is of short duration. Sociological interest has focused on how conditions can emerge which lead workers to be so angry that they indulge in wildcat action. (See *strikes; unofficial strikes.*)

Wissensociologie: used by Scheler to mean the sociology of knowledge. (See *relativnaturliche Weltanschauung; knowledge.*)

withdrawals from work: a concept developed to take account of the situation when workers may have stopped work, but are not yet on strike, either officially or unofficially. In many conflict situations at work, workers may stop to complain about an issue. Though production has stopped it is not yet a strike until management take the workers 'off the clock', that is from the time when wages will not be paid. Thus, many withdrawals from work never end up as *strikes,* because management are able to resolve the issue immediately, or to promise enough for the workers to go back to work.

work: though apparently obvious, work is a difficult concept for sociologists to define, but is usually conceived of as paid employment. The difficulties in defining work in a sociological way stem from two issues:

- The relationship between work and *leisure* is not always clear-cut, for example with some people being paid for carrying out activities which for most others would be conceived as *leisure* (sport for example).

- The relationship between *housework* and work is also problematic. While it is formally unpaid, housework can be conceived as receiving indirect payment, and it is certainly physically arduous, like many manual jobs. Yet housework is not usually seen as work. Therefore, sociologists break classifications of time down into the following categories:

	Element of compulsion	No compulsion
Element of payment	Work	Work-related time
No payment	Non-work obligations	Leisure

Work and non-work

work crime: law-breaking in the workplace, this ranges from the trivial such as taking paper clips home from work to the serious such as embezzlement. The interesting thing from the sociological point of view is the distinction between that kind of work crime which is seen as acceptable by everyone and work crime which is condemned. (See *white-collar crime; corporate crime.*)

work enrichment programmes: a general movement which argued that in order to increase production, workers need to be given much more responsibility in their job, so that they become involved and committed to their work. The work enrichment programme was developed in opposition to *scientific management,* which saw the increasing *specialisation* of tasks and *de-skilling* of workers as taking control over work away from them. Proponents of work enrichment therefore argued for the *re-aggregation of tasks.* The most famous experiment in work enrichment was at the Volvo car factory in Sweden, which re-introduced work teams to build cars, rather than the extremely specialised *assembly-line.* Though eventually abandoned, the Volvo experiment was used to show that the *detailed division of labour* was not the only way that efficient production could be organised.

work experience: the opportunity for school pupils to spend a period at work, both to learn something of a particular kind of job, and to experience the discipline of work. Work experience forms part of the school experience for a growing number of pupils, and is delivered either as a block of time, such as a fortnight, or on a trickle system, such as half a day a week for a term. (See *new vocationalism; work shadowing.*)

work motivation theories: explanations developed by early forms of industrial sociology of what makes workers work harder. Though there were various types of work motivation theory, such as *expectancy theory* or *incentive theory,* they were all based on underlying assumptions of the basic nature of human beings. So, for example, sociologists who saw human beings as basically economically rational, tended to put forward types of incentive theory when explaining work motivation.

work satisfaction: basically, a condition in which workers are happy in their work. However, sociologists dispute what actually makes workers happy in this sense. While some sociologists focus on the material rewards of work as the key element in promoting work satisfaction, others argue that other factors such as *intrinsic satisfaction* are equally important. The assumption behind the concept of work satisfaction is that satisfied workers will be productive workers. (See *alienation; work motivation theories.*)

work shadowing: a form of *work experience* in which, rather than perform simple tasks in the workplace, the pupil or student 'shadows' a high-level worker such as a manager or senior executive by following her/him throughout the working day over a given period of time. This form of work experience is usually reserved for sixth form students or undergraduates.

work situation: used by Lockwood in his consideration of the *proletarianisation* of clerical workers to describe the physical context of the environment in which men and women labour. Lockwood included a whole range of factors in the work situation, such as the size of offices, the degree of automation, the extent of *bureaucratisation* etc. (See *market situation; status situation.*)

work-related time: the period of the working day where the worker is not at work, but is carrying out activities necessary to do work. For example, getting the bus to work would be work-related time. (See *leisure.*)

work-to-rule: where workers take industrial action by exactly obeying the rules of the enterprise. This has the paradoxical effect of slowing down production. The reason for this is that rules are developed over time and many survive in the rule-book long past the time they have served any useful purpose. By implementing every single rule, the workers are able to disrupt production, yet do not lose basic pay. (See *strikes.*)

working class: the position in the social structure which is characterised by manual labour. The numbers in the working class have been declining as manual work is replaced by automated machines. (See *middle class; proletariat.*)

working mothers: mothers who are in part-time or full-time paid employment. This number has been growing steadily over the last few decades, and in 1994, 64% of all women with children under 16 were 'economically active' (i.e. in paid work). Even among mothers of children under five, 52% were in work. Many mothers, especially of young children, are in part-time work. Attention has been focused on the problems for many working mothers (and would-be working mothers) arising from the shortage of adequate *childcare* facilities, including workplace crèches. The Conservative Government has expressed a commitment to providing more nursery and play-school facilities, largely with the involvement of the private sector. Currently, Britain lags behind many other countries in this respect. (See *voucher schemes.*)

working-class Conservatives: those manual workers who consistently vote Conservative and who describe themselves as Conservative supporters. The importance of the working-class Conservatives is that they are the crucial fraction of the working class that allowed the Conservative Party to win elections, when manual workers were the majority of the population. If everybody voted according to their *class interest*, then the party of the working class (the *Labour Party*), should always win elections. The fact that they do not is due to the existence of significant numbers of working-class Conservatives. However, not all working-class Conservatives have the same reason for supporting the Conservatives. (See *deferential voters; secularists.*)

working class sub-cultures: groups within the *working class* who share similar attitudes, styles, dress and identity which separate them both from the majority of the working class and the rest of society. The *sub-culture* exists within the dominant culture, though it may be resistant to it. Members of working-class youth sub-cultures often dress in a similar fashion, so that they are easily identifiable.

world-accommodating sects: see *new religious movements*

world-affirming sects: see *new religious movements*

world-rejecting sects: see *new religious movements*

world system theory: a view which approaches *development* from the viewpoint of a global economy, seeing the economies of the world as inter-connected and inter-dependent in many ways. World System theory differs from both *modernisation* and *under-development* theory in resisting a simple and fixed division of the world into two or three 'worlds'. Rather, it argues that there are core and periphery countries in the global economy and that these change constantly under the dynamic global impact of *capitalism*. The historic role of capitalism has been to transform traditional and feudal societies into modern capitalist ones. The result of capitalist development has therefore been to extend the reach of capitalist *relations of production* into every corner of the world, to produce a constantly changing and ambiguous world.

xenophobia: fear of foreigners or those from a distinctly separate ethnic background, which often leads to hatred of members of these groups.

young adults: a term used to describe the way in which children in the nineteenth century were treated by their parents. It is used to denote the lack of *childhood* at that time, in that there was no special treatment of the young, but adult standards were imposed on young people from a very early age. This meant that there was little awareness of the child's need for play or affection, so that parent-child relationships were distant. (See *black legend.*)

youth culture: a concept which suggests that all the young people in a society at any one time share a similar way of life and adopt similar attitudes. The idea of a youth culture emerged in the post-War period, when there seemed to be a rebellious spirit among young people. The extension of youth into the late teens, as the time of compulsory education was extended, also influenced the development of a youth culture. Another important factor was the relative *affluence* of the post-War period, when young people had disposable income to spend on leisure activities. This led to the development of a *popular culture* among the young, based around music. However, the notion that all young people have something in common has been heavily criticised, especially by those who argue that it ignores real differences in class, gender and ethnicity. It may be that young people in the post-War period are more affluent than in previous generations, but some are still more affluent than others. (See *generational units.*)

youth training schemes: a series of attempts in the 1980s and 1990s to provide young people with work experience and transferable skills, to prepare them for work in the post-modern economy. They have varied from voluntary, short-term schemes to compulsory long-term ones and have been criticised by some sociologists for a number of reasons:

- they do not give young workers useful skills
- they were devised to reduce unemployment figures rather than provide opportunities
- they are ideological devices to blame lack of appropriate education rather than capitalism for *unemployment.*

(See *Manpower Services Commission; Training and Enterprise Councils.*)

youth unemployment: where significant numbers of people under 21 years of age are without a job. The appearance of significant youth unemployment occurred in the 1980s leading to the concern that large and sustained levels of youth unemployment was producing a generation without experience of work. This has led to sociological investigation of the idea of an *underclass*.

Zeitgeist: literally, 'spirit of the time', it is used to describe the feeling of an era, its sense of art, *culture*, right/wrong, optimism/pessimism etc. The *Zeitgeist* is encapsulated in the *language* of a society, in which the spirit is given concrete expression.

zero-sum relationship: a situation of *power* between two individuals or social formations in which the winner in the struggle takes all that the loser can offer. The balance of the outcome of the power struggle is always zero, with the loser registering all the minuses and the winner all the pluses. The implication of this view of power is that it is always exercised over someone for the benefit of the winner in the struggle. (See *non zero-sum relationship*.)

zone: an area of a city which has some particular characteristic to provide it with a unity and identity. Zones are therefore 'natural' areas of cities, composed for example of similar *housing stock*, or inhabited by people of similar ethnic origin.

zone of transition: one of the areas suggested by Burgess in his *urban zones theory* which was characterised by social disorganisation, and therefore high rates of *suicide* and *crime*. The zone of transition was often inhabited by recent immigrants into the city, who were forced to take low-cost housing in the least desirable area. There was also a high turnover of people in the zone of transition, as groups moved up to better housing or sought work in other locations or other cities.

Zweckrational: logical behaviour which is aimed at achieving a specific end result. For example, building a bridge in order to cross a river is *Zweckrational* action. Weber identified *Zweckrational* action as one of the two types of *action* which were dominant in modern societies and which stood in contrast to *traditional* and *affective action*. (See *Wertrational*.)

SOCIOLOGY REVISION LISTS

The following pages provide revision lists for Advanced Level Sociology tests or exams. This is to help readers use their A-Z as effectively as possible.

MAIN CONCEPTS REQUIRED FOR SUCCESS IN SOCIOLOGY ADVANCED LEVEL EXAMS

In Sociology, as in other subjects, one of the characteristics of a good student is the ability to use subject-specific concepts in a relevant and informed manner. All the concepts you will meet in your Sociology course are important, and you should try to understand and learn them all, and to use them in your written work. However, it can be argued that certain concepts are absolutely essential to an informed understanding of a given topic area, and it is these we have listed here. They should form the basis of your revision for examinations, and a thorough grasp of these concepts will enable you to more easily understand the issues and debates which form a central part of sociological knowledge and insight.

1   Theory and methods

2   Family and households

3   Education and training

4   Work, organisations and leisure

5   Social stratification

6   Culture and identity

7   Crime and deviance

8   World sociology

9   Sociology of locality

10 Wealth, poverty and welfare

11 Health

12 Power and politics

13 Mass media

14 Religion

1 Theory and methods

Action
Conflict
Consensus
Feminism
Interactionism
Interviews
Objectivity
Participant observation
Perspectives
Positivism

Practical constraints
Qualitative data
Quantitative data
Questionnaire
Social change
Social order
Social policy
Social structure
Sociology as a science
Theory

2 Family and households

Childhood
Conjugal roles
Cohabitation
Core functions of the family
Death of the family
Divorce
Domestic labour
Extended family
Family fit
Family size

Family structure
Household
Lone-parent families
Loss of family functions
Marriage
Nuclear family
Patriarchy
Socialisation
Symmetrical family
Universality of the family

3 Education and training

Allocation process
Clash of cultures
Classroom interaction
Compensatory education
Comprehensivisation
Correspondence principle
Cultural capital
Cultural deprivation
Cultural reproduction
Curriculum

Educational standards
Equality of opportunity
Hidden curriculum
Home background
Language codes
National curriculum
New vocationalism
Parental attitudes to education
Secondary socialisation
Under-achievement

4 Work, organisations and leisure

Affluent workers
Alienation
Anomie
Automation
Bureaucracy
De-skilling
Domestic economy
Formal economy
Human Relations School
Industrial conflict
Leisure

Logic of industrialism
Organisations
Scientific management
Separation of home and work
Strike statistics
Technological determinism
Unemployment
Work
Work satisfaction

5 Social stratification

Age-set
Caste
Class boundaries debate
Class consciousness
Class structure
Embourgeoisement
Feminisation of work
Indicators of class
Middle class
Occupational structure

Persistence theories
Prestige
Problem of consciousness
Proletarianisation
Social class
Social closure
Social mobility
Stratification
Upper class
Working class

6 Culture and identity

Age
Culture
Discourse
Empowerment
Ethnicity
Gender
Gender codes
Hyperreality
Identity
Identity construction

Mass culture
Modernity
Norms
Other
Post-modernism
Self
Status
Sub-culture
Surveillance
Values

7 Crime and deviance

Crime
Crimes of the powerful
Crimes without victims
Critical criminology
Culture structure
Dark figure
Deviance
Differential Association theory
Drift
Folk devils

Juvenile delinquency
Labelling theory
New deviancy theory
Self-fulfilling prophecy
Social construction
Social control
Social order
Street crime
Suicide
Victim studies

8 World sociology

Aid
Colonialism
Dependency theory
Development
Dual economy thesis
First world
Five stages of economic growth
Globalisation
Green revolution
Industrialisation

Metropolis
Modernisation theory
Newly Industrialising countries
North-South
Pacific Rim
Third world
Trans-national companies
Under-development
Urbanisation
World system theory

9 Sociology of locality

Community
Environmentalism
Gentrification
Golden Age of the Village Community
Housing classes
Housing segregation
Inner city
Locality
Loss of community thesis
Modernisation

Neighbourhood
Rural-urban continuum
Satellite towns
Suburbanisation
Urban dispersal
Urban housing
Urban managers
Urban Renewal Programmes
Urban Zones theory
Urbanism

10 Wealth, poverty and welfare

Absolute poverty
Collectivism
Culture of poverty
Cycle of poverty
Feminisation of poverty
Index of deprivation
Inequality
Inheritance
Poverty
Poverty line

Relative poverty
Situational constraints
Subjective poverty
Taxation
Underclass
Victim-blaming
Wealth
Welfare
Welfare dependency
Welfare state

11 Health

Artefact explanation
Body
Disability
Health
Health targets
Iatrogenesis
Illness
Infant mortality rate
Life chances
Medical model

Medical technology
Medicalisation
Mental illness
Mortality rate
National Health Service
Primary healthcare
Private medicine
Reproductive technologies
Sick role
Social selection explanation

12 Power and politics

Authority
Democracy
Deviant voters
Hegemony
Ideology
Legitimation
New Social Movements
Pluralism
Political culture
Political identification

Political participation
Political party
Politics
Power
Pressure groups
Problem of order
Re-alignment theories
Ruling class
State
Unitary elite theory

13 Mass media

Agenda-setting
Allocative control
Amplification of deviance
Conglomeration
Decoding
Empty bucket theory
Gate-keepers
Headlining
Mass media
Mass society

Media effects
Media industries
Media representations
Mediation
News-values
Operational control
Opinion leaders
Selective exposure
Signification
Text

14 Religion

Church
Church attendance statistics
Demystification
Denomination
Ecumenicalism
Fundamentalism
Golden Age of Religion
Individuation
Liberation theology
New Christian Right

New Religious Movements
Profane
Protestant ethic thesis
Quantum theory of religion
Religion
Religiosity
Religious observance
Sacred
Sect
Secularisation

EXAMINERS' TERMS

INTRODUCTION

The terms used by examiners in Sociology to begin questions are important clues to the skill domains which the question is targeting. It is important for candidates to be able to identify these skills by analysing carefully the actual words being used to ask questions.

Knowledge and Understanding

Describe: Show your knowledge of something by providing a fuller account of it.

Examine the view: Provide detailed arguments surrounding a particular viewpoint. This often indicates that you should also evaluate the viewpoint, in which case you would need to provide criticisms of the view, as well as arguments in support of it.

Explain: Show that you understand something by providing some detailed knowledge about it, remembering to see whether you also need to answer the implied question 'why?'.

Give a definition of: This is the same as 'what is meant by'.

Outline: Briefly describe the most important points of the theory, viewpoint or approach identified by the question.

What do sociologists mean by: This is the same as 'what is meant by', but suggests that the concept in question might be used in a slightly different way by sociologists from the way it is used in everyday language, or in the mass media.

What do you understand by: Explain your knowledge of something.

What is meant by: Give a definition of something (usually a concept), making sure that you mention all the important features, albeit briefly. These might include, if appropriate, the area of sociology with which the term is usually associated (e.g. deviance, mass media) and possibly a relevant sociological perspective (e.g. feminism, Marxism). The degree of detail you provide should be guided by the number of marks allocated.

With reference to other sources: You must bring in knowledge other than that included in any material given to you.

Interpretation and Application
(the Interboard Syllabus refers to this skill as 'Analysis')

According to Item D: This indicates you are being asked to interpret the material in the item in some way, e.g. to identify a reason, work out a percentage, interpret a trend.

Examine the problems of: This is often referring to a methodological issue. You must identify the problems, and say how sociologists have dealt with these problems, or how they might be able to do so.

Give three examples of: This is asking you to show apply your knowledge of something to other contexts. Make sure that you give the required number of examples.

How might:? This is asking you to apply your knowledge and understanding to a particular situation.

Identify: Depending on the rest of the phrase, show that you can recognise a perspective, viewpoint or trend, or provide reasons, or apply your understanding to solve a problem. The degree of depth and detail will depend on the mark allocation.

Illustrate with reference to the material from Item A: You must not simply copy wording or figures from the material provided, but must interpret and explain the meaning, and apply it to a particular example or examples.

State two reasons why: Make sure that you give two reasons, applying your knowledge to the situation identified in the question.

Using Item C: You must interpret and apply material from the item in your answer, in any appropriate way.

With reference to Item B: You must interpret and apply the relevant material in the specified item at some point in your response.

Evaluation

It is particularly important here, as with the other skills, that your discussion and argument remains focused on the particular issues raised by the question. Keep referring back to the question to ensure that you keep this focus.

Assess: Come to a judgement of the usefulness of something by examining all sides of the argument referred to in the question, and also the quality of the evidence offered to support it and/or criticise it.

Assess the advantages and disadvantages: Similar to 'assess the strengths and weaknesses'. You must clearly state what are perceived as the advantages and disadvantages of the issue, method, etc., identified by the question, and come to a conclusion regarding whether or not the advantages outweigh the disadvantages, or under what conditions they might do so.

Critically discuss: Put forward all sides of an argument raised by a question before coming to a conclusion about it.

Critically examine: This is usually asking you to look critically at arguments for and against a particular viewpoint.

Discuss: The same as 'Critically discuss:'.

Evaluate: Similar to 'assess'. Weigh up the evidence and arguments to come to a conclusion about something.

Examine sociological contributions to: Identify the different kinds of contribution and come to a conclusion regarding their usefulness to understanding the issue raised by the question.

Examine the evidence for and against the view:. You will have to explain and examine the pros and cons of a viewpoint and then reach a conclusion about it.

How far do: This is usually followed by a phrase such as 'sociologists agree with:', and you must explain the position(s) clearly and then come to a conclusion. Remember that the word 'sociologists' can embrace sociologists of different viewpoints and perspectives, which you might need to discuss in order to reach the conclusion.

How successful: This is asking you to come to a conclusion regarding whether something has adequately explained or helped your understanding of a particular issue.

How useful is: You must make your mind up how far something is helpful in explaining or researching a social phenomenon.

Identify the strengths and weaknesses: Although it looks like a 'Knowledge' question, to be able to identify what are strengths and what are weaknesses you will need to evaluate the arguments, evidence etc.

To what extent: This is asking you to come to a conclusion about the degree to which something is useful, valid, reliable, supported by the evidence etc. It implies that the conclusion should not be a simple 'yes, it does' or 'no, it does not', but one which discusses how far it does or it does not.